individual may grow up amid the proper influences. Change the system and everything follows. But when it is asked why immoral persons, the product of a vicious system, should take it upon themselves to reform the institutions of society we encounter again a moral dilemma. Helvetius is sure only that the first step and subsequent steps will be taken. The vicious legislator will perceive the error of his ways and pass good laws. Society will reform itself without the aid of the decalogue or the threats and admonitions of priests. Whether such an ethical theory is sound or no, need not, for the moment, concern us. The important point, historically, is that the hold of the Church upon mankind was weakened in a vital place; questions of right and wrong were henceforth increasingly to be decided upon the grounds of social expediency. The Utilitarianism of Jeremy Bentham and his disciples, James and Stuart Mill, is based upon the teachings of Helvetius. And to Utilitarianism, during the first third of the century, is due much of the moral impetus for needed social reforms in England.

To us of today it seems odd that an encyclopedia should have been one of the chief instruments of reform in the hands of the French philosophers. Yet such in effect was the work edited by Diderot and published in many volumes over a period of years. Its staff of contributors numbered most of the great scholars of France in all departments of human knowledge, men impatient of the restrictions imposed by church and state upon the inquiring mind. Its survey of man's achievements in the arts and sciences revealed the extent of human knowledge and the infinite possibilities of science. It was a work conceived and executed in the scientific spirit, and while it dared not openly attack church and state it undermined the authority of both by a thousand

subtle indirections. It fostered the critical mind and pinned its faith to human reason freed from traditional bonds. Church and State recognized the *Encyclopedia* as an insidious enemy, but despite the difficulties placed in the path of its publication it was completed, printed, and widely read. Its influence in encouraging scientific inquiry and the criticism of traditional faiths and institutions is indeterminate but was undoubtedly vast.

All the radical doctrines of the revolutionary French philosophy are set forth in Holbach's *System of Nature,* a work of far-reaching influence, not only in France but in England. The doctrine of Necessity, "Divine Necessity" as radicals apostrophized it, is there enunciated without qualification or fear. That such a book could have been published and its author go unscathed is proof that earlier attacks upon the Church and State had been effective. The hand of authority had been weakened. Holbach boldly preaches a mechanistic philosophy in which there is no place for God. God is no more than a name, the first cause in an unbroken chain of causes. Speculation as to the nature of this cause is fruitless; it is by the very nature of man's mind forever unknowable. Unalterable law is the rule of life, and man, as a part of nature, can be no other than he is. Every act is predetermined by causes beyond his control and free-will is a meaningless term coined by theologians. It follows, therefore, that no man should be punished for unsocial conduct. The criminal, like the good man, is the product of destiny. But society, for its protection, must seek to reform the criminal and show him the error of his ways, substituting social for anti-social stimuli and thus determining conduct. There is a fallacy concealed in this argument, as, analogously, in the theory of morals which Helvetius formulated. It is hard to see how in a deterministic universe men can ever be other

than they are. To deny all freedom of choice would seem to strike at the root all possibility of social betterment. The practical consequences of the doctrine, as of other revolutionary doctrines, were, however, many and important. The humane treatment of the insane—for insanity was for the first time attributed to physical causes; the reform of prisons, criminal procedure, and the code of punishments; the abolition of slavery—all these enlightened practices had their origin in the new social philosophy. It is an odd consequence of attacks upon traditional religion that man's treatment of his kind should have been made thereby more humane, more in the spirit of Christ.

It is evident that the revolutionary philosophers, despite their mechanistic theories and their desire to overthrow existing institutions, were animated by a religious fervor. Their passion for human welfare and their willingness to endure suffering and persecution in behalf of their convictions proclaim a faith in spiritual forces which their intellectual professions often seem to deny. The spirit, if not the letter, of faith was theirs. Yet they gloried in the epithet "atheist" which was hurled at them. In the eyes of the narrowly orthodox, of the conservative pillars of society, all radicals were atheists. Tom Paine, deist, believer in God and immortality, though not an orthodox Christian, was denounced as an atheist and the charge clings to him to this day. Shelley, whose faith is not easily defined, for it altered with the development of his genius, proudly proclaimed himself an atheist; yet few men have lived so wholly in accord with the teachings of Christ. Shelley meant that he was a rebel, that he hated the tyranny of Church and State, that he would have no traffic with those who professed a hollow orthodoxy. It is not surprising that he and others of his kind were misunderstood by those who

confuse the word with the deed, the form with the spirit which underlies the form.

The doctrines of the French revolutionary philosophers and the political and social reforms which were put into effect during the French Revolution had their influence upon English writers and thinkers and ultimately upon social and political institutions. But whereas a small group of Jacobins in England advocated that the English people imitate the French, the political leaders of England and the greater part of the populace were intimidated by the excesses of the Terror and became even more conservative than they were by nature. Such young and ardent poets as Wordsworth, Coleridge, and Southey, who welcomed the overthrow of tyranny in France, though not wholly alienated by French excesses, and deploring these as inevitable concomitants of change, drew back when France under Napoleon became the dread of Europe. In all three conservatism triumphed and the Wordsworth and Coleridge of later years are scarcely recognizable as the young idealists of 1791. Southey became completely reactionary. Hazlitt and Hunt among the noted writers contemporary with the Revolution are almost alone in holding to their youthful convictions. Shelley and Byron were born half a generation later and had never experienced the high hopes and consequent disillusionment of such a man as Wordsworth. Of Byron, too, it may be said that his radicalism was but half hearted, and of Shelley that he was by nature a radical and would have been such in any age and under any conditions.

In the French revolutionary philosophy were anomalies and paradoxes of which the thinkers were not themselves aware. It is not apparent, logically, wherein selfishness is best realized in altruism. A man pursuing his own pleasure will not easily be convinced that in the

sacrifice of that pleasure for the good of others he will find a greater pleasure. This, if a truth, is not one to be grasped by the processes of reason. Nor is it logically intelligible how, in a deterministic universe, men may mold their destinies to ends of their own devising. The theory of free will is denied, but its substance retained. In truth the French revolutionary thinkers were animated by humanitarian ideals for which there is no justification in pure reason. The passion to aid one's fellow men is born of the heart, not the head. Emotion, instinct, intuition were the sources of their ardor, but because the age was a rational age, all the processes and apparatus of science were invoked to give weight and a seeming logical sanction to that which had a wholly different origin.

The romantic age, both in its humanitarian passion and in its return to nature, asserts the truth of instinct and intuition as against the truth of the reason, which is the domain of science. The conflict is well expressed in the poetry of Wordsworth which proclaims that

"One impulse from a vernal wood
May teach you more of man,
Of moral evil and of good,
Than all the sages can."

He expresses his contempt for the lore of books and for the curiosity which leads one "to peep and botanize upon his mother's grave." Wordsworth is asserting the dominance of heart over head, proclaiming the truths of intuition as greater, for human happiness, than the truths of science.

The Romantic Movement is thus in one aspect a revolt against the pressing weight of science, against the exces-

sive rationalism of the 18th century. As science advances and the individual man feels his impotence and littleness amid the processes of nature, he periodically reasserts his dignity, his sense that he is more than a trivial fact amid the overwhelming facts of the universe. The individualism of the Romantic Movement so variously manifest, particularly in its poets, is the expression of this protest. It does not reconcile intuition and the methods of science, for this is too great a task, one not yet achieved. Only in the poetry of Shelley is there an approach to such a synthesis; and it has remained for a modern scientist and philosopher, not a professed literary critic, to explain Shelley's fusion of the two seemingly opposed and incompatible faculties by which man apprehends truth. A. N. Whitehead in a chapter entitled "The Romantic Reaction" of his book *Science and the Modern World* points out that in Shelley's maturer work the facts of science and the methods of scientific thinking are reconciled with the poetic or intuitive perception of the meaning of life. Shelley is both scientist and pantheist. He accepts the reign of law and yet conceives of the universe as a living thing, to the secret of whose life man may approach by other than scientific processes. The ensuing nineteenth century, says Mr. Whitehead, derives only in part from the Romantic Movement, for the significance of Shelley's achievement was not perceived, and the movement itself died down. "The faith of the century was derived from three sources: one source was the romantic movement, showing itself in religious revival, in art, and in political aspiration: another source was the gathering advance of science which opened avenues of thought: a third source was the advance in technology which completely changed the conditions of human life."

II

In England the period from 1792-1832 is one of political and social reaction. Prior to the French Revolution there had been a movement to reform the rotten boroughs and to make Parliament more truly representative. It seems probable that but for the example of France and for the long Napoleonic wars, a period hostile to all reform, some progress in democracy would have been made before 1832. But the moderate English liberals were frightened, and the aristocracy and the Tory ministry persecuted the radicals and cowed the populace by holding before them the dread of a French invasion. Those who advocated reform were treated as enemies to their country. The masses of the people, moreover, were without political power and were impoverished by a war which raised the cost of living and produced its inevitable crop of profiteering millionaires. When, later, they were led to support the Reform Bill, they but unwittingly aided their enemies, the new capitalistic class of employers, to enjoy a share of political power. The Reform Bill enfranchised the wealthy manufacturing classes and did nothing for the farm laborers and factory workers. Economic and political reforms of benefit to the lower classes were achieved only much later, seventy-five and a hundred years after the enunciation of the democratic ideals of which they were the fruit. Some qualification should be made, however: the abolition of slavery in the English colonies, and some slight improvement in the conduct of prisons and in criminal procedure were sooner, though tardily, realized. Belatedly, too, inadequate industrial reforms followed in the wake of that revolution in the processes of manufacture in which, during this period, the energies of the English were largely absorbed.

For England, too, experienced its revolution, not a political revolution but one which was as profound in its effects as the revolution in France. Indeed the alteration in the ways of human life effected by the application of steam power to the processes of manufacture was greater than that produced by all political changes from that day to this. The period of the Industrial Revolution marks the transition from the old order of life to the new. We of today are more remote from the age of Dr. Johnson than that age is from the time of Chaucer. During the period of the romantic writers the whole background of life was rapidly changing and perhaps it was the unconscious recognition of that fact which accounts in part for the romanticists' interest in the past. The novels of Scott turn wistfully from an age of the power loom and the spinning jenny to a past thought of as more glorious, a time when man, not the machine, ruled the world, and there were nobler aims in life than money getting.

The introduction of steam power and the decay of cottage industry was accompanied by the enclosure acts; these, operating together, destroyed the old English peasantry, dispossessed them of their land, and either reduced them to the state of paupers or drove them to the new manufacturing cities of the north of England there to become, quite literally, wage slaves. The details of this radical transformation which was nothing less than destructive of the old England are too numerous to record here. J. L. and Barbara Hammond's *The Village Laborer* (1760-1832) and its companion volumes *The Town Laborer* and *The Skilled Laborer* give a full and vivid picture of the time. The poems of Crabbe depict the same facts in more emotional terms. And in the *Rural Rides* of Cobbett the later phases of the transformation of English life, especially as it affected the

farmers and farm laborers, are movingly set forth. The literary record of the new order of society, the adaptation of the worker to the life of urban industry such as we know today, is to be found in the novels of the Victorian period, the works of Disraeli, Mrs. Gaskell, and Charles Kingsley.

Different as seem the French Revolution and the Industrial Revolution they are but offshoots from a common trunk, spring from the same intellectual cause. The scientific spirit is at the source of each, in France leading to free speculation and the overthrow or modification of existing institutions and beliefs. Traditional and religious codes and revelations no longer suffice for the explanation and guidance of life. The human mind looks to itself for the interpretation of life and for rules of conduct. Henceforth the inquiring mind, the scientific spirit, is to share with religion the direction of human affairs, if indeed it is not almost wholly to supplant it. In England the scientific spirit, by reason of the accidents of circumstance and a different genius in the English people, takes a more practical direction. It is in the application of scientific knowledge to industry that the English were most notably successful. Social changes followed of necessity but largely as the result of industrial pressure and little as a result of the critical examination of social institutions. Yet here generalization is hazardous, for undoubtedly the effects of French political thinking are to be traced in the reforms of the nineteenth century. Social changes in England have, however, always been slow, and social innovation has never gone the lengths that it went in France. The structure of society has altered only when existing conditions have proved intolerable. For the rest, the freedom of thought which has characterized English life for two hundred years has fostered the spirit of inquiry.

In the nineteenth century England not only took the lead in industry but in the field of scientific research produced men to rival the thinkers of France and Germany.

In philosophy and the social sciences as evidenced by the prose writers of the Romantic Period, England, as I have intimated, can present no such array of brilliant thinkers as those who, in France, gave a philosophic meaning to the Revolution. Yet there are names of importance. Godwin and Bentham, and after Bentham, the Mills, took over from French thought ideas which appealed to them. Bentham and his disciples developed Utilitarianism and on this theory of social morality advocated their specific reforms. So practical a reformer as Francis Place was animated by the same philosophy. In Godwin, French revolutionary doctrine forms the basis for an anarchistic theory which, if for nothing more, is important in that it inspired the youthful Shelley. Mary Wollstonecraft derives in part from the French writers, Rousseau and Condorcet, though contributing many bold and original speculations. Thomas Paine popularizes radical doctrine and makes it intelligible to simple men. He has had a vast but indeterminate influence upon the thought of the English working class, an influence which bore fruit in the Chartist movement. And lastly there is Cobbett, owing little to anyone as a thinker, a man of practical philosophy rooted in observation. Perhaps Cobbett deserves no characterization as a political theorist. But he is at any rate a practical reformer, an admirable social chronicler, and, as a writer, superior to all the rest.

Great prose writers of the Romantic Movement are not so numerous as great poets, for poetry is the characteristic medium of the time. Yet there are several writers of the first rank: Hazlitt and Lamb as essayists,

DeQuincey as a writer of poetic prose, Landor as a master in a type of writing, the imaginary conversation, of his own invention; Cobbett, already mentioned, a great writer of an unliterary type; Sydney Smith, an admirable and racy magazine writer; Leigh Hunt, writer of light essays often charming. All of these are represented by characteristic excerpts in the following pages. Fiction writers it was impossible to include in a volume so small, a limitation which I regret chiefly because it shuts out Peacock, the wittiest and most instructive prose satirist of the age. But excerpts would in any case do him an injustice and the student of this period should read *Nightmare Abbey, Melincourt, Headlong Hall,* and the rest of Peacock's delightful novels entire. In them all the currents of thought and literary styles of the age are lightly satirized. Literary criticism it was not necessary to include, inasmuch as a companion volume of this series, *Critical Essays of the Early Nineteenth Century,* edited by the late Professor Alden, covers this field. Letters, too, must be excluded, though in them the age is rich; the letters of Keats, Byron, and Lamb are among the finest in English literature.

The best prose of the period reveals one characteristic romantic quality: it is usually autobiographical and confessional in its nature. DeQuincey's finest work springs from his experiences as a child and as an opium eater. Hazlitt's and Lamb's best essays, Hunt's also, are eminently personal and utilize the writer's memories or exploit his individual philosophy. Landor is the exception to this generalization. But Landor is a figure apart, despite a romantic strain that may be traced in him. Landor, one feels, is not essentially the product of his age but one who blends characteristics traditionally opposed. These, for lack of better terms, we call Classical and Romantic. It would be juster to say that Landor

resembles Goethe, that his balance, sanity, and impersonal tone are the ideals of true classicism.

Of all these writers I like best Hazlitt and Cobbett. If Lamb's essays were as good as his letters I should class him with the other two. But his essays are a little mannered. The letters seem to me more natural, less pretentious, to have less of the literary taint. Hazlitt at his best seems to be speaking, not writing; and Cobbett's prose has the racy colloquialism of good talk. Compare writing such as this with characteristic prose of the 18th century: Godwin's style is admirably lucid but it lacks the personal note, lacks too a certain careless roughness which to my taste is a merit both in Hazlitt and Cobbett. I do not like prose that seems studied or which reflects its literary origins. Too much grace, too much refinement, may be a defect in a prose style which seeks to put into the reader's mind what the author intends with the least possible friction and ostentation. English prose, I think, in its best modern examples is more nearly in the spirit of Malory's *Morte D'Arthur* or Foxe's *Book of Martyrs* than in the spirit of the 17th and 18th century masters of Latin derivation. Perhaps there is such a thing as a genius of the language, an inherent form to which the best writing, if not influenced by other languages, unconsciously reverts. And if this is so, Cobbett should take a higher place than is usually granted him. I should like to put in a word, too, for poor Tom Paine, whom literary historians treat with so much contempt. Surely a man whose words could rouse the courage of the Colonists as did his in the dark days of the American Revolution, had some gift of style. What is style unless it be the power so to arrange words that men's thoughts are altered and their emotions fired thereby?

CARL H. GRABO.

CONTENTS

	PAGE
INTRODUCTION........CARL H. GRABO..........	vii

WILLIAM HAZLITT............................ 1
On Familiar Style...................... 3
On Living To One's-Self................ 12
On Reading Old Books.................. 29
On The Pleasure of Hating.............. 43
On The Feeling of Immortality In Youth...... 58
On The Fear of Death.................. 74

CHARLES LAMB............................ 87
Witches, and Other Night-Fears.......... 89
Blakesmoor In H——Shire.............. 97
Christ's Hospital Five and Thirty Years Ago... 103
The South-Sea House.................. 119
Old China........................... 129
Mrs. Battle's Opinions on Whist.......... 136
A Dissertation Upon Roast Pig.......... 144
Dream-Children: A Reverie............ 153

THOMAS DE QUINCEY........................ 158
Selections from Confessions of an English Opium-Eater............................ 160
From The Pleasures of Opium.......... 180
From The Pains of Opium............. 190
Levana and Our Ladies of Sorrow...... 210

WILLIAM COBBETT........................ 219
From Rural Rides.................... 221
From Advice To Young Men and (Incidentally) To Young Women................. 242

LEIGH HUNT........................... 259
Cruelty To Children.................. 261
The Old Gentleman.................. 265
Colour.............................. 270

	PAGE
A Cat By The Fire	274
My Books	281

WALTER SAVAGE LANDOR 303
  Imaginary Conversations 305
    Henry VIII, and Anne Boleyn 305
    The Lady Lisle and Elizabeth Gaunt 313
    The Empress Catharine and Princess Dashkof 317
    The Maid of Orleans and Agnes Sorel 325
    Admiral Blake and Humphrey Blake 334
    Metellus and Marius 338

SYDNEY SMITH 344
  A Little Moral Advice 346
    A Fragment on the Cultivation and Improvement of the Animal Spirits 346
  Noodle's Oration 349
  Proceedings of The Society For The Suppression of Vice 352
    A Review.

ROBERT SOUTHEY 368
  Derwentwater 369
  Memoir of The Cats of Greta Hall 373
  The Manufacturing System 381
  Siege of Zaragoza (1808) 388

THOMAS PAINE 408
  From The Rights of Man 410

WILLIAM GODWIN 437
  From Political Justice 440

MARY WOLLSTONECRAFT 460
  A Vindication of The Rights of Woman 462
    Chapter IX—Of The Pernicious Effects Which Arise From The Unnatural Distinctions Established in Society

ROMANTIC PROSE OF THE EARLY
NINETEENTH CENTURY

WILLIAM HAZLITT

STEVENSON's saying that none of us can write like Hazlitt, good fellows as we are, seems to many readers, no doubt, a polite exaggeration. Wherein is Hazlitt's simple straightforward style remarkable? The virtuosity of De Quincey in passages of the *Opium Eater* and elsewhere is apparent. In Hazlitt there is no ostentation; there are no tricks. The sentences are for the most part short; the words are in no way unusual, though precise, and are neither too many nor too few. It is a style remarkable for the ease with which it conceals its art. The author's mind is revealed in the printed page as though seen through an unflawed crystal; it is neither dimmed nor distorted. Hazlitt talks to his auditors in a conversational and friendly tone, and the sentences rise and fall as with the modulations of the voice. No one who has not himself written much can know how difficult and how rare is a mastery of language such as this.

The root of the matter lies in Hazlitt's concern with his thoughts, which are copious, closely packed, and arresting. He wishes not to startle the reader with some fine phrase or purple passage but to convey with exactness his ideas. It is not a style to be emulated unless one has much to impart. Pose, affectation, thinness of utterance, can have no commerce with such plain speaking, which is not "literary" in the less happy meaning of that unfortunate word. No doubt it is Hazlitt's very freedom from the more obvious graces which accounts for the tardy recognition of his greatness. Keats held that the depth of Hazlitt's literary criticism was one

of the three wonders of the age, but I recall no other contemporary pronouncement so enthusiastic. Coleridge in his *Table Talk* speaks somewhat acidly of his former disciple. Jeffrey in reviewing *The Characters of Shakespeare's Plays,* commends the work civilly enough, but with no evident appreciation of Hazlitt's greatness either as critic or stylist. Of all his contemporaries Lamb, with the exception of Keats, is Hazlitt's warmest admirer.

There are personal reasons for these failures of contemporary criticism to rate Hazlitt at his proper worth. He was a good hater, enjoyed the brutal literary warfare of his age, and was in no wise dependent for his happiness upon his fellows. These anti-social traits, together with the unpopularity of his political views, explain the dislike in which he was held. Yet it was in part to these qualities that was due the detachment of his literary judgments. He writes of his contemporaries as though he were the voice of posterity itself.

Many of the excellences of Hazlitt's familiar essays, as of his literary criticism, are due to this cool detachment. Hazlitt is without sentimental weakness; he is not one to flatter humanity but tells the truth as he sees it. This truth-telling, which some may label malice or cynicism, imparts to his comments on life a certain acidity which acts as a preservative. A pickle will retain its relish when sweeter foods have gone stale. "Nothing makes women seem so much like angels as always to see, never to converse with them" he observes casually in his essay on Footmen. The pungency of this ungallant epigram is more exhilarating than a dozen sugary platitudes. A man given to such remarks will, to be sure, never be wholly popular. Lamb, his only rival among modern essayists, is to-day more widely read and admired. Yet it remains to be seen whether Hazlitt

will not, in the long run, have the greater influence on English literature and, on the ground of style, a sounder one.

A word must be said of Hazlitt's practise of quotation and half quotation. No essayist in English weaves so much of other men's utterance with his own. He is full of phrases and lines remembered—not always accurately —from the poets and prose writers he had so often read and reread. These borrowings he assimilates to his own style. They are never seemingly sought but spring to his pen spontaneously as suggested by the train of his argument. In Leigh Hunt's essays one has sometimes the impression that the excerpts are the meat of the matter and the essay written to set them off; or that the author sought for his illustration rather than found it ready to his hand. Hazlitt is never guilty of such a weakness. He has no need of borrowings, but lends to them by his own words as much richness as they impart to him.

ON FAMILIAR STYLE

It is not easy to write a familiar style. Many people mistake a familiar for a vulgar style, and suppose that to write without affectation is to write at random. On the contrary, there is nothing that requires more precision, and, if I may so say, purity of expression, than the style I am speaking of. It utterly rejects not only all unmeaning pomp, but all low, cant phrases, and loose, unconnected, *slipshod* allusions. It is not to take the first word that offers, but the best word in common use; it is not to throw words together in any combinations we please, but to follow and avail ourselves of the true idiom of the language. To write a genuine familiar or truly English style is to write as any one would speak in common conversation who had

a thorough command and choice of words, or who could discourse with ease, force, and perspicuity, setting aside all pedantic and oratorical flourishes. Or to give another illustration, to write naturally is the same thing in regard to common conversation as to read naturally is in regard to common speech. It does not follow that it is an easy thing to give the true accent and inflection to the words you utter, because you do not attempt to rise above the level of ordinary life and colloquial speaking. You do not assume, indeed, the solemnity of the pulpit, or the tone of stage-declamation; neither are you at liberty to gabble on at a venture, without emphasis or discretion, or to resort to vulgar dialect or clownish pronunciation. You must steer a middle course. You are tied down to a given and appropriate articulation, which is determined by the habitual associations between sense and sound, and which you can only hit by entering into the author's meaning, as you must find the proper words and style to express yourself by fixing your thoughts on the subject you have to write about. Any one may mouth out a passage with a theatrical cadence, or get upon stilts to tell his thoughts; but to write or speak with propriety and simplicity is a more difficult task. Thus it is easy to affect a pompous style, to use a word twice as big as the thing you want to express: it is not so easy to pitch upon the very word that exactly fits it. Out of eight or ten words equally common, equally intelligible, with nearly equal pretensions, it is a matter of some nicety and discrimination to pick out the very one, the preferableness of which is scarcely perceptible, but decisive. The reason why I object to Dr. Johnson's style is that there is no discrimination, no selection, no variety in it. He uses none but "tall, opaque words," taken from the "first row of the rubric"

ON FAMILIAR STYLE

—words with the greatest number of syllables, or Latin phrases with merely English terminations. If a fine style depended on this sort of arbitrary pretension, it would be fair to judge of an author's elegance by the measurement of his words and the substitution of foreign circumlocutions (with no precise associations) for the mother-tongue.[1] How simple it is to be dignified without ease, to be pompous without meaning! Surely it is but a mechanical rule for avoiding what is low, to be always pedantic and affected. It is clear you cannot use a vulgar English word, if you never use a common English word at all. A fine tact is shown in adhering to those which are perfectly common, and yet never falling into any expressions which are debased by disgusting circumstances, or which owe their signification and point to technical or professional allusions. A truly natural or familiar style can never be quaint or vulgar, for this reason, that it is of universal force and applicability, and that quaintness and vulgarity arise out of the immediate connection of certain words with coarse and disagreeable or with confined ideas. The last form what we understand by *cant* or *slang* phrases.—To give an example of what is not very clear in the general statement. I should say that the phrase *To cut with a knife,* or *To cut a piece of wood,* is perfectly free from vulgarity, because it is perfectly common; but to *cut an acquaintance* is not quite unexceptionable, because it is not perfectly common or intelligible, and has hardly yet escaped out of the limits of slang phraseology. I should hardly therefore use the word in this sense without putting it in italics as a license of expression, to be received *cum*

[1] I have heard of such a thing as an author who makes it a rule never to admit a monosyllable into his vapid verse. Yet the charm and sweetness of Marlowe's lines depended often on their being made up almost entirely of monosyllables.

end of the last century, but I should be shy of using any that had not been employed by any approved author during the whole of that time. Words, like clothes, get old-fashioned, or mean and ridiculous, when they have been for some time laid aside. Mr. Lamb is the only imitator of old English style I can read with pleasure; and he is so thoroughly imbued with the spirit of his authors that the idea of imitation is almost done away. There is an inward unction, a marrowy vein both in the thought and feeling, an intuition, deep and lively, of his subject, that carries off any quaintness or awkwardness arising from an antiquated style and dress. The matter is completely his own, though the manner is assumed. Perhaps his ideas are altogether so marked and individual as to require their point and pungency to be neutralised by the affectation of a singular but traditional form of conveyance. Tricked out in the prevailing costume, they would probably seem more startling and out of the way. The old English authors, Burton, Fuller, Coryate, Sir Thomas Browne, are a kind of mediators between us and the more eccentric and whimsical modern, reconciling us to his peculiarities. I do not however know how far this is the case or not, till he condescends to write like one of us. I must confess that what I like best of his papers under the signature of Elia (still I do not presume, amidst such excellence, to decide what is most excellent) is the account of "Mrs. Battle's Opinions on Whist," which is also the most free from obsolete allusions and turns of expression—

"A well of native English undefiled."

To those acquainted with his admired prototypes, these Essays of the ingenious and highly gifted author have the same sort of charm and relish that Erasmus's

ON FAMILIAR STYLE

Colloquies or a fine piece of modern Latin have to the classical scholar. Certainly, I do not know any borrowed pencil that has more power or felicity of execution than the one of which I have here been speaking.

It is as easy to write a gaudy style without ideas as it is to spread a pallet of showy colours, or to smear in a flaunting transparency. "What do you read?"—"Words, words, words."—"What is the matter?"—"*Nothing,*" it might be answered. The florid style is the reverse of the familiar. The last is employed as an unvarnished medium to convey ideas; the first is resorted to as a spangled veil to conceal the want of them. When there is nothing to be set down but words, it costs little to have them fine. Look through the dictionary, and cull out a *florilegium,* rival the *tulippomania. Rouge* high enough, and never mind the natural complexion. The vulgar, who are not in the secret, will admire the look of preternatural health and vigour; and the fashionable, who regard only appearances, will be delighted with the imposition. Keep to your sounding generalities, your tinkling phrases, and all will be well. Swell out an unmeaning truism to a perfect tympany of style. A thought, a distinction is the rock on which all this brittle cargo of verbiage splits at once. Such writers have merely *verbal* imaginations, that retain nothing but words. Or their puny thoughts have dragon-wings, all green and gold. They soar far above the vulgar failing of the *Sermo humi obrepens*—their most ordinary speech is never short of an hyperbole, splendid, imposing, vague, incomprehensible, magniloquent, a cento of sounding common-places. If some of us, whose "ambition is more lowly," pry a little too narrowly into nooks and corners to pick up a number of "unconsidered trifles," they never once direct their eyes or lift their hands to

seize on any but the most gorgeous, tarnished, threadbare, patch-work set of phrases, the left-off finery of poetic extravagance, transmitted down through successive generations of barren pretenders. If they criticise actors and actresses, a huddled phantasmagoria of feathers, spangles, floods of light, and oceans of sound float before their morbid sense, which they paint in the style of Ancient Pistol. Not a glimpse can you get of the merits or defects of the performers: they are hidden in a profusion of barbarous epithets and wilful rhodomontade. Our hypercritics are not thinking of these little fantoccini beings—

"That strut and fret their hour upon the stage"—

but of tall phantoms of words, abstractions, *genera* and *species,* sweeping clauses, periods that unite the Poles, forced alliterations, astounding antitheses—

"And on their pens *Fustian* sits plumed."

If they describe kings and queens, it is an Eastern pageant. The Coronation at either House is nothing to it. We get at four repeated images—a curtain, a throne, a sceptre, and a footstool. These are with them the wardrobe of a lofty imagination; and they turn their servile strains to servile uses. Do we read a description of pictures? It is not a reflection of tones and hues which "nature's own sweet and cunning hand laid on," but piles of precious stones, rubies, pearls, emeralds, Golconda's mines, and all the blazonry of art. Such persons are in fact besotted with words, and their brains are turned with the glittering but empty and sterile phantoms of things. Personifications, capital letters, seas of sunbeams, visions of glory, shining inscriptions, the figures of a transparency, Britannia with her shield, or Hope leaning

ON FAMILIAR STYLE

on an anchor, make up their stock-in-trade. They may be considered as *hieroglyphical* writers. Images stand out in their minds isolated and important merely in themselves, without any ground-work of feeling—there is no context in their imaginations. Words affect them in the same way, by the mere sound, that is, by their possible, not by their actual application to the subject in hand. They are fascinated by first appearances, and have no sense of consequences. Nothing more is meant by them than meets the ear: they understand or feel nothing more than meets their eye. The web and texture of the universe, and of the heart of man, is a mystery to them: they have no faculty that strikes a chord in unison with it. They cannot get beyond the daubings of fancy, the varnish of sentiment. Objects are not linked to feelings, words to things, but images revolve in splendid mockery, words represent themselves in their strange rhapsodies. The categories of such a mind are pride and ignorance—pride in outside show, to which they sacrifice every thing, and ignorance of the true worth and hidden structure both of words and things. With a sovereign contempt for what is familiar and natural, they are the slaves of vulgar affectation—of a routine of high-flown phrases. Scorning to imitate realities, they are unable to invent any thing, to strike out one original idea. They are not copyists of nature, it is true; but they are the poorest of all plagiarists, the plagiarists of words. All is far-fetched, dear-bought, artificial, oriental in subject and allusion; all is mechanical, conventional, vapid, formal, pedantic in style and execution. They startle and confound the understanding of the reader by the remoteness and obscurity of their illustrations; they soothe the ear by the monotony of the same everlasting round of circuitous metaphors. They are the *mock-*

school in poetry and prose. They flounder about between fustian in expression and bathos in sentiment. They tantalise the fancy, but never reach the head nor touch the heart. Their Temple of Fame is like a shadowy structure raised by Dulness to Vanity, or like Cowper's description of the Empress of Russia's palace of ice, "as worthless as in show 'twas glittering"—

"It smiled, and it was cold!"

ON LIVING TO ONE'S-SELF[1]

"Remote, unfriended, melancholy, slow,
Or by the lazy Scheldt or wandering Po."

I NEVER was in a better place or humour than I am at present for writing on this subject. I have a partridge getting ready for my supper, my fire is blazing on the hearth, the air is mild for the season of the year, I have had but a slight fit of indigestion to-day (the only thing that makes me abhor myself), I have three hours good before me, and therefore I will attempt it. It is as well to do it at once as to have it to do for a week to come.

If the writing on this subject is no easy task, the thing itself is a harder one. It asks a troublesome effort to ensure the admiration of others: it is a still greater one to be satisfied with one's own thoughts. As I look from the window at the wide bare heath before me, and through the misty moonlight air see the woods that wave over the top of Winterslow,

"While Heav'n's chancel-vault is blind with sleet,"

my mind takes its flight through too long a series of years, supported only by the patience of thought and secret yearnings after truth and good, for me to be at

[1] Written at Winterslow Hut, January 18th-19th, 1821.

ON LIVING TO ONE'S-SELF

a loss to understand the feeling I intend to write about; but I do not know that this will enable me to convey it more agreeably to the reader.

Lady Grandison, in a letter to Miss Harriet Byron, assures her that "her brother Sir Charles lived to himself"; and Lady L. soon after (for Richardson was never tired of a good thing) repeats the same observation; to which Miss Byron frequently returns in her answers to both sisters, "For you know Sir Charles lives to himself," till at length it passes into a proverb among the fair correspondents. This is not, however, an example of what I understand by *living to one's-self*, for Sir Charles Grandison was indeed always thinking of himself; but by this phrase I mean never thinking at all about one's-self, any more than if there was no such person in existence. The character I speak of is as little of an egotist as possible: Richardson's great favourite was as much of one as possible. Some satirical critic has represented him in Elysium "bowing over the *faded* hand of Lady Grandison" (Miss Byron that was)—he ought to have been represented bowing over his own hand, for he never admired any one but himself, and was the god of his own idolatry. Neither do I call it living to one's-self to retire into a desert (like the saints and martyrs of old) to be devoured by wild beasts, nor to descend into a cave to be considered as a hermit, nor to get to the top of a pillar or rock to do fanatic penance and be seen of all men. What I mean by living to one's-self is living in the world, as in it, not of it: it is as if no one knew there was such a person, and you wished no one to know it: it is to be a silent spectator of the mighty scene of things, not an object of attention or curiosity in it; to take a thoughtful, anxious interest in what is passing in the world, but not to feel the slightest inclination to make or

meddle with it. It is such a life as a pure spirit might be supposed to lead, and such an interest as it might take in the affairs of men, calm, contemplative, passive, distant, touched with pity for their sorrows, smiling at their follies without bitterness, sharing their affections, but not troubled by their passions, not seeking their notice, nor once dreamt of by them. He who lives wisely to himself and to his own heart looks at the busy world through the loop-holes of retreat, and does not want to mingle in the fray. "He hears the tumult, and is still." He is not able to mend it, nor willing to mar it. He sees enough in the universe to interest him without putting himself forward to try what he can do to fix the eyes of the universe upon him. Vain the attempt! He reads the clouds, he looks at the stars, he watches the return of the seasons, the falling leaves of autumn, the perfumed breath of spring, starts with delight at the note of a thrush in a copse near him, sits by the fire, listens to the moaning of the wind, pores upon a book, or discourses the freezing hours away, or melts down hours to minutes in pleasing thought. All this while he is taken up with other things, forgetting himself. He relishes an author's style without thinking of turning author. He is fond of looking at a print from an old picture in the room, without teasing himself to copy it. He does not fret himself to death with trying to be what he is not, or to do what he cannot. He hardly knows what he is capable of, and is not in the least concerned whether he shall ever make a figure in the world. He feels the truth of the lines—

"The man whose eye is ever on himself,
    Doth look on one, the least of nature's works;
    One who might move the wise man to that scorn
    Which wisdom holds unlawful ever."

He looks out of himself at the wide, extended prospect of nature, and takes an interest beyond his narrow pretensions in general humanity. He is free as air, and independent as the wind. Woe be to him when he first begins to think what others say of him. While a man is contented with himself and his own resources, all is well. When he undertakes to play a part on the stage, and to persuade the world to think more about him than they do about themselves, he is got into a track where he will find nothing but briars and thorns, vexation and disappointment. I can speak a little to this point. For many years of my life I did nothing but think. I had nothing else to do but solve some knotty point, or dip in some abstruse author, or look at the sky, or wander by the pebbled sea-side—

"To see the children sporting on the shore,
And hear the mighty waters rolling evermore."

I cared for nothing, I wanted nothing. I took my time to consider whatever occurred to me, and was in no hurry to give a sophistical answer to a question— there was no printer's devil waiting for me. I used to write a page or two perhaps in half a year; and remember laughing heartily at the celebrated experimentalist Nicholson, who told me that in twenty years he had written as much as would make three hundred octavo volumes. If I was not a great author, I could read with ever fresh delight, "never ending, still beginning," and had no occasion to write a criticism when I had done. If I could not paint like Claude, I could admire "the witchery of the soft blue sky" as I walked out, and was satisfied with the pleasure it gave me. If I was dull, it gave me little concern: if I was lively, I indulged my spirits. I wished well to the world, and believed as favourably of it as I could. I was like a

stranger in a foreign land, at which I looked with wonder, curiosity, and delight, without expecting to be an object of attention in return. I had no relations to the state, no duty to perform, no ties to bind me to others: I had neither friend nor mistress, wife nor child. I lived in a world of contemplation, and not of action.

This sort of dreaming existence is the best. He who quits it to go in search of realities generally barters repose for repeated disappointments and vain regrets. His time, thoughts, and feelings are no longer at his own disposal. From that instant he does not survey the objects of nature as they are in themselves, but looks asquint at them to see whether he cannot make them the instruments of his ambition, interest, or pleasure; for a candid, undesigning, undisguised simplicity of character, his views become jaundiced, sinister, and double: he takes no farther interest in the great changes of the world but as he has a paltry share in producing them: instead of opening his senses, his understanding, and his heart to the resplendent fabric of the universe, he holds a crooked mirror before his face, in which he may admire his own person and pretensions, and just glance his eye aside to see whether others are not admiring him too. He no more exists in the impression which "the fair variety of things" makes upon him, softened and subdued by habitual contemplation, but in the feverish sense of his own upstart self-importance. By aiming to fix, he is become the slave of opinion. He is a tool, a part of a machine that never stands still, and is sick and giddy with the ceaseless motion. He has no satisfaction but in the reflection of his own image in the public gaze—but in the repetition of his own name in the public ear. He himself is mixed up with and spoils everything. I wonder Buonaparte was not tired of the N. N.'s stuck

all over the Louvre and throughout France. Goldsmith (as we all know) when in Holland went out into a balcony with some handsome Englishwomen, and on their being applauded by the spectators, turned round, and said peevishly, "There are places where I also am admired.". He could not give the craving appetite of an author's vanity one day's respite. I have seen a celebrated talker of our own time turn pale and go out of the room when a showy-looking girl has come into it, who for a moment divided the attention of his hearers.—Infinite are the mortifications of the bare attempt to emerge from obscurity; numberless the failures; and greater and more galling still the vicissitudes and tormenting accompaniments of success—

——— "Whose top to climb
Is certain falling, or so slippery, that
The fear's as bad as falling."

"Would to God," exclaimed Oliver Cromwell, when he was at any time thwarted by the Parliament, "that I had remained by my wood-side to tend a flock of sheep, rather than have been thrust on such a government as this!" When Buonaparte got into his carriage to proceed on his Russian expedition, carelessly twirling his glove, and singing the air, "Malbrook to the war is going," he did not think of the tumble he has got since, the shock of which no one could have stood but himself. We see and hear chiefly of the favourites of Fortune and the Muse, of great generals, of first-rate actors, of celebrated poets. These are at the head; we are struck with the glittering eminence on which they stand, and long to set out on the same tempting career,—not thinking how many discontented half-pay lieutenants are in vain seeking promotion all their lives, and obliged to put up with "the insolence of office, and the spurns

which patient merit of the unworthy takes"; how many half-starved strolling players are doomed to penury and tattered robes in country places, dreaming to the last of a London engagement; how many wretched daubers shiver and shake in the ague-fit of alternate hopes and fears, waste and pine away in the atrophy of genius, or else turn drawing-masters, picture-cleaners, or newspaper-critics; how many hapless poets have sighed out their souls to the Muse in vain, without ever getting their effusions farther known than the Poet's Corner of a country newspaper, and looked and looked with grudging, wistful eyes at the envious horizon that bounded their provincial fame!—Suppose an actor, for instance, "after the heart-aches and the thousand natural pangs that flesh is heir to," *does* get at the top of his profession, he can no longer bear a rival near the throne; to be second or only equal to another is to be nothing: he starts at the prospect of a successor, and retains the mimic sceptre with a convulsive grasp: perhaps as he is about to seize the first place which he has long had in his eye, an unsuspected competitor steps in before him, and carries off the prize, leaving him to commence his irksome toil again. He is in a state of alarm at every appearance or rumour of the appearance of a new actor: "a mouse that takes up its lodging in a cat's ear"[1] has a mansion of peace to him: he dreads every hint of an objection, and least of all can forgive praise mingled with censure: to doubt is to insult; to discriminate is to degrade: he dare hardly look into a criticism unless some one has *tasted* it for him, to see that there is no offence in it: if he does not draw crowded houses every night, he can neither eat nor sleep; or if all these terrible inflictions are removed, and he can "eat his meal in peace," he then becomes

[1] Webster's Duchess of Malfy.

surfeited with applause and dissatisfied with his profession: he wants to be something else, to be distinguished as an author, a collector, a classical scholar, a man of sense and information, and weighs every word he utters, and half retracts it before he utters it, lest if he were to make the smallest slip of the tongue it should get buzzed abroad that *Mr. —— was only clever as an actor!* If ever there was a man who did not derive more pain than pleasure from his vanity, that man, says Rousseau, was no other than a fool. A country-gentleman near Taunton spent his whole life in making some hundreds of wretched copies of second-rate pictures, which were bought up at his death by a neighbouring baronet, to whom

"Some Demon whisper'd, L——, have a taste!"

A little Wilson in an obscure corner escaped the man of *virtù*, and was carried off by a Bristol picture-dealer for three guineas, while the muddled copies of the owner of the mansion (with the frames) fetched thirty, forty, sixty, a hundred ducats a piece. A friend of mine found a very fine Canaletti in a state of strange disfigurement, with the upper part of the sky smeared over and fantastically variegated with English clouds; and on inquiring of the person to whom it belonged whether something had not been done to it, received for answer "that a gentleman, a great artist in the neighbourhood, had retouched some parts of it." What infatuation! Yet this candidate for the honours of the pencil might probably have made a jovial fox-hunter or respectable justice of the peace, if he could only have stuck to what nature and fortune intended him for. Miss —— can by no means be persuaded to quit the boards of the theatre at ——, a little country town in the West of England. Her salary has been

abridged, her person ridiculed, her acting laughed at; nothing will serve—she is determined to be an actress, and scorns to return to her former business as a milliner. Shall I go on? An actor in the same company was visited by the apothecary of the place in an ague-fit, who, on asking his landlady as to his way of life, was told that the poor gentleman was very quiet and gave little trouble, that he generally had a plate of mashed potatoes for his dinner, and lay in bed most of his time, repeating his part. A young couple, every way amiable and deserving, were to have been married, and a benefit-play was bespoke by the officers of the regiment quartered there, to defray the expense of a license and of the wedding-ring, but the profits of the night did not amount to the necessary sum, and they have, I fear, "virgined it e'er since!" Oh for the pencil of Hogarth or Wilkie to give a view of the comic strength of the company at ———, drawn up in battle-array in the Clandestine Marriage, with a *coup d'oeil* of the pit, boxes, and gallery, to cure for ever the love of the *ideal*, and the desire to shine and make holiday in the eyes of others, instead of retiring within ourselves and keeping our wishes and our thoughts at home!

Even in the common affairs of life, in love, friendship, and marriage, how little security have we when we trust our happiness in the hands of others! Most of the friends I have seen have turned out the bitterest enemies, or cold, uncomfortable acquaintance. Old companions are like meats served up too often, that lose their relish and their wholesomeness. He who looks at beauty to admire, to adore it, who reads of its wondrous power in novels, in poems, or in plays, is not unwise; but let no man fall in love, for from that

moment he is "the baby of a girl." I like very well to repeat such lines as these in the play of Mirandola—

> —— "With what a waving air she goes
> Along the corridor! How like a fawn!
> Yet statelier. Hark! No sound, however soft,
> Nor gentlest echo telleth when she treads,
> But every motion of her shape doth seem
> Hallowed by silence."

But however beautiful the description, defend me from meeting with the original!

> "The fly that sips treacle
> Is lost in the sweets;
> So he that tastes woman
> Ruin meets."

The song is Gay's, not mine, and a bitter-sweet it is. How few out of the infinite number of those that marry and are given in marriage wed with those they would prefer to all the world! nay, how far the greater proportion are joined together by mere motives of convenience, accident, recommendation of friends, or indeed not unfrequently by the very fear of the event, by repugnance and a sort of fatal fascination! yet the tie is for life, not to be shaken off but with disgrace or death: a man no longer lives to himself, but is a body (as well as mind) chained to another, in spite of himself—

> "Like life and death in disproportion met."

So Milton (perhaps from his own experience) makes Adam exclaim in the vehemence of his despair,

> "For either
> He never shall find out fit mate, but such
> As some misfortune brings him or mistake

Or whom he wishes most shall seldom gain
Through her perverseness, but shall see her gain'd
By a far worse; or if she love, withheld
By parents; or his happiest choice too late
Shall meet, already link'd and wedlock-bound
To a fell adversary, his hate and shame;
Which infinite calamity shall cause
To human life, and household peace confound."

If love at first sight were mutual, or to be conciliated by kind offices; if the fondest affection were not so often repaid and chilled by indifference and scorn; if so many lovers both before and since the madman in Don Quixote had not "worshipped a statue, hunted the wind, cried aloud to the desert;" if friendship were lasting; if merit were renown, and renown were health, riches, and long life; or if the homage of the world were paid to conscious worth and the true aspirations after excellence, instead of its gaudy signs and outward trappings; then indeed I might be of opinion that it is better to live to others than one's-self; but as the case stands, I incline to the negative side of the question.[1]

"I have not loved the world, nor the world me;
I have not flattered its rank breath, nor bow'd
To its idolatries a patient knee —
Nor coin'd my cheek to smiles—nor cried aloud
In worship of an echo; in the crowd

---

[1] Shenstone and Gray were two men, one of whom pretended to live to himself, and the other really did so. Gray shrunk from the public gaze (he did not even like his portrait to be prefixed to his works) into his own thoughts and indolent musings; Shenstone affected privacy that he might be sought out by the world; the one courted retirement in order to enjoy leisure and repose, as the other coquetted with it merely to be interrupted with the importunity of visitors and the flatteries of absent friends.

ON LIVING TO ONE'S-SELF

They could not deem me one of such; I stood
Among them, but not of them; in a shroud
Of thoughts which were not their thoughts, and still could,
Had I not filed my mind which thus itself subdued.

I have not loved the world, nor the world me—
But let us part fair foes; I do believe,
Though I have found them not, that there may be
Words which are things—hopes which will not deceive,
And virtues which are merciful nor weave
Snares for the failing: I would also deem
O'er others' griefs that some sincerely grieve;
That two, or one, are almost what they seem—
That goodness is no name, and happiness no dream."

Sweet verse embalms the spirit of sour misanthropy; but woe betide the ignoble prose-writer who should thus dare to compare notes with the world, or tax it roundly with imposture.

If I had sufficient provocation to rail at the public, as Ben Jonson did at the audience in the Prologues to his plays, I think I should do it in good set terms, nearly as follows. There is not a more mean, stupid, dastardly, pitiful, selfish, spiteful, envious, ungrateful animal than the Public. It is the greatest of cowards, for it is afraid of itself. From its unwieldy, overgrown dimensions, it dreads the least opposition to it, and shakes like isinglass at the touch of a finger. It starts at its own shadow, like the man in the Hartz mountains, and trembles at the mention of its own name. It has a lion's mouth, the heart of a hare, with ears erect and sleepless eyes. It stands "listening its fears." It is so in awe of its own opinion that it never dares to form

any, but catches up the first idle rumour, lest it should be behindhand in its judgment, and echoes it till it is deafened with the sound of its own voice. The idea of what the public will think prevents the public from ever thinking at all, and acts as a spell on the exercise of private judgment, so that, in short, the public ear is at the mercy of the first impudent pretender who chooses to fill it with noisy assertions, or false surmises, or secret whispers. What is said by one is heard by all; the supposition that a thing is known to all the world makes all the world believe it, and the hollow repetition of a vague report drowns the "still, small voice" of reason. We may believe or know that what is said is not true; but we know or fancy that others believe it,—we dare not contradict or are too indolent to dispute with them, and therefore give up our internal, and, as we think, our solitary conviction to a sound without substance, without proof, and often without meaning. Nay more, we may believe and know not only that a thing is false, but that others believe and know it to be so, that they are quite as much in the secret of the imposture as we are, that they see the puppets at work, the nature of the machinery, and yet if any one has the art or power to get the management of it, he shall keep possession of the public ear by virtue of a cant phrase or nickname, and by dint of effrontery and perseverance make all the world believe and repeat what all the world know to be false. The ear is quicker than the judgment. We know that certain things are said; by that circumstance alone we know that they produce a certain effect on the imagination of others, and we conform to their prejudices by mechanical sympathy, and for want of sufficient spirit to differ with them. So far then is

public opinion from resting on a broad and solid basis, as the aggregate of thought and feeling in a community, that it is slight and shallow and variable to the last degree—the bubble of the moment; so that we may safely say the public is the dupe of public opinion, not its parent. The public is pusillanimous and cowardly, because it is weak. It knows itself to be a great dunce, and that it has no opinions but upon suggestion. Yet it is unwilling to appear in leading-strings, and would have it thought that its decisions are as wise as they are weighty. It is hasty in taking up its favourites, more hasty in laying them aside, lest it should be supposed deficient in sagacity in either case. It is generally divided into two strong parties, each of which will allow neither common sense nor common honesty to the other side. It reads the Edinburgh and Quarterly Reviews, and believes them both—or if there is a doubt, malice turns the scale. Taylor and Hessey told me that they had sold nearly two editions of the Characters of Shakespeare's Plays in about three months, but that after the Quarterly Review of them came out they never sold another copy. The public, enlightened as they are, must have known the meaning of that attack as well as those who made it. It was not ignorance then, but cowardice, that led them to give up their own opinion. A crew of mischievous critics at Edinburgh having affixed the epithet of the *Cockney School* to one or two writers born in the metropolis, all the people in London became afraid of looking into their works, lest they too should be convicted of cockneyism. Oh brave public! This epithet proved too much for one of the writers in question, and stuck like a barbed arrow in his heart. Poor Keats! What was sport to

the town was death to him. Young, sensitive, delicate, he was like

> "A bud bit by an envious worm,
> Ere he could spread his sweet leaves to the air,
> Or dedicate his beauty to the sun"—

and unable to endure the miscreant cry and idiot laugh, withdrew to sigh his last breath in foreign climes.—The public is as envious and ungrateful as it is ignorant, stupid, and pigeon-livered—

> "A huge-sized monster of ingratitudes."

It reads, it admires, it extols, only because it is the fashion, not from any love of the subject or the man. It cries you up or runs you down out of mere caprice and levity. If you have pleased it, it is jealous of its own involuntary acknowledgment of merit, and seizes the first opportunity, the first shabby pretext, to pick a quarrel with you and be quits once more. Every petty caviller is erected into a judge, every tale-bearer is implicitly believed. Every little low paltry creature that gaped and wondered, only because others did so, is glad to find you (as he thinks) on a level with himself. An author is not then, after all, a being of another order. Public admiration is forced, and goes against the grain. Public obloquy is cordial and sincere: every individual feels his own importance in it. They give you up bound hand and foot into the power of your accusers. To attempt to defend yourself is a high crime and misdemeanour, a contempt of court, an extreme piece of impertinence. Or if you prove every charge unfounded, they never think of retracing their error or making you amends. It would be a compromise of their dignity; they consider themselves as the party injured, and resent your innocence as an

imputation on their judgment. The celebrated Bub Doddington, when out of favour at court, said "he would not *justify* before his sovereign: it was for Majesty to be displeased, and for him to believe himself in the wrong!" The public are not quite so modest. People already begin to talk of the Scotch Novels as overrated. How then can common authors be supposed to keep their heads long above water? As a general rule, all those who live by the public starve, and are made a bye-word and a standing jest into the bargain. Posterity is no better (not a bit more enlightened or more liberal), except that you are no longer in their power, and that the voice of common fame saves them the trouble of deciding on your claims. The public now are the posterity of Milton and Shakespeare. Our posterity will be the living public of a future generation. When a man is dead, they put money in his coffin, erect monuments to his memory, and celebrate the anniversary of his birthday in set speeches. Would they take any notice of him if he were living? No!—I was complaining of this to a Scotchman who had been attending a dinner and a subscription to raise a monument to Burns. He replied he would sooner subscribe twenty pounds to his monument than have given it him while living; so that if the poet were to come to life again, he would treat him just as he was treated in fact. This was an honest Scotchman. What *he* said, the rest would do.

Enough: my soul, turn from them, and let me try to regain the obscurity and quiet that I love, "far from the madding strife," in some sequestered corner of my own, or in some far-distant land! In the latter case, I might carry with me as a consolation the passage in Bolingbroke's Reflections on Exile, in which he describes in glowing colours the resources which a man may

always find within himself, and of which the world cannot deprive him.

"Believe me, the providence of God has established such an order in the world, that of all which belongs to us, the least valuable parts can alone fall under the will of others. Whatever is best is safest; lies out of the reach of human power; can neither be given nor taken away. Such is this great and beautiful work of nature, the world. Such is the mind of man, which contemplates and admires the world, whereof it makes the noblest part. These are inseparably ours, and as long as we remain in one we shall enjoy the other. Let us march therefore intrepidly wherever we are led by the course of human accidents. Wherever they lead us, on what coast soever we are thrown by them, we shall not find ourselves absolutely strangers. We shall feel the same revolution of seasons, and the same sun and moon[1] will guide the course of our year. The same azure vault, bespangled with stars, will be every where spread over our heads. There is no part of the world from whence we may not admire those planets which roll, like ours, in different orbits round the same central sun; from whence we may not discover an object still more stupendous, that army of fixed stars hung up in the immense space of the universe, innumerable suns whose beams enlighten and cherish the unknown worlds which roll around them: and whilst I am ravished by such contemplations as these, whilst my soul is thus raised up to heaven, it imports me little what ground I tread upon."

[1] "Plut. of Banishment. He compares those who cannot live out of their own country to the simple people who fancied the moon of Athens was a finer moon than that of Corinth,
Labentem coelo quae ducitis annum.
VIRG. *Georg.*"

ON READING OLD BOOKS

I HATE to read new books. There are twenty or thirty volumes that I have read over and over again, and these are the only ones that I have any desire ever to read at all. It was a long time before I could bring myself to sit down to the Tales of My Landlord, but now that author's works have made a considerable addition to my scanty library. I am told that some of Lady Morgan's are good, and have been recommended to look into Anastasius; but I have not yet ventured upon that task. A lady, the other day, could not refrain from expressing her surprise to a friend, who said he had been reading Delphine:—she asked,—If it had not been published some time back? Women judge of books as they do of fashions or complexions, which are admired only "in their newest gloss." That is not my way. I am not one of those who trouble the circulating libraries much, or pester the booksellers for mail-coach copies of standard periodical publications. I cannot say that I am greatly addicted to black-letter, but I profess myself well versed in the marble bindings of Andrew Millar, in the middle of the last century; nor does my taste revolt at Thurloe's State Papers, in Russia leather; or an ample impression of Sir William Temple's Essays, with a portrait after Sir Godfrey Kneller in front. I do not think altogether the worse of a book for having survived the author a generation or two. I have more confidence in the dead than the living. Contemporary writers may generally be divided into two classes—one's friends or one's foes. Of the first we are compelled to think too well, and of the last we are disposed to think too ill, to receive much genuine pleasure from the perusal, or to judge fairly of the merits of either. One candidate for literary fame, who

happens to be of our acquaintance, writes finely, and like a man of genius; but unfortunately has a foolish face, which spoils a delicate passage:—another inspires us with the highest respect for his personal talents and character, but does not quite come up to our expectations in print. All these contradictions and petty details interrupt the calm current of our reflections. If you want to know what any of the authors were who lived before our time, and are still objects of anxious inquiry, you have only to look into their works. But the dust and smoke and noise of modern literature have nothing in common with the pure, silent air of immortality.

When I take up a work that I have read before (the oftener the better) I know what I have to expect. The satisfaction is not lessened by being anticipated. When the entertainment is altogether new, I sit down to it as I should to a strange dish,—turn and pick out a bit here and there, and am in doubt what to think of the composition. There is a want of confidence and security to second appetite. New-fangled books are also like made-dishes in this respect, that they are generally little else than hashes and *rifaccimentos* of what has been served up entire and in a more natural state at other times. Besides, in thus turning to a well-known author, there is not only an assurance that my time will not be thrown away, or my palate nauseated with the most insipid or vilest trash,—but I shake hands with, and look an old, tried, and valued friend in the face,—compare notes, and chat the hours away. It is true, we form dear friendships with such ideal guests—dearer, alas! and more lasting, than those with our most intimate acquaintance. In reading a book which is an old favourite with me (say the first novel I ever read) I not only have the pleasure of imagination and of a critical relish of the work, but

the pleasures of memory added to it. It recalls the same feelings and associations which I had in first reading it, and which I can never have again in any other way. Standard productions of this kind are links in the chain of our conscious being. They bind together the different scattered divisions of our personal identity. They are land-marks and guides in our journey through life. They are pegs and loops on which we can hang up, or from which we can take down, at pleasure, the wardrobe of a moral imagination, the relics of our best affections, the tokens and records of our happiest hours. They are "for thoughts and for remembrance!" They are like Fortunatus's Wishing-Cap—they give us the best riches—those of Fancy; and transport us, not over half the globe, but (which is better) over half our lives, at a word's notice!

My father Shandy solaced himself with Bruscambille. Give me for this purpose a volume of Peregrine Pickle or Tom Jones. Open either of them any where—at the Memoirs of Lady Vane, or the adventures at the masquerade with Lady Bellaston, or the disputes between Thwackum and Square, or the escape of Molly Seagrim, or the incident of Sophia and her muff, or the edifying prolixity of her aunt's lecture—and there I find the same delightful, busy, bustling scene as ever, and feel myself the same as when I was first introduced into the midst of it. Nay, sometimes the sight of an odd volume of these good old English authors on a stall, or the name lettered on the back among others on the shelves of a library, answers the purpose, revives the whole train of ideas, and sets "the puppets dallying." Twenty years are struck off the list, and I am a child again. A sage philosopher, who was not a very wise man, said, that he should like very well to be young again, if he could take his experience

along with him. This ingenious person did not seem to be aware, by the gravity of his remark, that the great advantage of being young is to be without this weight of experience, which he would fain place upon the shoulders of youth, and which never comes too late with years. Oh! what a privilege to be able to let this hump, like Christian's burthen, drop from off one's back, and transport one's-self, by the help of a little musty duodecimo, to the time when "ignorance was bliss," and when we first got a peep at the raree-show of the world, through the glass of fiction—gazing at mankind, as we do at wild beasts in a menagerie, through the bars of their cages,—or at curiosities in a museum, that we must not touch! For myself, not only are the old ideas of the contents of the work brought back to my mind in all their vividness, but the old associations of the faces and persons of those I then knew, as they were in their life-time—the place where I sat to read the volume, the day when I got it, the feeling of the air, the fields, the sky—return, and all my early impressions with them. This is better to me —those places, those times, those persons, and those feelings that come across me as I retrace the story and devour the page, are to me better far than the wet sheets of the last new novel from the Ballantyne press, to say nothing of the Minerva press in Leadenhall-street. It is like visiting the scenes of early youth. I think of the time "when I was in my father's house, and my path ran down with butter and honey,"—when I was a little, thoughtless child, and had no other wish or care but to con my daily task, and be happy!—Tom Jones, I remember, was the first work that broke the spell. It came down in numbers once a fortnight, in Cooke's pocket-edition, embellished with cuts. I had hitherto read only in school-books, and a tiresome

ecclesiastical history (with the exception of Mrs. Radcliffe's Romance of the Forest): but this had a different relish with it,—"sweet in the mouth," though not "bitter in the belly." It smacked of the world I lived in, and in which I was to live—and shewed me groups, "gay creatures" not "of the elements," but of the earth; not "living in the clouds," but travelling the same road that I did;—some that had passed on before me, and others that might soon overtake me. My heart had palpitated at the thoughts of a boarding-school ball, or gala-day at Midsummer or Christmas: but the world I had found out in Cooke's edition of the British Novelists was to me a dance through life, a perpetual gala-day. The six-penny numbers of this work regularly contrived to leave off just in the middle of a sentence, and in the nick of a story, where Tom Jones discovers Square behind the blanket; or where Parson Adams, in the inextricable confusion of events, very undesignedly gets to bed to Mrs. Slip-slop. Let me caution the reader against this impression of Joseph Andrews; for there is a picture of Fanny in it which he should not set his heart on, lest he should never meet with any thing like it; or if he should, it would, perhaps, be better for him that he had not. It was just like —— ——! With what eagerness I used to look forward to the next number, and open the prints! Ah! never again shall I feel the enthusiastic delight with which I gazed at the figures, and anticipated the story and adventures of Major Bath and Commodore Trunnion, of Trim and my Uncle Toby, of Don Quixote and Sancho and Dapple, of Gil Blas and Dame Lorenza Sephora, of Laura and the fair Lucretia, whose lips open and shut like buds of roses. To what nameless ideas did they give rise,—with what airy delights I filled up the outlines, as I hung in silence

over the page!—Let me still recall them, that they may breathe fresh life into me, and that I may live that birthday of thought and romantic pleasure over again! Talk of the *ideal!* This is the only true ideal—the heavenly tints of Fancy reflected in the bubbles that float upon the spring-tide of human life.

Oh! Memory! shield me from the world's poor strife,
And give those scenes thine everlasting life!

The paradox with which I set out is, I hope, less startling than it was; the reader will, by this time, have been let into my secret. Much about the same time, or I believe rather earlier, I took a particular satisfaction in reading Chubb's Tracts, and I often think I will get them again to wade through. There is a high gusto of polemical divinity in them; and you fancy that you hear a club of shoemakers at Salisbury, debating a disputable text from one of St. Paul's Epistles in a workmanlike style, with equal shrewdness and pertinacity. I cannot say much for my metaphysical studies, into which I launched shortly after with great ardour, so as to make a toil of a pleasure. I was presently entangled in the briars and thorns of subtle distinctions,—of "fate, free-will, fore-knowledge absolute," though I cannot add that "in their wandering mazes I found no end;" for I did arrive at some very satisfactory and potent conclusions; nor will I go so far, however ungrateful the subject might seem, as to exclaim with Marlowe's Faustus—"Would I had never seen Wittenberg, never read book"—that is, never studied such authors as Hartley, Hume, Berkeley, &c. Locke's Essay on the Human Understanding is, however, a work from which I never derived either pleasure or profit; and Hobbes, dry and powerful as he is, I did

not read till long afterwards. I read a few poets, which did not much hit my taste,—for I would have the reader understand, I am deficient in the faculty of imagination; but I fell early upon French romances and philosophy, and devoured them tooth-and-nail. Many a dainty repast have I made of the New Eloise; —the description of the kiss; the excursion on the water; the letter of St. Preux, recalling the time of their first loves; and the account of Julia's death; these I read over and over again with unspeakable delight and wonder. Some years after, when I met with this work again, I found I had lost nearly my whole relish for it (except some few parts) and was, I remember, very much mortified with the change in my taste, which I sought to attribute to the smallness and gilt edges of the edition I had bought, and its being perfumed with rose-leaves. Nothing could exceed the gravity, the solemnity with which I carried home and read the Dedication to the Social Contract, with some other pieces of the same author, which I had picked up at a stall in a coarse leathern cover. Of the Confessions I have spoken elsewhere, and may repeat what I have said—"Sweet is the dew of their memory, and pleasant the balm of their recollection!" Their beauties are not "scattered like stray-gifts o'er the earth," but sown thick on the page, rich and rare. I wish I had never read the Emilius, or read it with less implicit faith. I had no occasion to pamper my natural aversion to affectation or pretence, by romantic and artificial means. I had better have formed myself on the model of Sir Fopling Flutter. There is a class of persons whose virtues and most shining qualities sink in, and are concealed by, an absorbent ground of modesty and reserve; and such a one I do, without vanity, profess

myself.[1] Now these are the very persons who are likely to attach themselves to the character of Emilius, and of whom it is sure to be the bane. This dull, phlegmatic, retiring humour is not in a fair way to be corrected, but confirmed and rendered desperate, by being in that work held up as an object of imitation, as an example of simplicity and magnanimity—by coming upon us with all the recommendations of novelty, surprise, and superiority to the prejudices of the world —by being stuck upon a pedestal, made amiable, dazzling, a *leurre de dupe!* The reliance on solid worth which it inculcates, the preference of sober truth to gaudy tinsel, hangs like a mill-stone round the neck of the imagination—"a load to sink a navy"—impedes our progress, and blocks up every prospect in life. A man, to get on, to be successful, conspicuous, applauded, should not retire upon the centre of his conscious resources, but be always at the circumference of appearances. He must envelop himself in a halo of mystery— he must ride in an equipage of opinion—he must walk with a train of self-conceit following him—he must not strip himself to a buff-jerkin, to the doublet and hose of his real merits, but must surround himself with a *cortege* of prejudices, like the signs of the Zodiac—he must seem any thing but what he is, and then he may pass for any thing he pleases. The world love to be amused by hollow professions, to be deceived by flattering appearances, to live in a state of hallucination; and can forgive every thing but the plain, downright, simple honest truth—such as we see it chalked out in

[1] Nearly the same sentiment was wittily and happily expressed by a friend, who had some lottery puffs, which he had been employed to write, returned on his hands for their too great severity of thought and classical terseness of style, and who observed on that occasion, that "Modest merit never can succeed!"

the character of Emilius.—To return from this digression, which is a little out of place here.

Books have in a great measure lost their power over me; nor can I revive the same interest in them as formerly. I perceive when a thing is good, rather than feel it. It is true,

> Marcian Colonna is a dainty book;

and the reading of Mr. Keats's Eve of St. Agnes lately made me regret that I was not young again. The beautiful and tender images there conjured up, "come like shadows—so depart." The "tiger-moth's wings," which he has spread over his rich poetic blazonry, just flit across my fancy; the gorgeous twilight window which he has painted over again in his verse, to me "blushes" almost in vain "with blood of queens and kings." I know how I should have felt at one time in reading such passages; and that is all. The sharp luscious flavour, the fine *aroma* is fled, and nothing but the stalk, the bran, the husk of literature is left. If any one were to ask me what I read now, I might answer with my Lord Hamlet in the play—"Words, words, words."—"What is the matter?"—"*Nothing!*" —They have scarce a meaning. But it was not always so. There was a time when to my thinking, every word was a flower or a pearl, like those which dropped from the mouth of the little peasant-girl in the Fairy tale, or like those that fall from the great preacher in the Caledonian Chapel! I drank of the stream of knowledge that tempted, but did not mock my lips, as of the river of life, freely. How eagerly I slaked my thirst of German sentiment, "as the hart that panteth for the water-springs;" how I bathed and revelled, and added

my floods of tears to Goethe's Sorrows of Werter, and to Schiller's Robbers—

Giving my stock of more to that which had too much!

I read, and assented with all my soul to Coleridge's fine Sonnet, beginning—

> Schiller! that hour I would have wish'd to die,
> If through the shuddering midnight I had sent,
> From the dark dungeon of the tow'r time-rent,
> That fearful voice, a famish'd father's cry!

I believe I may date my insight into the mysteries of poetry from the commencement of my acquaintance with the authors of the Lyrical Ballads; at least, my discrimination of the higher sorts—not my predilection for such writers as Goldsmith or Pope: nor do I imagine they will say I got my liking for the Novelists, or the comic writers,—for the characters of Valentine, Tattle, or Miss Prue, from them. If so, I must have got from them what they never had themselves. In points where poetic diction and conception are concerned, I may be at a loss, and liable to be imposed upon: but in forming an estimate of passages relating to common life and manners, I cannot think I am a plagiarist from any man. I there "know my cue without a prompter." I may say of such studies—*Intus et in cute*. I am just able to admire those literal touches of observation and description, which persons of loftier pretensions overlook and despise. I think I comprehend something of the characteristic part of Shakespeare; and in him indeed, all is characteristic, even the nonsense and poetry. I believe it was the celebrated Sir Humphrey Davy who used to say, that Shakespeare was rather a metaphysician than a poet. At any rate, it was not ill said. I wish that I had

sooner known the dramatic writers contemporary with Shakespeare; for in looking them over about a year ago, I almost revived my old passion for reading, and my old delight in books, though they were very nearly new to me. The Periodical Essayists I read long ago. The Spectator I liked extremely: but the Tatler took my fancy most. I read the others soon after, the Rambler, the Adventurer, the World, the Connoisseur: I was not sorry to get to the end of them, and have no desire to go regularly through them again. I consider myself a thorough adept in Richardson. I like the longest of his novels best, and think no part of them tedious; nor should I ask to have any thing better to do than to read them from beginning to end, to take them up when I chose, and lay them down when I was tired, in some old family mansion in the country, till every word and syllable relating to the bright Clarissa, the divine Clementina, the beautiful Pamela, "with every trick and line of their sweet favour," were once more "graven in my heart's table."[1] I have a sneaking kindness for Mackenzie's Julia de Roubigne—for the deserted mansion, and straggling gilliflowers on the mouldering garden-wall; and still more for his Man of Feeling; not that it is better, nor so good; but at the time I read it, I sometimes thought of the heroine, Miss Walton, and of Miss —— together, and "that ligament, fine as it was, was never broken!"—One of the poets

[1] During the peace of Amiens, a young English officer, of the name of Lovelace, was presented at Buonaparte's levee. Instead of the usual question, "Where have you served, Sir?" the First Consul immediately addressed him, "I perceive your name, Sir, is the same as that of the hero of Richardson's Romance!" Here was a Consul. The young man's uncle, who was called Lovelace, told me this anecdote while we were stopping together at Calais. I had also been thinking that his was the same name as that of the hero of Richardson's Romance. This is one of my reasons for liking Buonaparte.

that I have always read with most pleasure, and can wander about in for ever with a sort of voluptuous indolence, is Spenser; and I like Chaucer even better. The only writer among the Italians I can pretend to any knowledge of, is Boccaccio, and of him I cannot express half my admiration. His story of the Hawk I could read and think of from day to day, just as I would look at a picture of Titian's!—

I remember, as long ago as the year 1798, going to a neighbouring town (Shrewsbury, where Farquhar has laid the plot of his Recruiting Officer) and bringing home with me, "at one proud swoop," a copy of Milton's Paradise Lost, and another of Burke's Reflections on the French Revolution—both which I have still; and I still recollect, when I see the covers, the pleasure with which I dipped into them as I returned with my double prize. I was set up for one while. That time is past "with all its giddy raptures:" but I am still anxious to preserve its memory, "embalmed with odours."—With respect to the first of these works, I would be permitted to remark here in passing, that it is a sufficient answer to the German criticism which has since been started against the character of Satan (*viz.* that it is not one of disgusting deformity, or pure, defecated malice) to say that Milton has there drawn, not the abstract principle of evil, not a devil incarnate, but a fallen angel. This is the scriptural account, and the poet has followed it. We may safely retain such passages as that well-known one—

—— His form had not yet lost
All her original brightness; nor appear'd
Less than archangel ruin'd; and the excess
Of glory obscur'd—

for the theory, which is opposed to them, "falls flat

upon the grunsel edge, and shames its worshippers." Let us hear no more then of this monkish cant, and bigoted outcry for the restoration of the horns and tail of the devil!—Again, as to the other work, Burke's Reflections, I took a particular pride and pleasure in it, and read it to myself and others for months afterwards. I had reason for my prejudice in favour of this author. To understand an adversary is some praise: to admire him is more. I thought I did both: I knew I did one. From the first time I ever cast my eyes on any thing of Burke's (which was an extract from his Letter to a Noble Lord in a three-times a week paper, The St. James's Chronicle, in 1796), I said to myself, "This is true eloquence: this is a man pouring out his mind on paper." All other style seemed to me pedantic and impertinent. Dr. Johnson's was walking on stilts; and even Junius's (who was at that time a favourite with me) with all his terseness, shrunk up into little antithetic points and well-trimmed sentences. But Burke's style was forked and playful as the lightning, crested like the serpent. He delivered plain things on a plain ground; but when he rose, there was no end of his flights and circumgyrations—and in this very Letter, "he, like an eagle in a dove-cote, fluttered *his* Volscians" (the Duke of Bedford and the Earl of Lauderdale)[1] "in Corioli." I did not care for his doctrines. I was then, and am still, proof against their contagion; but I admired the author, and was considered as not a very staunch partisan of the opposite side, though I thought myself that an abstract proposition was one thing—a masterly transition, a brilliant metaphor, another. I conceived too that he might be wrong in his main argument, and yet deliver

[1] He is there called "Citizen Lauderdale." Is this the present Earl?

fifty truths in arriving at a false conclusion. I remember Coleridge assuring me, as a poetical and political set-off to my sceptical admiration, that Wordsworth had written an Essay on Marriage, which, for manly thought and nervous expression, he deemed incomparably superior. As I had not, at that time, seen any specimens of Mr. Wordsworth's prose style, I could not express my doubts on the subject. If there are greater prose-writers than Burke, they either lie out of my course of study, or are beyond my sphere of comprehension. I am too old to be a convert to a new mythology of genius. The niches are occupied, the tables are full. If such is still my admiration of this man's misapplied powers, what must it have been at a time when I myself was in vain trying, year after year, to write a single Essay, nay, a single page or sentence; when I regarded the wonders of his pen with the longing eyes of one who was dumb and a changeling; and when, to be able to convey the slightest conception of my meaning to others in words, was the height of an almost hopeless ambition! But I never measured others' excellences by my own defects: though a sense of my own incapacity, and of the steep, impassable ascent from me to them, made me regard them with greater awe and fondness. I have thus run through most of my early studies and favourite authors, some of whom I have since criticised more at large. Whether those observations will survive me, I neither know nor do I much care: but to the works themselves, "worthy of all acceptation," and to the feelings they have always excited in me since I could distinguish a meaning in language, nothing shall ever prevent me from looking back with gratitude and triumph. To have lived in the cultivation of an intimacy with such works, and

to have familiarly relished such names, is not to have lived quite in vain.

There are other authors whom I have never read, and yet whom I have frequently had a great desire to read, from some circumstance relating to them. Among these is Lord Clarendon's History of the Grand Rebellion, after which I have a hankering, from hearing it spoken of by good judges—from my interest in the events, and knowledge of the characters from other sources, and from having seen fine portraits of most of them. I like to read a well-penned character, and Clarendon is said to have been a master in this way. I should like to read Froissart's Chronicles, Hollingshed and Stowe, and Fuller's Worthies. I intend, whenever I can, to read Beaumont and Fletcher all through. There are fifty-two of their plays, and I have only read a dozen or fourteen of them. A Wife for a Month, and Thierry and Theodoret, are, I am told, delicious, and I can believe it. I should like to read the speeches in Thucydides, and Guicciardini's History of Florence, and Don Quixote in the original. I have often thought of reading the Loves of Persiles and Sigismunda, and the Galatea of the same author. But I somehow reserve them like "another Yarrow." I should also like to read the last new novel (if I could be sure it was so) of the author of Waverley:—no one would be more glad than I to find it the best!—

ON THE PLEASURE OF HATING

THERE is a spider crawling along the matted floor of the room where I sit (not the one which has been so well allegorised in the admirable *Lines to a Spider,* but another of the same edifying breed); he runs with heedless, hurried haste, he hobbles awkwardly towards me,

he stops: he sees the giant shadow before him, and, at a loss whether to retreat or proceed, meditates his huge foe. But as I do not start up and seize upon the straggling caitiff, as he would upon a hapless fly within his toils, he takes heart, and ventures on, with mingled cunning, impudence, and fear. As he passes me, I lift up the matting to assist his escape, am glad to get rid of the unwelcome intruder, and shudder at the recollection after he is gone. A child, a woman, a clown, or a moralist a century ago, would have crushed the little reptile to death: my philosophy has got beyond that. I bear the creature no ill-will, but still I hate the very sight of it. The spirit of malevolence survives the practical exertion of it. We learn to curb our will and keep our overt actions within the bounds of humanity, long before we can subdue our sentiments and imaginations to the same mild tone. We give up the external demonstration, the *brute* violence, but cannot part with the essence or principle of hostility. We do not tread upon the poor little animal in question (that seems barbarous and pitiful!) but we regard it with a sort of mystic horror and superstitious loathing. It will ask another hundred years of fine writing and hard thinking to cure us of the prejudice, and make us feel towards this ill-omened tribe with something of "the milk of human kindness," instead of their own shyness and venom.

Nature seems (the more we look into it) made up of antipathies: without something to hate, we should lose the very spring of thought and action. Life would turn to a stagnant pool, were it not ruffled by the jarring interests, the unruly passions, of men. The white streak in our own fortunes is brightened (or just rendered visible) by making all around it as dark as possible; so the rainbow paints its form upon the cloud. Is it

pride? Is it envy? Is it the force of contrast? Is it weakness or malice? But so it is, that there is a secret affinity, a *hankering* after evil in the human mind, and that it takes a perverse, but a fortunate delight in mischief, since it is a never-failing source of satisfaction. Pure good soon grows insipid, wants variety and spirit. Pain is a bitter-sweet, which never surfeits. Love turns, with a little indulgence, to indifference or disgust: hatred alone is immortal. Do we not see this principle at work every where? Animals torment and worry one another without mercy: children kill flies for sport: every one reads the accidents and offences in a newspaper, as the cream of the jest: a whole town runs to be present at a fire, and the spectator by no means exults to see it extinguished. It is better to have it so, but it diminishes the interest; and our feelings take part with our passions rather than with our understandings. Men assemble in crowds, with eager enthusiasm, to witness a tragedy: but if there were an execution going forward in the next street, as Mr. Burke observes, the theatre would be left empty. A strange cur in a village, an idiot, a crazy woman, are set upon and baited by the whole community. Public nuisances are in the nature of public benefits. How long did the Pope, the Bourbons, and the Inquisition keep the people of England in breath, and supply them with nick-names to vent their spleen upon! Had they done us any harm of late? No: but we have always a quantity of superfluous bile upon the stomach, and we wanted an object to let it out upon. How loth were we to give up our pious belief in ghosts and witches, because we liked to persecute the one, and frighten ourselves to death with the other! It is not the quality so much as the quantity of excitement that we are anxious about: we cannot bear a state of indifference and *ennui*: the mind seems to abhor

a *vacuum* as much as ever matter was supposed to do. Even when the spirit of the age (that is, the progress of intellectual refinement, warring with our natural infirmities) no longer allows us to carry our vindictive and headstrong humours into effect, we try to revive them in description, and keep up the old bugbears, the phantoms of our terror and our hate, in imagination. We burn Guy Fawkes in effigy, and the hooting and buffeting and maltreating that poor tattered figure of rags and straw makes a festival in every village in England once a year. Protestants and Papists do not now burn one another at the stake: but we subscribe to new editions of *Fox's Book of Martyrs;* and the secret of the success of the *Scotch Novels* is much the same: they carry us back to the feuds, the heart-burnings, the havoc, the dismay, the wrongs and the revenge of a barbarous age and people—to the rooted prejudices and deadly animosities of sects and parties in politics and religion, and contending chiefs and clans in war and intrigue. We feel the full force of the spirit of hatred with all of them in turn. As we read, we throw aside the trammels of civilisation, the flimsy veil of humanity. "Off, you lendings!" The wild beast resumes its sway within us, we feel like hunting-animals, and as the hound starts in his sleep and rushes on the chase in fancy, the heart rouses itself in its native lair, and utters a wild cry of joy, at being restored once more to freedom and lawless, unrestrained impulses. Every one has his full swing, or goes to the Devil his own way. Here are no Jeremy Bentham Panopticons, none of Mr. Owen's impassable Parallelograms, (Rob Roy would have spurned and poured a thousand curses on them), no long calculations of self-interest: the will takes its instant way to its object, as the mountain-torrent flings itself over the precipice: the greatest possible good

ON THE PLEASURE OF HATING

of each individual consists in doing all the mischief he can to his neighbour: that is charming, and finds a sure and sympathetic chord in every breast! So Mr. Irving, the celebrated preacher, has rekindled the old, original, almost exploded hell-fire in the aisles of the Caledonian Chapel, as they introduce the real water of the New River at Sadler's Wells, to the delight and astonishment of his fair audience. *'Tis pretty, though a plague,* to sit and peep into the pit of Tophet, to play at *snap-dragon* with flames and brimstone (it gives a smart electrical shock, a lively fillip to delicate constitutions), and to see Mr. Irving, like a huge Titan, looking as grim and swarthy as if he had to forge tortures for all the damned! What a strange being man is! Not content with doing all he can to vex and hurt his fellows here, "upon this bank and shoal of time," where one would think there were heart-aches, pain, disappointment, anguish, tears, sighs, and groans enough, the bigoted maniac takes him to the top of the high peak of school divinity to hurl him down the yawning gulf of penal fire; his speculative malice asks eternity to wreak its infinite spite in, and calls on the Almighty to execute its relentless doom! The cannibals burn their enemies and eat them in good-fellowship with one another: meek Christian divines cast those who differ from them but a hair's breadth, body and soul, into hell-fire, for the glory of God and the good of his creatures! It is well that the power of such persons is not co-ordinate with their wills: indeed, it is from the sense of their weakness and inability to control the opinions of others, that they thus "outdo termagant," and endeavour to frighten them into conformity by big words and monstrous denunciations.

The pleasure of hating, like a poisonous mineral, eats into the heart of religion, and turns it to rankling

spleen and bigotry; it makes patriotism an excuse for carrying fire, pestilence, and famine into other lands: it leaves to virtue nothing but the spirit of censoriousness, and a narrow, jealous, inquisitorial watchfulness over the actions and motives of others. What have the different sects, creeds, doctrines in religion been but so many pretexts set up for men to wrangle, to quarrel, to tear one another in pieces about, like a target as a mark to shoot at? Does any one suppose that the love of country in an Englishman implies any friendly feeling or disposition to serve another bearing the same name? No, it means only hatred to the French or the inhabitants of any other country that we happen to be at war with for the time. Does the love of virtue denote any wish to discover or amend our own faults? No, but it atones for an obstinate adherence to our own vices by the most virulent intolerance to human frailties. This principle is of a most universal application. It extends to good as well as evil: if it makes us hate folly, it makes us no less dissatisfied with distinguished merit. If it inclines us to resent the wrongs of others, it impels us to be as impatient of their prosperity. We revenge injuries: we repay benefits with ingratitude. Even our strongest partialities and likings soon take this turn. "That which was luscious as locusts, anon becomes bitter as coloquintida;" and love and friendship melt in their own fires. We hate old friends: we hate old books: we hate old opinions; and at last we come to hate ourselves.

I have observed that few of those, whom I have formerly known most intimate, continue on the same friendly footing, or combine the steadiness with the warmth of attachment. I have been acquainted with two or three knots of inseparable companions, who saw each other "six days in the week," that have broken

ON THE PLEASURE OF HATING

up and dispersed. I have quarrelled with almost all my old friends, (they might say this is owing to my bad temper, but) they have also quarrelled with one another. What is become of "that set of whist-players," celebrated by ELIA in his notable *Epistle to Robert Southey, Esq.* (and now I think of it—that I myself have celebrated in this very volume) "that for so many years called Admiral Burney friend?" They are scattered, like last year's snow. Some of them are dead, or gone to live at a distance, or pass one another in the street like strangers; or if they stop to speak, do it as coolly and try to *cut* one another as soon as possible. Some of us have grown rich, others poor. Some have got places under Government, others a *niche* in the Quarterly Review. Some of us have dearly earned a name in the world; whilst others remain in their original privacy. We despise the one, and envy and are glad to mortify the other. Times are changed; we cannot revive our old feelings; and we avoid the sight and are uneasy in the presence of those who remind us of our infirmity, and put us upon an effort at seeming cordiality, which embarrasses ourselves and does not impose upon our *quondam* associates. Old friendships are like meats served up repeatedly, cold, comfortless, and distasteful. The stomach turns against them. Either constant intercourse and familiarity breed weariness and contempt; or if we meet again after an interval of absence, we appear no longer the same. One is too wise, another too foolish, for us; and we wonder we did not find this out before. We are disconcerted and kept in a state of continual alarm by the wit of one, or tired to death of the dullness of another. The *good things* of the first (besides leaving stings behind them) by repetition grow stale, and lose their startling effect; and the insipidity of the last becomes intolerable. The

most amusing or instructive companion is at best like a favourite volume, that we wish after a time to *lay upon the shelf;* but as our friends are not willing to be laid there, this produces a misunderstanding and ill-blood between us. Or if the zeal and integrity of friendship is not abated, or its career interrupted by any obstacle arising out of its own nature, we look out for other subjects of complaint and sources of dissatisfaction. We begin to criticise each other's dress, looks, and general character. "Such a one is a pleasant fellow, but it is a pity he sits so late!" Another fails to keep his appointments, and that is a sore that never heals. We get acquainted with some fashionable young men or with a mistress, and wish to introduce our friend; but he is awkward and a sloven, the interview does not answer, and this throws cold water on our intercourse. Or he makes himself obnoxious to opinion—and we shrink from our own convictions on the subject as an excuse for not defending him. All or any of these causes mount up in time to a ground of coolness or irritation—and at last they break out into open violence as the only amends we can make ourselves for suppressing them so long, or the readiest means of banishing recollections of former kindness so little compatible with our present feelings. We may try to tamper with the wounds or patch up the carcase of departed friendship; but the one will hardly bear the handling, and the other is not worth the trouble of embalming! The only way to be reconciled to old friends is to part with them for good: at a distance we may chance to be thrown back (in a waking dream) upon old times and old feelings: or at any rate we should not think of renewing our intimacy, till we have fairly *spit our spite,* or said, thought, and felt all the ill we can of each other. Or if we can pick a quarrel with some one

else, and make him the scapegoat, this is an excellent contrivance to heal a broken bone. I think I must be friends with Lamb again, since he has written that magnanimous Letter to Southey, and told him a piece of his mind! I don't know what it is that attaches me to H—— so much, except that he and I, whenever we meet, sit in judgment on another set of old friends, and "carve them as a dish fit for the gods." There was L—— H——, John Scott, Mrs. M——, whose dark raven locks made a picturesque background to our discourse, B——, who is grown fat, and is, they say, married, R——; these had all separated long ago, and their foibles are the common link that holds us together. We do not affect to condole or whine over their follies; we enjoy, we laugh at them till we are ready to burst our sides, *"sans* intermission, for hours by the dial." We serve up a course of anecdotes, *traits,* master-strokes of character, and cut and hack at them till we are weary. Perhaps some of them are even with us. For my own part, as I once said, I like a friend the better for having faults that one can talk about. "Then," said Mrs. M——, "you will never cease to be a philanthropist!" Those in question were some of the choice-spirits of the age, not "fellows of no mark or likelihood;" and we so far did them justice: but it is well they did not hear what we sometimes said of them. I care little what any one says of me, particularly behind my back, and in the way of critical and analytical discussion: it is looks of dislike and scorn that I answer with the worst venom of my pen. The expression of the face wounds me more than the expressions of the tongue. If I have in one instance mistaken this expression, or resorted to this remedy where I ought not, I am sorry for it. But the face was too fine over which it mantled, and I am too old

to have misunderstood it! . . . I sometimes go up to ——'s; and as often as I do, resolve never to go again. I do not find the old homely welcome. The ghost of friendship meets me at the door, and sits with me all dinner-time. They have got a set of fine notions and new acquaintance. Allusions to past occurrences are thought trivial, nor is it always safe to touch upon more general subjects. M. does not begin as he formerly did every five minutes, "Fawcett used to say," &c. That topic is something worn. The girls are grown up, and have a thousand accomplishments. I perceive there is a jealousy on both sides. They think I give myself airs, and I fancy the same of them. Every time I am asked, "If I do not think Mr. Washington Irving a very fine writer?" I shall not go again till I receive an invitation for Christmas Day in company with Mr. Liston. The only intimacy I never found to flinch or fade was a purely intellectual one. There was none of the cant of candour in it, none of the whine of mawkish sensibility. Our mutual acquaintance were considered merely as subjects of conversation and knowledge, not at all of affection. We regarded them no more in our experiments than "mice in an air-pump:" or like malefactors, they were regularly cut down and given over to the dissecting-knife. We spared neither friend nor foe. We sacrificed human infirmities at the shrine of truth. The skeletons of character might be seen, after the juice was extracted, dangling in the air like flies in cobwebs: or they were kept for future inspection in some refined acid. The demonstration was as beautiful as it was new. There is no surfeiting on gall: nothing keeps so well as a decoction of spleen. We grow tired of every thing but turning others into ridicule, and congratulating ourselves on their defects.

We take a dislike to our favourite books, after a

time, for the same reason. We cannot read the same works for ever. Our honeymoon, even though we wed the Muse, must come to an end; and is followed by indifference, if not by disgust. There are some works, those indeed that produce the most striking effect at first by novelty and boldness of outline, that will not bear reading twice: others of a less extravagant character, and that excite and repay attention by a greater nicety of details, have hardly interest enough to keep alive our continued enthusiasm. The popularity of the most successful writers operates to wean us from them, by the cant and fuss that is made about them, by hearing their names everlastingly repeated, and by the number of ignorant and indiscriminate admirers they draw after them:—we as little like to have to drag others from their unmerited obscurity, lest we should be exposed to the charge of affectation and singularity of taste. There is nothing to be said respecting an author that all the world have made up their minds about: it is a thankless as well as hopeless task to recommend one that nobody has ever heard of. To cry up Shakespeare as the god of our idolatry, seems like a vulgar national prejudice: to take down a volume of Chaucer, or Spenser, or Beaumont and Fletcher, or Ford, or Marlowe, has very much the look of pedantry and egotism. I confess it makes me hate the very name of Fame and Genius when works like these are "gone into the wastes of time," while each successive generation of fools is busily employed in reading the trash of the day, and women of fashion gravely join with their waiting-maids in discussing the preference between the Paradise Lost and Mr. Moore's Loves of the Angels. I was pleased the other day on going into a shop to ask, "If they had any of the *Scotch Novels?*" to be told—"That they had just sent out the last, Sir

Andrew Wylie!"—Mr. Galt will also be pleased with this answer! The reputation of some books is raw and *unaired;* that of others is worm-eaten and mouldy. Why fix our affections on that which we cannot bring ourselves to have faith in, or which others have long ceased to trouble themselves about? I am half afraid to look into Tom Jones, lest it should not answer my expectations at this time of day; and if it did not, I should certainly be disposed to fling it into the fire, and never look into another novel while I lived. But surely, it may be said, there are some works that, like nature, can never grow old; and that must always touch the imagination and passions alike! Or there are passages that seem as if we might brood over them all our lives, and not exhaust the sentiments of love and admiration they excite: they become favourites, and we are fond of them to a sort of dotage. Here is one:

———"Sitting in my window
Printing my thoughts in lawn, I saw a god,
I thought (but it was you), enter our gates;
My blood flew out and back again, as fast
As I had puffed it forth and sucked it in
Like breath; then was I called away in haste
To entertain you: never was a man
Thrust from a sheepcote to a sceptre, raised
So high in thoughts as I; you left a kiss
Upon these lips then, which I mean to keep
From you for ever. I did hear you talk
Far above singing!"

A passage like this indeed leaves a taste on the palate like nectar, and we seem in reading it to sit with the gods at their golden tables: but if we repeat it often in ordinary moods, it loses its flavour, becomes vapid, "the wine of *poetry* is drank, and but the lees remain."

ON THE PLEASURE OF HATING

Or, on the other hand, if we call in the aid of extraordinary circumstances to set it off to advantage, as the reciting it to a friend, or after having our feelings excited by a long walk in some romantic situation, or while we

—"play with Amaryllis in the shade,
Or with the tangles of Neæra's hair"—

we afterwards miss the accompanying circumstances, and instead of transferring the recollection of them to the favourable side, regret what we have lost, and strive in vain to bring back "the irrevocable hour"—wondering in some instances how we survive it, and at the melancholy blank that is left behind! The pleasure rises to its height in some moment of calm solitude or intoxicating sympathy, declines ever after, and from the comparison and a conscious falling-off, leaves rather a sense of satiety and irksomeness behind it. . . . "Is it the same in pictures?" I confess it is, with all but those from Titian's hand. I don't know why, but an air breathes from his landscapes, pure, refreshing, as if it came from other years; there is a look in his faces that never passes away. I saw one the other day. Amidst the heartless desolation and glittering finery of Fonthill, there is a portfolio of the Dresden Gallery. It opens, and a young female head looks from it; a child, yet woman grown; with an air of rustic innocence and the graces of a princess, her eyes like those of doves, the lips about to open, a smile of pleasure dimpling the whole face, the jewels sparkling in her crisped hair, her youthful shape compressed in a rich antique dress, as the bursting leaves contain the April buds! Why do I not call up this image of gentle sweetness, and place it as a perpetual barrier between mischance and me?—It is because pleasure asks a

greater effort of the mind to support it than pain; and we turn, after a little idle dalliance, from what we love to what we hate!

As to my old opinions, I am heartily sick of them. I have reason, for they have deceived me sadly. I was taught to think, and I was willing to believe, that genius was not a bawd, that virtue was not a mask, that liberty was not a name, that love had its seat in the human heart. Now I would care little if these words were struck out of the dictionary, or if I had never heard them. They are become to my ears a mockery and a dream. Instead of patriots and friends of freedom, I see nothing but the tyrant and the slave, the people linked with kings to rivet on the chains of despotism and superstition. I see folly join with knavery, and together make up public spirit and public opinions. I see the insolent Tory, the blind Reformer, the coward Whig! If mankind had wished for what is right, they might have had it long ago. The theory is plain enough; but they are prone to mischief, "to every good work reprobate." I have seen all that had been done by the mighty yearnings of the spirit and intellect of men, "of whom the world was not worthy," and that promised a proud opening to truth and good through the vista of future years, undone by one man, with just glimmering of understanding enough to feel that he was a king, but not to comprehend how he could be king of a free people! I have seen this triumph celebrated by poets, the friends of my youth and the friends of man, but who were carried away by the infuriate tide that, setting in from a throne, bore down every distinction of right reason before it; and I have seen all those who did not join in applauding this insult and outrage on humanity proscribed, hunted down (they and their friends made a bye-word of), so that it

has become an understood thing that no one can live by his talents or knowledge who is not ready to prostitute those talents and that knowledge to betray his species, and prey upon his fellow-man. "This was some time a mystery: but the time gives evidence of it." The echoes of liberty had awakened once more in Spain, and the morning of human hope dawned again: but that dawn has been overcast by the foul breath of bigotry, and those reviving sounds stifled by fresh cries from the time-rent towers of the Inquisition: man yielding (as it is fit he should) first to brute force, but more to the innate perversity and dastard spirit of his own nature, which leaves no room for farther hope or disappointment. And England, that arch-reformer, that heroic deliverer, that mouther about liberty and tool of power, stands gaping by, not feeling the blight and mildew coming over it, nor its very bones crack and turn to a paste under the grasp and circling folds of this new monster—Legitimacy! In private life do we not see hypocrisy, servility, selfishness, folly, and impudence succeed, while modesty shrinks from the encounter, and merit is trodden under foot? How often is "the rose plucked from the forehead of a virtuous love to plant a blister there!" What chance is there of the success of real passion? What certainty of its continuance? Seeing all this as I do, and unravelling the web of human life into its various threads of meanness, spite, cowardice, want of feeling, and want of understanding, of indifference towards others and ignorance of ourselves—seeing custom prevail over all excellence, itself giving way to infamy—mistaken as I have been in my public and private hopes, calculating others from myself, and calculating wrong; always disappointed where I placed most reliance; the dupe of friendship, and the fool of love;—have I not reason to

ON THE FEELING OF IMMORTALITY IN YOUTH

"Life is a pure flame, and we live by an invisible sun within us."

—Sir Thomas Browne.

No young man believes he shall ever die. It was a saying of my brother's, and a fine one. There is a feeling of Eternity in youth, which makes us amends for every thing. To be young is to be as one of the Immortal Gods. One half of time indeed is flown—

[1] The only exception to the general drift of this Essay (and that is an exception in theory—I know of none in practice) is, that in reading we always take the right side, and make the case properly our own. Our imaginations are sufficiently excited, we have nothing to do with the matter but as a pure creation of the mind, and we therefore yield to the natural, unwarped impression of good and evil. Our own passions, interests, and prejudices out of the question, or in an abstracted point of view, we judge fairly and conscientiously; for conscience is nothing but the abstract idea of right and wrong. But no sooner have we to act or suffer than the spirit of contradiction or some other demon comes into play, and there is an end of common sense and reason. Even the very strength of the speculative faculty, or the desire to square things with an *ideal* standard of perfection (whether we can or no) leads perhaps to half the absurdities and miseries of mankind. We are hunting after what we cannot find, and quarrelling with the good within our reach. Among the thousands that have read *The Heart of Midlothian* there assuredly never was a single person who did not wish Jeanie Deans success. Even Gentle George was sorry for what he had done, when it was over, though he would have played the same prank the next day: and the *unknown* author, in his immediate character of contributor to Blackwood and the Sentinel is about as respectable a personage as Daddy Ratton himself. On the stage, every one takes part with Othello against Iago. Do boys at school, in reading Homer, generally side with the Greeks or Trojans?

FEELING OF IMMORTALITY IN YOUTH

the other half remains in store for us with all its countless treasures; for there is no line drawn, and we see no limit to our hopes and wishes. We make the coming age our own.—

"The vast, the unbounded prospect lies before us."

Death, old age, are words without a meaning, that pass by us like the idle air which we regard not. Others may have undergone, or may still be liable to them—we "bear a charmed life," which laughs to scorn all such sickly fancies. As in setting out on a delightful journey, we strain our eager gaze forward—

"Bidding the lovely scenes at distance hail,"—

and see no end to the landscape, new objects presenting themselves as we advance; so, in the commencement of life, we set no bounds to our inclinations, nor to the unrestricted opportunities of gratifying them. We have as yet found no obstacle, no disposition to flag; and it seems that we can go on so for ever. We look round in a new world, full of life, and motion, and ceaseless progress; and feel in ourselves all the vigour and spirit to keep pace with it, and do not foresee from any present symptoms how we shall be left behind in the natural course of things, decline into old age, and drop into the grave. It is the simplicity, and as it were *abstractedness* of our feelings in youth, that (so to speak) identifies us with nature, and (our experience being slight and our passions strong) deludes us into a belief of being immortal like it. Our short-lived connection with existence, we fondly flatter ourselves, is an indissoluble and lasting union—a honeymoon that knows neither coldness, jar, nor separation. As infants smile and sleep, we are rocked in the cradle of our wayward fancies, and lulled into security by the

roar of the universe around us—we quaff the cup of life with eager haste without draining it, instead of which it only overflows the more—objects press around us, filling the mind with their magnitude and with the throng of desires that wait upon them, so that we have no room for the thoughts of death. From the plenitude of our being, we cannot change all at once to dust and ashes, we cannot imagine "this sensible, warm motion, to become a kneaded clod"—we are too much dazzled by the brightness of the waking dream around us to look into the darkness of the tomb. We no more see our end than our beginning: the one is lost in oblivion and vacancy, as the other is hid from us by the crowd and hurry of approaching events. Or the grim shadow is seen lingering in the horizon, which we are doomed never to overtake, or whose last, faint, glimmering outline touches upon Heaven and translates us to the skies! Nor would the hold that life has taken of us permit us to detach our thoughts from present objects and pursuits, even if we would. What is there more opposed to health, than sickness; to strength and beauty, than decay and dissolution; to the active search of knowledge than mere oblivion? Or is there none of the usual advantage to bar the approach of Death, and mock his idle threats; Hope supplies their place, and draws a veil over the abrupt termination of all our cherished schemes. While the spirit of youth remains unimpaired, ere the "wine of life is drank up," we are like people intoxicated or in a fever, who are hurried away by the violence of their own sensations: it is only as present objects begin to pall upon the sense, as we have been disappointed in our favorite pursuits, cut off from our closest ties, that passion loosens its hold upon the breast, that we by degrees become weaned from the world, and allow our-

selves to contemplate, "as in a glass, darkly," the possibility of parting with it for good. The example of others, the voice of experience, has no effect upon us whatever. Casualties we must avoid: the slow and deliberate advances of age we can play at *hide-and-seek* with. We think ourselves too lusty and too nimble for that blear-eyed decrepit old gentleman to catch us. Like the foolish fat scullion, in Sterne, when she hears that Master Bobby is dead, our only reflection is—"So am not I!" The idea of death, instead of staggering our confidence, rather seems to strengthen and enhance our possession and our enjoyment of life. Others may fall around us like leaves, or be mowed down like flowers by the scythe of Time: these are but tropes and figures to the unreflecting ears and overweening presumption of youth. It is not till we see the flowers of Love, Hope, and Joy, withering around us, and our own pleasures cut up by the roots, that we bring the moral home to ourselves, that we abate something of the wanton extravagance of our pretensions, or that the emptiness and dreariness of the prospect before us reconciles us to the stillness of the grave!

"Life! thou strange thing, that hast a power
  to feel
Thou art, and to perceive that others are."[1]

Well might the poet begin his indignant invective against an art, whose professed object is its destruction, with this animated apostrophe to life. Life is indeed a strange gift, and its privileges are most miraculous. Nor is it singular that when the splendid boon is first granted us, our gratitude, our admiration, and our delight should prevent us from reflecting on our own nothingness, or from thinking it will ever be recalled.

[1] Fawcett's Art of War, a poem, 1794.

Our first and strongest impressions are taken from the mighty scene that is opened to us, and we very innocently transfer its durability as well as magnificence to ourselves. So newly found, we cannot make up our minds to parting with it yet and at least put off that consideration to an indefinite term. Like a clown at a fair, we are full of amazement and rapture, and have no thoughts of going home, or that it will soon be night. We know our existence only from external objects, and we measure it by them. We can never be satisfied with gazing; and nature will still want us to look on and applaud. Otherwise, the sumptuous entertainment, "the feast of reason and the flow of soul," to which they were invited, seems little better than a mockery and a cruel insult. We do not go from a play till the scene is ended, and the lights are ready to be extinguished. But the fair face of things still shines on; shall we be called away, before the curtain falls, or ere we have scarce had a glimpse of what is going on? Like children, our step-mother Nature holds us up to see the raree-show of the universe; and then, as if life were a burthen to support, lets us instantly down again. Yet in that short interval, what "brave sublunary things" does not the spectacle unfold; like a bubble, at one minute reflecting the universe, and the next, shook to air!—To see the golden sun and the azure sky, the outstretched ocean, to walk upon the green earth, and to be lord of a thousand creatures, to look down giddy precipices or over distant flowery vales, to see the world spread out under one's finger in a map, to bring the stars near, to view the smallest insects in a microscope, to read history, and witness the revolutions of empires and the succession of generations, to hear of the glory of Sidon and Tyre, of Babylon and Susa, as of a faded pageant, and to say all these were, and are now nothing,

FEELING OF IMMORTALITY IN YOUTH 63

to think that we exist in such a point of time, and in such a corner of space, to be at once spectators and a part of the moving scene, to watch the return of the seasons, of spring and autumn, to hear

"——The stockdove plain amid the forest deep,
That drowsy rustles to the sighing gale"—

to traverse desert wilderness, to listen to the midnight choir, to visit lighted halls, or plunge into the dungeon's gloom, or sit in crowded theatres and see life itself mocked, to feel heat and cold, pleasure and pain, right and wrong, truth and falsehood, to study the works of art and refine the sense of beauty to agony, to worship fame and to dream of immortality, to have read Shakespeare and belong to the same species as Sir Isaac Newton;[1] to be and to do all this, and then in a moment to

[1] Lady Wortley Montagu says, in one of her letters, that "she would much rather be a rich *effendi*, with all his ignorance, than Sir Isaac Newton, with all his knowledge." This was not perhaps an impolitic choice, as she had a better chance of becoming one than the other, there being many rich effendis to one Sir Isaac Newton. The wish was not a very intellectual one. The same petulance of rank and sex breaks out every where in these "*Letters.*" She is constantly reducing the poets or philosophers who have the misfortune of her acquaintance, to the figure they might make at her Ladyship's levee or toilette, not considering that the public mind does not sympathize with this process of a fastidious imagination. In the same spirit, she declares of Pope and Swift, that "had it not been for the *good-nature* of mankind, these two superior beings were entitled, by their birth and hereditary fortune, to be only a couple of link-boys." Gulliver's Travels, and the Rape of the Lock, go for nothing in this critical estimate, and the world raised the authors to the rank of superior beings, in spite of their disadvantages of birth and fortune, *out of pure good-nature!* So, again, she says of Richardson, that he had never got beyond the servant's hall, and was utterly unfit to describe the manners of people of quality; till in the capricious workings of her vanity, she persuades herself that Clarissa is very like what she was at her age, and that Sir Thomas and Lady Grandison strongly resembled what she had heard of her mother and remembered

be nothing, to have it all snatched from one like a juggler's ball or a phantasmagoria; there is something revolting and incredible to sense in the transition, and no wonder that, aided by youth and warm blood, and the flush of enthusiasm, the mind contrives for a long time to reject it with disdain and loathing as a monstrous and improbable fiction, like a monkey on a house-

of her father. It is one of the beauties and advantages of literature, that it is the means of abstracting the mind from the narrowness of local and personal prejudices, and of enabling us to judge of truth and excellence by their inherent merits alone. Woe be to the pen that would undo this fine illusion (the only reality), and teach us to regulate our notions of genius and virtue by the circumstances in which they happen to be placed! You would not expect a person whom you saw in a servant's hall, or behind a counter, to write Clarissa; but after he had written the work, to *pre-judge* it from the situation of the writer, is an unpardonable piece of injustice and folly. His merit could only be the greater from the contrast. If literature is an elegant accomplishment, which none but persons of birth and fashion should be allowed to excel in, or to exercise with advantage to the public, let them by all means take upon them the task of enlightening and refining mankind: if they decline this responsibility as too heavy for their shoulders, let those who do the drudgery in their stead, however inadequately, for want of their polite example, receive the meed that is their due, and not be treated as low pretenders who have encroached upon the provinces of their betters. Suppose Richardson to have been acquainted with the great man's steward, or valet, instead of the great man himself, I will venture to say that there was more difference between him who lived in an *ideal world,* and had the genius and felicity to open that world to others, and his friend the steward, than between the lacquey and the mere lord, or between those who lived in different rooms of the same house, who dined on the same luxuries at different tables, who rode outside or inside of the same coach, and were proud of wearing or of bestowing the same tawdry livery. If the lord is distinguished from his valet by any thing else, it is by education and talent, which he has in common with the author. But if the latter shews these in the highest degree, it is asked what are his pretensions? Not birth or fortune, for neither of these would enable him to write Clarissa. One man is born with a title and estate, another with genius. That is sufficient; and we have no right to question the genius for want of the

FEELING OF IMMORTALITY IN YOUTH 65

top, that is loath, amidst its fine discoveries and specious antics, to be tumbled headlong into the street, and crushed to atoms, the sport and laughter of the multitude!

The change, from the commencement to the close of life, appears like a fable, after it has taken place; how should we treat it otherwise than as a chimera before it

gentility, unless the former ran in families, or could be bequeathed with a fortune, which is not the case. Were it so, the flowers of literature, like jewels and embroidery, would be confined to the fashionable circles; and there would be no pretenders to taste or elegance but those whose names were found in the court list. No one objects to Claude's Landscapes as the work of a pastry-cook, or withholds from Raphael the epithet of *divine,* because his parents were not rich. This impertinence is confined to men of letters; the evidence of the senses baffles the envy and foppery of mankind. No quarter ought to be given to this *aristocratic* tone of criticism whenever it appears. People of quality are not contented with carrying all the external advantages for their own share, but would persuade you that all the intellectual ones are packed up in the same bundle. Lord Byron was a later instance of this double and unwarrantable style of pretension—*monstrum ingens, biforme.* He could not endure a lord who was not a wit, nor a poet who was not a lord. Nobody but himself answered his own standard of perfection. Mr. Moore carries a proxy in his pocket from some noble persons to estimate literary merit by the same rule. Lady Mary calls Fielding names, but she afterwards makes atonement by doing justice to his frank, free, hearty nature, where she says "his spirits gave him raptures with his cook-maid, and cheerfulness when he was starving in a garret, and his happy constitution made him forget everything when he was placed before a venison-pasty or over a flask of champagne." She does not want shrewdness and spirit when her petulance and conceit do not get the better of her, and she has done ample and merited execution on Lord Bolingbroke. She is, however, very angry at the freedoms taken with the Great; *smells a rat* in this indiscriminate scribbling, and the familiarity of writers with the reading public; and inspired by her Turkish costume, foretells a French and English revolution as the consequence of transferring the patronage of letters from the *quality* to the mob, and of supposing that ordinary writers or readers can have any notions in common with their superiors.

has come to pass? There are some things that happened so long ago, places or persons we have formerly seen, of which such dim traces remain, we hardly know whether it was sleeping or waking they occurred; they are like dreams within the dream of life, a mist, a film before the eye of memory, which, as we try to recall them more distinctly, elude our notice altogether. It is but natural that the lone interval that we thus look back upon, should have appeared long and endless in prospect. There are others so distinct and fresh, they seem but of yesterday—their very vividness might be deemed a pledge of their permanence. Then, however far back our impressions may go, we find others still older (for our years are multiplied in youth); descriptions of scenes that we have read, and people before our time, Priam and the Trojan war; and even then, Nestor was old and dwelt delighted on his youth, and spoke of the race of heroes that were no more;—what wonder that, seeing this long line of being pictured in our minds, and reviving as it were in us, we should give ourselves involuntary credit for an indeterminate existence? In the Cathedral at Peterborough there is a monument to Mary, Queen of Scots, at which I used to gaze when a boy, while the events of the period, all that had happened since, passed in review before me. If all this mass of feeling and imagination could be crowded into a moment's compass, what might not the whole of life be supposed to contain? We are heirs of the past; we count on the future as our natural reversion. Besides, there are some of our early impressions so exquisitely tempered, it appears that they must always last—nothing can add to or take away from their sweetness and purity—the first breath of spring, the hyacinth dipped in the dew, the mild lustre of the evening-star, the rainbow after a storm—while we have the full en-

FEELING OF IMMORTALITY IN YOUTH 67

joyment of these, we must be young; and what can ever alter us in this respect? Truth, friendship, love, books, are also proof against the canker of time; and while we live but for them, we can never grow old. We take out a new lease of existence from the objects on which we set our affections, and become abstracted, impassive, immortal in them. We cannot conceive how certain sentiments should ever decay or grow cold in our breasts; and, consequently, to maintain them in their first youthful glow and vigour, the flame of life must continue to burn as bright as ever, or rather, they are the fuel that feed the sacred lamp, that kindle "the purple light of love," and spread a golden cloud around our heads! Again, we not only flourish and survive in our affections (in which we will not listen to the possibility of a change, any more than we foresee the wrinkles on the brow of a mistress), but we have a farther guarantee against the thoughts of death in our favourite studies and pursuits and in their continual advance. Art we know is long; life, we feel, should be so too. We see no end of the difficulties we have to encounter: perfection is slow of attainment, and we must have time to accomplish it in. Rubens complained that when he had just learned his art, he was snatched away from it: we trust we shall be more fortunate! A wrinkle in an old head takes whole days to finish it properly: but to catch "the Raphael grace, the Guido air," no limit should be put to our endeavours. What a prospect for the future What a task we have entered upon! and shall we be arrested in the middle of it? We do not reckon our time thus employed lost, or our pains thrown away, or our progress slow—we do not droop or grow tired, but "gain a new vigour at our endless task;"—and shall Time grudge us the opportunity to finish what we have auspiciously begun, and

have formed a sort of compact with nature to achieve? The fame of the great names we look up to is also imperishable; and shall not we, who contemplate it with such intense yearnings, imbibe a portion of ethereal fire, the *divinae particula auroe,* which nothing can extinguish? I remember to have looked at a print of Rembrandt for hours together, without being conscious of the flight of time, trying to resolve it into its component parts, to connect its strong and sharp gradations, to learn the secret of its reflected lights, and found neither satiety nor pause in the prosecution of my studies. The print over which I was poring would last long enough; why should the idea in my mind, which was finer, more impalpable, perish before it? At this, I redoubled the ardour of my pursuit, and by the very subtlety and refinement of my inquiries, seemed to bespeak for them an exemption from corruption and the rude grasp of Death.[1]

Objects, on our first acquaintance with them, have that singleness and integrity of impression that it seems as if nothing could destroy or obliterate them, so firmly are they stamped and rivetted on the brain. We repose on them with a sort of voluptuous indolence, in full faith and boundless confidence. We are absorbed in the present moment, or return to the same point—idling away a great deal of time in youth, thinking we have enough to spare. There is often a local feeling in the air, which is as fixed as if it were marble; we loiter in dim cloisters, losing ourselves in thought and in their glimmering arches; a winding road before us seems as long as the journey of life, and as full of events. Time and experience dissipate this illusion; and by reducing

[1] Is it not this that frequently keeps artists alive so long, *viz.* the constant occupation of their minds with vivid images, with little of the *wear-and-tear* of the body?

them to detail, circumscribe the limits of our expectations. It is only as the pageant of life passes by and the masques turn their back upon us, that we see through the deception, or believe that the train will have an end. In many cases, the slow progress and monotonous texture of our lives, before we mingle with the world and are embroiled in its affairs, has a tendency to aid the same feeling. We have a difficulty, when left to ourselves, and without the resource of books or some more lively pursuit, to "beguile the slow and creeping hours of time," and argue that if it moves on always at this tedious snail's-pace, it can never come to an end. We are willing to skip over certain portions of it that separate us from favourite objects, that irritate ourselves at the unnecessary delay. The young are prodigal of life from a superabundance of it; the old are tenacious on the same score, because they have little left, and cannot enjoy even what remains of it.

For my part, I set out in life with the French Revolution, and that event had considerable influence on my early feelings, as on those of others. Youth was then doubly such. It was the dawn of a new era, a new impulse had been given to men's minds, and the sun of Liberty rose upon the sun of Life in the same day, and both were proud to run their race together. Little did I dream, while my first hopes and wishes went hand in hand with those of the human race, that long before my eyes should close, that dawn would be overcast, and set once more in the night of despotism—"total eclipse!" Happy that I did not. I felt for years, and during the best part of my existence, *heart-whole* in that cause, and triumphed in the triumphs over the enemies of man! At that time, while the fairest aspirations of the human mind seemed about to be realized, ere the image of man was defaced and his

breast mangled in scorn, philosophy took a higher, poetry could afford a deeper range. At that time, to read the "Robbers," was indeed delicious, and to hear

> "From the dungeon of the tower time-rent,
> That fearful voice, a famish'd father's cry."

could be borne only amidst the fulness of hope, the crash of the fall of the strong-holds of power, and the exulting sounds of the march of human freedom. What feelings the death-scene in Don Carlos sent into the soul! In that headlong career of lofty enthusiasm, and the joyous opening of the prospects of the world and our own, the thought of death crossing it, smote doubly cold upon the mind; there was a stifling sense of oppression and confinement, an impatience of our present knowledge, a desire to grasp the whole of our existence in one strong embrace, to sound the mystery of life and death, and in order to put an end to the agony of doubt and dread, to burst through our prison-house, and confront the King of Terrors in his grisly palace! . . . As I was writing out this passage, my miniature-picture when a child lay on the mantle-piece, and I took it out of the case to look at it. I could perceive few traces of myself in it; but there was the same placid brow, the dimpled mouth, the same timid, inquisitive glance as ever. But its careless smile did not seem to reproach me with having become recreant to the sentiments that were then sown in my mind, or with having written a sentence that could call up a blush in this image of ingenuous youth!

"That time is past with all its giddy raptures." Since the future was barred to my progress, I have turned for consolation to the past, gathering up the fragments of my early recollections, and putting them into a form that might live. It is thus, that when we find our per-

sonal and substantial identity vanishing from us, we strive to gain a reflected and substituted one in our thoughts: we do not like to perish wholly, and wish to bequeath our names at least to posterity. As long as we can keep alive our cherished thoughts and nearest interests in the minds of others, we do not appear to have retired altogether from the stage, we still occupy a place in the estimation of mankind, exercise a powerful influence over them, and it is only our bodies that are trampled into dust or dispersed into air. Our darling speculations still find favour and encouragement, and we make as good a figure in the eyes of our descendants, nay, perhaps, a better than we did in our life-time. This is one point gained; the demands of our self-love are so far satisfied. Besides, if by the proofs of intellectual superiority we survive ourselves in this world, by exemplary virtue or unblemished faith, we are taught to ensure an interest in another and a higher state of being, and to anticipate at the same time the applauses of men and angels.

"Even from the tomb the voice of nature cries;
Even in our ashes live their wonted fires."

As we advance in life, we acquire a keener sense of the value of time. Nothing else, indeed, seems of any consquence; and we become misers in this respect. We try to arrest its few last tottering steps, and to make it linger on the brink of the grave. We can never leave off wondering how that which has ever been should cease to be, and would still live on, that we may wonder at our own shadow, and when "all the life of life is flown," dwell on the retrospect of the past. This is accompanied by a mechanical tenaciousness of whatever we possess, by a distrust and a sense of fallacious hollowness in all we see. Instead of the full, pulpy feeling

of youth, every thing is flat and insipid. The world is a painted witch, that puts us off with false shews and tempting appearances. The ease, the jocund gaiety, the unsuspecting security of youth are fled: nor can we, without flying in the face of common sense,

"From the last dregs of life, hope to receive
What its first sprightly runnings could not give."

If we can slip out of the world without notice or mischance, can tamper with bodily infirmity, and frame our minds to the becoming composure of *still-life,* before we sink into total insensibility, it is as much as we ought to expect. We do not in the regular course of nature die all at once: we have mouldered away gradually long before; faculty after faculty, attachment after attachment, we are torn from ourselves piece-meal while living; year after year takes something from us; and death only consigns the last remnant of what we were to the grave. The revulsion is not so great, and a quiet *euthanasia* is a winding-up of the plot, that is not out of reason or nature.

That we should thus in a manner outlive ourselves, and dwindle imperceptibly into nothing, is not surprising, when even in our prime the strongest impressions leave so little traces of themselves behind, and the last object is driven out by the succeeding one. How little effect is produced on us at any time by the books we have read, the scenes we have witnessed, the sufferings we have gone through! Think only of the variety of feelings we experience in reading an interesting romance, or being present at a fine play—what beauty, what sublimity, what soothing, what heart-rending emotions! You would suppose these would last for ever, or at

least subdue the mind to a correspondent tone and harmony—while we turn over the page, while the scene is passing before us, it seems as if nothing could ever after shake our resolution, that "treason domestic, foreign levy, nothing could touch us farther!" The first splash of mud we get, on entering the street, the first pettifogging shop-keeper that cheats us out of twopence, and the whole vanishes clean out of our remembrance, and we become the idle prey of the most petty and annoying circumstances. The mind soars by an effort to the grand and lofty: it is at home, in the grovelling, the disagreeable, and the little. This happens in the height and hey-day of our existence, when novelty gives a stronger impulse to the blood and takes a faster hold of the brain, (I have known the impression on coming out of a gallery of pictures then last half a day)—as we grow old, we become more feeble and querulous, every object "reverbs its own hollowness," and both worlds are not enough to satisfy the peevish importunity and extravagant presumption of our desires! There are a few superior, happy beings, who are born with a temper exempt from every trifling annoyance. This spirit sits serene and smiling as in its native skies, and a divine harmony (whether heard or not) plays around them. This is to be at peace. Without this, it is in vain to fly into deserts, or to build a hermitage on the top of rocks, if regret and ill-humour follow us there: and with this, it is needless to make the experiment. The only true retirement is that of the heart; the only true leisure is the repose of the passions. To such persons it makes little difference whether they are young or old; and they die as they have lived, with graceful resignation.

ON THE FEAR OF DEATH

"And our little life is rounded with a sleep."

Perhaps the best cure for the fear of death is to reflect that life has a beginning as well as an end. There was a time when we were not: this gives us no concern— why then should it trouble us that a time will come when we shall cease to be? I have no wish to have been alive a hundred years ago, or in the reign of Queen Anne: why should I regret and lay it so much to heart that I shall not be alive a hundred years hence, in the reign of I cannot tell whom?

When Bickerstaff wrote his Essays, I knew nothing of the subjects of them; nay, much later, and but the other day, as it were, in the beginning of the reign of George III., when Goldsmith, Johnson, Burke, used to meet at the Globe, when Garrick was in his glory, and Reynolds was over head and ears with his portraits, and Sterne brought out the volumes of Tristram Shandy year by year, it was without consulting me: I had not the slightest intimation of what was going on: the debates in the House of Commons on the American War, or the firing at Bunker's Hill, disturbed not me: yet I thought this no evil—I neither ate, drank, nor was merry, yet I did not complain: I had not then looked out into this breathing world, yet I was well; and the world did quite as well without me as I did without it! Why then should I make all this outcry about parting with it, and being no worse off than I was before? There is nothing in the recollection that at a certain time we were not come into the world, that "the gorge rises at"—why should we revolt at the idea that we must one day go out of it? To die is only to be as we were before we were born; yet no one feels any remorse, or regret, or repugnance, in contemplating

ON THE FEAR OF DEATH

this last idea. It is rather a relief and disburthening of the mind: it seems to have been holiday-time with us then: we were not called to appear upon the stage of life, to wear robes or tatters, to laugh or cry, be hooted or applauded; we had lain *perdus* all this while, snug, out of harm's way; and had slept out our thousands of centuries without wanting to be waked up; at peace and free from care, in a long nonage, in a sleep deeper and calmer than that of infancy, wrapt in the softest and finest dust. And the worst that we dread is, after a short, fretful, feverish being, after vain hopes, and idle fears, to sink to final repose again, and forget the troubled dream of life! . . . Ye armed men, knights templars, that sleep in the stone aisles of that old Temple church, where all is silent above, and where a deeper silence reigns below (not broken by the pealing organ), are ye not contented where ye lie? Or would you come out of your long homes to go to the Holy War? Or do ye complain that pain no longer visits you, that sickness has done its worst, that you have paid the last debt to nature, that you hear no more of the thickening phalanx of the foe, or your lady's waning love; and that while this ball of earth rolls its eternal round, no sound shall ever pierce through to disturb your lasting repose, fixed as the marble over your tombs, breathless as the grave that holds you! And thou, oh! thou, to whom my heart turns, and will turn while it has feeling left, who didst love in vain, and whose first was thy last sigh, wilt not thou too rest in peace (or wilt thou cry to me complaining from thy clay-cold bed) when that sad heart is no longer sad, and that sorrow is dead which thou wert only called into the world to feel!

It is certain that there is nothing in the idea of a pre-existent state that excites our longing like the

prospect of a posthumous existence. We are satisfied to have begun life when we did; we have no ambition to have set out on our journey sooner; and feel that we have had quite enough to do to battle our way through since. We cannot say,

"The wars we well remember of King Nine,
  Of old Assaracus and Inachus divine."

Neither have we any wish: we are contented to read of them in story, and to stand and gaze at the vast sea of time that separates us from them. It was early days then: the world was not *well-aired* enough for us: we have no inclination to have been up and stirring. We do not consider the six thousand years of the world before we were born as so much time lost to us: we are perfectly indifferent about the matter. We do not grieve and lament that we did not happen to be in time to see the grand mask and pageant of human life going on in all that period; though we are mortified at being obliged to quit our stand before the rest of the procession passes.

It may be suggested in explanation of this difference, that we know from various records and traditions what happened in the time of Queen Anne, or even in the reigns of the Assyrian monarchs: but that we have no means of ascertaining what is to happen hereafter but by awaiting the event, and that our eagerness and curiosity are sharpened in proportion as we are in the dark about it. This is not at all the case; for at that rate we should be constantly wishing to make a voyage of discovery to Greenland or to the Moon, neither of which we have, in general, the least desire to do. Neither, in truth, have we any particular solicitude to pry into the secrets of futurity, but as a pretext for prolonging our own existence. It is not so much that

we care to be alive a hundred or a thousand years hence, any more than to have been alive a hundred or a thousand years ago: but the thing lies here, that we would all of us wish the present moment to last for ever. We would be as we are, and would have the world remain just as it is, to please us.

"The present eye catches the present object"— to have and to hold while it may; and abhors, on any terms, to have it torn from us, and nothing left in its room. It is the pang of parting, the unloosing our grasp, the breaking asunder some strong tie, the leaving some cherished purpose unfulfilled, that creates the repugnance to go, and "makes calamity of so long life," as it often is.

———"Oh! thou strong heart!
There's such a covenant 'twixt the world and thee
They're loth to break!"

The love of life, then, is an habitual attachment, not an abstract principle. Simply *to be* does not "content man's natural desire": we long to be in a certain time, place, and circumstance. We would much rather be now, "on this bank and shoal of time," than have our choice of any future period, than take a slice of fifty or sixty years out of the Millennium, for instance. This shows that our attachment is not confined either to *being* or to *well-being;* but that we have an inveterate prejudice in favour of our immediate existence, such as it is. The mountaineer will not leave his rock, nor the savage his hut; neither are we willing to give up our present mode of life, with all its advantages and disadvantages, for any other that could be substituted for it. No man would, I think, exchange his existence with any other man, however fortunate. We had as lief *not be,* as *not be ourselves.* There are some per-

sons of that reach of soul that they would like to live two hundred and fifty years hence, to see to what height of empire America will have grown up in that period, or whether the English constitution will last so long. These are points beyond me. But I confess I should like to live to see the downfall of the Bourbons. That is a vital question with me; and I shall like it the better, the sooner it happens!

No young man ever thinks he shall die. He may believe that others will, or assent to the doctrine that "all men are mortal" as an abstract proposition, but he is far enough from bringing it home to himself individually.[1] Youth, buoyant activity, and animal spirits, hold absolute antipathy with old age as well as with death; nor have we, in the hey-day of life, any more than in the thoughtfulness of childhood, the remotest conception how

> "This sensible warm motion can become
> A kneaded clod"—

nor how sanguine, florid health and vigour, shall "turn to withered, weak, and grey." Or if in a moment of idle speculation we indulge in this notion of the close of life as a theory, it is amazing at what a distance it seems; what a long, leisurely interval there is between; what a contrast its slow and solemn approach affords to our present gay dreams of existence! We eye the farthest verge of the horizon, and think what a way we shall have to look back upon, ere we arrive at our journey's end; and without our in the least suspecting it, the mists are at our feet, and the shadows of age encompass us. The two divisions of our lives have melted into each other: the extreme points close and meet with none of that romantic interval stretching

[1] All men think all men mortal but themselves."—YOUNG.

out between them that we had reckoned upon; and for the rich, melancholy, solemn hues of age, "the sear, the yellow leaf," the deepening shadows of an autumnal evening, we only feel a dank, cold mist, encircling all objects, after the spirit of youth is fled. There is no inducement to look forward; and what is worse, little interest in looking back to what has become so trite and common. The pleasures of our existence have worn themselves out, are "gone into the wastes of time," or have turned their indifferent side to us: the pains by their repeated blows have worn us out, and have left us neither spirit nor inclination to encounter them again in retrospect. We do not want to rip up old grievances, nor to renew our youth like the phœnix, nor to live our lives twice over. Once is enough. As the tree falls, so let it lie. Shut up the book and close the account once for all!

It has been thought by some that life is like the exploring of a passage that grows narrower and darker the farther we advance, without a possibility of ever turning back, and where we are stifled for want of breath at last. For myself, I do not complain of the narrow house. I felt it more formerly,[1] when the idea alone seemed to suppress a thousand rising hopes, and weighed upon the pulses of the blood. At present I rather feel a thinness and want of support, I stretch out my hand to some object and find none, I am too much in a world of abstraction; the naked map of life is spread out before me, and in the emptiness and desolation I see Death coming to meet me. In my youth I could not behold him for the crowd of objects and feelings, and Hope stood always between us, say-

[1] I remember once, in particular, having this feeling in reading Schiller's Don Carlos, where there is a description of death, in a degree that almost stifled me.

ing, "Never mind that old fellow!" If I had lived indeed, I should not care to die. But I do not like a contract of pleasure broken off unfulfilled, a marriage with joy unconsummated, a promise of happiness rescinded. My public and private hopes have been left a ruin, or remain only to mock me. I would wish them to be re-edified. I should like to see some prospect of good to mankind, such as my life began with. I should like to leave some sterling work behind me. I should like to have some friendly hand to consign me to the grave. On these conditions I am ready, if not willing, to depart. I shall then write on my tomb— GRATEFUL AND CONTENTED! But I have thought and suffered too much to be willing to have thought and suffered in vain.—In looking back, it sometimes appears to me as if I had in a manner slept out my life in a dream or shadow on the side of the hill of knowledge, where I have fed on books, on thoughts, on pictures, and only heard in half-murmurs the trampling of busy feet, or the noises of the throng below. Waked out of this dim, twilight existence, and startled with the passing scene, I have felt a wish to descend to the world of realities, and join in the chase. But I fear too late, and that I had better return to my bookish chimeras and indolence once more! *Zanetto, lascia le donne, et studia la matematica.* I will think of it.

It is not wonderful that the contemplation and fear of death become more familiar to us as we approach nearer to it: that life seems to ebb with the decay of blood and youthful spirits; and that as we find everything about us subject to chance and change, as our strength and beauty die, as our hopes and passions, our friends and our affections leave us, we begin by degrees to feel ourselves mortal!

I have never seen death but once, and that was in an

ON THE FEAR OF DEATH

infant. It is years ago. The look was calm and placid, and the face was fair and firm. It was as if a waxen image had been laid out in the coffin, and strewed with innocent flowers. It was not like death, but more like an image of life! No breath moved the lips, no pulse stirred, no sight or sound would enter those eyes or ears more. While I looked at it, I saw no pain was there; it seemed to smile at the short pang of life which was over: but I could not bear the coffin-lid to be closed —it seemed to stifle me; and still as the nettles wave in a corner of the churchyard over his little grave, the welcome breeze helps to refresh me, and ease the tightness at my breast!

An ivory or marble image, like Chantry's monument of the two children, is contemplated with pure delight. Why do we not grieve and fret that the marble is not alive, or fancy that it has a shortness of breath? It never was alive; and it is the difficulty of making the transition from life to death, the struggle between the two in our imagination, that confounds their properties painfully together, and makes us conceive that the infant that is but just dead, still wants to breathe, to enjoy, and look about it, and is prevented by the icy hand of death, locking up its faculties and benumbing its senses; so that, if it could, it would complain of its own hard state. Perhaps religious considerations reconcile the mind to this change sooner than any others, by representing the spirit as fled to another sphere, and leaving the body behind it. So in reflecting on death generally, we mix up the idea of life with it, and thus make it the ghastly monster it is. We think, how we should feel, not how the dead feel.

"Still from the tomb the voice of nature cries;
Even in our ashes live their wonted fires!"

There is an admirable passage on this subject in Tucker's *Light of Nature Pursued,* which I shall transcribe, as by much the best illustration I can offer of it.

"The melancholy appearance of a lifeless body, the mansion provided for it to inhabit, dark, cold, close and solitary, are shocking to the imagination; but it is to the imagination only, not the understanding; for whoever consults this faculty will see at first glance, that there is nothing dismal in all these circumstances: if the corpse were kept wrapped up in a warm bed, with a roasting fire in the chamber, it would feel no comfortable warmth therefrom; were store of tapers lighted up as soon as day shuts in, it would see no objects to divert it; were it left at large it would have no liberty, nor if surrounded with company would be cheered thereby; neither are the distorted features, expressions of pain, uneasiness, or distress. This every one knows, and will readily allow upon being suggested, yet still cannot behold, nor even cast a thought upon those objects without shuddering; for knowing that a living person must suffer grievously under such appearances, they become habitually formidable to the mind, and strike a mechanical horror, which is increased by the customs of the world around us."

There is usually one pang added voluntarily and unnecessarily to the fear of death, by our affecting to compassionate the loss which others will have in us. If that were all, we might reasonably set our minds at rest. The pathetic exhortation on country tombstones, "Grieve not for me, my wife and children dear," &c., is for the most part speedily followed to the letter. We do not leave so great a void in society as we are inclined to imagine, partly to magnify our own importance, and partly to console ourselves by sympathy. Even in the same family the gap is not so great; the

wound closes up sooner than we should expect. Nay, *our room* is not unfrequently thought better than *our company*. People walk along the streets the day after our deaths just as they did before, and the crowd is not diminished. While we were living, the world seemed in a manner to exist only for us, for our delight and amusement, because it contributed to them. But our hearts cease to beat, and it goes on as usual, and thinks no more about us than it did in our life-time. The million are devoid of sentiment, and care as little for you or me as if we belonged to the moon. We live the week over in the Sunday's paper, or are decently interred in some obituary at the month's end! It is not surprising that we are forgotten so soon after we quit this mortal stage; we are scarcely noticed while we are on it. It is not merely that our names are not known in China—they have hardly been heard of in the next street. We are hand in glove with the universe, and think the obligation is mutual. This is an evident fallacy. If this, however, does not trouble us now, it will not hereafter. A handful of dust can have no quarrel to pick with its neighbours, or complaint to make against Providence, and might well exclaim, if it had but an understanding and a tongue, "Go thy ways, old world, swing round in blue ether, voluble to every age, you and I shall no more jostle!"

It is amazing how soon the rich and titled, and even some of those who have wielded great political power, are forgotten.

> "A little rule, a little sway,
>   Is all the great and mighty have
>   Betwixt the cradle and the grave"—

and, after its short date, they hardly leave a name behind them. "A great man's memory may, at the

common rate, survive him half a year." His heirs and successors take his titles, his power, and his wealth—all that made him considerable or courted by others; and he has left nothing else behind him either to delight or benefit the world. Posterity are not by any means so disinterested as they are supposed to be. They give their gratitude and admiration only in return for benefits conferred. They cherish the memory of those to whom they are indebted for instruction and delight; and they cherish it just in proportion to the instruction and delight they are conscious they receive. The sentiment of admiration springs immediately from this ground, and cannot be otherwise than well founded.[1]

The effeminate clinging to life as such, as a general or abstract idea, is the effect of a highly civilised and artificial state of society. Men formerly plunged into all the vicissitudes and dangers of war, or staked their all upon a single die, or some one passion, which if they could not have gratified life became a burden to them—now our strongest passion is to think, our chief amusement is to read new plays, new poems, new novels, and this we may do at our leisure, in perfect security, *ad infinitum*. If we look into the old histories and romances, before the *belles-lettres* neutralised human affairs and reduced passion to a state of mental equivocation, we find the heroes and heroines not setting their lives "at a pin's fee," but rather courting opportunities

[1] It has been usual to raise a very unjust clamour against the enormous salaries of public singers, actors, and so on. This matter seems reducible to a *moral equation*. They are paid out of money raised by voluntary contributions in the strictest sense; and if they did not bring certain sums into the treasury, the Managers would not engage them. These sums are exactly in proportion to the number of individuals to whom their performance gives an extraordinary degree of pleasure. The talents of a singer, actor, &c., are therefore worth just as much as they will fetch.

of throwing them away in very wantonness of spirit. They raise their fondness for some favourite pursuit to its height, to a pitch of madness, and think no price too dear to pay for its full gratification. Every thing else is dross. They go to death as to a bridal bed, and sacrifice themselves or others without remorse at the shrine of love, of honour, of religion, or any other prevailing feeling. Romeo runs his "sea-sick, weary bark upon the rocks" of death, the instant he finds himself deprived of his Juliet; and she clasps his neck in their last agonies, and follows him to the same fatal shore. One strong idea takes possession of the mind and over-rules every other; and even life itself, joyless without that, becomes an object of indifference or loathing. There is at least more of imagination in such a state of things, more vigour of feeling and promptitude to act than in our lingering, languid, protracted attachment to life for its own poor sake. It is, perhaps, also better, as well as more heroical, to strike at some daring or darling object, and if we fail in that, to take the consequences manfully, than to renew the lease of a tedious, spiritless, charmless existence, merely (as Pierre says) "to lose it afterwards in some vile brawl" for some worthless object. Was there not a spirit of martyrdom as well as a spice of reckless energy of barbarism in this bold defiance of death? Had not religion something to do with it: the implicit belief in a future life, which rendered this of less value, and embodied something beyond it to the imagination; so that the rough soldier, the infatuated lover, the valorous knight, &c., could afford to throw away the present venture, and take a leap into the arms of futurity, which the modern sceptic shrinks back from, with all his boasted reason and vain philosophy, weaker than a woman! I cannot help thinking so myself; but I have endeavoured to explain

this point before, and will not enlarge farther on it here.

A life of action and danger moderates the dread of death. It not only gives us fortitude to bear pain, but teaches us at every step the precarious tenure on which we hold our present being. Sedentary and studious men are the most apprehensive on this score. Dr. Johnson was an instance in point. A few years seemed to him soon over, compared with those sweeping contemplations on time and infinity with which he had been used to pose himself. In the *still-life* of a man of letters there was no obvious reason for a change. He might sit in an arm-chair and pour out cups of tea to all eternity. Would it had been possible for him to do so! The most rational cure after all for the inordinate fear of death is to set a just value on life. If we merely wish to continue on the scene to indulge our headstrong humours and tormenting passions, we had better begone at once; and if we only cherish a fondness for existence according to the good we derive from it, the pang we feel at parting with it will not be very severe!

CHARLES LAMB

HAZLITT in an appreciative passage remarks of Lamb's style that, despite its archaisms and its borrowings from Elizabethan and Jacobean writers, it is appropriate to its author and therefore genuine. What in another would seem affectation is in Lamb the dress peculiar to his genius. But Hazlitt notes also that Lamb's best work is in his more serious vein; and it is in this that Lamb is least peculiar and mannered. The criticisms are not, perhaps, wholly reconcilable. Hazlitt was not forgetful of Lamb's charm both as man and writer and his concession to it, a rare instance in his ever-just criticism, is, if a weakness, an amiable one. Much as Lamb's literary friends, who were many and diverse, quarreled among themselves, him they loved and admired. He continued to remain the friend both of Southey and Hazlitt, with but one interval of coldness in each instance due to no fault of his.

The charm of Lamb's personality is manifest in his essays and even more, to my thinking, in his letters. With few authors does the reader feel so intimate; much of the pleasure one has in reading him is the sense of listening to the brilliant conversation of a gifted friend. Lamb could say harsh things of acquaintances now and again in letters to his friends. But his strictures are humorous or deliberately exaggerated and doubtless deserved. In few authors have essential kindness and charity been so blent with shrewd insight. Lamb, though he perceived the imperfections of his friends, bore with them. He was, therefore, in his own day, and has remained, greatly beloved. An anecdote is

characteristic: having expressed his hatred of someone and his auditor exhibiting surprise, Lamb remarked that of course he didn't know the man or he couldn't hate him.

The romantic qualities in Lamb are obvious. His harking back to his beloved Elizabethan and Jacobean writers, for whose rehabilitation he did much, is one. The personal autobiographical quality of his work is another. In his best essays Lamb draws much upon his memories of his childhood, of the Inns of Law, of the East India House, of odd characters he has known. His vein is narrow as was, in a sense, his life. He travelled little and his days were mostly spent in unattractive tasks. It was only in his reading and in the experiences of his friends that he wandered far. A confirmed cockney, he made slurring remarks upon the beauties of the mountains beloved of Wordsworth, largely, to be sure, that he might provoke Wordsworth. Yet it is true that he was never for long happy beyond the sight and sound of London where he had been born and bred. There is not in Lamb that hearty enjoyment of the out-of-doors which is one of the strains in Hazlitt's nature. But Hazlitt was happiest when alone, and Lamb when among his friends. He was a social being.

Lamb's fondness for old words, for recondite quotations, his faculty of exaggeration for humorous effect, his puns and jokes are all a part of his peculiar manner. A page of his writing declares its author unmistakably. No less characteristic is the genuine vein of pathos in his work. *Dream Children* is a moving and a tender thing. The memories with which so much of his work is crowded are touched with a delicate melancholy. In this respect his work has a wider range than Hazlitt's. There is little pathos in Hazlitt that I recall and his

melancholy is more robust. To Hazlitt, with his gusto for life and his delight in books and pictures, these more delicate shades of feeling are foreign. The differences in the two explain the greater popularity of Lamb's work despite the fact that, in my judgment, Hazlitt as critic, stylist, and observer of life is the greater of the two.

In a book so small as this the selections from Lamb's work are necessarily inadequate and do not represent his entire range. I have selected essays which seem to me among his best. Another choice might easily be defended as preferable. But if these few essays serve to send new readers to Lamb's works—unfortunately only too limited—they will have met the purpose for which they were chosen.

WITCHES, AND OTHER NIGHT-FEARS

WE are too hasty when we set down our ancestors in the gross for fools, for the monstrous inconsistencies (as they seem to us) involved in their creed of witchcraft. In the relations of this visible world we find them to have been as rational, and shrewd to detect an historic anomaly, as ourselves. But when once the invisible world was supposed to be opened, and the lawless agency of bad spirits assumed, what measures of probability, of decency, of fitness, or proportion—of that which distinguishes the likely from the palpable absurd—could they have to guide them in the rejection or admission of any particular testimony?—that maidens pined away, wasting inwardly as their waxen images consumed before a fire—that corn was lodged and cattle lamed—that whirlwinds uptore in diabolic revelry the oaks of the forest—or that spits and kettles only danced a fearful-innocent vagary about some

rustic's kitchen when no wind was stirring—were all equally probable where no law of agency was understood. That the prince of the powers of darkness, passing by the flower and pomp of the earth, should lay preposterous siege to the weak fantasy of indigent eld—has neither likelihood nor unlikelihood *à priori* to us, who have no measure to guess at his policy, or standard to estimate what rate those anile souls may fetch in the devil's market. Nor, when the wicked are expressly symbolised by a goat, was it to be wondered at so much, that *he* should come sometimes in that body, and assert his metaphor.—That the intercourse was opened at all between both worlds was perhaps the mistake—but that once assumed, I see no reason for disbelieving one attested story of this nature more than another on the score of absurdity. There is no law to judge of the lawless, or canon by which a dream may be criticised.

I have sometimes thought that I could not have existed in the days of received witchcraft; that I could not have slept in a village where one of those reputed hags dwelt. Our ancestors were bolder or more obtuse. Amidst the universal belief that these wretches were in league with the author of all evil, holding hell tributary to their muttering, no simple Justice of the Peace seems to have scrupled issuing, or silly Headborough serving, a warrant upon them—as if they should subpœna Satan!—Prospero in his boat, with his books and wand about him suffers himself to be conveyed away at the mercy of his enemies to an unknown island. He might have raised a storm or two, we think, on the passage. His acquiescence is in exact analogy to the non-resistance of witches to the constituted powers.— What stops the Fiend in Spenser from tearing Guyon to pieces—or who had made it a condition of his prey,

that Guyon must take assay of the glorious bait—we have no guess. We do not know the laws of that country.

From my childhood I was extremely inquisitive about witches and witch-stories. My maid, and more legendary aunt, supplied me with good store. But I shall mention the accident which directed my curiosity originally into this channel. In my father's book-closet, the History of the Bible, by Stackhouse, occupied a distinguished station. The pictures with which it abounds—one of the ark, in particular, and another of Solomon's temple, delineated with all the fidelity of ocular admeasurement, as if the artist had been upon the spot—attracted my childish attention. There was a picture, too, of the Witch raising up Samuel, which I wish that I had never seen. We shall come to that hereafter. Stackhouse is in two huge tomes—and there was a pleasure in removing folios of that magnitude, which, with infinite straining, was as much as I could manage, from the situation which they occupied upon an upper shelf. I have not met with the work from that time to this, but I remember it consisted of Old Testament stories, orderly set down, with the *objection* appended to each story, and the *solution* of the objection regularly tacked to that. The *objection* was a summary of whatever difficulties had been opposed to the credibility of the history, by the shrewdness of ancient or modern infidelity, drawn up with an almost complimentary excess of candour. The *solution* was brief, modest, and satisfactory. The bane and antidote were both before you. To doubts so put, and so quashed, there seemed to be an end for ever. The dragon lay dead, for the foot of the veriest babe to trample on. But—like as was rather feared than realised from that slain monster in Spenser—from the womb of those

crushed errors young dragonets would creep, exceeding the prowess of so tender a Saint George as myself to vanquish. The habit of expecting objections to every passage, set me upon starting more objections, for the glory of finding a solution of my own for them. I became staggered and perplexed, a sceptic in long coats. The pretty Bible stories which I had read, or heard read in church, lost their purity and sincerity of impression, and were turned into so many historic or chronologic theses to be defended against whatever impugners. I was not to disbelieve them, but—the next thing to that—I was to be quite sure that some one or other would or had disbelieved them. Next to making a child an infidel, is the letting him know that there are infidels at all. Credulity is the man's weakness, but the child's strength. O, how ugly sound scriptural doubts from the mouth of a babe and a suckling!—I should have lost myself in these mazes, and have pined away, I think, with such unfit sustenance as these husks afforded, but for a fortunate piece of ill-fortune, which about this time befel me. Turning over the picture of the ark with too much haste, I unhappily made a breach in its ingenious fabric— driving my inconsiderate fingers right through the two larger quadrupeds—the elephant, and the camel—that stare (as well they might) out of the two last windows next the steerage in that unique piece of naval architecture. Stackhouse was henceforth locked up, and became an interdicted treasure. With the book, the *objections* and *solutions* gradually cleared out of my head, and have seldom returned since in any force to trouble me.—But there was one impression which I had imbibed from Stackhouse, which no lock or bar could shut out, and which was destined to try my childish nerves rather more seriously.—That detestable picture!

I was dreadfully alive to nervous terrors. The night-time solitude, and the dark, were my hell. The sufferings I endured in this nature would justify the expression. I never laid my head on my pillow, I suppose, from the fourth to the seventh or eighth year of my life—so far as memory serves in things so long ago—without an assurance, which realised its own prophecy, of seeing some frightful spectre. Be old Stackhouse then acquitted in part, if I say, that to his picture of the Witch raising up Samuel—(O that old man covered with a mantle!) I owe—not my midnight terrors, the hell of my infancy—but the shape and manner of their visitation. It was he who dressed up for me a hag that nightly sate upon my pillow—a sure bed-fellow, when my aunt or my maid was far from me. All day long, while the book was permitted me, I dreamed waking over his delineation, and at night (if I may use so bold an expression) awoke into sleep, and found the vision true. I durst not, even in the daylight, once enter the chamber where I slept, without my face turned to the window, aversely from the bed where my witch-ridden pillow was.—Parents do not know what they do when they leave tender babes alone to go to sleep in the dark. The feeling about for a friendly arm—the hoping for a familiar voice—when they wake screaming—and find none to soothe them—what a terrible shaking it is to their poor nerves! The keeping them up till midnight, through candle-light and the unwholesome hours, as they are called,—would, I am satisfied, in a medical point of view, prove the better caution.—That detestable picture, as I have said, gave the fashion to my dreams—if dreams they were—for the scene of them was invariably the room in which I lay. Had I never met with the picture, the fears

would have come self-pictured in some shape or other—

> Headless bear, black man, or ape—

but, as it was, my imaginations took that form.—It is not book, or picture, or the stories of foolish servants, which create these terrors in children. They can at most but give them a direction. Dear little T. H. who of all children has been brought up with the most scrupulous exclusion of every taint of superstition—who was never allowed to hear of goblin or apparition, or scarcely to be told of bad men, or to read or hear of any distressing story—finds all this world of fear, from which he has been so rigidly excluded *ab extra,* in his own "thick-coming fancies;" and from his little midnight pillow, this nurse-child of optimism will start at shapes, unborrowed of tradition, in sweats to which the reveries of the cell-damned murderer are tranquillity.

Gorgons, and Hydras, and Chimæras—dire stories of Celæno and the Harpies—may reproduce themselves in the brain of superstition—but they were there before. They are transcripts, types—the archetypes are in us, and eternal. How else should the recital of that, which we know in a waking sense to be false, come to affect us at all?—or

> ——Names, whose sense we see not,
> Fray us with things that be not?

Is it that we naturally conceive terror from such objects, considered in their capacity of being able to inflict upon us bodily injury?—O, least of all! These terrors are of older standing. They date beyond body—or, without the body, they would have been the same. All the cruel, tormenting, defined devils in Dante—tearing, mangling, choking, stifling, scorching demons—are they

WITCHES, AND OTHER NIGHT-FEARS

one half so fearful to the spirit of a man, as the simple idea of a spirit unembodied following him—

> Like one that on a lonesome road
> Doth walk in fear and dread,
> And having once turn'd round, walks on,
> And turns no more his head;
> Because he knows a frightful fiend
> Doth close behind him tread.*

That the kind of fear here treated of is purely spiritual—that it is strong in proportion as it is objectless upon earth—that it predominates in the period of sinless infancy—are difficulties, the solution of which might afford some probable insight into our ante-mundane condition, and a peep at least into the shadowland of pre-existence.

My night-fancies have long ceased to be afflictive. I confess an occasional night-mare; but I do not, as in early youth, keep a stud of them. Fiendish faces, with the extinguished taper, will come and look at me; but I know them for mockeries, even while I cannot elude their presence, and I fight and grapple with them. For the credit of my imagination, I am almost ashamed to say how tame and prosaic my dreams are grown. They are never romantic, seldom even rural. They are of architecture and of buildings—cities abroad which I have never seen, and hardly have hope to see. I have traversed, for the seeming length of a natural day, Rome, Amsterdam, Paris, Lisbon—their churches, palaces, squares, market-places, shops, suburbs, ruins, with an inexpressible sense of delight—a map-like distinctness of trace—and a daylight vividness of vision, that was all but being awake.—I have formerly travelled among the Westmoreland fells—my highest Alps,—but

* Mr. Coleridge's Ancient Mariner.

they are objects too mighty for the grasp of my dreaming recognition; and I have again and again awoke with ineffectual struggles of the inner eye, to make out a shape in any way whatever, of Helvellyn. Methought I was in that country, but the mountains were gone. The poverty of my dreams mortifies me. There is Coleridge, at his will can conjure up icy domes, and pleasure-houses for Kubla Khan, and Abyssinian maids, and songs of Abara, and caverns,

> Where Alph, the sacred river, runs,

to solace his night solitudes—when I cannot muster a fiddle. Barry Cornwall has his tritons and his nereids gambolling before him in nocturnal visions, and proclaiming sons born to Neptune—when my stretch of imaginative activity can hardly, in the night season, raise up the ghost of a fish-wife. To set my failures in somewhat a mortifying light—it was after reading the noble Dream of this poet, that my fancy ran strong upon these marine spectra; and the poor plastic power, such as it is, within me set to work, to humour my folly in a sort of dream that very night. Methought I was upon the ocean billows at some sea nuptials, riding and mounted high, with the customary train sounding their conchs before me, (I myself, you may be sure, the *leading god,*) and jollily we went careering over the main, till just where Ino Lucothea should have greeted me (I think it was Ino) with a white embrace, the billows gradually subsiding, fell from a sea-roughness to a sea-calm, and thence to a river-motion, and that river (as happens in the familiarisation of dreams) was no other than the gentle Thames, which landed me, in the wafture of a placid wave or two, alone, safe and inglorious, somewhere at the foot of Lambeth palace.

The degree of the soul's creativeness in sleep might

furnish no whimsical criterion of the quantum of poetical faculty resident in the same soul waking. An old gentleman, a friend of mine, and a humourist, used to carry this notion so far, that when he saw any stripling of his acquaintance ambitious of becoming a poet, his first question would be,—"Young man, what sort of dreams have you?" I have so much faith in my old friend's theory, that when I feel that idle vein returning upon me, I presently subside into my proper element of prose, remembering those eluding nereids, and that inauspicious inland landing.

BLAKESMOOR IN H——SHIRE

I do not know a pleasure more affecting than to range at will over the deserted apartments of some fine old family mansion. The traces of extinct grandeur admit of a better passion than envy: and contemplations on the great and good, whom we fancy in succession to have been its inhabitants, weave for us illusions, incompatible with the bustle of modern occupancy, and vanities of foolish present aristocracy. The same difference of feeling, I think, attends us between entering an empty and a crowded church. In the latter it is chance but some present human frailty—an act of inattention on the part of some of the auditory—or a trait of affectation, or worse, vain-glory, on that of the preacher—puts us by our best thoughts, disharmonising the place and the occasion. But wouldst thou know the beauty of holiness?—go alone on some week-day, borrowing the keys of good Master Sexton, traverse the cool aisles of some country church: think of the piety that has kneeled there—the congregations, old and young, that have found consolation there—the meek pastor—the docile parishioner. With no disturbing emotions, no cross

conflicting comparisons, drink in the tranquillity of the place, till thou thyself become as fixed and motionless as the marble effigies that kneel and weep around thee.

Journeying northward lately, I could not resist going some few miles out of my road to look upon the remains of an old great house with which I had been impressed in this way in infancy. I was apprised that the owner of it had lately pulled it down; still I had a vague notion that it could not all have perished, that so much solidity with magnificence could not have been crushed all at once into the mere dust and rubbish which I found it.

The work of ruin had proceeded with a swift hand indeed, and the demolition of a few weeks had reduced it to—an antiquity.

I was astonished at the indistinction of everything. Where had stood the great gates? What bounded the courtyard? Whereabouts did the out-houses commence? A few bricks only lay as representatives of that which was so stately and so spacious.

Death does not shrink up his human victim at this rate. The burnt ashes of a man weigh more in their proportion.

Had I seen these brick-and-mortar knaves at their process of destruction, at the plucking of every pannel I should have felt the varlets at my heart. I should have cried out to them to spare a plank at least out of the cheerful store-room, in whose hot window-seat I used to sit and read Cowley, with the grass-plot before, and the hum and flappings of that one solitary wasp that ever haunted it about me—it is in mine ears now, as oft as summer returns; or a pannel of the yellow room.

Why, every plank and pannel of that house for me had magic in it. The tapestried bed-rooms—tapestry

BLAKESMOOR IN H——SHIRE

so much better than painting—not adorning merely, but peopling the wainscots—at which childhood ever and anon would steal a look, shifting its coverlid (replaced as quickly) to exercise its tender courage in a momentary eye-encounter with those stern bright visages, staring reciprocally—all Ovid on the walls, in colours vivider than his descriptions. Actæon in mid sprout, with the unappeasable prudery of Diana; and the still more provoking and almost culinary coolness of Dan Phœbus, eel-fashion, deliberately divesting of Marsyas.

Then, that haunted room—in which old Mrs. Battle died—whereinto I have crept, but always in the day time, with a passion of fear; and a sneaking curiosity, terror-tainted, to hold communication with the past.— *How shall they build it up again?*

It was an old deserted place, yet not so long deserted but that traces of the splendour of past inmates were everywhere apparent. Its furniture was still standing— even to the tarnished gilt leather battledores, and crumbling feathers of shuttlecocks in the nursery, which told that children had once played there. But I was a lonely child, and had the range at will of every apartment, knew every nook and corner, wondered and worshipped everywhere.

The solitude of childhood is not so much the mother of thought, as it is the feeder of love, and silence, and admiration. So strange a passion for the place possessed me in those years, that, though there lay—I shame to say how few roods distant from the mansion —half hid by trees, what I judged some romantic lake, such was the spell which bound me to the house, and such my carefulness not to pass its strict and proper precincts, that the idle waters lay unexplored for me; and not till late in life, curiosity prevailing over elder

devotion, I found, to my astonishment, a pretty brawling brook had been the Lacus Incognitus of my infancy. Variegated views, extensive prospects—and those at no great distance from the house—I was told of such—what were they to me, being out of the boundaries of my Eden?—So far from a wish to roam, I would have drawn, methought, still closer the fences of my chosen prison; and have been hemmed in by a yet securer cincture of those excluding garden walls. I could have exclaimed with that garden-loving poet—

> Bind me, ye woodbines, in your twines;
> Curl me about, ye gadding vines;
> And oh so close your circles lace,
> That I may never leave this place;
> But, lest your fetters prove too weak,
> Ere I your silken bondage break,
> Do you, O brambles, chain me too,
> And, courteous briars, nail me through.

I was here as in a lonely temple. Snug firesides—the low-built roof—parlours ten feet by ten—frugal boards, and all the homeliness of home—these were the condition of my birth—the wholesome soil which I was planted in. Yet, without impeachment to their tenderest lessons, I am not sorry to have had glances of something beyond; and to have taken, if but a peep, in childhood, at the contrasting accidents of a great fortune.

To have the feeling of gentility, it is not necessary to have been born gentle. The pride of ancestry may be had on cheaper terms than to be obliged to an importunate race of ancestors; and the coatless antiquary in his unemblazoned cell, revolving the long line of a Mowbray's or De Clifford's pedigree, at those sounding names may warm himself into as gay a vanity as those who do inherit them. The claims of birth are ideal

merely, and what herald shall go about to strip me of an idea? Is it trenchant to their swords? can it be hacked off as a spur can? or torn away like a tarnished garter?

What, else, were the families of the great to us? what pleasure should we take in their tedious genealogies, or their capitulatory brass monuments? What to us the uninterrupted current of their bloods, if our own did not answer within us to a cognate and corresponding elevation?

Or wherefore else, O tattered and diminished 'Scutcheon that hung upon the time-worn walls of thy princely stairs, BLAKESMOOR! have I in childhood so oft stood poring upon the mystic characters—thy emblematic supporters, with their prophetic "Resurgam"—till, every dreg of peasantry purging off, I received unto myself Very Gentility? Thou wert first in my morning eyes; and of nights, hast detained my steps from bedward, till it was but a step from gazing at thee to dreaming on thee.

This is the only true gentry by adoption; the veritable change of blood, and not, as empirics have fabled, by transfusion.

Who it was by dying that had earned the splendid trophy, I know not, I inquired not; but its fading rags, and colours cobweb-stained, told that its subject was of two centuries back.

And what if my ancestor at that date was some Damœtas—feeding flocks, not his own, upon the hills of Lincoln—did I in less earnest vindicate to myself the family trappings of his once proud Aegon?—repaying by a backward triumph the insults he might possibly have heaped in his life-time upon my poor pastoral progenitor.

If it were presumption so to speculate, the present

owners of the mansion had least reason to complain. They had long forsaken the old house of their fathers for a newer trifle; and I was left to appropriate to myself what images I could pick up, to raise my fancy, or to soothe my vanity.

I was the true descendant of those old W——s; and not the present family of that name, who had fled the old waste places.

Mine was that gallery of good old family portraits, which as I have gone over, giving them in fancy my own family name, one—and then another—would seem to smile—reaching forward from the canvas, to recognise the new relationship; while the rest looked grave, as it seemed, at the vacancy in their dwelling, and thoughts of fled posterity.

That Beauty with the cool blue pastoral drapery, and a lamb—that hung next the great bay window—with the bright yellow H——shire hair, and eye of watchet hue —so like my Alice!—I am persuaded she was a true Elia—Mildred Elia, I take it.

Mine too, BLAKESMOOR, was thy noble Marble Hall, with its mosaic pavements, and its Twelve Cæsars— stately busts in marble—ranged round: of whose countenances, young reader of faces as I was, the frowning beauty of Nero, I remember, had most of my wonder; but the mild Galba had my love. There they stood in the coldness of death, yet freshness of immortality.

Mine too, thy lofty Justice Hall, with its one chair of authority, high-backed and wickered, once the terror of luckless poacher, or self-forgetful maiden—so common since, that bats have roosted in it.

Mine too—whose else?—thy costly fruit-garden, with its sun-baked southern wall; the ampler pleasure-garden, rising backwards from the house in triple terraces, with flower-pots now of palest lead, save that a

speck here and there, saved from the elements, bespake their pristine state to have been gilt and glittering; the verdant quarters backwarder still; and, stretching still beyond, in old formality, thy firry wilderness, the haunt of the squirrel, and the day-long murmuring wood-pigeon, with that antique image in the centre, God or Goddess I wist not; but child of Athens or old Rome paid never a sincerer worship to Pan or to Sylvanus in their native groves, than I to that fragmentary mystery.

Was it for this, that I kissed my childish hands too fervently in your idol worship, walks and windings of BLAKESMOOR! for this, or what sin of mine, has the plough passed over your pleasant places? I sometimes think that as men, when they die, do not die all, so of their extinguished habitations there may be a hope—a germ to be revivified.

CHRIST'S HOSPITAL FIVE AND THIRTY YEARS AGO

IN Mr. Lamb's "Works," published a year or two since, I find a magnificent eulogy on my old school, such as it was, or now appears to him to have been, between the years 1782 and 1789. It happens, very oddly, that my own standing at Christ's was nearly corresponding with his; and, with all gratitude to him for his enthusiasm for the cloisters, I think he has contrived to bring together whatever can be said in praise of them, dropping all the other side of the argument most ingeniously.

I remember L. at school; and can well recollect that he had some peculiar advantages, which I and others of his schoolfellows had not. His friends lived in town, and were near at hand; and he had the privilege of going to see them, almost as often as he wished, through

some invidious distinction, which was denied to us. The present worthy sub-treasurer to the Inner Temple can explain how that happened. He had his tea and hot rolls in a morning, while we were battening upon our quarter of a penny loaf—our *crug*—moistened with attenuated small beer, in wooden piggins, smacking of the pitched leathern jack it was poured from. Our Monday's milk porritch, blue and tasteless, and the pease soup of Saturday, coarse and choking, were enriched for him with a slice of "extraordinary bread and butter," from the hot-loaf of the Temple. The Wednesday's mess of millet, somewhat less repugnant—(we had three banyan to four meat days in the week)—was endeared to his palate with a lump of double-refined, and a smack of ginger (to make it go down the more glibly) or the fragrant cinnamon. In lieu of our *half-pickled* Sundays, or *quite fresh* boiled beef on Thursdays (strong as *caro equina*), with detestable marigolds floating in the pail to poison the broth—our scanty mutton scrags on Fridays—and rather more savoury, but grudging, portions of the same flesh, rotten-roasted or rare, on the Tuesdays (the only dish which excited our appetites, and disappointed our stomachs, in almost equal proportion)—he had his hot plate of roast veal, or the more tempting griskin (exotics unknown to our palates), cooked in the paternal kitchen (a great thing), and brought him daily by his maid or aunt! I remember the good old relative (in whom love forbade pride) squatting down upon some odd stone in a by-nook of the cloisters, disclosing the viands (of higher regale than those cates which the ravens ministered to the Tishbite); and the contending passions of L. at the unfolding. There was love for the bringer; shame for the thing brought, and the manner of its bringing; sympathy for those who were too many to share in it; and, at top of

all, hunger (eldest, strongest of the passions!) predominant, breaking down the stony fences of shame, and awkwardness, and a troubling over-consciousness.

I was a poor friendless boy. My parents, and those who should care for me, were far away. Those few acquaintances of theirs, which they could reckon upon being kind to me in the great city, after a little forced notice, which they had the grace to take of me on my first arrival in town, soon grew tired of my holiday visits. They seemed to them to recur too often, though I thought them few enough; and, one after another, they all failed me, and I felt myself alone among six hundred playmates.

O the cruelty of separating a poor lad from his early homestead! The yearnings which I used to have towards it in those unfledged years! How, in my dreams, would my native town (far in the west) come back, with its church, and trees, and faces! How I would wake weeping, and in the anguish of my heart exclaim upon sweet Calne in Wiltshire!

To this late hour of my life, I trace impressions left by the recollection of those friendless holidays. The long warm days of summer never return but they bring with them a gloom from the haunting memory of those *whole-day-leaves,* when, by some strange arrangement, we were turned out, for the live-long day, upon our own hands, whether we had friends to go to, or none. I remember those bathing excursions to the New River, which L. recalls with such relish, better, I think, than he can—for he was a home-seeking lad, and did not much care for such water-pastimes.—How merrily we would sally forth into the fields; and strip under the first warmth of the sun; and wanton like young dace in the streams; getting us appetites for noon, which those of us that were penniless (our scanty morning

crust long since exhausted) had not the means of allaying—while the cattle, and the birds, and the fishes, were at feed about us, and we had nothing to satisfy our cravings—the very beauty of the day, and the exercise of the pastime, and the sense of liberty, setting a keener edge upon them!—How faint and languid, finally we would return, towards nightfall, to our desired morsel, half-rejoicing, half-reluctant, that the hours of our uneasy liberty had expired!

It was worse in the days of winter, to go prowling about the streets objectless—shivering at cold windows of print-shops, to extract a little amusement; or haply, as a last resort, in the hope of a little novelty, to pay a fifty-times repeated visit (where our individual faces should be as well known to the warden as those of his own charges) to the Lions in the Tower—to whose levee, by courtesy immemorial, we had a prescriptive title to admission.

L.'s governor (so we called the patron who presented us to the foundation) lived in a manner under his paternal roof. Any complaint which he had to make was sure of being attended to. This was understood at Christ's, and was an effectual screen to him against the severity of masters, or worse tyranny of the monitors. The oppressions of these young brutes are heart-sickening to call to recollection. I have been called out of my bed, and *waked for the purpose,* in the coldest winter nights—and this not once, but night after night—in my shirt, to receive the discipline of a leathern thong, with eleven other sufferers, because it pleased my callow overseer, when there has been any talking heard after we were gone to bed, to make the six last beds in the dormitory, where the youngest children of us slept, answerable for an offence they neither dared to commit, nor had the power to hinder.—The same exe-

CHRIST'S HOSPITAL

crable tyranny drove the younger part of us from the fires, when our feet were perishing with snow; and under the cruellest penalties, forbade the indulgence of a drink of water, when we lay in sleepless summer nights, fevered with the season, and the day's sports.

There was one H——, who, I learned, in after days, was seen expiating some maturer offence in the hulks. (Do I flatter myself in fancying that this might be the planter of that name, who suffered —— at Nevis, I think, or St. Kitts, —— some few years since? My friend Tobin was the benevolent instrument of bringing him to the gallows.) This petty Nero actually branded a boy, who had offended him, with a red-hot iron; and nearly starved forty of us, with exacting contributions, to the one half of our bread, to pamper a young ass, which, incredible as it may seem, with the connivance of the nurse's daughter (a young flame of his) he had contrived to smuggle in, and keep upon the leads of the *ward,* as they called our dormitories. This game went on for better than a week, till the foolish beast, not able to fare well but he must cry roast meat—happier than Caligula's minion, could he have kept his own counsel—but, foolisher, alas! than any of his species in the fables—waxing fat, and kicking, in the fulness of bread, one unlucky minute would needs proclaim his good fortune to the world below; and, laying out his simple throat, blew such a ram's horn blast, as (toppling down the walls of his own Jericho) set concealment any longer at defiance. The client was dismissed, with certain attentions, to Smithfield; but I never understood that the patron underwent any censure on the occasion. This was in the stewardship of L.'s admired Perry.

Under the same *facile* administration, can L. have forgotten the cool impunity with which the nurses used to carry away openly, in open platters, for their own

tables, one out of two of every hot joint, which the careful matron had been seeing scrupulously weighed out for our dinners? These things were daily practised in that magnificent apartment, which L. (grown connoisseur since, we presume) praises so highly for the grand paintings "by Verrio, and others," with which it is "hung round and adorned." But the sight of sleek, well-fed blue-coat boys in pictures was, at that time, I believe, little consolatory to him, or us, the living ones, who saw the better part of our provisions carried away before our faces by harpies; and ourselves reduced (with the Trojan in the hall of Dido)

"To feed our mind with idle portraiture."

L. has recorded the repugnance of the school to *gags*, or the fat of fresh beef boiled; and sets it down to some superstition. But these unctuous morsels are never grateful to young palates (children are universally fat-haters) and in strong, coarse, boiled meats, *unsalted*, are detestable. A *gag-eater* in our time was equivalent to a *goul*, and held in equal detestation. —— suffered under the imputation.

"——'Twas said,
He ate strange flesh."

He was observed, after dinner, carefully to gather up the remnants left at his table (not many, nor very choice fragments, you may credit me)—and, in an especial manner, these disreputable morsels, which he would convey away, and secretly stow in the settle that stood at his bed-side. None saw when he ate them. It was rumoured that he privately devoured them in the night. He was watched, but no traces of such midnight practices were discoverable. Some reported, that, on leave-days, he had been seen to carry out of the bounds

a large blue check handkerchief, full of something. This then must be the accursed thing. Conjecture next was at work to imagine how he could dispose of it. Some said he sold it to the beggars. This belief generally prevailed. He went about moping. None spake to him. No one would play with him. He was excommunicated; put out of the pale of the school. He was too powerful a boy to be beaten, but he underwent every mode of that negative punishment, which is more grievous than many stripes. Still he persevered. At length he was observed by two of his school-fellows, who were determined to get at the secret, and had traced him one leave-day for that purpose, to enter a large worn-out building, such as there exist specimens of in Chancery Lane, which are let out to various scales of pauperism with open door, and a common staircase. After him they silently slunk in, and followed by stealth up four flights, and saw him tap at a poor wicket, which was opened by an aged woman, meanly clad. Suspicion was now ripened into certainty. The informers had secured their victim. They had him in their toils. Accusation was formally preferred, and retribution most signal was looked for. Mr. Hathaway, the then steward (for this happened a little after my time), with that patient sagacity which tempered all his conduct, determined to investigate the matter, before he proceeded to sentence. The result was, that the supposed mendicants, the receivers or purchasers of the mysterious scraps, turned out to be the parents of ——, an honest couple come to decay,—whom this seasonable supply had, in all probability, saved from mendicancy; and that this young stork, at the expense of his own good name, had all this while been only feeding the old birds!—The governors on this occasion, much to their honour, voted a present relief to the family of ——, and presented

him with a silver medal. The lesson which the steward read upon RASH JUDGMENT, on the occasion of publicly delivering the medal to ——, I believe, would not be lost upon his auditory.—I had left school then, but I well remember ——. He was a tall, shambling youth, with a cast in his eye, not at all calculated to conciliate hostile prejudices. I have since seen him carrying a baker's basket. I think I heard he did not do quite so well by himself, as he had done by the old folks.

I was a hypochondriac lad; and the sight of a boy in fetters, upon the day of my first putting on the blue clothes, was not exactly fitted to assuage the natural terrors of initiation. I was of tender years, barely turned of seven; and had only read of such things in books, or seen them but in dreams. I was told he had *run away*. This was the punishment for the first offence.—As a novice I was soon after taken to see the dungeons. These were little, square, Bedlam cells, where a boy could just lie at his length upon straw and a blanket—a mattress, I think, was afterwards substituted—with a peep of light, let in askance, from a prison-orifice at top, barely enough to read by. Here the poor boy was locked in by himself all day, without sight of any but the porter who brought him his bread and water—who *might not speak to him;*—or of the beadle, who came twice a week to call him out to receive his periodical chastisement, which was almost welcome, because it separated him for a brief interval from solitude:—and here he was shut up by himself *of nights,* out of the reach of any sound, to suffer whatever horrors the weak nerves, and superstition incident to his time of life, might subject him to.* This was the penalty

* One or two instances of lunacy, or attempted suicide, accordingly, at length convinced the governors of the impolicy of this part of the sentence, and the midnight torture to the

for the second offence.—Wouldst thou like, reader, to see what became of him in the next degree?

The culprit, who had been a third time an offender, and whose expulsion was at this time deemed irreversible, was brought forth, as at some solemn *auto da fé* arrayed in uncouth and most appalling attire—all trace of his late "watchet weeds" carefully effaced, he was exposed in a jacket, resembling those which London lamplighters formerly delighted in, with a cap of the same. The effect of this divestiture was such as the ingenious devisers of it could have anticipated. With his pale and frighted features, it was as if some of those disfigurements in Dante had seized upon him. In this disguisement he was brought into the hall (*L.'s favourite state-room*), where awaited him the whole number of his schoolfellows, whose joint lessons and sports he was thenceforth to share no more; the awful presence of the steward, to be seen for the last time; of the executioner beadle, clad in his state robe for the occasion; and of two faces more, of direr import, because never but in these extremities visible. These were governors; two of whom, by choice, or charter, were always accustomed to officiate at these *Ultima Supplicia;* not to mitigate (so at least we understood it), but to enforce the uttermost stripe. Old Bamber Gascoigne, and Peter Aubert, I remember, were colleagues on one occasion, when the beadle turning rather pale, a glass of brandy was ordered to prepare him for the mysteries. The scourging was, after the old Roman fashion, long and stately. The lictor accompanied the criminal quite round the hall. We were generally too faint with attending

---

spirits was dispensed with.—This fancy of dungeons for children was a sprout of Howard's brain; for which (saving the reverence due to Holy Paul), methinks, I could willingly spit upon his statue.

to the previous disgusting circumstances, to make accurate report with our eyes of the degree of corporal suffering inflicted. Report, of course, gave out the back knotty and livid. After scourging, he was made over, in his *San Benito*, to his friends, if he had any (but commonly such poor runagates were friendless), or to his parish officer, who, to enhance the effect of the scene, had his station allotted to him on the outside of the hall gate.

These solemn pageantries were not played off so often as to spoil the general mirth of the community. We had plenty of exercise and recreation *after* school hours; and, for myself, I must confess, that I was never happier, than *in* them. The Upper and Lower Grammar Schools were held in the same room; and an imaginary line only divided their bounds. Their character was as different as that of the inhabitants on the two sides of the Pyrenees. The Rev. James Boyer was the Upper Master: but the Rev. Matthew Field presided over that portion of the apartment, of which I had the good fortune to be a member. We lived a life as careless as birds. We talked and did just what we pleased, and nobody molested us. We carried an accidence, or a grammar, for form; but, for any trouble it gave us, we might take two years in getting through the verbs deponent, and another two in forgetting all that we had learned about them. There was now and then the formality of saying a lesson, but if you had not learned it, a brush across the shoulders (just enough to disturb a fly) was the sole remonstrance. Field never used the rod; and in truth he wielded the cane with no great good will—holding it "like a dancer." It looked in his hands rather like an emblem than an instrument of authority; and an emblem, too, he was ashamed of. He was a good easy man, that did not care to ruffle his own

peace, nor perhaps set any great consideration upon the value of juvenile time. He came among us, now and then, but often stayed away whole days from us; and when he came, it made no difference to us—he had his private room to retire to, the short time he stayed, to be out of the sound of our noise. Our mirth and uproar went on. We had classics of our own, without being beholden to "insolent Greece or haughty Rome," that passed current among us—Peter Wilkins—the Adventures of the Hon. Capt. Robert Boyle—the Fortunate Blue-Coat Boy—and the like. Or we cultivated a turn for mechanic or scientific operation; making little sundials of paper; or weaving those ingenious parentheses, called *cat-cradles;* or making dry peas to dance upon the end of a tin pipe; or studying the art military over that laudable game "French and English," and a hundred other such devices to pass away the time—mixing the useful with the agreeable—as would have made the souls of Rousseau and John Locke chuckle to have seen us.

Matthew Field belonged to that class of modest divines who affect to mix in equal proportion the *gentleman,* the *scholar,* and the *Christian;* but, I know not how, the first ingredient is generally found to be the predominating dose in the composition. He was engaged in gay parties, or with his courtly bow at some episcopal levée, when he should have been attending upon us. He had for many years the classical charge of a hundred children, during the four or five first years of their education; and his very highest form seldom proceeded further than two or three of the introductory fables of Phædrus. How things were suffered to go on thus, I cannot guess. Boyer, who was the proper person to have remedied these abuses, always affected, perhaps felt, a delicacy in interfering in a province not strictly

his own. I have not been without my suspicions, that he was not altogether displeased at the contrast we presented to his end of the school. We were a sort of Helots to his young Spartans. He would sometimes, with ironic deference, send to borrow a rod of the Under Master, and then, with Sardonic grin, observe to one of his upper boys, "how neat and fresh the twigs looked." While his pale students were battering their brains over Xenophon and Plato, with a silence as deep as that enjoined by the Samite, we were enjoying ourselves at our ease in our little Goshen. We saw a little into the secrets of his discipline, and the prospect did but the more reconcile us to our lot. His thunders rolled innocuous for us; his storms came near, but never touched us; contrary to Gideon's miracle, while all around were drenched, our fleece was dry. His boys turned out the better scholars; we, I suspect, have the advantage in temper. His pupils cannot speak of him without something of terror allaying their gratitude; the remembrance of Field comes back with all the soothing images of indolence, and summer slumbers, and work like play, and innocent idleness, and Elysian exemptions, and life itself a "playing holiday."

Though sufficiently removed from the jurisdiction of Boyer, we were near enough (as I have said) to understand a little of his system. We occasionally heard sounds of the *Ululantes,* and caught glances of Tartarus. B. was a rabid pedant. His English style was cramped to barbarism. His Easter anthems (for his duty obliged him to those periodical flights) were grating as scrannel pipes.*—He would laugh, ay, and heartily,

---

* In this and every thing B. was the antipodes of his coadjutor. While the former was digging his brains for crude anthems, worth a pig-nut, F. would be recreating his gentlemanly fancy in the more flowery walks of the Muses. A little dramatic effusion of his, under the name of Vertumnus

but then it must be at Flaccus's quibble about Rex —— or at the *tristis severitas in vultu,* or *inspicere in patinas,* of Terence—thin jests, which at their first broaching could hardly have had *vis* enough to move a Roman muscle.—He had two wigs, both pedantic, but of different omen. The one serene, smiling, fresh powdered, betokening a mild day. The other, an old discoloured, unkempt, angry caxon, denoting frequent and bloody execution. Woe to the school, when he made his morning appearance in his *passy,* or *passionate wig.* No comet expounded surer.—J. B. had a heavy hand. I have known him double his knotty fist at a poor trembling child (the maternal milk hardly dry upon its lips) with a "Sirrah, do you presume to set your wits at me?" —Nothing was more common than to see him make a headlong entry into the schoolroom, from his inner recess, or library, and, with turbulent eye, singling out a lad, roar out, "Od's my life, Sirrah" (his favourite adjuration), "I have a great mind to whip you,"—then, with as sudden a retracting impulse, fling back into his lair—and, after a cooling lapse of some minutes (during which all but the culprit had totally forgotten the context) drive headlong out again, piecing out his imperfect sense, as if it had been some Devil's Litany, with the expletory yell—"*and I* WILL *too.*"—In his gentler moods, when the *rabidus furor* was assuaged, he had resort to an ingenious method, peculiar, for what I have heard, to himself, of whipping the boy, and reading the Debates, at the same time; a paragraph, and a lash between; which in those times, when parliamentary oratory was most at a height and flourishing in these

---

and Pomona, is not yet forgotten by the chroniclers of that sort of literature. It was accepted by Garrick, but the town did not give it their sanction.—B. used to say of it, in a way of half-compliment, half-irony, that it was *too classical for representation.*

realms, was not calculated to impress the patient with a veneration for the diffuser graces of rhetoric.

Once, and but once, the uplifted rod was known to fall ineffectual from his hand—when droll squinting W—— having been caught putting the inside of the master's desk to a use for which the architect had clearly not designed it, to justify himself, with great simplicity averred, that *he did not know that the thing had been forewarned.* This exquisite irrecognition of any law antecedent to the *oral* or *declaratory* struck so irresistibly upon the fancy of all who heard it (the pedagogue himself not excepted) that remission was unavoidable.

L. has given credit to B.'s great merits as an instructor. Coleridge, in his literary life, has pronounced a more intelligible and ample encomium on them. The author of the Country Spectator doubts not to compare him with the ablest teachers of antiquity. Perhaps we cannot dismiss him better than with the pious ejaculation of C.—when he heard that his old master was on his death-bed—"Poor J. B.!—may all his faults be forgiven; and may he be wafted to bliss by little cherub boys, all head and wings, with no *bottoms* to reproach his sublunary infirmities."

Under him were many good and sound scholars bred. —First Grecian of my time was Lancelot Pepys Stevens, kindest of boys and men, since Co-grammar-master (and inseparable companion) with Dr. T——e. What an edifying spectacle did this brace of friends present to those who remembered the anti-socialities of their predecessors!—You never met the one by chance in the street without a wonder, which was quickly dissipated by the almost immediate sub-appearance of the other. Generally arm in arm, these kindly coadjutors lightened for each other the toilsome duties of their profession, and when, in advanced age, one found it convenient to retire,

CHRIST'S HOSPITAL

the other was not long in discovering that it suited him to lay down the fasces also. Oh, it is pleasant, as it is rare, to find the same arm linked in yours at forty, which at thirteen helped it to turn over the *Cicero De Amicitia,* or some tale of Antique Friendship, which the young heart even then was burning to anticipate!—Co-Grecian with S. was Th——, who has since executed with ability various diplomatic functions at the Northern courts. Th—— was a tall, dark, saturnine youth, sparing of speech, with raven locks.—Thomas Fanshaw Middleton following him (now Bishop of Calcutta) a scholar and a gentleman in his teens. He has the reputation of an excellent critic; and is author (besides the Country Spectator) of a Treatise on the Greek Article, against Sharpe.—M. is said to bear his mitre high in India, where the *regni novitas* (I dare say) sufficiently justifies the bearing. A humility quite as primitive as that of Jewel or Hooker might not be exactly fitted to impress the minds of those Anglo-Asiatic diocesans with a reverence for home institutions, and the church which those fathers watered. The manners of M. at school, though firm, were mild, and unassuming.—Next to M. (if not senior to him) was Richards, author of the Aboriginal Britons, the most spirited of the Oxford Prize Poems: a pale, studious Grecian.—Then followed poor S——, ill-fated M——! of these the Muse is silent,

> Finding some of Edward's race
> Unhappy, pass their annals by.

Come back into memory, like as thou wert in the day-spring of thy fancies, with hope like a fiery column before thee—the dark pillar not yet turned—Samuel Taylor Coleridge—Logician, Metaphysician, Bard!— How have I seen the casual passer through the Cloisters stand still, entranced with admiration (while he weighed

the disproportion between the *speech* and the *garb* of the young Mirandula), to hear thee unfold, in thy deep and sweet intonations, the mysteries of Jamblichus, or Plotinus (for even in those years thou waxedst not pale at such philosophic draughts), or reciting Homer in his Greek, or Pindar —— while the walls of the old Grey Friars re-echoed to the accents of the *inspired charity-boy!* Many were the "wit-combats" (to dally awhile with the words of old Fuller) between him and C. V. Le G——, "which two I behold like a Spanish great galleon, and an English man-of-war; Master Coleridge, like the former, was built far higher in learning, solid, but slow in his performances. C. V. L., with the English man-of-war, lesser in bulk, but lighter in sailing, could turn with all tides, tack about, and take advantage of all winds, by the quickness of his wit and invention."

Nor shalt thou, their compeer, be quickly forgotten, Allen, with the cordial smile, and still more cordial laugh, with which thou wert wont to make the old Cloisters shake, in thy cognition of some poignant jest of theirs; or the anticipation of some more material, and, peradventure, practical one, of thine own. Extinct are those smiles, with that beautiful countenance, with which (for thou wert the *Nireus formosus* of the school), in the days of thy maturer waggery, thou didst disarm the wrath of infuriated town-damsel, who, incensed by provoking pinch, turning tigress-like round, suddenly converted by thy angel-look, exchanged the half-formed terrible *"bl——,"* for a gentler greeting—*"bless thy handsome face!"*

Next follow two, who ought to be now alive, and the friends of Elia—the junior Le G—— and F——; who impelled, the former by a roving temper, the latter by too quick a sense of neglect—ill capable of enduring the slights poor Sizars are sometimes subject to in our

seats of learning—exchanged their Alma Mater for the camp; perishing, one by climate, and one on the plains of Salamanca:—Le G—— sanguine, volatile, sweet-natured; F—— dogged, faithful, anticipative of insult, warm-hearted, with something of the old Roman height about him.

Fine, frank-hearted Fr——, the present master of Hertford, with Marmaduke T——, mildest of Missionaries—and both my good friends still—close the catalogue of Grecians in my time.

THE SOUTH-SEA HOUSE

READER, in thy passage from the Bank—where thou hast been receiving thy half-yearly dividends (supposing thou art a lean annuitant like myself)—to the Flower Pot, to secure a place for Dalston, or Shacklewell, or some other thy suburban retreat northerly,—didst thou never observe a melancholy looking, handsome, brick and stone edifice, to the left—where Threadneedle Street abuts upon Bishopsgate? I dare say thou hast often admired its magnificent portals ever gaping wide, and disclosing to view a grave court, with cloisters, and pillars, with few or no traces of goers-in or comers-out—a desolation something like Balclutha's*

This was once a house of trade,—a centre of busy interests. The throng of merchants was here—the quick pulse of gain—and here some forms of business are still kept up, though the soul be long since fled. Here are still to be seen stately porticos; imposing staircases; offices roomy as the state apartments in palaces—deserted, or thinly peopled with a few straggling clerks; the still more sacred interiors of court and committee

* "I passed by the walls of Balclutha, and they were desolate."—OSSIAN.

rooms, with venerable faces of beadles, door-keepers—directors seated in form on solemn days (to proclaim a dead dividend) at long worm-eaten tables, that have been mahogany, with tarnished gilt-leather coverings, supporting massy silver ink stands long since dry;—the oaken wainscots hung with pictures of deceased governors and sub-governors, of Queen Anne, and the two first monarchs of the Brunswick dynasty;—huge charts, which subsequent discoveries have antiquated;—dusty maps of Mexico, dim as dreams,—and soundings of the Bay of Panama!—The long passages hung with buckets, appended, in idle row, to walls, whose substance might defy any, short of the last, conflagration:—with vast ranges of cellarage under all, where dollars and pieces of eight once lay, an "unsunned heap," for Mammon to have solaced his solitary heart withal,—long since dissipated, or scattered into air at the blast of the breaking of that famous BUBBLE.——

Such is the SOUTH-SEA HOUSE. At least, such it was forty years ago, when I knew it,—a magnificent relic! What alterations may have been made in it since, I have had no opportunities of verifying. Time, I take for granted, has not freshened it. No wind has resuscitated the face of the sleeping waters. A thicker crust by this time stagnates upon it. The moths, that were then battening upon its obsolete ledgers and day-books, have rested from their depredations, but other light generations have succeeded, making fine fretwork among their single and double entries. Layers of dust have accumulated (a superfœtation of dirt!) upon the old layers, that seldom used to be disturbed, save by some curious finger, now and then, inquisitive to explore the mode of book-keeping in Queen Anne's reign; or, with less hallowed curiosity, seeking to unveil some of the mysteries of that tremendous HOAX, whose extent the petty pecu-

lators of our day look back upon with the same expression of incredulous admiration, and hopeless ambition of rivalry, as would become the puny face of modern conspiracy contemplating the Titan size of Vaux's superhuman plot.

Peace to the manes of the BUBBLE! Silence and destitution are upon thy walls, proud house, for a memorial!

Situated as thou art, in the very heart of stirring and living commerce,—amid the fret and fever of speculation—with the Bank, and the 'Change, and the India-house about thee, in the hey-day of present prosperity, with their important faces, as it were, insulting thee, their *poor neighbour out of business*—to the idle and merely contemplative,—to such as me, old house! there is a charm in thy quiet:—a cessation—a coolness from business—an indolence almost cloistral—which is delightful! With what reverence have I paced thy great bare rooms and courts at eventide! They spoke of the past:—the shade of some dead accountant, with visionary pen in ear, would flit by me, stiff as in life. Living accounts and accountants puzzle me. I have no skill in figuring. But thy great dead tomes, which scarce three degenerate clerks of the present day could lift from their enshrining shelves—with their old fantastic flourishes, and decorative rubric interlacings—their sums in triple columniations, set down with formal superfluity of cyphers—with pious sentences at the beginning, without which our religious ancestors never ventured to open a book of business, or bill of lading—the costly vellum covers of some of them almost persuading us that we are got into some *better library,*—are very agreeable and edifying spectacles. I can look upon these defunct dragons with complacency. The heavy, odd-shaped ivory-handled penknives (our ancestors had everything on a larger scale than we have hearts for) are as good as any thing from

Herculaneum. The pounce-boxes of our days have gone retrograde.

The very clerks which I remember in the South-Sea House—I speak of forty years back—had an air very different from those in the public offices that I have had to do with since. They partook of the genius of the place!

They were mostly (for the establishment did not admit of superfluous salaries) bachelors. Generally (for they had not much to do) persons of a curious and speculative turn of mind. Old-fashioned, for a reason mentioned before. Humorists, for they were of all descriptions; and, not having been brought together in early life (which has a tendency to assimilate the members of corporate bodies to each other), but, for the most part, placed in this house in ripe or middle age, they necessarily carried into it their separate habits and oddities, unqualified, if I may so speak, as into a common stock. Hence they formed a sort of Noah's ark. Odd fishes. A lay-monastery. Domestic retainers in a great house, kept more for show than use. Yet pleasant fellows, full of chat—and not a few among them had arrived at considerable proficiency on the German flute.

The cashier at that time was one Evans, a Cambro-Briton. He had something of the choleric complexion of his countrymen stamped on his visage, but was a worthy sensible man at bottom. He wore his hair, to the last, powdered and frizzed out, in the fashion which I remember to have seen in caricatures of what were termed, in my young days, *Maccaronies*. He was the last of that race of beaux. Melancholy as a gib-cat over his counter all the forenoon, I think I see him, making up his cash (as they call it) with tremulous fingers, as if he feared every one about him was a defaulter; in his hypochondry ready to imagine himself one; haunted, at least, with the

idea of the possibility of his becoming one: his tristful visage clearing up a little over his roast neck of veal at Anderton's at two (where his picture still hangs, taken a little before his death by desire of the master of the coffee-house, which he had frequented for the last five-and-twenty years), but not attaining the meridian of its animation till evening brought on the hour of tea and visiting. The simultaneous sound of his well-known rap at the door with the stroke of the clock announcing six, was a topic of never-failing mirth in the families which this dear old bachelor gladdened with his presence. Then was his *forte,* his glorified hour! How would he chirp, and expand, over a muffin! How would he dilate into secret history! His countryman, Pennant himself, in particular, could not be more eloquent than he in relation to old and new London—the site of old theatres, churches, streets gone to decay—where Rosamond's pond stood—the Mulberry Gardens—and the Conduit in Cheap—with many a pleasant anecdote, derived from paternal tradition, of those grotesque figures which Hogarth has immortalised in his picture of *Noon,*—the worthy descendants of those heroic confessors, who, flying to this country, from the wrath of Louis the Fourteenth and his dragoons, kept alive the flame of pure religion in the sheltering obscurities of Hog Lane, and the vicinity of the Seven Dials!

Deputy, under Evans, was Thomas Tame. He had the air and stoop of a nobleman. You would have taken him for one, had you met him in one of the passages leading to Westminster Hall. By stoop, I mean that gentle bending of the body forwards, which, in great men, must be supposed to be the effect of an habitual condescending attention to the applications of their inferiors. While he held you in converse, you felt strained to the height in the colloquy. The conference over, you

were at leisure to smile at the comparative insignificance of the pretensions which had just awed you. His intellect was of the shallowest order. It did not reach to a saw or a proverb. His mind was in its original state of white paper. A sucking babe might have posed him. What was it then? Was he rich? Alas, no! Thomas Tame was very poor. Both he and his wife looked outwardly gentlefolks, when I fear all was not well at all times within. She had a neat meagre person, which it was evident she had not sinned in over-pampering; but in its veins was noble blood. She traced her descent, by some labyrinth of relationship, which I never thoroughly understood,—much less can explain with any heraldic certainty at this time of day,—to the illustrious but unfortunate house of Derwentwater. This was the secret of Thomas's stoop. This was the thought—the sentiment—the bright solitary star of your lives,—ye mild and happy pair,—which cheered you in the night of intellect, and in the obscurity of your station! This was to you instead of riches, instead of rank, instead of glittering attainments: and it was worth them altogether. You insulted none with it; but, while you wore it as a piece of defensive armour only, no insult likewise could reach you through it. *Decus et solamen.*

Of quite another stamp was the then accountant, John Tipp. He neither pretended to high blood, nor in good truth cared one fig about the matter. He "thought an accountant the greatest character in the world, and himself the greatest accountant in it." Yet John was not without his hobby. The fiddle relieved his vacant hours. He sang, certainly, with other notes than to the Orphean lyre. He did, indeed, scream and scrape most abominably. His fine suite of official rooms in Threadneedle Street, which, without anything very substantial appended to them, were enough to enlarge a man's notions of

himself that lived in them, (I know not who is the occupier of them now)* resounded fortnightly to the notes of a concert of "sweet breasts," as our ancestors would have called them, culled from club-rooms and orchestras —chorus singers—first and second violincellos—double basses—and clarionets—who ate his cold mutton, and drank his punch, and praised his ear. He sate like Lord Midas among them. But at the desk Tipp was quite another sort of creature. Thence all ideas, that were purely ornamental, were banished. You could not speak of anything romantic without rebuke. Politics were excluded. A newspaper was thought too refined and abstracted. The whole duty of man consisted in writing off dividend warrants. The striking of the annual balance in the company's books (which, perhaps, differed from the balance of last year in the sum of £25 1s. 6d.) occupied his days and nights for a month previous. Not that Tipp was blind to the deadness of *things* (as they call them in the city) in his beloved house, or did not sigh for a return of the old stirring days when South Sea hopes were young—(he was indeed equal to the wielding of any the most intricate accounts of the most flourishing company in these or those days):—but to a genuine accountant the difference of proceeds is as nothing. The fractional farthing is as dear to his heart as the thousands which stand before it. He is the true actor, who, whether his part be a prince or a peasant, must act it with like intensity. With Tipp form was everything. His life was formal. His actions seemed

* I have since been informed that the present tenant of them is a Mr. Lamb, a gentleman who is happy in the possession of some choice pictures, and among them a rare portrait of Milton, which I mean to do myself the pleasure of going to see, and at the same time to refresh my memory with the sight of old scenes. Mr. Lamb has the character of a right courteous and communicative collector.

ruled with a ruler. His pen was not less erring than his heart. He made the best executor in the world: he was plagued with incessant executorships accordingly, which excited his spleen and soothed his vanity in equal ratios. He would swear (for Tipp swore) at the little orphans, whose rights he would guard with a tenacity like the grasp of the dying hand, that commended their interests to his protection. With all this there was about him a sort of timidity—(his few enemies used to give it a worse name)—a something which in reverence to the dead, we will place, if you please, a little on this side of the heroic. Nature certainly had been pleased to endow John Tipp with a sufficient measure of the principle of self-preservation. There is a cowardice which we do not despise, because it has nothing base or treacherous in its elements; it betrays itself, not you: it is mere temperament; the absence of the romantic and the enterprising; it sees a lion in the way, and will not, with Fortinbras, "greatly find quarrel in a straw," when some supposed honour is at stake. Tipp never mounted the box of a stage-coach in his life; or leaned against the rails of a balcony; or walked upon the ridge of a parapet; or looked down a precipice; or let off a gun; or went upon a waterparty; or would willingly let you go if he could have helped it: neither was it recorded of him, that for lucre, or for intimidation, he ever forsook friend or principle.

Whom next shall we summon from the dusty dead, in whom common qualities become uncommon? Can I forget thee, Henry Man, the wit, the polished man of letters, the *author,* of the South-Sea House? who never enteredst thy office in the morning or quittedst it in mid-day (what didst *thou* in an office?) without some quirk that left a sting! Thy gibes and thy jokes

THE SOUTH-SEA HOUSE

are now extinct, or survive but in two forgotten volumes, which I had the good fortune to rescue from a stall in Barbican, not three days ago, and found thee terse, fresh, epigrammatic, as alive. Thy wit is a little gone by in these fastidious days—thy topics are staled by the "new-born gauds" of the time:—but great thou used to be in Public Ledgers, and in Chronicles, upon Chatham, and Shelburne, and Rockingham, and Howe, and Burgoyne, and Clinton, and the war which ended in the tearing from Great Britain her rebellious colonies,—and Keppel, and Wilkes, and Sawbridge, and Bull, and Dunning, and Pratt, and Richmond—and such small politics.——

A little less facetious, and a great deal more obstreperous, was fine rattling, rattleheaded Plumer. He was descended,—not in a right line, reader (for his lineal pretensions, like his personal, favoured a little of the sinister bend)—from the Plumers of Hertfordshire. So tradition gave him out; and certain family features not a little sanctioned the opinion. Certainly old Walter Plumer (his reputed author) had been a rake in his day, and visited much in Italy, and had seen the world. He was uncle, bachelor-uncle, to the fine old whig still living, who has represented the county in so many successive parliaments, and has a fine old mansion near Ware. Walter flourished in George the Second's days, and was the same who was summoned before the House of Commons about a business of franks, with the old Duchess of Marlborough. You may read of it in Johnson's "Life of Cave." Cave came off cleverly in that business. It is certain our Plumer did nothing to discountenance the rumour. He rather seemed pleased whenever it was, with all gentleness, insinuated. But,

besides his family pretensions, Plumer was an engaging fellow, and sang gloriously.——

Not so sweetly sang Plumer as thou sangest, mild, child-like, pastoral M——; a flute's breathing less divinely whispering than thy Arcadian melodies, when, in tones worthy of Arden, thou didst chant that song sung by Amiens to the banished Duke, which proclaims the winter wind more lenient than for a man to be ungrateful. Thy sire was old surly M——, the unapproachable churchwarden of Bishopsgate. He knew not what he did, when he begat thee, like spring, gentle offspring of blustering winter:—only unfortunate in thy ending, which should have been mild, conciliatory, swan-like.——

Much remains to sing. Many fantastic shapes rise up, but they must be mine in private:—already I have fooled the reader to the top of his bent;—else could I omit that strange creature Woollet, who existed in trying the question, and *bought litigations?*—and still stranger, inimitable, solemn Hepworth, from whose gravity Newton might have deduced the law of gravitation. How profoundly would he nib a pen—with what deliberation would he wet a wafer!——

But it is time to close—night's wheels are rattling fast over me—it is proper to have done with this solemn mockery.

Reader, what if I have been playing with thee all this while—peradventure the very *names,* which I have summoned up before thee, are fantastic—insubstantial—like Henry Pimpernel, and old John Naps of Greece:——

Be satisfied that something answering to them has had a being. Their importance is from the past.

OLD CHINA

I HAVE an almost feminine partiality for old china. When I go to see any great house, I enquire for the china-closet, and next for the picture gallery. I cannot defend the order of preference, but by saying, that we have all some taste or other, of too ancient a date to admit of our remembering distinctly that it was an acquired one. I can call to mind the first play, and the first exhibition, that I was taken to; but I am not conscious of a time when china jars and saucers were introduced into my imagination.

I had no repugnance then—why should I now have? —to those little, lawless, azure-tinctured grotesques, that under the notion of men and women, float about, uncircumscribed by any element, in that world before perspective—a china tea-cup.

I like to see my old friends—whom distance cannot diminish—figuring up in the air (so they appear to our optics), yet on *terra firma* still—for so we must in courtesy interpret that speck of deeper blue—which the decorous artist, to prevent absurdity, had made to spring up beneath their sandals.

I love the men with women's faces, and the women, if possible, with still more womanish expressions.

Here is a young and courtly Mandarin, handing tea to a lady from a salver—two miles off. See how distance seems to set off respect! And here the same lady, or another—for likeness is identity on tea-cups—is stepping into a little fairy boat, moored on the hither side of this calm garden river, with a dainty mincing foot, which in a right angle of incidence (as angles go in our world) must infallibly land her in the midst of a flowery mead—a furlong off on the other side of the same strange stream!

Farther on—if far or near can be predicated of their world—see horses, trees, pagodas, dancing the hays.

Here—a cow and rabbit couchant, and co-extensive—so objects show, seen through the lucid atmosphere of fine Cathay.

I was pointing out to my cousin last evening, over our Hyson (which we are old fashioned enough to drink unmixed still of an afternoon), some of these *speciosa miracula* upon a set of extraordinary old blue china (a recent purchase) which we were now for the first time using; and could not help remarking how favourable circumstances had been to us of late years, that we could afford to please the eye sometimes with trifles of this sort—when a passing sentiment seemed to overshade the brows of my companion. I am quick at detecting these summer clouds in Bridget.

"I wish the good old times would come again," she said, "when we were not quite so rich. I do not mean, that I want to be poor; but there was a middle state"—so she pleased to ramble on—"in which I am sure we were a great deal happier. A purchase is but a purchase, now that you have money enough and to spare. Formerly it used to be a triumph. When we coveted a cheap luxury (and, O! how much ado I had to get you to consent in those times!)—we were used to have a debate two or three days before, and to weigh the *for* and *against,* and think what we might spare it out of, and what saving we could hit upon, that should be an equivalent. A thing was worth buying then, when we felt the money that we paid for it.

"Do you remember the brown suit, which you made to hang upon you, till all your friends cried shame upon you, it grew so thread-bare—and all because of that folio Beaumont and Fletcher, which you dragged home late at night from Barker's in Covent Garden? Do

OLD CHINA

you remember how we eyed it for weeks before we could make up our minds to the purchase, and had not come to a determination till it was near ten o'clock of the Saturday night, when you set off from Islington, fearing you should be too late—and when the old bookseller with some grumbling opened his shop, and by the twinkling taper (for he was setting bedwards) lighted out the relic from his dusty treasures—and when you lugged it home, wishing it were twice as cumbersome—and when you presented it to me—and when we were exploring the perfectness of it (*collating* you called it)—and while I was repairing some of the loose leaves with paste, which your impatience would not suffer to be left till daybreak—was there no pleasure in being a poor man? or can those neat black clothes which you wear now, and are so careful to keep brushed, since we have become rich and finical, give you half the honest vanity, with which you flaunted it about in that overworn suit—your old corbeau—for four or five weeks longer than you should have done, to pacify your conscience for the mighty sum of fifteen—or sixteen shillings was it?—a great affair we thought it then—which you had lavished on the old folio. Now you can afford to buy any book that pleases you, but I do not see that you ever bring me home any nice old purchases now.

"When you came home with twenty apologies for laying out a less number of shillings upon that print after Lionardo, which we christened the 'Lady Blanch;' when you looked at the purchase, and thought of the money—and thought of the money, and looked again at the picture—was there no pleasure in being a poor man? Now, you have nothing to do but to walk into Colnaghi's, and buy a wilderness of Lionardos. Yet do you?

"Then, do you remember our pleasant walks to

Enfield, and Potter's Bar, and Waltham, when we had a holyday—holydays, and all other fun, are gone, now we are rich—and the little hand-basket in which I used to deposit our day's fare of savoury cold lamb and salad—and how you would pry about at noontide for some decent house, where we might go in, and produce our store—only paying for the ale that you must call for—and speculate upon the looks of the landlady, and whether she was likely to allow us a tablecloth—and wish for such another honest hostess, as Izaak Walton has described many a one on the pleasant banks of the Lea, when he went a-fishing—and sometimes they would prove obliging enough, and sometimes they would look grudgingly upon us—but we had cheerful looks still for one another, and would eat our plain food savorily, scarcely grudging Piscator his Trout Hall? Now,—when we go out a day's pleasuring, which is seldom moreover, we *ride* part of the way—and go into a fine inn, and order the best of dinners, never debating the expense—which, after all, never has half the relish of those chance country snaps, when we were at the mercy of uncertain usage, and a precarious welcome.

"You are too proud to see a play anywhere now but in the pit. Do you remember where it was we used to sit, when we saw the Battle of Hexham, and the Surrender of Calais, and Bannister and Mrs. Bland in the Children in the Wood—when we squeezed out our shillings a-piece to sit three or four times in a season in the one-shilling gallery—where you felt all the time that you ought not to have brought me—and more strongly I felt obligation to you for having brought me—and the pleasure was the better for a little shame—and when the curtain drew up, what cared we for our place in the house, or what mattered it where we were sitting, when our thoughts were with Rosalind in Arden,

or with Viola at the Court of Illyria? You used to say, that the Gallery was the best place of all for enjoying a play socially—that the relish of such exhibitions must be in proportion to the infrequency of going—that the company we met there, not being in general readers of plays, were obliged to attend the more, and did attend, to what was going on, on the stage—because a word lost would have been a chasm, which it was impossible for them to fill up. With such reflections we consoled our pride then—and I appeal to you, whether, as a woman, I met generally with less attention and accommodation, than I have done since in more expensive situations in the house? The getting in indeed, and the crowding up those inconvenient staircases, was bad enough,—but there was still a law of civility to woman recognised to quite as great an extent as we ever found in the other passages—and how a little difficulty overcome heightened the snug seat, and the play, afterwards! Now we can only pay our money and walk in. You cannot see, you say, in the galleries now. I am sure we saw, and heard too, well enough then—but sight, and all, I think, is gone with our poverty.

"There was pleasure in eating strawberries, before they became quite common—in the first dish of peas, while they were yet dear—to have them for a nice supper, a treat. What treat can you have now? If we were to treat ourselves now—that is, to have dainties a little above our means, it would be selfish and wicked. It is very little more that we allow ourselves beyond what the actual poor can get at, that makes what I call a treat—when two people living together, as we have done, now and then indulge themselves in a cheap luxury, which both like; while each apologises, and is willing to take both halves of the blame to his single

share. I see no harm in people making much of themselves in that sense of the word. It may give them a hint how to make much of others. But now—what I mean by the word—we never do make much of ourselves. None but the poor can do it. I do not mean the veriest poor of all, but persons as we were, just above poverty.

"I know what you were going to say, that it is mighty pleasant at the end of the year to make all meet,—and much ado we used to have every Thirty-first Night of December to account for our exceedings—many a long face did you make over your puzzled accounts, and in contriving to make it out how we had spent so much—or that we had not spent so much—or that it was impossible we should spend so much next year—and still we found our slender capital decreasing—but then, betwixt ways, and projects, and compromises of one sort or another, and talk of curtailing this charge, and doing without that for the future—and the hope that youth brings, and laughing spirits (in which you were never poor till now) we pocketed up our loss, and in conclusion, with 'lusty brimmers' (as you used to quote it out of *hearty cheerful Mr. Cotton,* as you called him), we used to welcome in the 'coming guest.' Now we have no reckoning at all at the end of the old year—no flattering promises about the new year doing better for us."

Bridget is so sparing of her speech on most occasions, that when she gets into a rhetorical vein, I am careful how I interrupt it. I could not help, however, smiling at the phantom of wealth which her dear imagination had conjured up out of a clear income of a poor—hundred pounds a year. "It is true we were happier when we were poorer, but we were also younger, my cousin. I am afraid we must put up with the excess,

for if we were to shake the superflux into the sea, we should not much mend ourselves. That we had much to struggle with, as we grew up together, we have reason to be most thankful. It strengthened, and knit our compact closer. We could never have been what we have been to each other, if we had always had the sufficiency which you now complain of. The resisting power—those natural dilations of the youthful spirit, which circumstances cannot straiten—with us are long since passed away. Competence to age is supplementary youth, a sorry supplement indeed, but I fear the best that is to be had. We must ride, where we formerly walked: live better, and lie softer—and shall be wise to do so—than we had means to do in those good old days you speak of. Yet could those days return—could you and I once more walk our thirty miles a-day—could Bannister and Mrs. Bland again be young, and you and I be young to see them—could the good old one-shilling gallery days return—they are dreams, my cousin, now—but could you and I at this moment, instead of this quiet argument, by our well-carpeted fire-side, sitting on this luxurious sofa—be once more struggling up those inconvenient staircases, pushed about, and squeezed, and elbowed by the poorest rabble of poor gallery scramblers—could I once more hear those anxious shrieks of yours—and the delicious *Thank God, we are safe,* which always followed when the topmost stair, conquered, let in the first light of the whole cheerful theatre down beneath us—I know not the fathom line that ever touched a descent so deep as I would be willing to bury more wealth in than Crœsus had, or the great Jew R—— is supposed to have, to purchase it. And now do just look at that merry little Chinese waiter holding an umbrella, big enough for a

bed-tester, over the head of that pretty insipid half-Madonaish chit of a lady in that very blue summer house."

MRS. BATTLE'S OPINIONS ON WHIST

"A CLEAR fire, a clean hearth,* and the rigour of the game." This was the celebrated *wish* of old Sarah Battle (now with God) who, next to her devotions, loved a good game of whist. She was none of your lukewarm gamesters, your half and half players, who have no objection to take a hand, if you want one to make up a rubber; who affirm that they have no pleasure in winning; that they like to win one game and lose another; that they can while away an hour very agreeably at a card-table, but are indifferent whether they play or no; and will desire an adversary, who has slipt a wrong card, to take it up and play another.† These insufferable triflers are the curse of a table. One of these flies will spoil a whole pot. Of such it may be said, that they do not play at cards, but only play at playing at them.

Sarah Battle was none of that breed. She detested them, as I do, from her heart and soul; and would not, save upon a striking emergency, willingly seat herself at the same table with them. She loved a thorough-paced partner, a determined enemy. She took, and gave, no concessions. She hated favours. She never made a revoke, nor ever passed it over in her adversary without exacting the utmost forfeiture. She fought a good fight: cut and thrust. She held not her good sword

---

* This was before the introduction of rugs, Reader. You must remember the intolerable crash of the unswept cinders betwixt your foot and the marble.

† As if a sportsman should tell you he liked to kill a fox one day and lose him the next.

(her cards) "like a dancer." She sat bolt upright; and neither showed you her cards, nor desired to see yours. All people have their blind side—their superstitions; and I have heard her declare, under the rose, that Hearts was her favourite suit.

I never in my life—and I knew Sarah Battle many of the best years of it—saw her take out her snuff-box when it was her turn to play; or snuff a candle in the middle of a game; or ring for a servant, till it was fairly over. She never introduced or connived at miscellaneous conversation during its process. As she emphatically observed, cards were cards: and if I ever saw unmingled distaste in her fine last-century countenance, it was at the airs of a young gentleman of a literary turn, who had been with difficulty persuaded to take a hand; and who, in his excess of candour, declared, that he thought there was no harm in unbending the mind now and then, after serious studies, in recreations of that kind! She could not bear to have her noble occupation, to which she wound up her faculties, considered in that light. It was her business, her duty, the thing she came into the world to do,—and she did it. She unbent her mind afterwards—over a book.

Pope was her favourite author: his Rape of the Lock her favourite work. She once did me the favour to play over with me (with the cards) his celebrated game of Ombre in that poem; and to explain to me how far it agreed with, and in what points it would be found to differ from, tradrille. Her illustrations were apposite and poignant; and I had the pleasure of sending the substance of them to Mr. Bowles: but I suppose they came too late to be inserted among his ingenious notes upon that author.

Quadrille, she has often told me, was her first love; but whist had engaged her maturer esteem. The former,

she said, was showy and specious, and likely to allure young persons. The uncertainty and quick shifting of partners—a thing which the constancy of whist abhors; the dazzling supremacy and regal investiture of Spadille —absurd, as she justly observed, in the pure aristocracy of whist, where his crown and garter gave him no proper power above his brother-nobility of the Aces;— the giddy vanity, so taking to the inexperienced, of playing alone;—above all, the overpowering attractions of a *Sans Prendre Vole*,—to the triumph of which there is certainly nothing parallel or approaching, in the contingencies of whist;—all these, she would say, make quadrille a game of captivation to the young and enthusiastic. But whist was the *solider* game: that was her word. It was a long meal; not like quadrille, a feast of snatches. One or two rubbers might co-extend in duration with an evening. They gave time to form rooted friendships, to cultivate steady enmities. She despised the chance-started, capricious, and ever fluctuating alliances of the other. The skirmishes of quadrille, she would say, reminded her of the petty ephemeral embroilments of the little Italian states, depicted by Machiavel; perpetually changing postures and connexions; bitter foes to-day, sugared darlings to-morrow; kissing and scratching in a breath;—but the wars of whist were comparable to the long, steady, deep-rooted, rational, antipathies of the great French and English nations.

A grave simplicity was what she chiefly admired in her favourite game. There was nothing silly in it, like the nob in cribbage—nothing superfluous. No *flushes* —that most irrational of all pleas that a reasonable being can set up:—that any one should claim four by virtue of holding cards of the same mark and colour, without reference to the playing of the game, or the

individual worth or pretensions of the cards themselves! She held this to be a solecism; as pitiful an ambition at cards as alliteration is in authorship. She despised superficiality, and looked deeper than the colours of things. Suits were soldiers, she would say, and must have a uniformity of array to distinguish them; but what should we say to a foolish squire, who should claim a merit for dressing up his tenantry in red jackets, that never were to be marshalled—never to take the field?—She even wished that whist were more simple than it is; and, in my mind, would have stript it of some appendages, which, in the state of human frailty, may be venially, and even commendably allowed of. She saw no reason for the deciding of the trump by the turn of the card. Why not one suit always trumps?— Why two colours, when the mark of the suits would have sufficiently distinguished them without it?—

"But the eye, my dear Madam, is agreeably refreshed with the variety. Man is not a creature of pure reason —he must have his senses delightfully appealed to. We see it in Roman Catholic countries, where the music and the paintings draw in many to worship, whom your quaker spirit of unsensualising would have kept out.— You, yourself, have a pretty collection of paintings— but confess to me, whether, walking in your gallery at Sandham, among those clear Vandykes, or among the Paul Potters in the ante-room, you ever felt your bosom glow with an elegant delight, at all comparable to *that* you have it in your power to experience most evenings over a well-arranged assortment of the court cards?— the pretty antic habits, like heralds in a procession—the gay triumph-assuring scarlets—the contrasting deadly-killing sables—the 'hoary majesty of spades'—Pam in all his glory!—

"All these might be dispensed with; and, with their

naked names upon the drab pasteboard, the game might go on very well, pictureless. But the *beauty* of cards would be extinguished for ever. Stripped of all that is imaginative in them, they must degenerate into mere gambling.—Imagine a dull deal board, or drum head, to spread them on, instead of that nice verdant carpet (next to nature's), fittest arena for those courtly combatants to play their gallant jousts and tourneys in!— Exchange those delicately-turned ivory markers—(work of Chinese artist, unconscious of their symbol—or as profanely slighting their true application as the arrantest Ephesian journeyman that turned out those little shrines for the goddess)—exchange them for little bits of leather (our ancestors' money) or chalk and a slate!"—

The old lady, with a smile, confessed the soundness of my logic; and to her approbation of my arguments on her favourite topic that evening, I have always fancied myself indebted for the legacy of a curious cribbage board, made of the finest Sienna marble, which her maternal uncle (Old Walter Plumer, whom I have elsewhere celebrated brought with him from Florence:— this, and a trifle of five hundred pounds came to me at her death.

The former bequest (which I do not least value) I have kept with religious care; though she herself, to confess a truth, was never greatly taken with cribbage. It was an essentially vulgar game, I have heard her say,—disputing with her uncle, who was very partial to it. She could never heartily bring her mouth to pronounce *"go,"* or *"that's a go."* She called it an ungrammatical game. The pegging teased her. I once knew her to forfeit a rubber (a five dollar stake), because she would not take advantage of the turn-up knave, which would have given it her, but which she must have

claimed by the disgraceful tenure of declaring *"two for his heels."* There is something extremely genteel in this sort of self-denial. Sarah Battle was a gentlewoman born.

Piquet she held the best game at the cards for two persons, though she would ridicule the pedantry of the terms—such as pique repique—the capot—they savoured (she thought) of affectation. But games for two, or even three, she never greatly cared for. She loved the quadrate, or square. She would argue thus:—Cards are warfare: the ends are gain, with glory. But cards are war, in disguise of a sport: when single adversaries encounter, the ends proposed are too palpable. By themselves, it is too close a fight: with spectators, it is not much bettered. No looker-on can be interested, except for a bet, and then it is a mere affair of money; he cares not for your luck *sympathetically,* or for your play.—Three are still worse; a mere naked war of every man against every man, as in cribbage, without league or alliance; or a rotation of petty and contradictory interests, a succession of heartless leagues, and not much more hearty infractions of them, as in tradrille. But in square games (*she meant whist*) all that is possible to be attained in card-playing is accomplished. There are the incentives of profit with honour, common to every species—though the *latter* can be but very imperfectly enjoyed in those other games, where the spectator is only feebly a participator. But the parties in whist are spectators and principals too. They are a theatre to themselves, and a looker-on is not wanted. He is rather worse than nothing, and an impertinence. Whist abhors neutrality, or interests beyond its sphere. You glory is some surprising stroke of skill or fortune, not because a cold—or even an interested—by-stander witnesses it, but because your *partner*

sympathises in the contingency. You win for two. You triumph for two. Two are exalted. Two again are mortified; which divides their disgrace, as the conjunction doubles (by taking off the invidiousness) your glories. Two losing to two are better reconciled, than one to one in that close butchery. The hostile feeling is weakened by multiplying the channels. War becomes a civil game.—By such reasonings as these the old lady was accustomed to defend her favourite pastime.

No inducement could ever prevail upon her to play at any game where chance entered into the composition, *for nothing*. Chance, she would argue—and here again, admire the subtlety of her conclusion!—chance is nothing, but where something else depends upon it. It is obvious, that cannot be *glory*. What rational cause of exultation could it give to a man to turn up size ace a hundred times together by himself? or before spectators, where no stake was depending?—Make a lottery of a hundred thousand tickets with but one fortunate number —and what possible principle of our nature, except stupid wonderment, could it gratify to gain that number as many times successively, without a prize?—Therefore she disliked the mixture of chance in backgammon, where it was not played for money. She called it foolish, and those people idiots, who were taken with a lucky hit under such circumstances. Games of pure skill were as little to her fancy. Played for a stake, they were a mere system of over-reaching. Played for glory, they were a mere setting of one man's wit—his memory, or combination-faculty rather—against another's; like a mock-engagement at a review, bloodless and profitless.— She could not conceive a *game* wanting the spritely infusion of chance,—the handsome excuses of good fortune. Two people playing at chess in a corner of a room whilst whist was stirring in the centre, would

inspire her with unsufferable horror and ennui. Those well-cut similitudes of Castles, and Knights, the *imagery* of the board, she would argue (and I think in this case justly) were entirely misplaced, and senseless. Those hard head-contests can in no instance ally with the fancy. They reject form and colour. A pencil and dry slate (she used to say) were the proper arena for such combatants.

To those puny objectors against cards, as nurturing the bad passions, she would retort, that man is a gaming animal. He must be always trying to get the better in something or other:—that this passion can scarcely be more safely expended than upon a game at cards: that cards are a temporary illusion; in truth, a mere drama; for we do but *play* at being mightily concerned, where a few idle shillings are at stake, yet, during the illusion, we *are* as mightily concerned as those whose stake is crowns and kingdoms. They are a sort of dream-fighting; much ado; great battling, and little blood shed; mighty means for disproportioned ends; quite as diverting, and a great deal more innoxious, than many of those more serious *games* of life, which men play, without esteeming them to be such.——

With great deference to the old lady's judgment on these matters, I think I have experienced some moments in my life, when playing at cards *for nothing* has even been very agreeable. When I am in sickness, or not in the best spirits, I sometimes call for the cards, and play a game at piquet *for love* with my cousin Bridget— Bridget Elia.

I grant there is something sneaking in it: but with a toothache or a sprained ankle,—when you are subdued and humble,—you are glad to put up with an inferior spring of action.

There is such a thing in nature, I am convinced, as *sick whist*.

I grant it is not the highest style of man—I deprecate the manes of Sarah Battle—she lives not, alas! to whom I should apologise.—

At such times those *terms* which my old friend objected to, come in as something admissible.—I love to get a tierce or a quatorze, though they mean nothing. I am subdued to an inferior interest. Those shadows of winning amuse me.

That last game I had with my sweet cousin (I capotted her)—(dare I tell thee how foolish I am?)—I wished it might have lasted for ever, though we gained nothing, and lost nothing, though it was a mere shade of play: I would be content to go on in that idle folly for ever. The pipkin should be ever boiling, that was to prepare the gentle lenitive to my foot, which Bridget was doomed to apply after the game was over: and as I do not much relish appliances, there it should ever bubble. Bridget and I should be ever playing.

A DISSERTATION UPON ROAST PIG

MANKIND, says a Chinese manuscript, which my friend M. was obliging enough to read and explain to me, for the first seventy thousand ages ate their meat raw, clawing or biting it from the living animal, just as they do in Abyssinia to this day. This period is not obscurely hinted at by their great Confucius in the second chapter of his Mundane Mutations, where he designates a kind of golden age by the term Cho-fang, literally the Cook's holiday. The manuscript goes on to say, that the art of roasting, or rather broiling (which I take to be the elder brother) was accidentally discovered in the manner following. The swine-herd, Ho-ti, having gone out

A DISSERTATION UPON ROAST PIG 145

into the woods one morning, as his manner was, to collect mast for his hogs, left his cottage in the care of his eldest son Bo-bo, a great lubberly boy, who being fond of playing with fire, as younkers of his age commonly are, let some sparks escape into a bundle of straw, which kindling quickly, spread the conflagration over every part of their poor mansion, till it was reduced to ashes. Together with the cottage (a sorry antediluvian make-shift of a building, you may think it), what was of much more importance, a fine litter of new-farrowed pigs, no less than nine in number, perished. China pigs have been esteemed a luxury all over the East from the remotest periods that we read of. Bo-bo was in utmost consternation, as you may think, not so much for the sake of the tenement, which his father and he could easily build up again with a few dry branches, and the labour of an hour or two, at any time, as for the loss of the pigs. While he was thinking what he should say to his father, and wringing his hands over the smoking remnants of one of those untimely sufferers, an odour assailed his nostrils, unlike any scent which he had before experienced. What could it proceed from?—not from the burnt cottage—he had smelt that smell before—indeed this was by no means the first accident of the kind which had occurred through the negligence of this unlucky young fire-brand. Much less did it resemble that of any known herb, weed, or flower. A premonitory moistening at the same time overflowed his nether lip. He knew not what to think. He next stooped down to feel the pig, if there were any signs of life in it. He burnt his fingers, and to cool them he applied them in his booby fashion to his mouth. Some of the crumbs of the scorched skin had come away with his fingers, and for the first time in his life (in the world's life indeed, for before him no man had known

it) he tasted—*crackling!* Again he felt and fumbled at the pig. It did not burn him so much now, still he licked his fingers from a sort of habit. The truth at length broke into his slow understanding, that it was the pig that smelt so, and the pig that tasted so delicious; and, surrendering himself up to the newborn pleasure, he fell to tearing up whole handfuls of the scorched skin with the flesh next it, and was cramming it down his throat in his beastly fashion, when his sire entered amid the smoking rafters, armed with retributory cudgel, and finding how affairs stood, began to rain blows upon the young rogue's shoulders, as thick as hailstones, which Bo-bo heeded not any more than if they had been flies. The tickling pleasure, which he experienced in his lower regions, had rendered him quite callous to any inconveniences he might feel in those remote quarters. His father might lay on, but he could not beat him from his pig, till he had fairly made an end of it, when, becoming a little more sensible of his situation, something like the following dialogue ensued.

"You graceless whelp, what have you got there devouring? Is it not enough that you have burnt me down three houses with your dog's tricks, and be hanged to you, but you must be eating fire, and I know not what—what have you got there, I say?"

"O, father, the pig, the pig, do come and taste how nice the burnt pig eats."

The ears of Ho-ti tingled with horror. He cursed his son, and he cursed himself that ever he should beget a son that should eat burnt pig.

Bo-bo, whose scent was wonderfully sharpened since morning, soon raked out another pig, and fairly rending it asunder, thrust the lesser half by main force into the fists of Ho-ti, still shouting out "Eat, eat, eat the burnt pig, father, only taste—O Lord,"—with such-like bar-

A DISSERTATION UPON ROAST PIG

barous ejaculations, cramming all the while as if he would choke.

Ho-ti trembled every joint while he grasped the abominable thing, wavering whether he should not put his son to death for an unnatural young monster, when the crackling scorching his fingers, as it had done his son's, and applying the same remedy to them, he in his turn tasted some of its flavour, which, make what sour mouths he would for a pretence, proved not altogether displeasing to him. In conclusion (for the manuscript here is a little tedious) both father and son fairly sat down to the mess, and never left off till they had despatched all that remained of the litter.

Bo-bo was strictly enjoined not to let the secret escape, for the neighbours would certainly have stoned them for a couple of abominable wretches, who could think of improving upon the good meat which God had sent them. Nevertheless, strange stories got about. It was observed that Ho-ti's cottage was burnt down now more frequently than ever. Nothing but fires from this time forward. Some would break out in broad day, others in the night-time. As often as the sow farrowed, so sure was the house of Ho-ti to be in a blaze; and Ho-ti himself, which was the more remarkable, instead of chastising his son, seemed to grow more indulgent to him than ever. At length they were watched, the terrible mystery discovered, and father and son summoned to take their trial at Pekin, then an inconsiderable assize town. Evidence was given, the obnoxious food itself produced in court, and verdict about to be pronounced, when the foreman of the jury begged that some of the burnt pig, of which the culprits stood accused, might be handed into the box. He handled it, and they all handled it, and burning their fingers, as Bo-bo and his father had done before them, and nature prompting to

each of them the same remedy, against the face of all the facts, and the clearest charge which judge had ever given,—to the surprise of the whole court, townsfolk, strangers, reporters, and all present—without leaving the box, or any manner of consultation whatever, they brought in a simultaneous verdict of Not Guilty.

The judge, who was a shrewd fellow, winked at the manifest iniquity of the decision; and, when the court was dismissed, went privily, and bought up all the pigs that could be had for love or money. In a few days his Lordship's town house was observed to be on fire. The thing took wing, and now there was nothing to be seen but fires in every direction. Fuel and pigs grew enormously dear all over the district. The insurance offices one and all shut up shop. People built slighter and slighter every day, until it was feared that the very science of architecture would in no long time be lost to the world. Thus this custom of firing houses continued, till in process of time, says my manuscript, a sage arose, like our Locke, who made a discovery, that the flesh of swine, or indeed of any other animal, might be cooked (*burnt,* as they called it) without the necessity of consuming a whole house to dress it. Then first began the rude form of a gridiron. Roasting by the string, or spit, came in a century or two later, I forget in whose dynasty. By such slow degrees, concludes the manuscript, do the most useful, and seemingly the most obvious arts, make their way among mankind.——

Without placing too implicit faith in the account above given, it must be agreed, that if a worthy pretext for so dangerous an experiment as setting houses on fire (especially in these days) could be assigned in favour of any culinary object, that pretext and excuse might be found in ROAST PIG.

Of all the delicacies in the whole *mundus edibilis,*

A DISSERTATION UPON ROAST PIG 149

I will maintain it to be the most delicate—*princeps obsoniorum*.

I speak not of your grown porkers—things between pig and pork—those hobbydehoys—but a young and tender suckling—under a moon old—guiltless as yet of the sty—with no original speck of the *amor immunditiae*, the hereditary failing of the first parent, yet manifest—his voice as yet not broken, but something between a childish treble, and a grumble—the mild forerunner, or *praeludium*, of a grunt.

He must be roasted. I am not ignorant that our ancestors ate them seethed, or boiled—but what a sacrifice of the exterior tegument!

There is no flavour comparable, I will contend, to that of the crisp, tawny, well-watched, not over-roasted, *crackling*, as it is well called—the very teeth are invited to their share of the pleasure at this banquet in overcoming the coy, brittle resistance—with the adhesive oleaginous—O call it not fat—but an indefinable sweetness growing up to it—the tender blossoming of fat—fat cropped in the bud—taken in the shoot—in the first innocence—the cream and quintessence of the child-pig's yet pure food—the lean, no lean, but a kind of animal manna—or, rather, fat and lean, (if it must be so) so blended and running into each other, that both together make but one ambrosian result, or common substance.

Behold him, while he is doing—it seemeth rather a refreshing warmth, than a scorching heat, that he is so passive to. How equably he twirleth round the string!—Now he is just done. To see the extreme sensibility of that tender age, he hath wept out his pretty eyes—radiant jellies—shooting stars—

See him in the dish, his second cradle, how meek he lieth!—wouldst thou have had this innocent grow up to

the grossness and indocility which too often accompany maturer swinehood? Ten to one he would have proved a glutton, a sloven, an obstinate, disagreeable animal—wallowing in all manner of filthy conversation—from these sins he is happily snatched away—

> Ere sin could blight, or sorrow fade,
> Death came with timely care—

his memory is odoriferous—no clown curseth, while his stomach half rejecteth, the rank bacon—no coal-heaver bolteth him in reeking sausages—he hath a fair sepulchre in the grateful stomach of the judicious epicure—and for such a tomb might be content to die.

He is the best of Sapors. Pine-apple is great. She is indeed almost too transcendent—a delight, if not sinful, yet so like to sinning, that really a tender-conscienced person would do well to pause—too ravishing for mortal taste, she woundeth and excoriateth the lips that approach her—like lovers' kisses, she biteth—she is a pleasure bordering on pain from the fierceness and insanity of her relish—but she stoppeth at the palate—she meddleth not with the appetite—and the coarsest hunger might barter her consistently for a mutton chop.

Pig—let me speak his praise—is no less provocative of the appetite, than he is satisfactory to the criticalness of the censorious palate. The strong man may batten on him, and weakling refuseth not his mild juices.

Unlike to mankind's mixed characters, a bundle of virtues and vices, inexplicably intertwisted, and not to be unravelled without hazard, he is—good throughout. No part of him is better or worse than another. He helpeth, as far as his little means extend, all around. He is the least envious of banquets. He is all neighbours' fare.

I am one of those, who freely and ungrudgingly im-

A DISSERTATION UPON ROAST PIG

part a share of the good things of this life which fall to their lot (few as mine are in this kind) to a friend. I protest I take as great an interest in my friend's pleasures, his relishes, and proper satisfactions, as in mine own. "Presents," I often say, "endear Absents." Hares, pheasants, partridges, snipes, barn-door chickens (those "tame villatic fowl"), capons, plovers, brawn, barrels of oysters, I dispense as freely as I receive them. I love to taste them, as it were, upon the tongue of my friend. But a stop must be put somewhere. One would not, like Lear, "give everything." I make my stand upon pig. Methinks it is an ingratitude to the Giver of all good flavours, to extra-domiciliate, or send out of the house, slightingly (under pretext of friendship, or I know not what), a blessing so particularly adapted, predestined, I may say, to my individual palate—It argues an insensibility.

I remember a touch of conscience in this kind at school. My good old aunt, who never parted from me at the end of a holiday without stuffing a sweetmeat, or some nice thing, into my pocket, had dismissed me one evening with a smoking plum-cake, fresh from the oven. In my way to school (it was over London Bridge) a grey-headed old beggar saluted me (I have no doubt at this time of day that he was a counterfeit). I had no pence to console him with, and in the vanity of self-denial, and the very coxcombry of charity, schoolboy like, I made him a present of—the whole cake! I walked on a little, buoyed up, as one is on such occasions, with a sweet soothing of self-satisfaction; but before I had got to the end of the bridge, my better feelings returned, and I burst into tears, thinking how ungrateful I had been to my good aunt, to go and give her good gift away to a stranger, that I had never seen before, and who might be a bad man for

aught I knew; and then I thought of the pleasure my aunt would be taking in thinking that I—I myself, and not another—would eat her nice cake—and what should I say to her the next time I saw her—how naughty I was to part with her pretty present—and the odour of that spicy cake came back upon my recollection, and the pleasure and the curiosity I had taken in seeing her make it, and her joy when she sent it to the oven, and how disappointed she would feel that I had never had a bit of it in my mouth at last—and I blamed my impertinent spirit of alms-giving, and out-of-place hypocrisy of goodness, and above all I wished never to see the face again of that insidious, good-for-nothing, old grey impostor.

Our ancestors were nice in their method of sacrificing these tender victims. We read of pigs whipt to death with something of a shock, as we hear of any other obsolete custom. The age of discipline is gone by, or it would be curious to inquire (in a philosophical light merely) what effect this process might have towards intenerating and dulcifying a substance, naturally so mild and dulcet as the flesh of young pigs. It looks like refining a violet. Yet we should be cautious, while we condemn the inhumanity, how we censure the wisdom of the practice. It might impart a gusto—

I remember an hypothesis, argued upon by the young students, when I was at St. Omer's, and maintained with much learning and pleasantry on both sides, "Whether, supposing that the flavour of a pig who obtained his death by whipping (*per flagellationem extremam*) superadded a pleasure upon the palate of a man more intense than any possible suffering we can conceive in the animal, is man justified in using that method of putting the animal to death?" I forget the decision.

His sauce should be considered. Decidedly, a few bread crumbs, done up with his liver and brains, and a dash of mild sage. But, banish, dear Mrs. Cook, I beseech you, the whole onion tribe. Barbecue your whole hogs to your palate, steep them in shalots, stuff them out with plantations of the rank and guilty garlic; you cannot poison them, or make them stronger than they are—but consider, he is a weakling—a flower.

DREAM-CHILDREN: A REVERIE

CHILDREN love to listen to stories about their elders, when *they* were children: to stretch their imagination to the conception of a traditionary great-uncle or grandame, whom they never saw. It was in this spirit that my little ones crept about me the other evening to hear about their great-grandmother Field, who lived in a great house in Norfolk (a hundred times bigger than that in which they and papa lived) which had been the scene— so at least it was generally believed in that part of the country—of the tragic incidents which they had lately become familiar with from the ballad of the Children in the Wood. Certain it is that the whole story of the children and their cruel uncle was to be seen fairly carved out in wood upon the chimney-piece of the great hall, the whole story down to the Robin Redbreasts, till a foolish rich person pulled it down to set up a marble one of modern invention in its stead, with no story upon it. Here Alice put out one of her dear mother's looks, too tender to be called upbraiding. Then I went on to say, how religious and how good their great-grandmother Field was, how beloved and respected by every body, though she was not indeed the mistress of this great house, but had only the charge of it (and yet in some respects she might be said to be the mistress

of it too) committed to her by the owner, who preferred living in a newer and more fashionable mansion which he had purchased somewhere in the adjoining county; but still she lived in it in a manner as if it had been her own, and kept up the dignity of the great house in a sort while she lived, which afterwards came to decay, and was nearly pulled down, and all its old ornaments stripped and carried away to the owner's other house, where they were set up, and looked as awkward as if some one were to carry away the old tombs they had seen lately at the Abbey, and stick them up in Lady C.'s tawdry gilt drawing-room. Here John smiled, as much as to say, "that would be foolish indeed." And then I told how, when she came to die, her funeral was attended by a concourse of all the poor, and some of the gentry too, of the neighborhood for many miles round, to show their respect for her memory, because she had been such a good and religious woman; so good indeed that she knew all the Psaltery by heart, ay, and a great part of the Testament besides. Here little Alice spread her hands. Then I told what a tall, upright, graceful person their great-grandmother Field once was; and how in her youth she was esteemed the best dancer—here Alice's little right foot played an involuntary movement, till upon my looking grave, it desisted—the best dancer, I was saying, in the county, till a cruel disease, called a cancer, came, and bowed her down with pain; but it could never bend her good spirits, or make them stoop, but they were still upright, because she was so good and religious. Then I told how she was used to sleep by herself in a lone chamber of the great lone house; and how she believed that an apparition of two infants was to be seen at midnight gliding up and down the great staircase near where she slept, but she said "those innocents would do her no

harm;" and how frightened I used to be, though in those days I had my maid to sleep with me, because I was never half so good or religious as she—and yet I never saw the infants. Here John expanded all his eyebrows and tried to look courageous. Then I told how good she was to all her grand-children, having us to the great house in the holydays, where I in particular used to spend many hours by myself, in gazing upon the old busts of the Cæsars, that had been Emperors of Rome, till the old marble heads would seem to live again, or I be turned into marble with them; how I never could be tired with roaming about that huge mansion, with its vast empty rooms, with their worn-out hangings, fluttering tapestry, and carved oaken panels, with the gilding almost rubbed out—sometimes in the spacious old-fashioned gardens, which I had almost to myself, unless when now and then a solitary gardening man would cross me—and how the nectarines and peaches hung upon the walls, without my ever offering to pluck them, because they were forbidden fruit, unless now and then,—and because I had more pleasure in strolling about among the old melancholy-looking yew trees, or the firs, and picking up the red berries, and the fir apples, which were good for nothing but to look at— or in lying about upon the fresh grass, with all the fine garden smells around me—or basking in the orangery, till I could almost fancy myself ripening too along with the oranges and the limes in that grateful warmth—or in watching the dace that darted to and fro in the fish-pond, at the bottom of the garden, with here and there a great sulky pike hanging midway down the water in silent state, as if it mocked at their impertinent friskings,—I had more pleasure in these busy-idle diversions than in all the sweet flavours of peaches, nectarines, oranges, and such like common baits of children. Here

John slily deposited back upon the plate a bunch of grapes, which, not unobserved by Alice, he had meditated dividing with her, and both seemed willing to relinquish them for the present as irrelevant. Then in somewhat a more heightened tone, I told how, though their great-grandmother Field loved all her grandchildren, yet in an especial manner she might be said to love their uncle, John L———, because he was so handsome and spirited a youth, and a king to the rest of us; and, instead of moping about in solitary corners, like some of us, he would mount the most mettlesome horse he could get, when but an imp no bigger than themselves, and make it carry him half over the country in a morning, and join the hunters when there were any out—and yet he loved the old great house and gardens too, but had too much spirit to be always pent up within their boundaries—and how their uncle grew up to man's estate as brave as he was handsome, to the admiration of every body, but of their great-grandmother Field most especially; and how he used to carry me upon his back when I was a lame-footed boy—for he was a good bit older than me—many a mile when I could not walk for pain;—and how in after life he became lame-footed too, and I did not always (I fear) make allowances enough for him when he was impatient, and in pain, nor remember sufficiently how considerate he had been to me when I was lame-footed; and how when he died, though he had not been dead an hour, it seemed as if he had died a great while ago, such a distance there is betwixt life and death; and how I bore his death as I thought pretty well at first, but afterwards it haunted and haunted me; and though I did not cry or take it to heart as some do, and as I think he would have done if I had died, yet I missed him all day long, and knew not till then how much I had loved him. I missed his

DREAM CHILDREN: A REVERIE

kindness, and I missed his crossness, and wished him to be alive again, to be quarrelling with him (for we quarrelled sometimes), rather than not have him again, and was as uneasy without him, as he, their poor uncle, must have been when the doctor took off his limb. Here the children fell a crying, and asked if their little mourning which they had on was not for uncle John, and they looked up, and prayed me not to go on about their uncle, but to tell them some stories about their pretty dead mother. Then I told how for seven long years, in hope sometimes, sometimes in despair, yet persisting ever, I courted the fair Alice W——n; and, as much as children could understand, I explained to them what coyness, and difficulty, and denial meant in maidens—when suddenly, turning to Alice, the soul of the first Alice looked out at her eyes with such a reality of re-presentment, that I became in doubt which of them stood there before me, or whose that bright hair was; and while I stood gazing, both the children gradually grew fainter to my view, receding, and still receding till nothing at last but two mournful features were seen in the uttermost distance, which, without speech, strangely impressed upon me the effects of speech; "We are not of Alice, nor of thee, nor are we children at all. The children of Alice call Bartrum father. We are nothing; less than nothing, and dreams. We are only what might have been, and must wait upon the tedious shores of Lethe millions of ages before we have existence, and a name"—and immediately awaking, I found myself quietly seated in my bachelor armchair, where I had fallen asleep, with the faithful Bridget unchanged by my side—but John L. (or James Elia) was gone for ever.

THOMAS DE QUINCEY

Sydney Smith is remembered for his jests, Southey for his friendships and an unread epic or two, De Quincey for the *Opium-Eater* and a few prose poems. All were celebrated magazine writers, skilled in the somewhat formal manner of writing approved by the chief periodicals of their time. But magazine articles are usually ephemeral. The quality of timeliness which gives them vogue, the semi-popular presentation of material, the policy or prejudices of the editor (which may not be disregarded) all conspire to make the liveliest and soundest article uninteresting a hundred years hence.

De Quincey wrote, of necessity, for a living. A learned man and a scholarly writer in various fields, he read Kant and, as he said, thought he understood him. His speculations in political economy excited the commendation of Ricardo. He was at home in the German, Latin, and Greek literatures. Altogether his intellectual range and talents were remarkable and have their place in the anecdotal history of literature. Yet it is only the *Opium-Eater* and two or three short pieces which are much read today. These only, in De Quincey's phrase, are of the literature not of knowledge but of power. They are emotional, not informative.

There was in De Quincey a vein of feeling which, if narrow, was delicate and fine. The story of Ann in the *Opium-Eater* is told with power and beauty, and episodes of his childhood as he recalls them have a wistful charm. These are true incidents, and De Quincey is most compelling as a narrative writer when he relates

what he has himself experienced. The opium dreams are as strange as the exotic creations of fancy; yet they are intensely true and personal, and their power lies very considerably in the sympathy which they excite for the human soul which experienced them. De Quincey is the pathetic and heroic center of his story. We remember Carlyle's immortal description of him as "the beautifullest little child," but, too, of whom Carlyle said: "this child has been in hell."

As a stylist De Quincey is too often rhetorical; the form and manner of his writing distract from the thing said. Yet his best things, despite a virtuosity which cannot be ignored and which must, indeed, be admired even as one reads, are more than skilful exercises. It is possible, when listening to a great singer, both to marvel at the execution and to be carried away by the passion of the song. The listener experiences a twofold pleasure, in which admiration of technic enhances the intensity of the emotional effect. Some such operatic triumph is De Quincey's in his great moments. Thus in the passage in the *Opium-Eater* beginning "I dreamt that it was Easter Sunday and very early in the morning," the biblical cadence of the style with its coordinated sentences, almost wholly simple-compound in form, is calculated obviously to an emotional effect which culminates with the apparition of Ann. The shift from De Quincey's characteristic periodic style with its complex sentences is dramatic, like the sudden rallentando or pianissimo in the whirl-wind finale of a symphony. Yet despite its calculated artistry, the passage seems to me wholly moving even when many times read.

De Quincey is very much the musician, too, in his massing of words to complex and sonorous harmonies, as in the fugue-like passages depicting the pains of opium. *Levana and Our Ladies of Sorrow* is a tone

poem, orchestral in its effects, contrapuntal in its architectonics. It is emotionally compelling, nevertheless, and despite its elaborateness, simple in its effect, evoking pity for all who sorrow. More profoundly than other emotions De Quincey knew grief and compassion. These are the theme of his finest prose, wherein all his resources as a stylist move at the command of his sincerest feeling.

The extracts from the *Opium-Eater* which follow are based upon the first form of it which appeared in the *London Magazine*. Later De Quincey very considerably expanded it after his characteristic fashion. Yet he doubted whether the first and simpler form was not preferable. The modern reader has no hesitation in concurring.

Selections from
CONFESSIONS OF AN ENGLISH OPIUM-EATER

I have often been asked how I came to be a regular opium-eater; and have suffered, very unjustly, in the opinion of my acquaintance, from being reputed to have brought upon myself all the sufferings which I shall have to record, by a long course of indulgence in this practice purely for the sake of creating an artificial state of pleasurable excitement. This, however, is a misrepresentation of my case. True it is, that for nearly ten years I did occasionally take opium for the sake of the exquisite pleasure it gave me: but, so long as I took it with this view, I was effectually protected from all material bad consequences by the necessity of interposing long intervals between the several acts of indulgence, in order to renew the pleasurable sensations. It was not for the purpose of creating pleasure, but of mitigating pain in the severest degree, that I first began to use opium as an

article of daily diet. In the twenty-eighth year of my age, a most painful affection of the stomach, which I had first experienced about ten years before, attacked me in great strength. This affection had originally been caused by extremities of hunger suffered in my boyish days. During the season of hope and redundant happiness which succeeded (that is, from eighteen to twenty-four) it had slumbered: for the three following years it had revived at intervals: and now, under unfavourable circumstances, from depression of spirits, it attacked me with a violence that yielded to no remedies but opium. As the youthful sufferings which first produced this derangement of the stomach, were interesting in themselves, and in the circumstances that attended them, I shall briefly retrace them.

My father died when I was about seven years old, and left me to the care of four guardians. I was sent to various schools, great and small; and was very early distinguished for my classical attainments, especially for my knowledge of Greek. At thirteen, I wrote Greek with ease; and at fifteen my command of that language was so great that I not only composed Greek verses in lyric metres, but could converse in Greek fluently, and without embarrassment—an accomplishment which I have not since met with in any scholar of my times, and which, in my case, was owing to the practice of daily reading off the newspapers into the best Greek I could furnish *extempore:* for the necessity of ransacking my memory and invention for all sorts and combinations of periphrastic expressions, as equivalents for modern ideas, images, relations of things, etc., gave me a compass of diction which would never have been called out by a dull translation of moral essays, etc. "That boy," said one of my masters, pointing the attention of a stranger

to me, "that boy could harangue an Athenian mob better than you or I could address an English one." He who honoured me with this eulogy, was a scholar, "and a ripe and good one;" and, of all my tutors, was the only one whom I loved or reverenced. Unfortunately for me (and, as I afterwards learned, to this worthy man's great indignation), I was transferred to the care, first of a blockhead, who was in a perpetual panic lest I should expose his ignorance; and finally, to that of a respectable scholar, at the head of a great school on an ancient foundation. This man had been appointed to his situation by Brasenose College, Oxford; and was a sound, well-built scholar, but, like most men whom I have known from that college, coarse, clumsy and inelegant. A miserable contrast he presented, in my eyes, to the Etonian brilliancy of my favorite master: and, besides, he could not disguise from my hourly notice the poverty and meagerness of his understanding. It is a bad thing for a boy to be, and to know himself far beyond his tutors, whether in knowledge or in power of mind. This was the case, so far as regarded knowledge at least, not with myself only; for the two boys who jointly with myself composed the first form, were better Grecians than the headmaster, though not more elegant scholars, nor at all more accustomed to sacrifice to the graces. When I first entered, I remember that we read Sophocles; and it was a constant matter of triumph to us, the learned triumvirate of the first form, to see our "Archididascalus," as he loved to be called, conning our lesson before he went up, and laying a regular train, with lexicon and grammar, for blowing up and blasting, as it were, any difficulties he found in the choruses; whilst *we* never condescended to open our books until the moment of going up, and were generally employed in

writing epigrams upon his wig, or some such important matter. My two class-fellows were poor, and dependent, for their future prospects at the university, on the recommendation of the head-master: but I, who had a small patrimonial property, the income of which was sufficient to support me at college, wished to be sent thither immediately. I made earnest representations on the subject to my guardians, but all to no purpose. One, who was more reasonable, and had more knowledge of the world than the rest, lived at a distance: two of the other three resigned all their authority into the hands of the fourth; and this fourth, with whom I had to negotiate, was a worthy man in his way, but haughty, obstinate, and intolerant of all opposition to his will. After a certain number of letters and personal interviews, I found that I had nothing to hope for, not even a compromise of the matter, from my guardian; unconditional submission was what he demanded: and I prepared myself, therefore, for other measures. Summer was now coming on with hasty steps, and my seventeenth birthday was fast approaching; after which day I had sworn within myself that I would no longer be numbered amongst school-boys. Money being what I chiefly wanted, I wrote to a woman of high rank, who, though young herself, had known me from a child, and had latterly treated me with great distinction, requesting that she would "lend" me five guineas. For upwards of a week no answer came; and I was beginning to despond, when, at length, a servant put into my hands a double letter, with a coronet on the seal. The letter was kind and obliging: the fair writer was on the seacoast, and in that way the delay had arisen: she enclosed double of what I had asked, and good-naturedly hinted that if I should *never* repay her it would not

absolutely ruin her. Now, then, I was prepared for my scheme: ten guineas, added to about two which I had remaining from my pocket money, seemed to me sufficient for an indefinite length of time: and at that happy age, if no *definite* boundary can be assigned to one's power, the spirit of hope and pleasure makes it virtually infinite.

It is a just remark of Dr. Johnson's, and, what cannot often be said of his remarks, it is a very feeling one, that we never do anything consciously for the last time—of things, that is, which we have long been in the habit of doing—without sadness of heart. This truth I felt deeply, when I came to leave [Manchester], a place which I did not love, and where I had not been happy. On the evening before I left [Manchester] forever, I grieved when the ancient and lofty school-room resounded with the evening service, performed for the last time in my hearing; and at night, when the muster-roll of names was called over, and mine, as usual, was called first, I stepped forward, and, passing the head-master, who was standing by, I bowed to him, and looked earnestly in his face, thinking to myself, "He is old and infirm, and in this world I shall not see him again." I was right: I never *did* see him again, nor ever shall. He looked at me complacently, smiled good-naturedly, returned my salutation, or rather my valediction, and we parted, though he knew it not, forever. I could not reverence him intellectually: but he had been uniformly kind to me, and had allowed me many indulgences: and I grieved at the thought of the mortification I should inflict upon him.

The morning came which was to launch me into the world, and from which my whole succeeding life has, in many important points, taken its coloring. I lodged in the head-master's house, and had been allowed, from

my first entrance, the indulgence of a private room, which I used both as a sleeping-room and as a study. At half after three I rose, and gazed with deep emotion at the ancient towers of [the Collegiate Church], "drest in earliest light," and beginning to crimson with the radiant lustre of a cloudless July morning. I was firm and immovable in my purpose; but yet agitated by anticipation of uncertain danger and troubles; and, if I could have foreseen the hurricane and perfect hail-storm of affliction which soon fell upon me, well might I have been agitated. To this agitation the deep peace of the morning presented an affecting contrast, and in some degree a medicine. The silence was more profound than that of midnight: and to me the silence of a summer morning is more touching than all other silence, because the light being broad and strong, as that of noon-day at other seasons of the year, it seems to differ from perfect day chiefly because man is not yet abroad; and thus the peace of nature, and of the innocent creatures of God, seems to be secure and deep, only so long as the presence of man, and his restless and unquiet spirit, are not there to trouble its sanctity. I dressed myself, took my hat and gloves, and lingered a little in the room. For the last year and a half this room had been my "pensive citadel:" here I had read and studied through all the hours of night: and, though true it was that for the latter part of this time I, who was framed for love and gentle affections, had lost my gaiety and happiness, during the strife and fever of contention with my guardian; yet, on the other hand, as a boy so passionately fond of books, and dedicated to intellectual pursuits, I could not fail to have enjoyed many happy hours in the midst of general dejection. I wept as I looked round on the chair, hearth, writing-table, and other familiar

objects, knowing too certainly that I looked upon them for the last time. Whilst I write this, it is nineteen years ago: and yet, at this moment, I see distinctly as if it were yesterday the lineaments and expression of the object on which I fixed my parting gaze: it was a picture of the lovely———, which hung over the mantelpiece; the eyes and mouth of which were so beautiful, and the whole countenance so radiant with benignity and divine tranquillity, that I had a thousand times laid down my pen or my book, to gather consolation from it, as a devotee from his patron saint. Whilst I was yet gazing upon it, the deep tones of [Manchester] clock proclaimed that it was four o'clock. I went up to the picture, kissed it, and then gently walked out, and closed the door forever!

* * * * * * *

Soon after this, I contrived, by means which I must omit for want of room, to transfer myself to London. And now began the latter and fiercer stage of my long sufferings; without using a disproportionate expression, I might say, of my agony. For I now suffered, for upwards of sixteen weeks, the physical anguish of hunger in various degrees of intensity; but as bitter, perhaps, as ever any human being can have suffered who has survived it. I would not needlessly harass my readers' feelings by a detail of all that I endured; for extremities such as these, under any circumstances of heaviest misconduct or guilt, cannot be contemplated even in description without a rueful pity that is painful to the natural goodness of the human heart. Let it suffice, at least on this occasion, to say, that a few fragments of bread from the breakfast-table of one individual, who supposed me to be ill, but did not know of my being in utter want, and these at uncertain intervals, constituted my whole support. During the

former part of my sufferings, that is, generally in Wales, and always for the first two months in London, I was houseless, and very seldom slept under a roof. To this constant exposure to the open air I ascribe it mainly that I did not sink under my torments. Latterly, however, when colder and more inclement weather came on, and when, from the length of my sufferings, I had begun to sink into a more languishing condition, it was, no doubt, fortunate for me that the same person to whose breakfast-table I had access allowed me to sleep in a large unoccupied house, of which he was tenant. Unoccupied, I call it, for there was no household or establishment in it; nor any furniture, indeed, except a table and a few chairs. But I found, on taking possession of my new quarters, that the house already contained one single inmate, a poor friendless child, apparently ten years old; but she seemed hunger-bitten; and sufferings of that sort often make children look older than they are. From this forlorn child I learned that she had slept and lived there alone for some time before I came; and great joy the poor creature expressed, when she found that I was, in future, to be her companion through the hours of darkness. The house was large; and, from want of furniture, the noise of the rats made a prodigious echoing on the spacious stair-case and hall; and, amidst the real fleshly ills of cold, and, I fear, hunger, the forsaken child had found leisure to suffer still more, it appeared, from the self-created one of ghosts. I promised her protection against all ghosts whatsoever; but, alas! I could offer her no other assistance. We lay upon the floor, with a bundle of cursed law papers for a pillow; but with no other covering than a sort of large horseman's cloak; afterwards, however, we discovered, in a garret, an old sofa cover, a small piece of rug, and some

fragments of other articles, which added a little to our warmth. The poor child crept close to me for warmth, and for security against her ghostly enemies. When I was not more than usually ill, I took her into my arms, so that, in general, she was tolerably warm, and often slept when I could not; for, during the last two months of my sufferings, I slept much in the day-time, and was apt to fall into transient dozings at all hours. But my sleep distressed me more than my watching; for, besides the tumultuousness of my dreams, which were only not so awful as those which I shall have to describe hereafter as produced by opium, my sleep was never more than what is called *dog-sleep;* so that I could hear myself moaning, and was often, as it seemed to me, wakened suddenly by my own voice; and, about this time, a hideous sensation began to haunt me as soon as I fell into a slumber, which has since returned upon me at different periods of my life, viz., a sort of twitching, I know not where, but apparently about the region of the stomach, which compelled me violently to throw out my feet for the sake of relieving it. This sensation coming on as soon as I began to sleep, and the effort to relieve it constantly awaking me, at length I slept only from exhaustion; and from increasing weakness, as I said before, I was constantly falling asleep, and constantly waking. Meantime, the master of the house sometimes came in upon us suddenly, and very early, sometimes not till ten o'clock, sometimes not at all. He was in constant fear of bailiffs; improving on the plan of Cromwell, every night he slept in a different quarter of London; and I observed that he never failed to examine through a private window the appearance of those who knocked at the door, before he would allow it to be opened. He breakfasted alone; indeed, his tea equipage would hardly have ad-

mitted of his hazarding an invitation to a second person —any more than the quantity of esculent *matériel,* which, for the most part, was little more than a roll, or a few biscuits, which he had bought on his road from the place where he had slept. Or, if he *had* asked a party—as I once learnedly and facetiously observed to him—the several members of it must have *stood* in the relation to each other (not *sat* in any relation whatever) of succession, as the metaphysicians have it, and not of co-existence; in the relation of the parts of time, and not of the parts of space. During his breakfast, I generally contrived a reason for lounging in; and, with an air of as much indifference as I could assume, took up such fragments as he had left— sometimes, indeed, there were none at all. In doing this, I committed no robbery except upon the man himself, who was thus obliged, I believe, now and then to send out at noon for an extra biscuit; for, as to the poor child, *she* was never admitted into his study, if I may give that name to his chief depository of parchments, law writings, etc.; that room was to her the Bluebeard room of the house, being regularly locked on his departure to dinner, about six o'clock, which usually was his final departure for the night. Whether this child were an illegitimate daughter of Mr. [Brunell], or only a servant, I could not ascertain; she did not herself know; but certainly she was treated altogether as a menial servant. No sooner did Mr. [Brunell] make his appearance, than she went below stairs, brushed his shoes, coat, etc., and, except when she was summoned to run an errand, she never emerged from the dismal Tartarus of the kitchen, etc., to the upper air, until my welcome knock at night called up her little trembling footsteps to the front door. Of her life during the day-time, however, I knew little but

what I gathered from her own account at night; for, as soon as the hours of business commenced, I saw that my absence would be acceptable; and, in general, therefore, I went off, and sat in the parks, or elsewhere, until night-fall.

But who, and what, meantime, was the master of the house himself? Reader, he was one of those anomalous practitioners in lower departments of the law, who—what shall I say?—who, on prudential reasons, or from necessity, deny themselves all indulgence in the luxury of too delicate a conscience; (a periphrasis which might be abridged considerably, but *that* I leave to the reader's taste,) in many walks of life, a conscience is a more expensive encumbrance than a wife or a carriage; and just as people talk of "laying down" their carriages, so I suppose my friend, Mr. [Brunell], had "laid down" his conscience for a time, meaning, doubtless, to resume it as soon as he could afford it. The inner economy of such a man's daily life would present a most strange picture, if I could allow myself to amuse the reader at his expense. Even with my limited opportunities for observing what went on, I saw many scenes of London intrigues, and complex chicanery, "cycle and epicycle, orb in orb," at which I sometimes smile to this day—and at which I smiled then, in spite of my misery. My situation, however, at that time, gave me little experience, in my own person, of any qualities in Mr. [Brunell's] character but such as did him honour; and of his whole strange composition I must forget everything but that towards me he was obliging, and to the extent of his power, generous.

That power was not, indeed, very extensive; however, in common with rats, I sat rent free; and, as Dr. Johnson has recorded that he never but once in his life had as much wall-fruit as he could eat, so let

me be grateful, that on that single occasion I had as large a choice of apartments in a London mansion as I could possibly desire. Except the Bluebeard room, which the poor child believed to be haunted, all others, from the attics to the cellars, were at our service; "the world was all before us;" and we pitched our tent for the night in any spot we chose. This house I have already described as a large one; it stands in a conspicuous situation, and in a well-known part of London. Many of my readers will have passed it, I doubt not, within a few hours of reading this. For myself, I never fail to visit it when business draws me to London; about ten o'clock, this very night, August 15, 1821, being my birthday,—I turned aside from my evening walk, down Oxford street, purposely to take a glance at it: it is now occupied by a respectable family; and, by the lights in the front drawing room, I observed a domestic party, assembled perhaps at tea, and apparently cheerful and gay. Marvelous contrast in my eyes to the darkness—cold—silence—and desolation of that same house eighteen years ago, when its nightly occupants were one famishing scholar and a neglected child.—Her, by the bye, in after years, I vainly endeavored to trace. Apart from her situation, she was not what one would call an interesting child; she was neither pretty, nor quick in understanding, nor remarkably pleasing in manners. But, thank God! even in those years I needed not the embellishments of novel accessaries to conciliate my affections; plain human nature, in its humblest and most homely apparel, was enough for me; and I loved the child because she was my partner in wretchedness. If she is now living, she is probably a mother, with children of her own; but, as I have said, I could never trace her.

This I regret, but another person there was at that

time, whom I have since sought to trace with far deeper earnestness, and with far deeper sorrow at my failure. This person was a young woman, and one of that unhappy class who subsist upon the wages of prostitution. I feel no shame, nor have any reason to feel it, in avowing that I was then on familiar terms with many women in that unfortunate condition. The reader needs neither smile at this avowal, nor frown. For, not to remind my classical readers of the old Latin proverb—"*Sine Cerere,*" etc., it may well be supposed that in the existing state of my purse my connection with such a woman could not have been an impure one. But the truth is, that at no time of my life have I been a person to hold myself polluted by the touch or approach of any creature that wore a human shape; on the contrary, from my very earliest youth it has been my pride to converse familiarly, *more Socratico,* with all human beings, man, woman, and child, that chance might fling in my way; a practice which is friendly to the knowledge of human nature, to good feelings, and to that frankness of address which becomes a man who would be thought a philosopher. For a philosopher should not see with the eyes of the poor limitary creature, calling himself a man of the world, and filled with narrow and self-regarding prejudices of birth and education, but should look upon himself as a catholic creature, and as standing in an equal relation to high and low—to educated and uneducated, to the guilty and innocent. Being myself at that time of necessity a peripatetic, or a walker of the streets, I naturally fell in more frequently with those female peripatetics who are technically called street-walkers. Many of these women had occasionally taken my part against watchmen who wished to drive me off the steps of houses where I was sitting. But one amongst them,

the one on whose account I have at all introduced this subject—yet no! let me not class thee, oh noble-minded Ann ——, with that order of women; let me find, if it be possible, some gentler name to designate the condition of her to whose bounty and compassion, ministering to my necessities when all the world had forsaken me, I owe it that I am at this time alive. For many weeks I had walked at nights with this poor friendless girl up and down Oxford street, or had rested with her on steps and under the shelter of porticoes. She could not be so old as myself; she told me, indeed, that she had not completed her sixteenth year. By such questions as my interest about her prompted, I had gradually drawn forth her simple history. Hers was a case of ordinary occurrence (as I have since had reason to think), and one in which, if London beneficence had better adapted its arrangements to meet it, the power of the law might oftener be interposed to protect, and to avenge. But the stream of London charity flows in a channel which, though deep and mighty, is yet noiseless and underground; not obvious or readily accessible to poor houseless wanderers; and it cannot be denied that the outside air and framework of London society is harsh, cruel, and repulsive. In any case, however, I saw that part of her injuries might easily have been redressed; and I urged her often and earnestly to lay her complaint before a magistrate; friendless as she was, I assured her that she would meet with immediate attention; and that English justice, which was no respecter of persons, would speedily and amply avenge her on the brutal ruffian who had plundered her little property. She promised me often that she would; but she delayed taking the steps I pointed out from time to time: for she was timid and dejected to a degree which showed how deeply sorrow had taken

hold of her young heart; and perhaps she thought justly that the most upright judge, and the most righteous tribunals, could do nothing to repair her heaviest wrongs. Something, however, would perhaps have been done; for it had been settled between us at length, but unhappily on the very last time but one that I was ever to see her, that in a day or two we should go together before a magistrate, and that I should speak on her behalf. This little service it was destined, however, that I should never realize. Meantime, that which she rendered to me, and which was greater than I could ever have repaid her, was this: One night, when we were pacing slowly along Oxford street, and after a day when I had felt more than usually ill and faint, I requested her to turn off with me into Soho square; thither we went; and we sat down on the steps of a house, which, to this hour, I never pass without a pang of grief, and an inner act of homage to the spirit of that unhappy girl, in memory of the noble action which she there performed. Suddenly, as we sat, I grew much worse; I had been leaning my head against her bosom; and all at once I sank from her arms and fell backwards on the steps. From the sensations I then had, I felt an inner conviction of the liveliest kind that without some powerful and reviving stimulus, I should either have died on the spot —or should at least have sunk to a point of exhaustion from which all re-ascent under my friendless circumstances would soon have become hopeless. Then it was, at this crisis of my fate, that my poor orphan companion— who had herself met with little but injuries in this world—stretched out a saving hand to me. Uttering a cry of terror, but without a moment's delay, she ran off into Oxford street, and in less time than could be imagined, returned to me with a glass of

port wine and spices, that acted upon my empty stomach (which at that time would have rejected all solid food) with an instantaneous power of restoration; and for this glass the generous girl without a murmur paid out of her own humble purse at a time—be it remembered!—when she had scarcely wherewithal to purchase the bare necessaries of life, and when she could have no reason to expect that I should ever be able to reimburse her.—Oh! youthful benefactress! how often in succeeding years, standing in solitary places, and thinking of thee with grief of heart and perfect love, how often have I wished that, as in ancient times the curse of a father was believed to have a supernatural power, and to pursue its object with a fatal necessity of self-fulfillment,—even so the benediction of a heart oppressed with gratitude might have a like prerogative; might have power given it from above to chase—to haunt—to waylay—to overtake—to pursue thee into the central darkness of a London brothel, or, if it were possible, into the darkness of the grave—there to awaken thee with an authentic message of peace and forgiveness, and of final reconciliation!

I do not often weep: for not only do my thoughts on subjects connected with the chief interests of man daily, nay hourly, descend a thousand fathoms "too deep for tears;" not only does the sternness of my habits of thought present an antagonism to the feelings which prompt tears—wanting of necessity to those who, being protected usually by their levity from any tendency to meditative sorrow, would by that same levity be made incapable of resisting it on any casual access of such feelings:—but also, I believe that all minds which have contemplated such objects as deeply as I have done, must, for their own protection from utter despondency, have early encouraged and cherished

some tranquillizing belief as to the future balances and the hieroglyphic meanings of human sufferings. On these accounts I am cheerful to this hour; and, as I have said, I do not often weep. Yet some feelings, though not deeper or more passionate, are more tender than others; and often, when I walk at this time in Oxford street by dreamy lamp-light, and hear those airs played on a barrel-organ which years ago solaced me and my dear companion, as I must always call her, I shed tears, and muse with myself at the mysterious dispensation which so suddenly and so critically separated us forever. How it happened the reader will understand from what remains of this introductory narration.

Soon after the period of the last incident I have recorded, I met, in Albemarle street, a gentleman of his late majesty's household. This gentleman had received hospitalities, on different occasions, from my family; and he challenged me upon the strength of my family likeness. I did not attempt any disguise: I answered his questions ingenuously,—and, on his pledging his word of honor that he would not betray me to my guardians, I gave him an address to my friend the attorney's. The next day I received from him a £10 bank-note. The letter enclosing it was delivered with other letters of business to the attorney; but, though his look and manner informed me that he suspected its contents, he gave it up to me honorably and without demur.

* * * * * *

On reading the letters, one of my Jewish friends agreed to furnish two or three hundred pounds on my personal security—provided that I could persuade the young Earl, who was, by the way, not older than myself, to guarantee the payment on our coming of age:

the Jew's final object being, as I now suppose, not the trifling profit he could expect to make by me, but the prospect of establishing a connection with my noble friend, whose immense expectations were well known to him. In pursuance of this proposal on the part of the Jew, about eight or nine days after I had received the £10, I prepared to go down to Eton. Nearly £3 of the money I had given to my money-lending friend, on his alleging that the stamps must be bought, in order that the writings might be preparing whilst I was away from London. I thought in my heart that he was lying; but I did not wish to give him any excuse for charging his own delays upon me. A smaller sum I had given to my friend the attorney, who was connected with the money-lenders as their lawyer, to which, indeed, he was entitled for his unfurnished lodgings. About fifteen shillings I had employed in re-establishing, though in a very humble way, my dress. Of the remainder I gave one quarter to Ann, meaning on my return to have divided with her whatever might remain. These arrangements made,—soon after six o'clock, on a dark winter evening, I set off, accompanied by Ann, towards Piccadilly; for it was my intention to go down as far as Salt-hill on the Bath or Bristol mail. Our course lay through a part of the town which has now all disappeared, so that I can no longer retrace its ancient boundaries: Swallow street, I think it was called. Having time enough before us, however, we bore away to the left until we came into Golden Square: there, near the corner of Sherrard street, we sat down; not wishing to part in the tumult and blaze of Piccadilly. I had told her of my plans some time before: and I now assured her again that she should share in my good fortune, if I met with any; and that I would never forsake her, as soon as I had power to protect

her. This I fully intended, as much from inclination as from a sense of duty: for, setting aside gratitude, which in any case must have made me her debtor for life, I loved her as affectionately as if she had been my sister: and at this moment, with seven-fold tenderness, from pity at witnessing her extreme dejection. I had, apparently, most reason for dejection, because I was leaving the saviour of my life; yet I, considering the shock my health had received, was cheerful and full of hope. She, on the contrary, who was parting with one who had little means of serving her, except by kindness and brotherly treatment, was overcome by sorrow; so that, when I kissed her at our final farewell, she put her arms about my neck, and wept without speaking a word. I hoped to return in a week at farthest, and I agreed with her that on the fifth night from that, and every night afterwards, she should wait for me at six o'clock near the bottom of Great Titchfield street, which had been our customary haven, as it were, of rendezvous, to prevent our missing each other in the great Mediterranean of Oxford street. This, and other measures of precaution I took: one only I forgot. She had either never told me, or (as a matter of no great interest) I had forgotten, her surname. It is a general practice, indeed, with girls of humble rank in her unhappy condition, not (as novel-reading women of higher pretensions) to style themselves—*Miss Douglas, Miss Montague,* etc., but simply by their Christian names, *Mary, Jane, Frances,* etc. Her surname, as the surest means of tracing her hereafter, I ought now to have inquired: but the truth is, having no reason to think that our meeting could, in consequence of a short interruption, be more difficult or uncertain than it had been for so many weeks, I had scarcely for a moment adverted to it as necessary, or placed it

amongst my memoranda against this parting interview; and, my final anxieties being spent in comforting her with hopes, and in pressing upon her the necessity of getting some medicines for a violent cough and hoarseness with which she was troubled, I wholly forgot it until it was too late to recall her.

*   *   *   *   *   *

Meantime, what had become of poor Ann? For her I have reserved my concluding words: According to our agreement, I sought her daily, and waited for her every night, so long as I stayed in London, at the corner of Titchfield street. I inquired for her of every one who was likely to know her; and during the last hours of my stay in London I put into activity every means of tracing her that my knowledge of London suggested, and the limited extent of my power made possible. The street where she had lodged I knew, but not the house; and I remembered at last some account which she had given me of ill treatment from her landlord, which made it probable that she had quitted those lodgings before we parted. She had few acquaintances; most people, besides, thought that the earnestness of my inquiries arose from motives which moved their laughter, or their slight regard; and others, thinking I was in chase of a girl who had robbed me of some trifles, were naturally and excusably indisposed to give me any clue to her, if, indeed, they had any to give. Finally, as my despairing resource, on the day I left London I put into the hands of the only person who (I was sure) must know Ann by sight, from having been in company with us once or twice, an address to——in——shire, at that time the residence of my family. But, to this hour, I have never heard a syllable about her. This, amongst such troubles as most men meet with in this life, has been my heaviest affliction.—If she lived, doubtless we must have been

sometimes in search of each other, at the very same moment, through the mighty labyrinths of London; perhaps even within a few feet of each other—a barrier no wider in a London street often amounting in the end to a separation for eternity! During some years, I hoped that she *did* live; and I suppose that, in the literal and unrhetorical use of the word *myriad,* I may say that on my different visits to London, I have looked into many, many myriads of female faces, in the hope of meeting her. I should know her again amongst a thousand, if I saw her for a moment; for, though not handsome, she had a sweet expression of countenance, and a peculiar and graceful carriage of the head.—I sought her, I have said, in hope. So it was for years; but now I should fear to see her; and her cough, which grieved me when I parted with her, is now my consolation. I now wish to see her no longer; but think of her, more gladly, as one long since laid in the grave; in the grave, I would hope, of a Magdalen; taken away, before injuries and cruelty had blotted out and transfigured her ingenuous nature, or the brutalities of ruffians had completed the ruin they had begun.

From THE PLEASURES OF OPIUM

IT IS so long since I first took opium that if it had been a trifling incident in my life I might have forgotten its date: but cardinal events are not to be forgotten: and from circumstances connected with it I remember that it must be referred to the autumn of 1804. During that season I was in London, having come thither for the first time since my entrance at college. And my introduction to opium arose in the following way. From an early age I had been accustomed to wash my head in cold water at least once a day: being suddenly seized

THE PLEASURES OF OPIUM

with toothache, I attributed it to some relaxation caused by an accidental intermission of that practice; jumped out of bed; plunged my head into a basin of cold water; and with hair thus wetted went to sleep. The next morning, as I need hardly say, I awoke with excruciating rheumatic pains of the head and face, from which I had hardly any respite for about twenty days. On the twenty-first day, I think it was, and on a Sunday, that I went out into the streets; rather to run away, if possible, from my torments, than with any distinct purpose. By accident I met a college acquaintance who recommended opium. Opium, dread agent of unimaginable pleasure and pain! I had heard of it as I had of manna or of ambrosia, but no further: how unmeaning a sound was it at that time! what solemn chords does it now strike upon my heart! what heart-quaking vibrations of sad and happy remembrances! Reverting for a moment to these, I feel a mystic importance attached to the minutest circumstances connected with the place and the time, and the man, if man he was, that first laid open to me the Paradise of Opium-eaters. It was a Sunday afternoon, wet and cheerless: and a duller spectacle this earth of ours has not to show than a rainy Sunday in London. My road homewards lay through Oxford street; and near "the *stately* Pantheon," as Mr. Wordsworth has obligingly called it, I saw a druggist's shop. The druggist, unconscious minister of celestial pleasures!—as if in sympathy with the rainy Sunday, looked dull and stupid, just as any mortal druggist might be expected to look on a Sunday: and, when I asked for the tincture of opium, he gave it to me as any other man might do: and furthermore, out of my shilling, returned me what seemed to be real copper halfpence, taken out of a real wooden drawer. Nevertheless, in spite of such indications of humanity,

he has ever since existed in my mind as the beatific vision of an immortal druggist, sent down to earth on a special mission to myself. And it confirms me in this way of considering him, that, when I next came up to London, I sought him near the stately Pantheon, and found him not: and thus to me, who knew not his name (if indeed he had one) he seemed rather to have vanished from Oxford street than to have removed in any bodily fashion. The reader may choose to think of him as, possibly, no more than a sublunary druggist: it may be so; but my faith is better: I believe him to have evanesced, or evaporated. So unwillingly would I connect any mortal remembrances with that hour, and place, and creature, that first brought me acquainted with the celestial drug.

* * * * * *

With respect to the torpor supposed to follow, or rather, if we were to credit the numerous pictures of Turkish opium-eaters, to accompany the practice of opium-eating, I deny that also. Certainly, opium is classed under the head of narcotics; and some such effect it may produce in the end; but the primary effects of opium are always, and in the highest degree, to excite and stimulate the system: this first stage of its action always lasted with me, during my novitiate, for upwards of eight hours; so that it must be the fault of the opium-eater himself if he does not so time his exhibition of the dose, to speak medically, as that the whole weight of its narcotic influence may descend upon his sleep. Turkish opium-eaters, it seems, are absurd enough to sit, like so many equestrian statues, on logs of wood as stupid as themselves. But that the reader may judge of the degree in which opium is likely to stupefy the faculties of an Englishman, I shall, by way of treating the question illustratively, rather than argumentatively,

describe the way in which I myself often passed an opium evening in London, during the period between 1804 and 1812. It will be seen, that at least opium did not move me to seek solitude, and much less to seek inactivity, or the torpid state of self-involution ascribed to the Turks. I give this account at the risk of being pronounced a crazy enthusiast or visionary; but I regard *that* little: I must desire my reader to bear in mind that I was a hard student, and at severe studies for all the rest of my time; and certainly I had a right occasionally to relaxations as well as other people; these, however, I allowed myself but seldom.

The late Duke of [Norfolk] used to say, "Next Friday, by the blessing of Heaven, I propose to be drunk;" and in like manner I used to fix beforehand how often, within a given time, and when, I would commit a debauch of opium. This was seldom more than once in three weeks; for at that time I could not have ventured to call every day (as I did afterwards) for *"a glass of laudanum negus, warm, and without sugar."* No; as I have said, I seldom drank laudanum, at that time, more than once in three weeks; this was usually on a Tuesday or a Saturday night; my reason for which was this. In those days Grassini sang at the Opera: and her voice was delightful to me beyond all that I had ever heard. I know not what may be the state of the Opera house now, having never been within its walls for seven or eight years, but at that time it was by much the most pleasant place of public resort in London for passing an evening. Five shillings admitted one to the gallery, which was subject to far less annoyance than the pit of the theatres; the orchestra was distinguished by its sweet and melodious grandeur from all English orchestras, the composition of which, I confess, is not acceptable to my ear, from

the predominance of the clangorous instruments, and the absolute tyranny of the violin. The choruses were divine to hear; and when Grassini appeared in some interlude, as she often did, and poured forth her passionate soul as Andromache at the tomb of Hector, etc., I question whether any Turk, of all that ever entered the paradise of opium-eaters, can have had half the pleasure I had. But, indeed, I honor the Barbarians too much by supposing them capable of any pleasures approaching to the intellectual ones of an Englishman. For music is an intellectual or a sensual pleasure, according to the temperament of him who hears it. And, by the by, with the exception of the fine extravaganza on that subject in Twelfth Night, I do not recollect more than one thing said adequately on the subject of music in all literature; it is a passage in the *Religio Medici* of Sir T. Brown; and, though chiefly remarkable for its sublimity, has also a philosophic value, inasmuch as it points to the true theory of musical effects. The mistake of most people is to suppose that it is by the ear they communicate with music, and, therefore, that they are purely passive to its effects. But this is not so; it is by the reaction of the mind upon the notices of the ear (the *matter* coming by the senses, the *form* from the mind), that the pleasure is constructed; and therefore it is that people of equally good ear differ so much in this point from one another. Now opium, by greatly increasing the activity of the mind generally, increases, of necessity, that particular mode of its activity by which we are able to construct out of the raw material of organic sound an elaborate intellectual pleasure. But, says a friend, a succession of musical sounds is to me like a collection of Arabic characters: I can attach no ideas to them. Ideas! my good sir? there is no occasion for them; all that class of ideas which

THE PLEASURES OF OPIUM

can be available in such a case has a language of representative feelings. But this is a subject foreign to my present purposes; it is sufficient to say, that a chorus, etc., of elaborate harmony, displayed before me, as in a piece of arras work, the whole of my past life—not as if recalled by an act of memory, but as if present and incarnated in the music; no longer painful to dwell upon; but the detail of its incidents removed, or blended in some hazy abstraction; and its passions exalted, spiritualized, and sublimed. All this was to be had for five shillings. And over and above the music of the stage and the orchestra, I had all around me, in the intervals of the performance, the music of the Italian language talked by Italian women; for the gallery was usually crowded with Italians; and I listened with a pleasure such as that with which Weld the traveler lay and listened, in Canada, to the sweet laughter of Indian women; for the less you understand of a language the more sensible you are to the melody or harshness of its sounds; for such a purpose, therefore, it was an advantage to me that I was a poor Italian scholar, reading it but little, and not speaking it at all, nor understanding a tenth part of what I heard spoken.

These were my Opera pleasures; but another pleasure I had which, as it could be had only on a Saturday night, occasionally struggled with my love of the Opera; for, at that time, Tuesday and Saturday were the regular Opera nights. On this subject I am afraid I shall be rather obscure, but, I can assure the reader, not at all more so than Marinus in his life of Proclus, or many other biographers and autobiographers of fair reputation. This pleasure, I have said, was to be had only on a Saturday night. What then was Saturday night to me more than any other night? I had no labors that I rested from; no wages to receive: what needed I to

care for Saturday night, more than as it was a summons to hear Grassini? True, most logical reader: what you say is unanswerable. And yet so it was and is, that, whereas different men throw their feelings into different channels, and most are apt to show their interest in the concerns of the poor, chiefly by sympathy, expressed in some shape or other, with their distresses and sorrows, I, at that time, was disposed to express my interest by sympathizing with their pleasures. The pains of poverty I had lately seen too much of; more than I wished to remember: but the pleasures of the poor, their consolations of spirit, and their reposes from bodily toil, can never become oppressive to contemplate. Now Saturday night is the season for the chief, regular, and periodic return of rest to the poor: in this point the most hostile sects unite, and acknowledge a common link of brotherhood: almost all Christendom rests from its labors. It is a rest introductory to another rest, and divided by a whole day and two nights from the renewal of toil. On this account I feel always, on a Saturday night, as though I also were released from some yoke of labor, had some wages to receive, and some luxury of repose to enjoy. For the sake, therefore, of witnessing, upon as large a scale as possible, a spectacle with which my sympathy was so entire, I used often, on Saturday nights, after I had taken opium, to wander forth, without much regarding the direction or the distance, to all the markets and other parts of London to which the poor resort on a Saturday night for laying out their wages. Many a family party, consisting of a man, his wife, and sometimes one or two of his children, have I listened to, as they stood consulting on their ways and means, or the strength of their exchequer, or the price of household articles. Gradually I became familiar with their wishes, their difficulties, and their

opinions. Sometimes there might be heard murmurs of discontent: but far oftener expressions on the countenance, or uttered in words, of patience, hope, and tranquillity. And taken generally, I must say, that, in this point at least, the poor are far more philosophic than the rich—that they show a more ready and cheerful submission to what they consider as irremediable evils, or irreparable losses. Whenever I saw occasion, or could do it without appearing to be intrusive, I joined their parties; and gave my opinion upon the matter in discussion, which if not always judicious, was always received indulgently. If wages were a little higher, or expected to be so, or the quartern loaf a little lower, or it was reported that onions and butter were expected to fall, I was glad: yet, if the contrary were true, I drew from opium some means of consoling myself. For opium, like the bee, that extracts its materials indiscriminately from roses and from the soot of chimneys, can overrule all feelings into a compliance with the master key. Some of these rambles led me to great distances: for an opium-eater is too happy to observe the motion of time. And sometimes in my attempts to steer homewards upon nautical principles, by fixing my eye on the pole-star, and seeking ambitiously for a northwest passage, instead of circumnavigating all the capes and headlands I had doubled in my outward voyage, I came suddenly upon such knotty problems of alleys, such enigmatical entries, and such sphinx's riddles of streets without thoroughfares, as must, I conceive, baffle the audacity of porters, and confound the intellects of hackney-coachmen. I could almost have believed, at times, that I must be the first discoverer of some of these *terrae incognitae,* and doubted whether they had yet been laid down in the modern charts of London. For all this, however, I paid a heavy

price in distant years, when the human face tyrannized over my dreams, and the perplexities of my steps in London came back and haunted my sleep with the feeling of perplexities moral or intellectual, that brought confusion to the reason, or anguish and remorse to the conscience.

Thus I have shown that opium does not, of necessity, produce inactivity or torpor; but that, on the contrary, it often led me into markets and theatres. Yet, in candor, I will admit that markets and theatres are not the appropriate haunts of the opium-eater, when in the divinest state incident to his enjoyment. In that state crowds become an oppression to him; music, even, too sensual and gross. He naturally seeks solitude and silence, as indispensable conditions of those trances and profoundest reveries which are the crown or consummation of what opium can do for human nature. I, whose disease it was to meditate too much, and to observe too little, and who, upon my first entrance at college, was nearly falling into a deep melancholy from brooding too much on the sufferings which I had witnessed in London, was sufficiently aware of the tendencies of my own thoughts to do all I could to counteract them.—I was, indeed, like a person who, according to the old legend, had entered the cave of Trophonius: and the remedies I sought were to force myself into society, and to keep my understanding in continual activity upon matters of science. But for these remedies, I should certainly have become hypochondriacally melancholy. In after years, however, when my cheerfulness was more fully re-established, I yielded to my natural inclination for a solitary life. And, at that time, I often fell into these reveries upon taking opium; and more than once it has happened to me, on a summer night, when I have been at an open window, in a room

from which I could overlook the sea at a mile below me, and could command a view of the great town of L[iverpool], at about the same distance, that I have sat, from sun-set to sun-rise, motionless, and without wishing to move.

I shall be charged with mysticism, Behmenism, quietism, etc., but *that* shall not alarm me. Sir H. Vane, the younger, was one of our wisest men: and let my readers see if he, in his philosophical works, be half as unmystical as I am.—I say, then, that it has often struck me that the scene itself was somewhat typical of what took place in such a reverie. The town of L[iverpool] represented the earth, with its sorrows and its graves left behind, yet not out of sight, nor wholly forgotten. The ocean, in everlasting but gentle agitation, and brooded over by a dove-like calm, might not unfitly typify the mind and the mood which then swayed it. For it seemed to me as if then first I stood at a distance, and aloof from the uproar of life; as if the tumult, the fever, and the strife, were suspended; a respite granted from the secret burthens of the heart; a sabbath of repose; a resting from human labors. Here were the hopes which blossom in the paths of life, reconciled with the peace which is in the grave; motions of the intellect as unwearied as the heavens, yet for all anxieties a halcyon calm: a tranquillity that seemed no product of inertia, but as if resulting from mighty and equal antagonisms; infinite activities, infinite repose.

Oh! just, subtle, and mighty opium! that to the hearts of poor and rich alike, for the wounds that will never heal, and for "the pangs that tempt the spirit to rebel," bringest an assuaging balm; eloquent opium! that with thy potent rhetoric stealest away the purposes of wrath; and to the guilty man for one night givest back the

hopes of his youth, and hands washed pure from blood; and to the proud man a brief oblivion for

> Wrongs unredress'd and insults unavenged;

that summonest to the chancery of dreams, for the triumphs of suffering innocence, false witnesses; and confoundest perjury; and dost reverse the sentences of unrighteous judges: thou buildest upon the bosom of darkness, out of the fantastic imagery of the brain, cities and temples beyond the art of Phidias and Praxiteles—beyond the splendor of Babylon and Hekatompylos: and "from the anarchy of dreaming sleep," callest into sunny light the faces of long-buried beauties, and the blessed household countenances, cleansed from the "dishonors of the grave." Thou only givest these gifts to man; and thou hast the keys of Paradise, oh, just, subtle, and mighty opium!

THE PAINS OF OPIUM

IF ANY man, poor or rich, were to say that he would tell us what had been the happiest day in his life, and the why, and the wherefore, I suppose that we should all cry out—Hear him! Hear Him!—As to the happiest *day*, that must be very difficult for any wise man to name; because any event, that could occupy so distinguished a place in a man's retrospect of his life, or be entitled to have shed a special felicity on any one day, ought to be of such an enduring character, as that, accidents apart, it should have continued to shed the same felicity, or one not distinguishably less, on many years together. To the happiest *lustrum,* however, or even to the happiest *year,* it may be allowed to any man to point without discountenance from wisdom. This year, in my case, reader, was the one which we have

THE PAINS OF OPIUM

now reached; though it stood, I confess, as a parenthesis between years of a gloomier character. It was a year of brilliant water, to speak after the manner of jewelers, set as it were, and insulated, in the gloom and cloudy melancholy of opium. Strange as it may sound, I had a little before this time descended suddenly, and without any considerable effort, from 320 grains of opium, (*i. e.*, eight thousand drops of laudanum) per day, to forty grains, or one-eighth part. Instantaneously, and as if by magic, the cloud of profoundest melancholy which rested upon my brain, like some black vapors that I have seen roll away from the summits of mountains, drew off in one day ($νυχθημερον$); passed off with its murky banners as simultaneously as a ship that has been stranded, and is floated off by a spring tide—

That moveth altogether, if it move at all.

Now, then, I was again happy: I now took only 1000 drops of laudanum per day; and what was that? A latter spring had come to close up the season of youth: my brain performed its functions as healthily as ever before: I read Kant again; and again I understood him, or fancied that I did. Again my feelings of pleasure expanded themselves to all around me: and if any man from Oxford or Cambridge, or from neither, had been announced to me in my unpretending cottage, I should have welcomed him with as sumptuous a reception as so poor a man could offer. Whatever else was wanting to a wise man's happiness,—of laudanum I would have given him as much as he wished, and in a golden cup. And, by the way, now that I speak of giving laudanum away, I remember, about this time, a little incident, which I mention, because, trifling as it was, the reader will soon meet it again in my dreams, which it influenced more fearfully than could be imag-

ined. One day a Malay knocked at my door. What business a Malay could have to transact amongst English mountains, I cannot conjecture: but possibly he was on his road to a sea-port about forty miles distant.

The servant who opened the door to him was a young girl born and bred amongst the mountains, who had never seen an Asiatic dress of any sort: his turban, therefore, confounded her not a little; and, as it turned out that his attainments in English were exactly of the same extent as hers in the Malay, there seemed to be an impassable gulf fixed between all communication of ideas, if either party had happened to possess any. In this dilemma, the girl, recollecting the reputed learning of her master, and doubtless giving me credit for a knowledge of all the languages of the earth, besides, perhaps, a few of the lunar ones, came and gave me to understand that there was a sort of demon below, whom she clearly imagined that my art could exorcise from the house. I did not immediately go down; but, when I did, the group which presented itself, arranged as it was by accident, though not very elaborate, took hold of my fancy and my eye in a way that none of the statuesque attitudes exhibited in the ballets at the Opera House, though so ostentatiously complex, had ever done. In a cottage kitchen, but panelled on the wall with dark wood that from age and rubbing resembled oak, and looking more like a rustic hall of entrance than a kitchen, stood the Malay—his turban and loose trowsers of dingy white relieved upon the dark panelling: he had placed himself nearer to the girl than she seemed to relish; though her native spirit of mountain intrepidity contended with the feeling of simple awe which her countenance expressed as she gazed upon the tiger-cat before her. And a more striking picture there could not be imagined than the beautiful English face of the girl,

THE PAINS OF OPIUM

and its exquisite fairness, together with her erect and independent attitude, contrasted with the sallow and bilious skin of the Malay, enameled or veneered with mahogany, by marine air, his small, fierce, restless eyes, thin lips, slavish gestures and adorations. Half-hidden by the ferocious-looking Malay was a little child from a neighboring cottage who had crept in after him, and was now in the act of reverting its head, and gazing upwards at the turban and the fiery eyes beneath it, whilst with one hand he caught at the dress of the young woman for protection. My knowledge of the Oriental tongues is not remarkably extensive, being, indeed, confined to two words—the Arabic word for barley, and the Turkish for opium (madjoon), which I have learned from Anastasius. And, as I had neither a Malay dictionary, nor even Adelung's *Mithridates,* which might have helped me to a few words, I addressed him in some lines from the Iliad; considering that, of such languages as I possessed, Greek, in point of longitude, came geographically nearest to an Oriental one. He worshipped me in a most devout manner, and replied in what I suppose was Malay. In this way I saved my reputation with my neighbors, for the Malay had no means of betraying the secret. He lay down upon the floor for about an hour, and then pursued his journey. On his departure I presented him with a piece of opium. To him, as an Orientalist, I concluded that opium must be familiar, and the expression of his face convinced me that it was. Nevertheless, I was struck with some little consternation when I saw him suddenly raise his hand to his mouth, and, in the school-boy phrase, bolt the whole, divided into three pieces, at one mouthful. The quantity was enough to kill three dragoons and their horses, and I felt some alarm for the poor creature; but what could be done? I had given him the opium in

compassion for his solitary life on recollecting that if he had traveled on foot from London it must be nearly three weeks since he could have exchanged a thought with any human being. I could not think of violating the laws of hospitality by having him seized and drenched with an emetic, and thus frightening him into a notion that we were going to sacrifice him to some English idol. No; there was clearly no help for it; he took his leave, and for some days I felt anxious; but as I never heard of any Malay being found dead, I became convinced that he was used to opium, and that I must have done him the service I designed, by giving him one night of respite from the pains of wandering.

This incident I have digressed to mention, because this Malay, partly from the picturesque exhibition he assisted to frame, partly from the anxiety I connected with his image for some days, fastened afterwards upon my dreams, and brought other Malays with him worse than himself, that ran "amuck" at me, and led me into a world of troubles.—But to quit this episode, and to return to my intercalary year of happiness. I have said already, that on a subject so important to us all as happiness, we should listen with pleasure to any man's experience or experiments, even though he were but a plough-boy, who cannot be supposed to have ploughed very deep into such an intractable soil as that of human pains and pleasures, or to have conducted his researches upon any very enlightened principles. But I, who have taken happiness, both in a solid and a liquid shape, both boiled and unboiled, both East India and Turkey—who have conducted my experiments upon this interesting subject with a sort of galvanic battery—and have, for the general benefit of the world, inoculated myself, as it were, with the poison of 8000 drops of laudanum per day, just for the same reason as a French surgeon

THE PAINS OF OPIUM

inoculated himself lately with cancer—an English one, twenty years ago, with plague—and a third, I know not of what nation, with hydrophobia,—*I*, it will be admitted, must surely know what happiness is, if any body does. And, therefore, I will here lay down an analysis of happiness; and as the most interesting mode of communicating it, I will give it, not didactically, but wrapt up and involved in a picture of one evening, as I spent every evening during the intercalary year when laudanum, though taken daily, was to me no more than the elixir of pleasure. This done, I shall quit the subject of happiness altogether, and pass to a very different one—the *pains of opium*.

Let there be a cottage, standing in a valley, eighteen miles from any town—no spacious valley, but about two miles long, by three quarters of a mile in average width; the benefit of which provision is that all the families resident within its circuit will compose, as it were, one larger household personally familiar to your eye, and more or less interesting to your affections. Let the mountains be real mountains, between three and four thousand feet high; and the cottage, a real cottage; not, as a witty author has it, "a cottage with a double coach-house"; let it be, in fact—for I must abide by the actual scene—a white cottage, embowered with flowering shrubs, so chosen as to unfold a succession of flowers upon the walls, and clustering round the windows through all the months of spring, summer and autumn—beginning, in fact, with May roses, and ending with jasmine. Let it, however, *not* be spring, nor summer, nor autumn—but winter, in his sternest shape. This is a most important point in the science of happiness. And I am surprised to see people overlook it, and think it matter of congratulation that winter is going; or, if coming, is not likely to be a severe one.

On the contrary, I put up a petition annually for as much snow, hail, frost, or storm, of one kind or other, as the skies can possibly afford us. Surely everybody is aware of the divine pleasures which attend a winter fireside: candles at four o'clock, warm hearth-rugs, tea, a fair tea-maker, shutters closed, curtains flowing in ample draperies on the floor, whilst the wind and rain are raging audibly without,

> And at the doors and windows seem to call,
> As heav'n and earth they would together mell;
> Yet the least entrance find they none at all;
> Whence sweeter grows our rest secure in massy hall.
> *Castle of Indolence.*

*　　*　　*　　*　　*　　*

My studies have now been long interrupted. I cannot read to myself with any pleasure, hardly with a moment's endurance. Yet I read aloud sometimes for the pleasure of others, because reading is an accomplishment of mine; and, in the slang use of the word *accomplishment* as a superficial and ornamental attainment, almost the only one I possess; and formerly, if I had any vanity at all connected with any endowment or attainment of mine, it was with this; for I had observed that no accomplishment was so rare. Players are the worst readers of all; John Kemble reads vilely; and Mrs. Siddons, who is so celebrated, can read nothing well but dramatic compositions; Milton she cannot read sufferably. People in general either read poetry without any passion at all, or else overstep the modesty of nature, and read not like scholars. Of late, if I have felt moved by anything in books, it has been by the grand lamentations of Samson Agonistes, or the great harmonies of the Satanic speeches in "Paradise Regained," when read aloud by myself. A young lady

sometimes comes and drinks tea with us; at her request and M[argaret]'s I now and then read Wordsworth's poems to them. (Wordsworth, by the by, is the only poet I ever met who could read his own verses; often, indeed, he reads admirably.)

For nearly two years I believe that I read no book but one; and I owe it to the author, in discharge of a great debt of gratitude, to mention what that was. The sublimer and more passionate poets I still read, as I have said, by snatches, and occasionally. But my proper vocation, as I well knew, was the exercise of the analytic understanding. Now, for the most part, analytic studies are continuous, and not to be pursued by fits and starts, or fragmentary efforts. Mathematics, for instance, intellectual philosophy, etc., were all become insupportable to me; I shrunk from them with a sense of powerless and infantine feebleness that gave me an anguish the greater from remembering the time when I grappled with them to my own hourly delight, and for this further reason, because I had devoted the labor of my whole life, and had dedicated my intellect, blossoms and fruits, to the slow and elaborate toil of constructing one single work, to which I had presumed to give the title of an unfinished work of Spinoza's, viz.: *De emendatione humani intellectûs.* This was now lying locked up, as by frost, like any Spanish bridge or aqueduct, begun upon too great a scale for the resources of the architect; and, instead of surviving me as a monument of wishes at least, and aspirations, and a life of labor dedicated to the exaltation of human nature in that way in which God had best fitted me to promote so great an object, it was likely to stand a memorial to my children of hopes defeated, of baffled efforts, of materials uselessly accumulated, of foundations laid that were never to support a superstructure,—of the

grief and the ruin of the architect. In this state of imbecility I had, for amusement, turned my attention to political economy; my understanding, which formerly had been as active and restless as a hyena, could not, I suppose (so long as I lived at all), sink into utter lethargy; and political economy offers this advantage to a person in my state, that though it is eminently an organic science (no part, that is to say, but what acts on the whole, as the whole again reacts on each part), yet the several parts may be detached and contemplated singly. Great as was the prostration of my powers at this time, yet I could not forget my knowledge; and my understanding had been for too many years intimate with severe thinkers, with logic, and the great masters of knowledge, not to be aware of the utter feebleness of the main herd of modern economists. I had been led in 1811 to look into loads of books and pamphlets on many branches of economy; and, at my desire, M[argaret] sometimes read to me chapters from more recent works, or parts of parliamentary debates. I saw that these were generally the very dregs and rinsings of the human intellect; and that any man of sound head, and practiced in wielding logic with a scholastic adroitness, might take up the whole academy of modern economists, and throttle them between heaven and earth with his finger and thumb, or bray their fungus heads to powder with a lady's fan. At length, in 1819, a friend in Edinburgh sent me down Mr. Ricardo's book; and recurring to my own prophetic anticipation of the advent of some legislator for this science, I said, before I had finished the first chapter, "Thou art the man!" Wonder and curiosity were emotions that had long been dead in me. Yet I wondered once more; I wondered at myself that I could once again be stimulated to the effort of reading; and much more I wondered at the

book. Had this profound work been really written in England during the nineteenth century? Was it possible? I supposed thinking had been extinct in England. Could it be that an Englishman, and he not in academic bowers, but oppressed by mercantile and senatorial cares, had accomplished what all the universities of Europe, and a century of thought, had failed even to advance by one hair's breadth? All other writers had been crushed and overlaid by the enormous weight of facts and documents; Mr. Ricardo had deduced, *à priori,* from the understanding itself, laws which first gave a ray of light into the unwieldy chaos of materials, and had constructed what had been but a collection of tentative discussions into a science of regular proportions, now first standing on an eternal basis.

Thus did one single work of a profound understanding avail to give me a pleasure and an activity which I had not known for years:—it roused me even to write, or, at least, to dictate what M[argaret] wrote for me. It seemed to me that some important truths had escaped even "the inevitable eye" of Mr. Ricardo; and, as these were, for the most part, of such a nature that I could express or illustrate them more briefly and elegantly by algebraic symbols than in the usual clumsy and loitering diction of economists, the whole would not have filled a pocketbook; and being so brief, with M[argaret] for my amanuensis, even at this time, incapable as I was of all general exertion, I drew up my *Prolegomena to all future Systems of Political Economy.* I hope it will not be found redolent of opium; though, indeed, to most people, the subject itself is a sufficient opiate.

This exertion, however, was but a temporary flash; as the sequel showed—for I designed to publish my work: arrangements were made at a provincial press, about eighteen miles distant, for printing it. An addi-

tional compositor was retained, for some days, on this account. The work was even twice advertised; and I was, in a manner, pledged to the fulfillment of my intention. But I had a preface to write; and a dedication, which I wished to make a splendid one, to Mr. Ricardo. I found myself quite unable to accomplish all this. The arrangements were countermanded; the compositor dismissed; and my "Prolegomena" rested peacefully by the side of its elder and more dignified brother.

I have thus described and illustrated my intellectual torpor, in terms that apply, more or less, to every part of the four years during which I was under the Circean spells of opium. But for misery and suffering, I might, indeed, be said to have existed in a dormant state. I seldom could prevail on myself to write a letter; an answer of a few words, to any that I received, was the utmost that I could accomplish; and often *that* not until the letter had lain weeks, or even months, on my writing table. Without the aid of M[argaret] all records of bills paid, or *to be* paid, must have perished; and my whole domestic economy, whatever became of Political Economy, must have gone into irretrievable confusion.— I shall not afterwards allude to this part of the case; it is one, however, which the opium-eater will find, in the end, as oppressive and tormenting as any other, from the sense of incapacity and feebleness, from the direct embarrassments incident to the neglect or procrastination of each day's appropriate duties, and from the remorse which must often exasperate the stings of these evils to a reflective and conscientious mind. The opium-eater loses none of his moral sensibilities, or aspirations; he wishes and longs, as earnestly as ever, to realize what he believes possible, and feels to be exacted by duty; but his intellectual apprehension of what is possible infinitely outruns his power, not of

execution only, but even of power to attempt. He lies under the weight of incubus and nightmare; he lies in sight of all that he would fain perform, just as a man forcibly confined to his bed by the mortal languor of a relaxing disease, who is compelled to witness injury or outrage offered to some object of his tenderest love;— he curses the spells which chain him down from motion; —he would lay down his life if he might but get up and walk; but he is powerless as an infant, and cannot even attempt to rise.

* * * * * *

Many years ago, when I was looking over Piranesi's Antiquities of Rome, Mr. Coleridge, who was standing by, described to me a set of plates by that artist, called his *Dreams,* and which record the scenery of his own visions during the delirium of a fever; some of them (I describe only from memory of Mr. Coleridge's account) representing vast Gothic halls; on the floor of which stood all sorts of engines and machinery, wheels, cables, pulleys, levers, catapults, etc., etc., expressive of enormous power put forth, and resistance overcome. Creeping along the sides of the walls, you perceived a staircase; and upon it, groping his way upwards, was Piranesi himself; follow the stairs a little further, and you perceive it come to a sudden abrupt termination, without any balustrade, and allowing no step onwards to him who had reached the extremity, except into the depths below.

Whatever is to become of poor Piranesi, you suppose, at least, that his labors must in some way terminate here. But raise your eyes, and behold a second flight of stairs still higher; on which again Piranesi is perceived, but this time standing on the very brink of the abyss. Again elevate your eye, and a still more aerial flight of stairs is beheld; and again is poor Piranesi busy

on his aspiring labors; and so on, until the unfinished stairs and Piranesi both are lost in the upper gloom of the hall.—With the same power of endless growth and self-reproduction did my architecture proceed in dreams. In the early stage of my malady, the splendors of my dreams were indeed chiefly architectural; and I beheld such pomp of cities and palaces as was never yet beheld by the waking eye, unless in the clouds. From a great modern poet I cite part of a passage which describes, as an appearance actually beheld in the clouds, what in many of its circumstances I saw frequently in sleep:

> The appearance, instantaneously disclosed,
> Was of a mighty city—boldly say
> A wilderness of building, sinking far
> And self-withdrawn into a wondrous depth,
> Far sinking into splendor—without end!
> Fabric it seem'd of diamond, and of gold,
> With alabaster domes, and silver spires,
> And blazing terrace upon terrace, high
> Uplifted; here, serene pavilions bright
> In avenues disposed; there towers begirt
> With battlements that on their restless fronts
> Bore stars—illumination of all gems!
> By earthly nature had the effect been wrought
> Upon the dark materials of the storm
> Now pacified: on them, and on the coves,
> And mountain-steeps and summits, whereunto
> The vapors had receded,—taking there
> Their station under a cerulean sky, etc., etc.

The sublime circumstance—"battlements that on their *restless* fronts bore stars,"—might have been copied from my architectural dreams, for it often occurred.— We hear it reported of Dryden, and of Fuseli in modern times, that they thought proper to eat raw meat for

THE PAINS OF OPIUM

the sake of obtaining splendid dreams; how much better for such a purpose to have eaten opium! which yet I do not remember that any poet is recorded to have done, except the dramatist Shadwell; and in ancient days, Homer is, I think, rightly reputed to have known the virtues of opium.

To my architecture succeeded dreams of lakes and silvery expanses of water:—these haunted me so much that I feared, though possibly it will appear ludicrous to a medical man, that some dropsical state or tendency of the brain might thus be making itself, to use a metaphysical word, *objective;* and the sentient organ *project* itself as its own object.—For two months I suffered greatly in my head—a part of my bodily structure which had hitherto been so clear from all touch or taint of weakness, physically, I mean, that I used to say of it, as the last Lord Orford said of his stomach, that it seemed likely to survive the rest of my person.—Till now I had never felt a headache even, or any the slightest pain, except rheumatic pains caused by my own folly. However, I got over this attack, though it must have been verging on something very dangerous.

The waters now changed their character,—from translucent lakes, shining like mirrors, they now became seas and oceans. And now came a tremendous change, which, unfolding itself slowly like a scroll, through many months, promised an abiding torment; and, in fact, it never left me until the winding up of my case. Hitherto the human face had mixed often in my dreams, but not despotically, nor with any special power of tormenting. But now that which I have called the tyranny of the human face began to unfold itself. Perhaps some part of my London life might be answerable for this. Be that as it may, now it was that upon the rocking waters of the ocean the human face began to appear; the sea

appeared paved with innumerable faces, upturned to the heavens; faces, imploring, wrathful, despairing, surged upwards by thousands, by myriads, by generations, by centuries;—my agitation was infinite,—my mind tossed —and surged with the ocean.

May, 1818.

The Malay has been a fearful enemy for months. I have been every night, through his means, transported into Asiatic scenes. I know not whether others share in my feelings on this point; but I have often thought that if I were compelled to forego England, and to live in China, and among Chinese manners and modes of life and scenery, I should go mad. The causes of my horror lie deep; and some of them must be common to others. Southern Asia, in general, is the seat of awful images and associations. As the cradle of the human race, it would alone have a dim and reverential feeling connected with it. But there are other reasons. No man can pretend that the wild, barbarous, and capricious superstitions of Africa, or of savage tribes elsewhere, affect him in the way that he is affected by the ancient, monumental, cruel, and elaborate religions of Indostan, etc. The mere antiquity of Asiatic things, of their institutions, histories, modes of faith, etc., is so impressive, that to me the vast age of the race and name overpowers the sense of youth in the individual. A young Chinese seems to me an antediluvian man renewed. Even Englishmen, though not bred in any knowledge of such institutions, cannot but shudder at the mystic sublimity of *castes* that have flowed apart, and refused to mix, through such immemorial tracts of time; nor can any man fail to be awed by the names of the Ganges or the Euphrates. It contributes much to these feelings that southern Asia is, and has been for thousands of years, the part of the earth most swarming with human life;

THE PAINS OF OPIUM

the great *officina gentium*. Man is a weed in those regions. The vast empires also, into which the enormous population of Asia has always been cast, give a further sublimity to the feelings associated with all Oriental names or images. In China, over and above what it has in common with the rest of southern Asia, I am terrified by the modes of life, by the manners, and the barrier of utter abhorrence, and want of sympathy, placed between us by feelings deeper than I can analyze. I could sooner live with lunatics, or brute animals. All this, and much more than I can say, or have time to say, the reader must enter into before he can comprehend the unimaginable horror which these dreams of Oriental imagery, and mythological tortures, impressed upon me. Under the connecting feeling of tropical heat and vertical sun-lights, I brought together all creatures, birds, beasts, reptiles, all trees and plants, usages and appearances, that are found in all tropical regions, and assembled them together in China or Indostan. From kindred feelings, I soon brought Egypt and all her gods under the same law. I was stared at, hooted at, grinned at, chattered at, by monkeys, by paroquets, by cockatoos. I ran into pagodas; and was fixed for centuries at the summit, or in secret rooms; I was the idol; I was the priest; I was worshipped; I was sacrificed. I fled from the wrath of Brama through all the forests of Asia; Vishnu hated me; Seeva laid wait for me. I came suddenly upon Isis and Osiris; I had done a deed, they said, which the ibis and the crocodile trembled at. I was buried for a thousand years in stone coffins, with mummies and sphinxes, in narrow chambers at the heart of eternal pyramids. I was kissed, with cancerous kisses, by crocodiles; and laid, confounded with all unutterable slimy things, amongst reeds and Nilotic mud.

I thus give the reader some slight abstraction of my Oriental dreams, which always filled me with such amazement at the monstrous scenery, that horror seemed absorbed, for a while, in sheer astonishment. Sooner or later, came a reflux of feeling that swallowed up the astonishment, and left me, not so much in terror, as in hatred and abomination of what I saw. Over every form, and threat, and punishment, and dim sightless incarceration, brooded a sense of eternity and infinity that drove me into an oppression as of madness. Into these dreams only, it was, with one or two slight exceptions, that any circumstances of physical horror entered. All before had been moral and spiritual terrors. But here the main agents were ugly birds, or snakes, or crocodiles; especially the last. The cursed crocodile became to me the object of more horror than almost all the rest. I was compelled to live with him; and (as was always the case almost in my dreams) for centuries. I escaped sometimes, and found myself in Chinese houses, with cane tables, etc. All the feet of the tables, sofas, etc., soon became instinct with life: the abominable head of the crocodile, and his leering eyes, looked out at me, multiplied into a thousand repetitions: and I stood loathing and fascinated. And so often did this hideous reptile haunt my dreams, that many times the very same dream was broken up in the very same way: I heard gentle voices speaking to me (I hear everything when I am sleeping); and instantly I awoke: it was broad noon; and my children were standing, hand in hand, at my bed-side; come to show me their colored shoes, or new frocks, or to let me see them dressed for going out. I protest that so awful was the transition from the damned crocodile, and the other unutterable monsters and abortions of my dreams, to the sight of innocent *human* natures and of infancy,

that, in the mighty and sudden revulsion of mind, I wept, and could not forbear it, as I kissed their faces.

June, 1819.

I have had occasion to remark, at various periods of my life, that the deaths of those whom we love, and indeed the contemplation of death generally, is (*caeteris paribus*) more affecting in summer than in any other season of the year. And the reasons are these three, I think: first, that the visible heavens in summer appear far higher, more distant, and (if such a solecism may be excused) more infinite; the clouds, by which chiefly the eye expounds the distance of the blue pavilion stretched over our heads, are in summer more voluminous, massed, and accumulated in far grander and more towering piles; secondly, the light and the appearances of the declining and the setting sun are much more fitted to be types and characters of the Infinite; and, thirdly, which is the main reason, the exuberant and riotous prodigality of life naturally forces the mind more powerfully upon the antagonist thought of death, and the wintry sterility of the grave. For it may be observed, generally, that wherever two thoughts stand related to each other by a law of antagonism, and exist, as it were, by mutual repulsion, they are apt to suggest each other. On these accounts it is that I find it impossible to banish the thought of death when I am walking alone in the endless days of summer; and any particular death, if not more affecting, at least haunts my mind more obstinately and besiegingly in that season. Perhaps this cause, and a slight incident which I omit, might have been the immediate occasions of the following dream; to which, however, a predisposition must always have existed in my mind; but having been once roused, it never left me, and split into a thousand fantastic varieties, which often

suddenly reunited, and composed again the original dream.

I thought that it was a Sunday morning in May, that it was Easter Sunday, and as yet very early in the morning. I was standing, as it seemed to me, at the door of my own cottage. Right before me lay the very scene which could really be commanded from that situation, but exalted, as was usual, and solemnized by the power of dreams. There were the same mountains, and the same lovely valley at their feet; but the mountains were raised to more than Alpine height, and there was interspace far larger between them of meadows and forest lawns; the hedges were rich with white roses; and no living creature was to be seen, excepting that in the green churchyard there were cattle tranquilly reposing upon the verdant graves, and particularly round about the grave of a child whom I had tenderly loved, just as I had really beheld them, a little before sunrise in the same summer, when that child died. I gazed upon the well-known scene, and I said aloud (as I thought) to my self, "It yet wants much of sun-rise; and it is Easter Sunday; and that is the day on which they celebrate the first-fruits of resurrection. I will walk abroad; old griefs shall be forgotten to-day; for the air is cool and still, and the hills are high, and stretch away to heaven; and the forest-glades are as quiet as the churchyard; and with the dew I can wash the fever from my forehead, and then I shall be unhappy no longer." And I turned, as if to open my garden gate; and immediately I saw upon the left a scene far different; but which yet the power of dreams had reconciled into harmony with the other. The scene was an Oriental one; and there also it was Easter Sunday, and very early in the morning. And at a vast distance were visible, as a stain upon the horizon, the domes and

cupolas of a great city—an image or faint abstraction, caught perhaps in childhood from some picture of Jerusalem. And not a bow-shot from me, upon a stone, and shaded by Judean palms, there sat a woman; and I looked; and it was—Ann! She fixed her eyes upon me earnestly; and I said to her at length: "So then I have found you at last." I waited; but she answered me not a word. Her face was the same as when I saw it last, and yet again how different! Seventeen years ago, when the lamp-light fell upon her face, as for the last time I kissed her lips (lips, Ann, that to me were not polluted), her eyes were streaming with tears: the tears were now wiped away; she seemed more beautiful than she was at that time, but in all other points the same, and not older. Her looks were tranquil, but with unusual solemnity of expression; and I now gazed upon her with some awe, but suddenly her countenance grew dim, and, turning to the mountains, I perceived vapors rolling between us; in a moment all had vanished; thick darkness came on; and, in the twinkling of an eye, I was far away from mountains, and by lamp-light in Oxford street, walking again with Ann—just as we walked seventeen years before, when we were both children.

As a final specimen, I cite one of a different character, from 1820.

The dream commenced with a music which now I often heard in dreams—a music of preparation and of awakening suspense; a music like the opening of the Coronation Anthem, and which, like *that,* gave the feeling of a vast march—of infinite cavalcades filing off— and the tread of innumerable armies. The morning was come of the mighty day—a day of crisis and of final hope for human nature, then suffering some mysterious eclipse, and laboring in some dread extremity. Somewhere, I knew not where—somehow, I knew not

how—by some beings, I knew not whom—a battle, a strife, an agony, was conducting,—was evolving like a great drama, or piece of music; with which my sympathy was the more insupportable from my confusion as to its place, its cause, its nature, and its possible issue. I, as is usual in dreams (where, of necessity, we make ourselves central to every movement), had the power, and yet had not the power, to decide it. I had the power, if I could raise myself, to will it; and yet again had not the power, for the weight of twenty Atlantics was upon me, or the oppression of inexpiable guilt. "Deeper than ever plummet sounded," I lay inactive. Then, like a chorus, the passion deepened. Some greater interest was at stake; some mightier cause than ever yet the sword had pleaded, or trumpet had proclaimed. Then came sudden alarms; hurryings to and fro; trepidations of innumerable fugitives, I knew not whether from the good cause or the bad; darkness and lights; tempest and human faces; and at last, with the sense that all was lost, female forms, and the features that were worth all the world to me, and but a moment allowed,—and clasped hands, and heart-breaking partings, and then—everlasting farewells! And with a sigh, such as the caves of hell sighed when the incestuous mother uttered the abhorred name of death, the sound was reverberated—everlasting farewells! and again, and yet again reverberated—everlasting farewells!

And I awoke in struggles, and cried aloud—"I will sleep no more!"

LEVANA AND OUR LADIES OF SORROW

OFTENTIMES at Oxford I saw Levana in my dreams. I knew her by her Roman symbols. Who is Levana? Reader, that do not pretend to have leisure for very

LEVANA AND OUR LADIES OF SORROW

much scholarship, you will not be angry with me for telling you. Levana was the Roman goddess that performed for the new-born infant the earliest office of ennobling kindness—typical, by its mode, of that grandeur which belongs to man everywhere, and of that benignity in powers invisible which even in Pagan worlds sometimes descends to sustain it. At the very moment of birth, just as the infant tasted for the first time the atmosphere of our troubled planet, it was laid on the ground. *That* might bear different interpretations. But immediately, lest so grand a creature should grovel there for more than one instant, either the paternal hand, as proxy for the goddess Levana, or some near kinsman, as proxy for the father, raised it upright, bade it look erect as the king of all this world, and presented its forehead to the stars, saying, perhaps, in his heart, "Behold what is greater than yourselves!" This symbolic act represented the function of Levana. And that mysterious lady, who never revealed her face (except to me in dreams), but always acted by delegation, had her name from the Latin verb (as still it is the Italian verb) *levare*, to raise aloft.

This is the explanation of Levana. And hence it has arisen that some people have understood by Levana the tutelary power that controls the education of the nursery. She, that would not suffer at his birth even a prefigurative or mimic degradation for her awful ward, far less could be supposed to suffer the real degradation attaching to the non-development of his power. She therefore watches over human education. Now, the word *educo*, with the penultimate short, was derived (by a process often exemplified in the crystallisation of languages) from the word *educo*, with the penultimate long. Whatsoever *educes*, or develops, *educates*. By the education of Levana, therefore, is meant,—not the poor

machinery that moves by spelling-books and grammars, but by that mighty system of central forces hidden in the deep bosom of human life, which by passion, by strife, by temptation, by the energies of resistance, works forever upon children,—resting not day or night, any more than the mighty wheel of day and night themselves, whose moments, like restless spokes, are glimmering forever as they revolve.

If, then, *these* are the ministries by which Levana works, how profoundly must she reverence the agencies of grief! But you, reader, think that children generally are not liable to grief such as mine. There are two senses in the word *generally*,—the sense of Euclid, where it means *universally* (or in the whole extent of the *genus*), and a foolish sense of this word, where it means *usually*. Now, I am far from saying that children universally are capable of grief like mine. But there are more than you ever heard of who die of grief in this island of ours. I will tell you a common case. The rules of Eton require that a boy on the *foundation* should be there twelve years: he is superannuated at eighteen; consequently he must come at six. Children torn away from mothers and sisters at that age not unfrequently die. I speak of what I know. The complaint is not entered by the registrar as grief; but *that* it is. Grief of that sort, and at that age, has killed more than ever have been counted amongst its martyrs.

Therefore it is that Levana often communes with the powers that shake man's heart; therefore it is that she dotes upon grief. "These ladies," said I softly to myself, on seeing the ministers with whom Levana was conversing, "these are the Sorrows; and they are three in number: as the *Graces* are three, who dress man's life with beauty; the *Parcae* are three, who weave the dark arras of man's life in their mysterious loom always

with colours sad in part, sometimes angry with tragic crimson and black; the *Furies* are three, who visit with retributions, called from the other side of the grave, offences that walk upon this; and once even the *Muses* were but three, who fit the harp, the trumpet, or the lute, to the great burdens of man's impassioned creations. These are the Sorrows; all three of whom I know." The last words I say *now;* but in Oxford I said, "one of whom I know, and the others too surely I *shall* know. For already, in my fervent youth, I saw (dimly relieved upon the dark background of my dreams) the imperfect lineaments of the awful Sisters.

These Sisters—by what name shall we call them? If I say simply "The Sorrows," there will be a chance of mistaking the term; it might be understood of individual sorrow,—separate cases of sorrow,—whereas I want a term expressing the mighty abstractions that incarnate themselves in all individual sufferings of man's heart, and I wish to have these abstractions presented as impersonations,—that is, as clothed with human attributes of life, and with functions pointing to flesh. Let us call them, therefore, *Our Ladies of Sorrow.*

I know them thoroughly, and have walked in all their kingdoms. Three sisters they are, of one mysterious household; and their paths are wide apart; but of their dominion there is no end. Them I saw often conversing with Levana, and sometimes about myself. Do they talk, then? O no! Mighty phantoms like these disdain the infirmities of language. They may utter voices through the organs of man when they dwell in human hearts, but amongst themselves is no voice nor sound; eternal silence reigns in *their* kingdoms. They spoke not as they talked with Levana; they whispered not; they sang not; though oftentimes methought they *might* have sung; for I upon earth had heard their mysteries

oftentimes deciphered by harp and timbrel, by dulcimer and organ. Like God, whose servants they are, they utter their pleasure not by sounds that perish, or by words that go astray, but by signs in heaven, by changes on earth, by pulses in secret rivers, heraldries painted on darkness, and hieroglyphics written on the tablets of the brain. *They* wheeled in mazes; *I* spelled the steps. *They* telegraphed from afar; *I* read the signals. *They* conspired together; and on the mirrors of darkness *my* eye traced the plots. *Theirs* were the symbols; *mine* are the words.

What is it the Sisters are? What is it that they do? Let me describe their form and their presence, if form it were that still *fluctuated* in its outline, or presence it were that forever advanced to the front or forever receded amongst shades.

The eldest of the three is named *Mater Lachrymarum,* Our Lady of Tears. She it is that night and day raves and moans, calling for vanished faces. She stood in Rama, where a voice was heard of lamentation,—Rachel weeping for her children, and refusing to be comforted. She it was that stood in Bethlehem on the night when Herod's sword swept its nurseries of Innocents, and the little feet were stiffened forever which, heard at times as they trotted along floors overhead, woke pulses of love in household hearts that were not unmarked in heaven. Her eyes are sweet and subtle, wild and sleepy, by turns; oftentimes rising to the clouds, oftentimes challenging the heavens. She wears a diadem round her head. And I knew by my childish memories that she could go abroad upon the winds, when she heard the sobbing of litanies, or the thundering of organs, and when she beheld the mustering of summer clouds. This Sister, the elder, it is that carries keys more than papal at her girdle, which open every cottage and every palace.

She, to my knowledge, sat all last summer by the bedside of the blind beggar, him that so often and so gladly I talked with, whose pious daughter, eight years old, with the sunny countenance, resisted the temptations of play and village mirth, to travel all day long on dusty roads with her afflicted father. For this did God send her a great reward. In the spring time of the year, and whilst yet her own spring was budding, He recalled her to himself. But her blind father mourns forever over *her;* still he dreams at midnight that the little guiding hand is locked within his own; and still he wakens to a darkness that is *now* within a second and a deeper darkness. This *Mater Lachrymarum* also has been sitting all this winter of 1844-5 within the bedchamber of the Czar, bringing before his eyes a daughter (not less pious) that vanished to God not less suddenly, and left behind her a darkness not less profound. By the power of the keys it is that Our Lady of Tears glides, a ghostly intruder, into the chambers of sleepless men, sleepless women, sleepless children, from Ganges to the Nile, from Nile to Mississippi. And her, because she is the first-born of her house, and has the widest empire, let us honour with the title of "Madonna."

The second Sister is called *Mater Suspiriorum,* Our Lady of Sighs. She never scales the clouds, nor walks abroad upon the winds. She wears no diadem. And her eyes, if they were ever seen, would be neither sweet nor subtle; no man could read their story; they would be found filled with perishing dreams, and with wrecks of forgotten delirium. But she raises not her eyes; her head, on which sits a dilapidated turban, droops forever, forever fastens on the dust. She weeps not. She groans not. But she sighs inaudibly at intervals. Her sister, Madonna, is oftentimes stormy and frantic,

raging in the highest against heaven, and demanding back her darlings. But Our Lady of Sighs never clamours, never defies, dreams not of rebellious aspirations. She is humble to abjectness. Hers is the meekness that belongs to the hopeless. Murmur she may, but it is in her sleep. Whisper she may, but it is to herself in the twilight. Mutter she does at times, but it is in solitary places that are desolate as she is desolate, in ruined cities, and when the sun has gone down to his rest. This Sister is the visitor of the Pariah, of the Jew, of the bondsman to the oar in the Mediterranean galleys; of the English criminal in Norfolk Island, blotted out from the books of remembrance in sweet far-off England; of the baffled penitent reverting his eyes forever upon a solitary grave, which to him seems the altar overthrown of some past and bloody sacrifice, on which altar no oblations can now be availing, whether towards pardon that he might implore, or towards reparation that he might attempt. Every slave that at noonday looks up to the tropical sun with timid reproach, as he points with one hand to the earth, our general mother, but for *him* a stepmother, as he points with the other hand to the Bible, our general teacher, but against *him* sealed and sequestered; every woman sitting in darkness, without love to shelter her head, or hope to illumine her solitude, because the heaven-born instincts kindling in her nature germs of holy affections, which God implanted in her womanly bosom, having been stifled by social necessities, now burn sullenly to waste, like sepulchral lamps amongst the ancients; every nun defrauded of her unreturning Maytime by wicked kinsman, whom God will judge; every captive in every dungeon; all that are betrayed, and all that are rejected; outcasts by traditionary law, and children of *hereditary* disgrace: all these walk with

LEVANA AND OUR LADIES OF SORROW

Our Lady of Sighs. She also carries a key; but she needs it little. For her kingdom is chiefly amongst the tents of Shem, and the houseless vagrant of every clime. Yet in the very highest ranks of man she finds chapels of her own; and even in glorious England there are some that, to the world, carry their heads as proudly as the reindeer, who yet secretly have received her mark upon their foreheads.

But the third Sister, who is also the youngest——! Hush! whisper whilst we talk of *her!* Her kingdom is not large, or else no flesh should live; but within that kingdom all power is hers. Her head, turreted like that of Cybele, rises almost beyond the reach of sight. She droops not; and her eyes, rising so high, *might* be hidden by distance. But, being what they are, they cannot be hidden: through the treble veil of crape which she wears the fierce light of a blazing misery, that rests not for matins or for vespers, for noon of day or noon of night, for ebbing or for flowing tide, may be read from the very ground. She is the defier of God. She also is the mother of lunatics, and the suggestress of suicides. Deep lie the roots of her power; but narrow is the nation that she rules. For she can approach only those in whom a profound nature has been upheaved by central convulsions; in whom the heart trembles and the brain rocks under conspiracies of tempest from without and tempest from within. Madonna moves with uncertain steps, fast or slow, but still with tragic grace. Our Lady of Sighs creeps timidly and stealthily. But this youngest Sister moves with incalculable motions, bounding, and with tiger's leaps. She carries no key; for, though coming rarely amongst men, she storms all doors at which she is permitted to enter at all. And *her* name is *Mater Tenebrarum*,—our Lady of Darkness.

These were the *Semnai Theai* or Sublime Goddesses,

these were the *Eumenides* or Gracious Ladies (so called by antiquity in shuddering propitiation), of my Oxford dreams. Madonna spoke. She spoke by her mysterious hand. Touching my head, she beckoned to Our Lady of Sighs; and *what* she spoke, translated out of the signs which (except in dreams) no man reads, was this:—

"Lo! here is he whom in childhood I dedicated to my altars. This is he that once I made my darling. Him I led astray, him I beguiled; and from heaven I stole away his young heart to mine. Through me did he become idolatrous; and through me it was, by languishing desires, that he worshipped the worm, and prayed to the wormy grave. Holy was the grave to him; lovely was its darkness; saintly its corruption. Him, this young idolater, I have seasoned for thee, dear gentle Sister of Sighs! Do thou take him now to *thy* heart, and season him for our dreadful sister. And thou,"— turning to the *Mater Tenebrarum,* she said,—"wicked sister, that temptest and hatest, do thou take him from *her.* See that thy sceptre lie heavy on his head. Suffer not woman and her tenderness to sit near him in his darkness. Banish the frailties of hope; wither the relenting of love; scorch the fountains of tears; curse him as only *thou* canst curse. So shall he be accomplished in the furnace; so shall he see the things that ought *not* to be seen, sights that are abominable, and secrets that are unutterable. So shall he read elder truths, sad truths, grand truths, fearful truths. So shall he rise again *before* he dies. And so shall our commission be accomplished which before God we had,—to plague his heart until we had unfolded the capacities of his spirit."

WILLIAM COBBETT

HAZLITT in *The Spirit of the Age* has written the best characterization of Cobbett, an impressionistic sketch done in a happy hour by a master whose subject was to his liking. The two men had traits in common. Both were strongly individual; both were good haters; both enjoyed life tremendously, and extracted from it every scruple of its simple pleasures. Politically they were not unsympathetic, at least in Cobbett's latter days when he had become a radical. Yet the differences in men of such marked character are inevitably outstanding. Cobbett was the most admirable of husbands and fathers, in which capacities Hazlitt, it is clear, cannot be counted a success. And the robust, early-rising, temperate Cobbett would have looked upon Hazlitt's immoderate consumption of strong tea with disgust.

The mental backgrounds of the two are, of course, diverse. Cobbett was self-educated and, in the polite sense, despite his strong mind, uncultured. There were not many books which he greatly admired; and these were of a practical sort pertaining to trees and agriculture. His references to Shakespeare are sometimes slighting and he seems to have had little appreciation of poetry and the arts. Trees and a fertile landscape he loved; he had an expert's eye for the state of the crops, the character of soils, and all matters relevant to the business of farming. His is the self-made man's contempt for the polite acquisitions of society, for institutional learning, for the arts and graces. Not only does he think them of little worth in themselves but he remembers always the common laborer whose toil makes

them possible, the laborer who in Cobbett's day too often got no more than nine or eight, or even seven shillings a week for his toil.

Cobbett's *Political Register,* the journal which he edited, was for many years a power in England. No other man had, perhaps, so large a personal following. Few had so great an influence in molding the popular mind to the need and methods of political reform. He wrote prodigiously on political and agricultural topics. Were all his writings to be collected and published they would fill a hundred volumes. Inevitably much of this writing is of interest nowadays only to historians. His English grammar, vastly popular for many years, and his book on French which embodies his sensible methods for mastering that language, are now superseded. It is to his *Rural Rides* and the delightful *Advice to Young Men and (Incidentally) to Young Women* that the modern reader will turn for an expression of his racy personality. Like all good writers Cobbett stamps everything he does with his own peculiar genius. He is prodigal of himself. All that he reports and all his arguments are colored with his idiosyncrasies and prejudices and illustrated with anecdotes drawn from his experience. His autobiography is written in every paragraph.

Cobbett has, then, style, for it is as though the man's voice sounded from the written page. It is a downright, vigorous, racy style free from all literary influences. He had a masterly command of English idiom and the instinct of a good writer for the word suited to his sense and his audience. This audience was one of little education, men essentially much like himself. He was their voice. Through him the agricultural worker became articulate. He surpassed them in range and power, of course, for he was an exceptional man, but he felt with

them and liked them. Despite his many volumes and
his great celebrity he remained to the end of his life a
son of the soil, fearful and contemptuous of great cities;
London he called the Wen. The rise of the manufacturing classes, the vast increase in England's material
wealth stirred in him none of the enthusiasm of the new
school of political economists. He looked deeper to the
condition of the masses whom this wealth did not benefit.
That England could never return to the old and better
order of things which he had known as a boy he did not
appreciate. His remedies for the ills of the Industrial
Revolution would not have sufficed had he been given
the power to administer them. But men of greater
knowledge than his were equally unable to cope with
the new and complicated problems of the machine age.

From RURAL RIDES

REIGATE, (SURREY),
Saturday, 26 July, 1823.

Came from the Wen, through Croydon. It rained
nearly all the way. The corn is good. A great deal of
straw. The barley very fine; but all are backward;
and, if this weather continue much longer, there must
be that "heavenly blight" for which the wise friends of
"social order" are so fervently praying. But if the
wet now cease, or cease soon, what is to become of the
"poor souls of farmers" God only knows! In one article the wishes of our wise government appear to have
been gratified to the utmost; and that, too, without the
aid of any express form of prayer. I allude to the
hops, of which, it is said, that there will be, according
to all appearance, none at all! Bravo! Courage, my
Lord Liverpool! This article, at any rate, will not
choak us, will not distress us, will not make us miserable

by "over-production!"—The other day a gentleman (and a man of general good sense too) said to me: "What a deal of wet we have: what do you think of the weather *now?*"—"More rain," said I. "D—n those farmers," said he, "what luck they have! They will be as rich as Jews!"—Incredible as this may seem, it is a fact. But, indeed, there is no folly, if it relate to these matters, which is, nowadays, incredible. The hop affair is a pretty good illustration of the doctrine of "relief" from "diminished production." Mr. Ricardo may now call upon any of the hop-planters for proof of the correctness of his notions. They are ruined, for the greater part, if their all be embarked in hops. How are they to pay rent? I saw a planter, the other day, who sold his hops (Kentish) last fall for sixty shillings a hundred. The same hops will now fetch the owner of them eight pounds, or a hundred and sixty shillings.

Thus the *Quaker* gets rich, and the poor devil of a farmer is squeezed into a gaol. The *Quakers* carry on the far greater part of this work. They are, as to the products of the earth, what the *Jews* are to gold and silver. How they profit, or, rather, the degree in which they profit, at the expense of those who own and those who till the land, may be guessed at if we look at their immense worth, and if we, at the same time, reflect that they never work. Here is a sect of non-labourers. One would think that their religion bound them under a curse not to work. Some part of the people of all other sects work; sweat at work; do something that is useful to other people; but here is a sect of buyers and sellers. They make nothing; they cause nothing to come; they breed as well as other sects; but they make none of the raiment or houses, and cause none of the food to come. In order to justify some measure for paring the nails of this grasping sect, it is enough to say of them, which

we may with perfect truth, that, if all the other sects were to act like them, *the community must perish*. This is quite enough to say of this sect, of the monstrous privileges of whom we shall, I hope, one of these days, see an end. If I had the dealing with them, I would soon teach them to use the *spade* and the *plough,* and the *musket* too when necessary.

The rye, along the roadside, is ripe enough; and some of it is reaped and in shock. At Mearstam there is a field of cabbages, which, I was told, belonged to Colonel Joliffe. They appear to be early Yorks, and look very well. The rows seem to be about eighteen inches apart. There may be from 15,000 to 20,000 plants to the acre; and I dare say that they will weigh three pounds each, or more. I know of no crop of cattle food equal to this. If they be early Yorks, they will be in perfection in October, just when the grass is almost gone. No five acres of common grass land will, during the year, yield cattle food equal, either in quantity or quality, to what one acre of land, in early Yorks, will produce during three months.

PETWORTH,
Saturday, 12 *Nov.* 1825.

I was at this town in the summer of 1823, when I crossed Sussex from Worth to Huntington, in my way to Titchfield in Hampshire. We came this morning from Petersfield, with an intention to cross to Horsham, and go thence to Worth, and then into Kent; but Richard's horse seemed not to be fit for so strong a bout, and therefore we resolved to bend our course homewards, and first of all to fall back upon our resources at Thursley, which we intend to reach tomorrow, going through North Chapel, Chiddingfold, and Brook.

At about four miles from Petersfield we passed

through a village called Rogate. Just before we came to it, I asked a man who was hedging on the side of the road how much he got a day. He said 1*s.* 6*d.*: and told me that the allowed wages was 7*d.* a day for the man *and a gallon loaf a week for the rest of his family;* that is to say, one pound and two and a quarter ounces of bread for each of them; and nothing more! And this, observe, is one-third short of the bread allowance of gaols, to say nothing of the meat and lodging of the inhabitants of gaols. If the man have full work; if he get his eighteen-pence a day, the whole nine shillings does not purchase a gallon loaf each for a wife and three children, and two gallon loaves for himself. In the gaols, the convicted felons have a pound and a half each of bread a day to begin with: they have some meat generally, and it has been found absolutely necessary to allow them meat when they work at the tread-mill. It is impossible to make them work at the tread-mill without it. However, let us take the bare allowance of bread allowed in the gaols. This allowance is, for five people, fifty-two pounds and a half in the week; whereas, the man's nine shillings will buy but fifty-two pounds of bread; and this, observe, is a vast deal better than the state of things in the north of Hampshire, where the day-labourer gets but eight shillings a week. I asked this man how much a day they gave to a young able man who had no family, and who was compelled to come to the parish-officers for work. Observe, that there are a great many young men in this situation, because the farmers will not employ single men *at full wages,* these full wages being wanted for the married man's family, just to keep them alive according to the calculation that we have just seen. About the borders of the north of Hampshire they give to these single men two gallon loaves a week, or, in money, two shillings and

eight pence, and nothing more. Here, in this part of Sussex, they give the single man sevenpence a day, that is to say, enough to buy two pounds and a quarter of bread for six days in the week, and as he does not work on the Sunday, there is no sevenpence allowed for the Sunday, and of course nothing to eat: and this is the allowance, settled by the magistrates, for a young, hearty, labouring man; and that, too, in the part of England where, I believe, they live better than in any other part of it. The poor creature here has sevenpence a day for six days in the week to find him food, clothes, washing, and lodging! It is just sevenpence, less than one half of what the meanest foot soldier in the standing army receives; besides that the latter has clothing, candle, fire, and lodging into the bargain! Well may we call our happy state of things the "envy of surrounding nations, and the admiration of the world!" We hear of the efforts of Mrs. Fry, Mr. Buxton, and numerous other persons to improve the situation of felons in the gaols; but never, no never, do we catch them ejaculating one single pious sigh for these innumerable sufferers, who are doomed to become felons or to waste away their bodies by hunger.

When we came into the village of Rogate, I saw a little group of persons standing before a blacksmith's shop. The churchyard was on the other side of the road, surrounded by a low wall. The earth of the churchyard was about four feet and a half higher than the common level of the ground round about it; and you may see, by the nearness of the church windows to the ground, that this bed of earth has been made by the innumerable burials that have taken place in it. The group, consisting of the blacksmith, the wheelwright, perhaps, and three or four others, appeared to me to be in a deliberative mood. So I said, looking

significantly at the churchyard, "It has taken a pretty many thousands of your forefathers to raise that ground up so high." "Yes, sir," said one of them. "And," said I, "for about nine hundred years those who built that church thought about religion very differently from what we do." "Yes," said another. "And," said I, "do you think that all those who made that heap there are gone to the devil?" I got no answer to this. "At any rate," added I, "they never worked for a pound and a half of bread a day." They looked hard at me, and then looked hard at one another; and I, having trotted off, looked round at the first turning, and saw them looking after us still. I should suppose that the church was built about seven or eight hundred years ago, that is to say, the present church; for the first church built upon this spot was, I dare say, erected more than a thousand years ago. If I had had time, I should have told this group that, before the Protestant Reformation, the labourers of Rogate received fourpence a day from Michaelmas to Lady-day; fivepence a day from Lady-day to Michaelmas, except in harvest and grass-mowing time, when able labourers had sevenpence a day; and that, at this time, bacon was *not so much as a halfpenny a pound*: and, moreover, that the parson of the parish maintained out of the tithes all those persons in the parish that were reduced to indigence by means of old age or other cause of inability to labour. I should have told them this, and, in all probability, a great deal more, but I had not time; and, besides, they will have an opportunity of reading all about it in my little book called the *History of the Protestant Reformation*.

From Rogate we came on to Trotten, where a Mr. Twyford is the squire, and where there is a very fine and ancient church close by the squire's house. I saw the squire looking at some poor devils who were making

"wauste improvements, ma'am," on the road which passes by the squire's door. He looked uncommonly hard at me. It was a scrutinising sort of look, mixed, as I thought, with a little surprise, if not of jealousy, as much as to say, "I wonder who the devil you can be?" My look at the squire was with the head a little on one side, and with the cheek drawn up from the left corner of the mouth, expressive of anything rather than a sense of inferiority to the squire, of whom, however, I had never heard speak before. Seeing the good and commodious and capacious church, I could not help reflecting on the intolerable baseness of this description of men, who have remained mute as fishes, while they have been taxed to build churches for the convenience of the cotton-lords and the stock-jobbers. First, their estates have been taxed to pay interest of debts contracted with these stock-jobbers, and to make wars for the sale of the goods of the cotton-lords. This drain upon their estates has collected the people into great masses, and now the same interests are taxed to build churches for them in these masses. And yet the tame fellows remain as silent as if they had been born deaf and dumb and blind. As towards the labourers, they are sharp and vigorous and brave as heart could wish; here they are bold as Hector. They pare down the wretched souls to what is below gaol allowance. But as towards the taxers they are gentle as doves. With regard, however, to this Squire Twyford, he is not, as I afterwards found, without some little consolation; for one of his sons, I understand, is like Squire Rawlinson of Hampshire, *a police justice in London!* I hear that Squire Twyford was always a distinguished champion of loyalty; what they call a staunch friend of government; and it is therefore natural that the government should be a staunch friend to him. By the taxing of his estate,

and paying the stock-jobbers out of the proceeds, the people have been got together in great masses, and as there are justices wanted to keep them in order in those masses it seems but reasonable that the squire should, in one way or another, enjoy some portion of the profits of keeping them in order. However, this cannot be the case with every loyal squire; and there are many of them who, for want of a share in the distribution, have been totally extinguished. I should suppose Squire Twyford to be in the second rank upwards (dividing the whole of the proprietors of land into five ranks). It appears to me that pretty nearly the whole of this second rank is gone; that the stock-jobbers have eaten them clean up, having less mercy than the cannibals, who usually leave the hands and the feet; so that this squire has had pretty good luck.

From Trotten we came to Midhurst, and, having baited our horses, went into Cowdry Park to see the ruins of that once noble mansion, from which the Countess of Salisbury (the last of the Plantagenets) was brought by the tyrant Henry VIII. to be cruelly murdered, in revenge for the integrity and the other great virtues of her son, Cardinal Pole, as we have seen in Number Four, paragraph 115, of the *History of the Protestant Reformation*. This noble estate, one of the finest in the whole kingdom, was seized on by the king, after the possessor had been murdered on his scaffold. She had committed no crime. No crime was proved against her. The miscreant Thomas Cromwell finding that no form of trial would answer his purpose, invented a new mode of bringing people to their death; namely, a bill brought into parliament, condemning her to death. The estate was then granted to a Sir Anthony Brown, who was physician to the king. By the descendants of this Brown, one of whom was afterwards created Lord

Montague, the estate has been held to this day; and
Mr. Poyntz, who married the sole remaining heiress of
this family, a Miss Brown, is now the proprietor of the
estate, comprising, I believe, *forty or fifty manors,* the
greater part of which are in this neighbourhood, some
of them, however, extending more than twenty miles
from the mansion. We entered the park through a great
iron gate-way, part of which being wanting, the gap
was stopped up by a hurdle. We rode down to the
house and all round about and in amongst the ruins,
now in part covered with ivy, and inhabited by innumerable starlings and jackdaws. The last possessor was,
I believe, that Lord Montague who was put an end to
by the celebrated *nautical adventure* on the Rhine along
with the brother of Sir Glory. These two sensible
worthies took it into their heads to go down a place
something resembling the waterfall of an overshot mill.
They were drowned just as two young kittens or two
young puppies would have been. And as an instance
of the truth that it is an ill wind that blows nobody
good, had it not been for this sensible enterprise, never
would there have been a Westminster Rump to celebrate
the talents and virtues of Westminster's Pride and
England's Glory. It was this Lord Montague, I believe,
who had this ancient and noble mansion completely
repaired, and fitted up as a place of residence: and a
few days, or a very few weeks, at any rate, after the
work was completed, the house was set on fire (by accident, I suppose), and left nearly in the state in which
it now stands, except that the ivy has grown up about
it, and partly hidden the stones from our sight. You
may see, however, the hour of the day or night at which
the fire took place; for there still remains the brass of
the face of the clock, and the hand pointing to the hour.
Close by this mansion there runs a little river which

runs winding away through the valleys, and at last falls
into the Arron. After viewing the ruins, we had to
return into the turnpike-road, and then enter another
part of the park, which we crossed, in order to go to
Petworth. When you are in a part of this road through
the park, you look down and see the house in the middle
of a very fine valley, the distant boundary of which, to
the south and south-west, is the South Down Hills.
Some of the trees here are very fine, particularly some
most magnificent rows of the Spanish chestnut. I asked
the people at Midhurst where Mr. Poyntz himself lived;
and they told me at the *lodge* in the park, which was
formerly the residence of the head keeper. The land
is very good about here. It is fine rich loam at top,
with clay further down. It is good for all sorts of trees,
and they seem to grow here very fast.

We got to Petworth pretty early in the day. On
entering it you see the house of Lord Egremont, which
is close up against the park-wall, and which wall bounds
this little vale on two sides. There is a sort of town-
hall here, and on one side of it there is the bust of
Charles II., I should have thought; but they tell me it
is that of Sir William Wyndham, from whom Lord
Egremont is descended. But there is *another building*
much more capacious and magnificent than the town-
hall; namely, the Bridewell, which, from the modernness
of its structure, appears to be one of those "wauste
improvements, ma'am," which distinguish this *enlightened* age. This structure vies, in point of magnitude,
with the house of Lord Egremont itself, though that is
one of the largest mansions in the whole kingdom. The
Bridewell has a wall round it that I should suppose
to be twenty feet high. This place was not wanted
when the labourer got twice as much instead of half as
much as the common standing soldier. Here you see

the true cause why the young labouring man is *"content"* to exist upon 7*d.* a day, for six days in the week, and nothing for Sunday. Oh! we are a most free and enlightened people; our happy constitution in church and state has supplanted Popery and slavery; but we go to a Bridewell unless we quietly exist and work upon 7*d.* a day!

Saturday, 2 September.

After I got to Warminster yesterday it began to rain, which stopped me in my way to Frome in Sommersetshire, which lies about seven or eight miles from this place; but as I meant to be quite in the northern part of the county by to-morrow noon, or thereabouts, I took a post-chaise in the afternoon of yesterday and went to Frome, where I saw, upon my entrance into the town, between two and three hundred weavers, men and boys, cracking stones, moving earth, and doing other sorts of work, towards making a fine road into the town. I drove into the town, and through the principal streets and then I put my chaise up a little at one of the inns. This appears to be a sort of little Manchester. A very small Manchester, indeed; for it does not contain above ten to twelve thousand people, but it has all the *flash* of a Manchester, and the innkeepers and their people look and behave like the Manchester fellows. I was, I must confess, glad to find proofs of the irretrievable decay of the place. I remembered how ready the bluff manufacturers had been to *call in the troops* of various descriptions. "Let them," said I to myself, "call the troops in now, to make their trade revive. Let them now resort to their friends of the yeomanry and of the army; let them now threaten their poor workmen with the gaol, when they dare to ask for the means of preventing starvation in their families. Let them, who have, in fact, lived and thriven by the sword, now call

upon the parson-magistrate to bring out the soldiers to compel me, for instance, to give thirty shillings a yard for the superfine black broad-cloth (made at Frome), which Mr. Roe, at Kensington, offered me at seven shillings and sixpence a yard just before I left home! Yes, these men have ground down into powder those who were earning them their fortunes: let the grinders themselves now be ground, and, according to the usual wise and just course of Providence, let them be crushed by the system which they have delighted in, because it made others crouch beneath them." Their poor work-people cannot be worse off than they long have been. The parish pay, which they now get upon the roads, is 2s. 6d. a week for a man, 2s. for his wife, 1s. 3d. for each child under eight years of age, 3d. a week, in addition, to each child above eight, who can go to work: and if the children above eight years old, whether girls or boys, do not go to work upon the road, they have *nothing!* Thus a family of five people have just as much, and eightpence over, as goes down the throat of one single foot soldier; but, observe, the standing soldier, that "truly English institution," has clothing, fuel, candle, soap, and house-rent, over and above what is allowed to this miserable family! And yet the base reptiles, who are called "country gentlemen," and whom Sir James Graham calls upon us to commit all sorts of acts of injustice in order to preserve, never utter a whisper about the expenses of keeping the soldiers, while they are everlastingly railing against the working people of every description, and representing them, and them only, as the cause of the loss of their estates!

These poor creatures at Frome have pawned all their things, or nearly all. All their best clothes, their blankets and sheets; their looms; any little piece of

RURAL RIDES 233

furniture that they had, and that was good for anything. Mothers have been compelled to pawn all the tolerably good clothes that their children had. In case of a man having two or three shirts, he is left with only one, and sometimes without any shirt; and though this is a sort of manufacture that cannot very well come to a complete end; still it has received a blow from which it cannot possibly recover. The population of this Frome has been augmented to the degree of one-third within the last six or seven years. There are here all the usual signs of accommodation bills and all false paper stuff, called money: new houses in abundance, half finished; new gingerbread "places of worship," as they are called; great swaggering inns; parcels of swaggering fellows going about, with vulgarity imprinted upon their countenances, but with good clothes upon their backs.

I found the working people at Frome very intelligent; very well informed as to the cause of their misery; not at all humbugged by the canters, whether about religion or loyalty. When I got to the inn, I sent my post-chaise boy back to the road to tell one or two of the weavers to come to me at the inn. The landlord did not at first like to let such ragged fellows upstairs. I insisted, however, upon their coming up, and I had a long talk with them. They were very intelligent men; had much clearer views of what is likely to happen than the pretty gentlemen of Whitehall seem to have; and it is curious enough that they, these common weavers, should tell me, that they thought that the trade never would come back again to what it was before, or, rather, to what it has been for some years past. This is the impression everywhere; that the *puffing is over;* that we must come back again to something like reality. The first factories that I met with were at a village called Upton Lovell,

just before I came to Heytesbury. There they were a doing not more than a quarter work. There is only one factory, I believe, here at Warminster, and that has been suspended, during the harvest, at any rate. At Frome they are all upon about a quarter work. It is the same at Bradford and Trowbridge; and, as curious a thing as ever was heard of in the world is, that here are, through all these towns, and throughout this country, weavers from the north, singing about the towns ballads of distress! They had been doing it at Salisbury just before I was there. The landlord at Heytesbury told me that people that could afford it generally gave them something; and I was told that they did the same at Salisbury. The landlord at Heytesbury told me that every one of them had a *license to beg,* given them he said "by the government." I suppose it was some *pass* from a magistrate; though I know of no law that allows of such passes; and a pretty thing it would be to grant such licenses, or such passes, when the law so positively commands that the poor of every parish shall be maintained in and by every such parish.

However, all law of this sort, all salutary and humane law, really seems to be drawing towards an end in this now miserable country, where the thousands are caused to wallow in luxury, to be surfeited with food and drink, while the millions are continually on the point of famishing. In order to form an idea of the degradation of the people of this country, and of the abandonment of every English principle, what need we of more than this one disgraceful and truly horrible fact, namely, that *the common soldiers of the standing army in time of peace subscribe in order to furnish the meanest of diet to keep from starving the industrious people who are taxed to the amount of one-half of their wages, and out of which taxes the very pay of these soldiers comes!*

is not this one fact; this disgraceful, this damning fact; is not this enough to convince us that *there must be a change;* that there must be a complete and radical change; or that England must become a country of the basest slavery that ever disgraced the earth?

STROUD, (GLOUCESTERSHIRE),
Tuesday Forenoon, 12 *Sept.* 1826.

I set off from Malmsbury this morning at 6 o'clock, in as sweet and bright a morning as ever came out of the heavens, and leaving behind me as pleasant a house and as kind hosts as I ever met with in the whole course of my life, either in England or America; and that is saying a great deal indeed. This circumstance was the more pleasant, as I had never before either seen or heard of these kind, unaffected, sensible, *sans-facons,* and most agreeable friends. From Malmsbury I first came, at the end of five miles, to Tutbury, which is in Gloucestershire, there being here a sort of dell, or ravine, which, in this place, is the boundary line of the two counties, and over which you go on a bridge, one-half of which belongs to each county. And now, before I take my leave of Wiltshire, I must observe that, in the course of my life (days of *courtship* excepted, of course), I never passed seventeen pleasanter days than those which I have just spent in Wiltshire. It is, especially in the southern half, just the sort of country that I like; the weather has been pleasant; I have been in good houses and amongst good and beautiful gardens; and, in *every* case, I have not only been most kindly entertained, but my entertainers have been of just the stamp that I like.

I saw again, this morning, large flocks of *goldfinches* feeding on the thistle-seed on the roadside. The French call this bird by a name derived from the thistle, so

notorious has it always been that they live upon this seed. Thistle is, in French, *chardon;* and the French call this beautiful little bird *chardonaret.* I never could have supposed that such flocks of these birds would ever be seen in England. But it is a great year for all the feathered race, whether wild or tame: naturally so, indeed; for every one knows that it is the *wet,* and not the *cold,* that is injurious to the breeding of birds of all sorts, whether land-birds or water-birds. They say that there are, this year, double the usual quantity of ducks and geese: and, really, they do seem to swarm in the farmyards, wherever I go. It is a great mistake to suppose that ducks and geese *need* water, except to drink. There is, perhaps, no spot in the world, in proportion to its size and population, where so many of these birds are reared and fatted as in Long Island; and it is not in one case out of ten that they have any ponds to go to, or that they ever see any water other than water that is drawn up out of a well.

A little way before I got to Tutbury I saw a woman digging some potatoes in a strip of ground making part of a field nearly an oblong square, and which field appeared to be laid out in strips. She told me that the field was part of a farm (to the homestead of which she pointed); that it was, by the farmer, *let out* in strips to labouring people; that each strip contained a rood (or quarter of a statute acre); that each married labourer rented one strip; and that the annual rent was *a pound* for the strip. Now the taxes being all paid by the farmer; the fences being kept in repair by him; and, as appeared to me, the land being exceedingly good: all these things considered, the rent does not appear to be too high.—This fashion is certainly a *growing* one; it is a little step towards a coming back to the ancient small life and leaseholds and common-

RURAL RIDES 237

field! This field of strips was, in fact, a sort of common-field; and the "agriculturists," as the conceited asses of landlords call themselves, at their clubs and meetings, might, and they would if their skulls could admit any thoughts except such as relate to high prices and low wages; they might, and they would, begin to suspect that the "dark age" people were not so very foolish when they had so many common-fields, and when almost every man that had a family had also a bit of land, either large or small. It is a very curious thing that the enclosing of commons, that the shutting out of the labourers *from all share* in the land; that the prohibiting of them to look at a wild animal, almost at a lark or a frog; it is curious that this hard-hearted system should have gone on until at last it has produced effects so injurious and so dangerous to the grinders themselves that they have, of their own accord and for their own safety, begun to make a step towards the ancient system, and have, in the manner I have observed, made the labourers sharers, in some degree, in the uses, at any rate, of the soil. The far greater part of these strips of land have potatoes growing in them; but in some cases they have borne wheat, and in others barley, this year; and these have now turnips; very young most of them, but in some places very fine, and in every instance nicely hoed out. The land that will bear 400 bushels of potatoes to the acre will bear 40 bushels of wheat; and the ten bushels of wheat to the quarter of an acre would be a crop far more valuable than a hundred bushels of potatoes, as I have proved many times in the *Register*.

Just before I got into Tutbury I was met by a good many people, in twos, threes, or fives, some running, and some walking fast, one of the first of whom asked me if I had met an "old man" some distance back. I

asked what *sort* of a man: "A *poor* man." "I don't recollect, indeed; but what are you all pursuing him for?" "He has been *stealing.*" "What has he been stealing?" "Cabbages." "Where?" "Out of Mr. Glover, the hatter's, garden." "What! do you call that *stealing;* and would you punish a man, a poor man, and therefore, in all likelihood, a hungry man too, and moreover an old man; do you set up a hue-and-cry after, and would you punish such a man for taking a few cabbages, when that Holy Bible, which, I dare say, you profess to believe in, and perhaps assist to circulate, teaches you that the hungry man may, without committing any offence at all, go into his neighbour's vineyard and eat his fill of grapes, one bunch of which is worth a sack-full of cabbages?" "Yes; but he is a very bad character." "Why, my friend, very poor and almost starved people are apt to be 'bad characters'; but the Bible, in both Testaments, commands us to be merciful to the poor, to feed the hungry, to have compassion on the aged; and it makes no exception as to the 'character' of the parties." Another group or two of the pursuers had come up by this time; and I, bearing in mind the fate of Don Quixote when he interfered in somewhat similar cases, gave my horse the hint, and soon got away; but though doubtless I made no converts, I, upon looking back, perceived that I had slackened the pursuit! The pursuers went more slowly; I could see that they got to talking; it was now the step of deliberation rather than that of decision; and though I did not like to call upon Mr. Glover, I hope he was merciful. It is impossible for me to witness scenes like this; to hear a man called a thief for such a cause; to see him thus eagerly and vindictively pursued for having taken some cabbages in a garden: it is impossible for me to

behold such a scene, without calling to mind the practice
in the United States of America, where, if a man were
even to talk of prosecuting another (especially if that
other were poor or old) for taking from the land, or
from the trees, any part of a growing crop, for his own
personal and immediate use; if any man were even to
talk of prosecuting another for such an act, such talker
would be held in universal abhorrence: people would
hate him; and, in short, if rich as Ricardo or Baring,
he might live by himself; for no man would look upon
him as a neighbour.

Tutbury is a very pretty town, and has a beautiful
ancient church. The country is high along here for a
mile or two towards Avening, which begins a long and
deep and narrow valley, that comes all the way down
to Stroud. When I got to the end of the high country,
and the lower country opened to my view, I was at
about three miles from Tutbury, on the road to Avening,
leaving the Minchinghampton road to my right. Here
I was upon the edge of the high land, looking right
down upon the village of Avening, and seeing, just close
to it, a large and fine mansion-house, a beautiful park,
and, making part of the park, one of the finest, most
magnificent woods (of 200 acres, I dare say), lying
facing me, going from a valley up a gently-rising hill.
While I was sitting on my horse, admiring this spot,
a man came along with some tools in his hand, as if
going somewhere to work as plumber. "Whose beautiful
place is that?" said I. "One 'Squire Ricardo, I think
they call him, but . . ."—You might have "knocked
me down with a feather," as the old women say . . .
"but" (continued the plumber) "the Old Gentleman's
dead, and . . ." "God—the old gentleman and the
young gentleman too!" said I; and, giving my horse a

blow, instead of a word, on I went down the hill. Before I got to the bottom, my reflections on the present state of the "market" and on the probable results of "watching the turn of it," had made me better humoured; and as one of the first objects that struck my eye in the village was the sign of the Cross, and of the Red, or Bloody, Cross too, I asked the landlord some questions, which began a series of joking and bantering that I had with the people, from one end of the village to the other. I set them all a laughing; and though they could not know my name, they will remember me for a long while.—This estate of Gatcomb belonged, I am told, to a Mr. Shepperd, and to his fathers before him. I asked where this Shepperd was now? A tradesman-looking man told me that he did not know where he was; but that he had heard that he was living somewhere near to Bath! Thus they go! Thus they are squeezed out of existence. The little ones are gone; and the big ones have nothing left for it but to resort to the bands of holy matrimony with the turn of the market watchers and their breed. This the big ones are now doing apace; and there is this comfort at any rate; namely, that the connection cannot make them baser than they are, a boroughmonger being, of all God's creatures, the very basest.

From Avening I came on through Nailsworth, Woodchester, and Rodborough to this place. These villages lie on the sides of a narrow and deep valley, with a narrow stream of water running down the middle of it, and this stream turns the wheels of a great many mills and sets of machinery for the making of *woollen-cloth.* The factories begin at Avening, and are scattered all the way down the valley. There are steam-engines as well as water powers. The work and the trade is so

RURAL RIDES 241

flat that in, I should think, much more than a hundred acres of ground, which I have seen to-day, covered with rails or racks, for the drying of cloth, I do not think that I have seen one single acre where the racks had cloth upon them. The workmen do not get half wages; great numbers are thrown on the parish; but overseers and magistrates in this part of England do not presume that they are to leave anybody to starve to death; there is law here; this is in England, and not in "the north," where those who ought to see that the poor do not suffer, talk of their dying with hunger as Irish 'squires do; aye, and applaud them for their patient resignation!

The Gloucestershire people have no notion of dying with hunger; and it is with great pleasure that I remark that I have seen no woe-worn creature this day. The sub-soil here is a yellowish ugly stone. The houses are all built with this; and it being ugly, the stone is made white by a wash of some sort or other. The land on both sides of the valley, and all down the bottom of it, has plenty of trees on it; it is chiefly pasture land, so that the green and the white colours, and the form and great variety of the ground, and the water, and altogether make this a very pretty ride. Here are a series of spots, every one of which a lover of landscapes would like to have painted. Even the buildings of the factories are not ugly. The people seem to have been constantly well off. A pig in almost every cottage sty; that is the infallible mark of a happy people. At present this valley suffers; and though cloth will always be wanted, there will yet be much suffering even here, while at Uly and other places they say the suffering is great indeed.

From ADVICE TO YOUNG MEN AND (INCIDENTALLY) TO YOUNG WOMEN

The next thing is the GRAMMAR of your own language. Without understanding this, you can never hope to become fit for any thing beyond mere trade or agriculture. It is true, that we do (God knows!) but too often see men have great wealth, high titles, and boundless power heaped upon them, who can hardly write ten lines together correctly; but, remember, it is not *merit* that has been the cause of their advancement; the cause has been, in almost every such case the subserviency of the party to the will of some government, and the baseness of some nation who have quietly submitted to be governed by brazen fools. Do not you imagine, that you will have luck of this sort: do not you hope to be rewarded and honoured for that ignorance which shall prove a scourge to your country, and which will earn you the curses of the children yet unborn. Rely you upon your merit, and upon nothing else. Without a knowledge of grammar, it is impossible for you to write correctly, and, it is by mere accident if you speak correctly, and, pray bear in mind, that all well-informed persons judge of a man's mind (until they have other means of judging) by his writing or speaking. The labour necessary to acquire this knowledge is, indeed, not trifling: grammar is not, like arithmetic, a science consisting of several distinct departments, some of which may be dispensed with: it is a whole, and the whole must be learned, or, no part is learned. The subject is abstruse: it demands much reflection and much patience: but, when once the task is performed, it is performed *for life,* and in every day of that life it will be found to be, in a greater or less degree, a source of pleasure or of profit or of both together. And, what

ADVICE TO YOUNG MEN AND WOMEN 243

is the labour? It consists of no bodily exertion; it exposes the student to no cold, no hunger, no sufferings of any sort. The study need subtract from the hours of no business, nor, indeed, from the hours of necessary exercise: the hours usually spent on the tea and coffee slops and in the mere gossip which accompany them; those wasted hours of only *one year,* employed in the study of English grammar, would make you a correct speaker and writer for the rest of your life. You want no school, no room to study in, no expenses, and no troublesome circumstances of any sort. I learned grammar when I was a private soldier on the pay of sixpence a day. The edge of my berth, or that of the guard-bed, was my seat to study in; my knapsack was my writing-table; and the task did not demand anything like a year of my life. I had no money to purchase candle or oil; in winter-time it was rarely that I could get any evening-light but that of *the fire,* and only my *turn* even of that. And, if I, under such circumstances, and without parent or friend to advise or encourage me, accomplished this undertaking, what excuse can there be for *any youth,* however poor, however pressed with business, or however circumstanced as to room or other conveniences? To buy a pen or a sheet of paper I was compelled to forego some portion of food, though in a state of half starvation; I had no moment of time that I could call my own; and I had to read and to write amidst the talking, laughing, singing, whistling and brawling of at least half a score of the most thoughtless of men, and that, too, in the hours of their freedom from all control. Think not lightly of the *farthing* that I had to give, now and then, for ink, pen, or paper! That farthing was, alas! a *great sum* to me! I was as tall as I am now; I had great health and great exercise. The whole of the money, not expended for us at

market, was *two-pence a week* for each man. I remember, and well I may! that, upon one occasion I, after all absolutely necessary expenses, had, on a Friday, made shift to have a half-penny in reserve, which I had destined for the purchase of a red-herring in the morning; but, when I pulled off my clothes at night, so hungry then as to be hardly able to endure life, I found that I had *lost my half-penny!* I buried my head under the miserable sheet and rug, and cried like a child! And, again I say, if I, under circumstances like these, could encounter and overcome this task, is there, can there be, in the whole world, a youth to find an excuse for the non-performance? What youth, who shall read this, will not be ashamed to say, that he is not able to find time and opportunity for this most essential of all the branches of book-learning?

*   *   *   *   *   *

As it may be your lot (such has been mine) to live by your literary talent, I will, here, before I proceed to matter more applicable to persons in other states of life, observe, that I cannot form an idea of a mortal more wretched than a man of real talent, compelled to curb his genius, and to submit himself in the exercise of that genius, to those whom he knows to be far inferior to himself, and whom he must despise from the bottom of his soul. The late Mr. William Gifford, who was the son of a shoemaker at Ashburton in Devonshire; who was put to school and sent to the university at the expense of a generous and good clergyman of the name of Cookson, and who died, the other day, a sort of whipper-in of Murray's Quarterly Review; this was a man of real genius; and, to my certain personal knowledge, he detested, from the bottom of his soul, the whole of the paper-money and borough-mongering system, and despised those by whom the system was

ADVICE TO YOUNG MEN AND WOMEN 245

carried on. But he had imaginary wants; he had been bred up in company with the rich and the extravagant: expensive indulgences had been made necessary to him by habit; and when, in the year 1798, or thereabouts, he had to choose between a bit of bacon, a scrag of mutton, and a lodging at ten shillings a week, on the one side, and made-dishes, wine, a fine house, and a footman, on the other side, he chose the latter. He became the servile Editor of CANNING's Anti-jacobin newspaper; and he, who had more wit and learning than all the rest of the writers put together, became the miserable tool in circulating their attacks upon every thing that was hostile to a system which he deplored and detested. But he secured the made-dishes, the wine, the footman and the coachman. A sinecure as *"clerk of the Foreign Estreats,"* gave him £329 a year, a double commissionership of the lottery gave him £600 or £700 more; and, at a later period, his Editorship of the Quarterly Review gave him perhaps as much more. He rolled in his carriage for several years; he fared sumptuously, he was buried at *Westminster Abbey,* of which his friend and formerly his brother pamphleteer in defence of Pitt was the *Dean*: and never is he to be heard of more! Mr. Gifford would have been full as happy, his health would have been better, his life longer, and his name would have lived for ages, if he could have turned to the bit of bacon and scrag of mutton in 1798; for his learning and talents were such, his reasonings so clear and conclusive, and his wit so pointed and keen, that his writings must have been generally read, must have been of long duration; and indeed must have enabled him (he being always a single man) to live in his latter days in as good style as that which he procured by becoming a sinecurist, a pensioner, and a *hack,* all which he was from the moment he lent himself to

WILLIAM COBBETT

the Quarterly Review. Think of the mortification of such a man, when he was called upon to justify the power-of-imprisonment bill in 1817! But, to go into particulars would be tedious: his life was a life of luxurious misery, than which a worse is not to be imagined.

* * * * * *

The things which you ought to desire in a wife are, 1. Chastity; 2. sobriety; 3. industry; 4. frugality; 5. cleanliness; 6. knowledge of domestic affairs; 7. good temper; 8. beauty.

* * * * * *

When I first saw my wife, she was *thirteen years old*, and I was within about a month of *twenty-one*. She was the daughter of a Serjeant of artillery, and I was the Serjeant-Major of a regiment of foot, both stationed in forts near the city of St. John in the Province of New-Brunswick. I sat in the room with her, for about an hour, in company with others, and I made up my mind that she was the very girl for me. That I thought her beautiful is certain, for that I had always said should be an indispensable qualification; but I saw in her what I deemed marks of that sobriety of *conduct* of which I have said so much, and which has been by far the greatest blessing of my life. It was now dead of winter, and, of course, the snow several feet deep on the ground, and the weather piercing cold. It was my habit, when I had done my morning's writing, to go out at break of day to take a walk on a hill at the foot of which our barracks lay. In about three mornings after I had first seen her, I had, by an invitation to breakfast with me, got up two young men to join me in my walk; and our road lay by the house of her father and mother. It was hardly light, but she was out on the snow, scrubbing out a washing-tub. "That's the girl for me," said I, when we had got out of her hearing.

ADVICE TO YOUNG MEN AND WOMEN 247

One of these young men came to England soon afterwards; and he, who keeps an inn in Yorkshire, came over to Preston, at the time of the election, to verify whether I were the same man. When he found that I was, he appeared surprised; but what was his surprise, when I told him, that those tall young men, whom he saw around me, were the *sons* of that pretty little girl that he and I saw scrubbing out the washing-tub on the snow in New-Brunswick in the morning.

From the day that I first spoke to her, I never had a thought of her ever being the wife of any other man, more than I had a thought of her being transformed into a chest of drawers; and I formed my resolution at once, to marry her as soon as we could get permission, and to get out of the army as soon as I could. So that this matter was, at once, settled as firmly as if written in the book of fate. At the end of about six months, my regiment, and I along with it, were removed to Frederickton, a distance of a *hundred miles,* up the river of St. John; and, which was worse, the artillery were expected to go off to England a year or two before our regiment! The artillery went, and she along with them; and now it was that I acted a part becoming a real and sensible lover. I was aware, that, when she got to that gay place, WOOLWICH, the house of her father and mother, necessarily visited by numerous persons not the most select, might become unpleasant to her, and I did not like besides, that she should continue to *work hard.* I had saved a *hundred and fifty guineas,* the earnings of my early hours, in writing for the paymaster, the quartermaster, and others, in addition to the savings of my own pay. *I sent her all my money,* before she sailed; and wrote to her to beg of her, if she found her home uncomfortable, to hire a lodging with respectable people: and, at any rate, not to spare the

248 WILLIAM COBBETT

money, by any means; but to buy herself good clothes, and to live without hard work, until I arrived in England; and I, in order to induce her to lay out the money, told her that I should get plenty more before I came home.

As the malignity of the devil would have it, we were kept abroad *two years longer* than our time, MR. PITT (England not being so tame then as she is now) having knocked up a dust with Spain about Nootka Sound. Oh, how I cursed Nootka Sound, and poor bawling Pitt too, I am afraid! At the end of *four years,* however, home I came; landed at Portsmouth, and got my discharge from the army by the great kindness of poor LORD EDWARD FITZGERALD, who was then the Major of my regiment. I found my little girl *a servant of all work* (and hard work it was), at *five pounds a year,* in the house of a Captain Brisac; and, without hardly saying a word about the matter, she put into my hands *the whole of my hundred and fifty guineas unbroken!*

Need I tell the reader what my feelings were? Need I tell kind-hearted English parents what effect this anecdote *must* have produced on the minds of our children? Need I attempt to describe what effect this example ought to have on every young woman who shall do me the honour to read this book? Admiration of her conduct, and self-gratulation on this indubitable proof of the soundness of my own judgment were now added to my love of her beautiful person.

* * * * * *

Beauty. Though I have reserved this to the last of the things to be desired in a wife, I by no means think it the last in point of importance. The less favoured part of the sex say, that "beauty is but *skin-deep*"; and this is very true; but, it is very *agreeable,* though, for all that. Pictures are only paint-deep, or pencil-deep;

ADVICE TO YOUNG MEN AND WOMEN 249

but we admire them, nevertheless. "Handsome is that handsome *does*," used to say to me an old man, who had marked me out for his not over handsome daughter. "Please your *eye* and plague your heart" is an adage that want of beauty invented, I dare say, more than a thousand years ago. These adages would say, if they had but the courage, that beauty is inconsistent with chastity, with sobriety of conduct, and with all the female virtues. The argument is, that beauty exposes the possessor *to greater temptation* than women not beautiful are exposed to; and that, *therefore,* their fall is more probable. Let us see a little how this matter stands.

It is certainly true, that pretty girls will have more, and more ardent, admirers than ugly ones; but, as to the *temptation* when in their unmarried state, there are few so very ugly as to be exposed to no *temptation* at all; and, which is the most likely to resist; she who has a choice of lovers, or she who if she let the occasion slip may never have it again? Which of the two is most likely to set a high value upon her reputation, she whom all beholders admire, or she who is admired, at best, by mere chance? And as to women in the married state, this argument assumes, that, when they fall, it is from their own vicious disposition; when the fact is, that, if you search the annals of conjugal infidelity, you will find, that, nine times out of ten, the *fault is in the husband.* It is his neglect, his flagrant disregard, his frosty indifference, his foul example; it is to these that, nine times out of ten, he owes the infidelity of his wife; and, if I were to say ninety-nine times out of a hundred, the facts, if verified, would, I am certain, bear me out. And whence this neglect, this disregard, this frosty indifference; whence this foul example? Because it is easy, in so many cases, to find some women more

beautiful than the wife. This is no justification for the husband to plead; for he has, with his eyes open, made a solemn contract: if he have not beauty enough to please him, he should have sought it in some other woman: if, as is frequently the case, he have preferred rank or money to beauty, he is an unprincipled man, if he do any thing to make her unhappy who has brought him the rank or the money. At any rate, as conjugal infidelity is, in so many cases; as it is *generally* caused by the want of affection and due attention in the husband, it follows, of course, that it must more frequently happen in the case of ugly than in that of handsome women.

In point of *dress,* nothing need be said to convince any reasonable man, that beautiful women will be less expensive in this respect than women of a contrary description. Experience teaches us, that ugly women are always the most studious about their dress and, if we had never observed upon the subject, *reason* would tell us, that it must be so. Few women are handsome without knowing it; and if they know that their features naturally attract admiration, will they desire to draw it off, and to fix it on lace and silks and jewels?

As to *manners* and *temper* there are certainly some handsome women who are conceited and arrogant; but, as they have all the best reasons in the world for being pleased with themselves, they afford you the best chance of general good humour; and this good humour is a very valuable commodity in the married state. Some that are called handsome, and that are such at the first glance, are dull, inanimate things, that might as well have been made of wax, or of wood. But, the truth is, that this is *not beauty,* for this is not to be found *only* in the *form* of the features, but in the movements of them also. Besides, here nature is very impartial; for

ADVICE TO YOUNG MEN AND WOMEN 251

she gives animation promiscuously to the handsome as well as to the ugly; and the want of this in the former is surely as bearable as in the latter.

But, the great use of female beauty, the great practical advantage of it is, that it naturally and unavoidably tends to *keep the husband in good humour with himself,* to make him, to use the dealer's phrase, *pleased with his bargain.* When old age approaches, and the parties have become endeared to each other by a long series of joint cares and interests, and when children have come and bound them together by the strongest ties that nature has in store; at this age the features and the person are of less consequence; but, in the *young days* of matrimony, when the roving eye of the bachelor is scarcely become steady in the head of the husband, it is dangerous for him to see, every time he stirs out, a face more captivating than that of the person to whom he is bound for life. Beauty is, in some degree, a matter of *taste*: what one man admires, another does not; and it is fortunate for us that it is thus. But still there are certain things that all men admire; and a husband is always pleased when he perceives that a portion, at least, of these things are in his own possession: he takes this possession as a *compliment to himself*: there must, he will think the world will believe, have been *some merit in him,* some charm, seen or unseen, to have caused him to be blessed with the acquisition.

* * * * * * *

The Province of New Brunswick, in North America, in which I passed my years from the age of eighteen to that of twenty-six, consists, in general, of heaps of rocks, in the interstices of which grow the pine, the spruce, and various sorts of fir trees, or, where the woods have been burnt down, the bushes of the rasp-

WILLIAM COBBETT

berry or those of the huckleberry. The province is cut asunder lengthwise, by a great river, called the St. John, about two hundred miles in length, and, at half way from the mouth full a mile wide. Into this main river run innumerable smaller rivers, there called *creeks*. On the sides of these creeks the land is, in places, clear of rocks; it is, in these places, generally good and productive; the trees that grow here are the birch, the maple, and others of the deciduous class; natural meadows here and there present themselves; and some of these spots far surpass in rural beauty any other that my eyes ever beheld; the creeks, abounding towards their sources in water-falls of endless variety, as well in form as in magnitude, and always teeming with fish, while water-fowl enliven their surface, and while wild-pigeons, of the gayest plumage, flutter, in thousands upon thousands, amongst the branches of the beautiful trees, which, sometimes, for miles together, form an arch over the creeks.

I, in one of my rambles in the woods, in which I took great delight, came to a spot at a very short distance from the source of one of these creeks. Here was every thing to delight the eye, and especially of one like me, who seem to have been born to love rural life, and trees and plants of all sorts. Here were about two hundred acres of natural meadow, interspersed with patches of maple-trees in various forms and of various extent; the creek (there about thirty miles from its point of joining the St. John) ran down the middle of the spot, which formed a sort of dish, the high and rocky hills rising all round it, except at the outlet of the creek, and these hills crowned with lofty pines: in the hills were the sources of the creek, the waters of which came down in cascades, for any one of which many a nobleman in England would, if he

ADVICE TO YOUNG MEN AND WOMEN 253

could transfer it, give a good slice of his fertile estate; and in the creek, at the foot of the cascades, there were, in the season, salmon the finest in the world, and so abundant, and so easily taken, as to be used for manuring the land.

If nature, in her very best humour, had made a spot for the express purpose of captivating me, she could not have exceeded the efforts which she had here made. But I found something here besides these rude works of nature; I found something in the fashioning of which *man* had had something to do. I found a large and well-built log dwelling house, standing (in the month of September) on the edge of a very good field of Indian Corn, by the side of which there was a piece of buck-wheat just then mowed. I found a homestead, and some very pretty cows. I found all the things by which an easy and happy farmer is surrounded: and I found still something besides all these; something that was destined to give me a great deal of pleasure and also a great deal of pain, both in their extreme degree; and both of which, in spite of the lapse of forty years, now make an attempt to rush back into my heart.

Partly from misinformation, and partly from miscalculation, I had lost my way; and, quite alone, but armed with my sword and a brace of pistols, to defend myself against the bears, I arrived at the log-house in the middle of a moonlight night, the hoar frost covering the trees and the grass. A stout and clamorous dog, kept off by the gleaming of my sword, waked the master of the house, who got up, received me with great hospitality, got me something to eat, and put me into a feather-bed, a thing that I had been a stranger to for some years. I, being very tired, had tried to pass the night in the woods, between the trunks of two

WILLIAM COBBETT

large trees, which had fallen side by side, and within a yard of each other. I had made a nest for myself of dry fern, and had made a covering by laying boughs of spruce across the trunk of the trees. But unable to sleep on account of the cold; becoming sick from the great quantity of water that I had drank during the heat of the day, and being, moreover, alarmed at the noise of the bears, and lest one of them should find me in a defenceless state, I had roused myself up, and had crept along as well as I could. So that no hero of eastern romance ever experienced a more enchanting change.

I had got into the house of one of those YANKEE LOYALISTS, who, at the close of the revolutionary war, (which, until it had succeeded, was called a rebellion) had accepted of grants of land in the King's Province of New Brunswick; and who, to the great honour of England, had been furnished with all the means of making new and comfortable settlements. I was suffered to sleep till breakfast time, when I found a table, the like of which I have since seen so many in the United States, loaded with good things. The master and the mistress of the house, aged about fifty, were like what an English farmer and his wife were half a century ago. There were two sons, tall and stout, who appeared to have come in from work, and the youngest of whom was about my age, then twenty-three. But there was *another member* of the family, aged nineteen, who (dressed according to the neat and simple fashion of New England, whence she had come with her parents five or six years before) had her long light-brown hair twisted nicely up, and fastened on the top of her head, in which head were a pair of lively blue eyes, associated with features of which that softness and that sweetness, so characteristic of American girls,

ADVICE TO YOUNG MEN AND WOMEN 255

were the predominant expressions, the whole being set
off by a complexion indicative of glowing health, and
forming, figure, movements, and all taken together, an
assemblage of beauties, far surpassing any that I had
ever seen but *once* in my life. That *once* was, too,
two years agone; and, in such a case and at such an
age, two years, two whole years, is a long, long while!
It was a space as long as the eleventh part of my then
life! Here was the *present* against the *absent*: here
was the power of the *eyes* pitted against that of the
memory: here were all the senses up in arms to subdue
the influence of the thoughts: here was vanity, here
was passion, here was the spot of all spots in the world,
and here were also the life, and the manners and the
habits and the pursuits that I delighted in: here was
every thing that imagination can conceive, united in a
conspiracy against the poor little brunette in England!
What, then, did I fall in love at once with this bouquet
of lilies and roses? Oh! by no means. I was, however,
so enchanted with *the place;* I so much enjoyed its
tranquillity, the shade of the maple trees, the business
of the farm, the sports of the water and of the woods,
that I stayed at it to the last possible minute, prom-
ising, at my departure, to come again as often as I
possibly could; a promise which I most punctually fulfilled.

Winter is the great season for jaunting and *dancing*
(called *frolicking*) in America. In this province the
river and the creeks were the only *roads* from settlement to settlement. In summer we travelled in *canoes;*
in winter in *sleighs* on the ice or snow. During more
than two years I spent all the time I could with my
Yankee friends: they were all fond of me: I talked
to them about country affairs, my evident delight in
which they took as a compliment to themselves: the

father and mother treated me as one of their children;
the sons as a brother; and the daughter, who was as
modest and as full of sensibility as she was beautiful,
in a way to which a chap much less sanguine than I
was would have given the tenderest interpretation;
which treatment I, especially in the last-mentioned
case, most cordially repaid.

It is when you meet in company with others of your
own age that you are, in love matters, put, most frequently, to the test, and exposed to detection. The
next door neighbour might, in that country, be ten
miles off. We used to have a frolic, sometimes at one
house and sometimes at another. Here, where female
eyes are very much on the alert, no secret can long be
kept; and very soon father, mother, brothers and the
whole neighbourhood looked upon the thing as certain,
not excepting herself, to whom I, however, had never
once even talked of marriage, and had never even told
her that I *loved* her. But I had a thousand times done
these by *implication*, taking into view the interpretation
that she would naturally put upon my looks, appellations and acts; and it was of this, that I had to
accuse myself. Yet I was not a *deceiver;* for my
affection for her was very great: I was uneasy if she
showed the slightest regard for any other young man: I
was unhappy if the smallest matter affected her health
and spirits: I quitted her in dejection, and returned to
her with eager delight: many a time, when I could get
leave but for a day, I paddled in a canoe two whole
succeeding nights, in order to pass the day with her.
If this was not love, it was first cousin to it; for as
to any *criminal* intention I no more thought of it, in
her case, than if she had been my sister. Many times
I put to myself the questions: "What am I at? Is not
this wrong? *Why do I go?*" But I still went.

ADVICE TO YOUNG MEN AND WOMEN 257

Then, farther in my excuse, my *prior engagement,* though carefully left unalluded to by both parties, was, in that thin population, and owing to the singular circumstances of it, and to the great talk that there always was about me, *perfectly well known* to her and all her family. It was a matter of so much notoriety and conversation in the Province, that GENERAL CARLETON (brother of the late Lord Dorchester), who was the Governor when I was there, when he, about fifteen years afterwards, did me the honour, on his return to England, to come and see me at my house in Duke Street, Westminster, asked before he went away, to see my *wife,* of whom *he had heard so much* before her marriage. So that here was no *deception* on my part: but still I ought not to have suffered even the most distant hope to be entertained by a person so innocent, so amiable, for whom I had so much affection and to whose heart I had no right to give a single twinge. I ought, from the very first, to have prevented the possibility of her ever feeling pain on my account. I was young, to be sure; but I was old enough to know what was my duty in this case, and I ought, dismissing my own feelings, to have had the resolution to perform it.

The *last parting* came; and now came my just punishment! The time was known to every body, and was irrevocably fixed; for I had to move with a regiment, and the embarkation of a regiment is an *epoch* in a thinly settled province. To describe this parting would be too painful even at this distant day, and with this frost of age upon my head. The kind and virtuous father came forty miles to see me just as I was going on board in the river. *His* looks and words I have never forgotten. As the vessel descended, she passed the mouth of *that creek* which I had so often

WILLIAM COBBETT

entered with delight; and though England, and all that England contained, were before me, I lost sight of this creek with an aching heart.

On what trifles run the great events in the life of man! If I had received a *cool* letter from my intended wife; if I had only heard a rumour of any thing from which fickleness in her might have been inferred; if I had found in her any, even the smallest, abatement of affection; if she had but let go any one of the hundred strings by which she held my heart; if any of these, never would the world have heard of me. Young as I was; able as I was as a soldier; proud as I was of the admiration and commendations of which I was the object; fond as I was, too, of the command, which, at so early an age, my rare conduct and great natural talents had given me; sanguine as was my mind, and brilliant as were my prospects: yet I had seen so much of the meannesses, the unjust partialities, the insolent pomposity, the disgusting dissipations of that way of life, that I was weary of it: I longed, exchanging my fine laced coat for the Yankee farmer's home-spun, to be where I should never behold the supple crouch of servility, and never hear the hectoring voice of authority, again; and, on the lonely banks of this branch covered creek, which contained (she out of the question) every thing congenial to my taste and dear to my heart, I, unapplauded, unfeared, unenvied and uncalumniated, should have lived and died.

LEIGH HUNT

CARLYLE in his *Reminiscences* ascribes to Leigh Hunt the eye of genius, and mingles with his compassion for Hunt's "hugger-mugger" domestic economy clear respect for his parts. Hunt was beloved of Shelley; he befriended and for a time was admired by Keats. He was thought well of by Byron until the unhappy Italian pilgrimage in which he was accompanied by Mrs. Hunt and the seven little Hunts. Lamb, Coleridge, and Hazlitt were among his many friends. These are notable names, evidence that there was more to the man than posterity can discern in his verse and prose. Only the admirable *Autobiography* would seem wholly to do him justice.

Both in his verse and prose he wrote, if not too much, at least with too facile a pen; for, despite an unerring eye for the genius of others and impeccable native taste, he seems not to have been rigorously critical of himself. The journalistic work which he began almost as a boy and continued with varying degrees of financial non-success throughout a long life was no doubt responsible for the superficiality which mars much of his prose. He was a dramatic critic and reviewer of books while scarcely out of his teens; a writer of editorials imprisoned for his radical opinions; a reformer feared by a corrupt and reactionary government. All this is to his credit as journalist and patriot but does not necessarily bespeak—indeed almost inevitably precludes—literary achievement of the very first order.

It is evident that he possessed charm. His friend-

259

ships and the kindly comments of many contemporaries attest the fact. The charm is manifest both in his prose and in his lighter—and better—verse. But the lightness and gaiety and good humor pall a little, like professional optimism. Good journalist that he was, he could turn all his experience, all his observations of life, whether profound or trivial, into copy. He could write a readable light essay on, literally, any topic whatsoever. But essays which are to endure must be weighted with deeper thought than he usually bestowed upon his; or if not thought, a truer sentiment, for his too often verges on sentimentality and is tinged with mawkishness.

Hunt was a genuine book lover, was widely, if superficially, read, and possessed an intuitive good taste for what was excellent. It is in his essays upon his books or those in which he displays his vast knowledge of literary anecdote and gossip that he seems to me best. Some, too, of his lighter observational essays upon types of people, such as that entitled "An Old Gentleman," are in the tradition of the character writers and their successors, Steele, Addison, and Goldsmith, and not unworthy of these masters. They ask good powers of observation and a light touch, both of which Hunt possessed. Yet the reader must here pick his way a little, for the essays of this class are uneven.

Much of Hunt's work, the question of its literary standing aside, is valuable for its record of contemporary life and customs, its gossip of the theater and of literary celebrities. Hunt will always hold a secure place as one of the lesser literary historians and annalists. Whoever would possess an intimate knowledge of the life of the first half of the nineteenth century will find in his work much which will instruct and please.

CRUELTY TO CHILDREN

[*Companion,* May 7, 1828]

READERS of newspapers are constantly being shocked with the unnatural conduct of parents towards their children. Some are detected in locking them up, and half-starving them: others tax them beyond their strength, and scourge them dreadfully for not bearing it: others take horrible dislikes to their children, and vex and torture them in every way they can think of, short of subjecting themselves to the gallows. In most cases the tyranny is of long duration before it is exposed. A whole neighbourhood are saddened by the cries of the poor victim, till they are obliged to rise up in self-defence, and bring the offender to justice. By this we may judge how many miseries are taking place, of which people have no suspicion; how many wretches have crimes of this sort, to account for the evil in their looks; and how many others, more criminal because more lying, go about in decent repute, while some oppressed and feeble relative, awfully patient, is awaiting in solitude the horror of the returning knock at the door.

It is sometimes alleged by offenders of this description, that the children have real faults, and are really provoking; that their conduct is very 'aggravating,' as the phrase is; and that 'nothing can mend them but blows,'—*which never do.* But whence come the faults of children? And how were they suffered to grow to such a height? Really,—setting aside these monsters of unpaternity,—parents are too apt to demand a great deal in their children, which they themselves do not possess. The child, on the mere will of the parents, and without any of their experience, is expected to have good sense, good temper, and heavens knows how many other good qualities; while the parents perhaps, not-

261

262 LEIGH HUNT

withstanding all the lessons they have received from
time and trouble, have little or nothing of any of them.
Above all, they forget that, in originating the bodies of
their children, they originate their minds and tempera-
ments; that a child is but a continuation of his father
and mother, or their fathers and mothers, and kindred;
that it is further modified, and made what it is, by education and bringing up; and that on all these accounts
the parents have no excuse for abusing and tormenting
it, unless with equal wisdom and a glorious impartiality
they should abuse and torment *themselves* in like manner
—scourge their own flesh, and condemn themselves to
a crust and a black hole. If a father were to give his
own sore legs a good flogging for inheriting ill humours
from his ancestors, he might with some show of reason
proceed to punish the continuation of them in those of
his child. If a cruel mother got into a handsome tub
of cold water, of a winter morning, and edified the
neighbours with the just and retributive shrieks which
she thence poured forth for a couple of hours, crying out
to her deceased 'mammy' that she would be a good
elderly woman in future, and not a scold and a reprobate, then she might, like a proper madwoman (for she
is but an improper one now), put her child into the tub
after her, and make it shriek out 'mammy' in its turn.

But let us do justice to all one's fellow creatures, not
forgetting these very 'aggravating' parents. To regard
even them as something infernal, and forget that they
as well as their children have become what they are
from circumstances over which they had no control, is
to fall into their own error, and forget our common
humanity. We believe that the very worst of these
domestic tyrants (and it is an awful lesson for the best
of them) would have been shocked in early life, if they
could have been shown, in a magic glass, what sort of

CRUELTY TO CHILDREN

beings they would become. Suppose one of them a young man, blooming with health, and not ill-natured, but subject to fits of sulkiness or passion, and not very wise; and suppose that in this glass he sees an old ill-looking fellow, scowling, violent, outrageous, tormenting with a bloody scourge his own child, who is meagre, squalid, and half starved:—'Good God!' he would cry, 'can that be myself? Can that be my arm, and my face? And that my own poor little child? There *are* devils then, and I am doomed to be one of them.' And the tears would pour into his eyes.—No; not so, poor wretch: thou art no devil; there is no such thing as devilism, or pure malice for its own sake; the very cruellest actions are committed to relieve the cravings of their own want of excitement, more than to hurt another. But though no devil, you are very ignorant, and are not aware of this. The energies of the universe, being on a great scale, are liable, in their progress from worse to better, to great roughness in the working, and appalling sounds of discord. The wiser you become, the more you diminish this jarring, and tend to produce that amelioration. Learn this, and be neither appalled nor appalling; or if your reflections do not travel so far, and you are in no danger of continuing your evil course by the subtle desperations of superstition, be content to know, that nobody ill-treats another who is satisfied with his own conduct. If the case were otherwise, it would be worse; for you would not have the excuse, even of a necessity for relieving your own sensations. But it never *is* so, sophisticate about it as you may. The very pains you take to reconcile yourself *to* yourself, may show you how much need you have of doing so. It is nothing else which makes the silliest little child sulky; and the same folly makes the grown man a tyrant. When you begin to ill-treat your child, you begin to

punish in him your own faults; and you most likely do nothing but beat them in upon him with every stroke of the scourge: for why should he be wiser than you? Why should he be able to throw off the ill-humours, of which your greater energies cannot get rid?

These thoughts we address to those who are worthy of them; and who, not being tyrants, may yet become such, for want of reflection. Vulgar offenders can be mended only with the whole progress of society, and the advancement of education. There is one thing we must not omit to say; which is, that the best parents are apt to expect too much of their children, and to forget how much error they may have committed in the course of bringing them up. Nobody is in fault, in a criminal sense. Children have their excuses; and parents have their excuses; but the wiser any of us become, the less we exact from others, and the more we do to deserve their regard. The great art of being a good parent consists in setting a good example, and in maintaining that union of dispassionate firmness with habitual good-humour, which a child never *thinks* of treating with disrespect.

We have here been speaking principally of the behaviour of parents to *little children*. When violent disputes take place between parents and children grown up,—young men and women,—there are generally great faults on both sides; though, for an obvious reason, the parent, who has had the training and formation of the other, is likely to be most in the wrong. But unhappily, very excellent people may sometimes find themselves hampered in a calamity of this nature; and out of that sort of weakness, which is so confounded with strength, turn their very sense of being in the right to the same hostile and implacable purpose, as if it were the reverse. We can only say, that from all we have seen in the

THE OLD GENTLEMAN 265

world, and indeed from the whole experience of mankind, they who are conscious of being right, are the first to make a movement towards reconciliation, let the cause of quarrel be what it may; and that there is no surer method, in the eyes of any who know what human nature is, both to sustain the real dignity of the right side, and to amend the wrong one. To kind-hearted fathers in general, who have the misfortune to get into a dilemma of this sort, we would recommend the pathetic story of a French general, who was observed after the death of his son in battle, never to hold up his head. He said to a friend, 'My boy was used to think me severe; and he had too much reason to do so. He did not know how I loved him at the bottom of my heart; *and it is now too late.*'

THE OLD GENTLEMAN

[*Indicator,* Feb. 2, 1820]

Our Old Gentleman, in order to be exclusively himself, must be either a widower or a bachelor. Suppose the former. We do not mention his precise age, which would be invidious;—nor whether he wears his own hair or a wig; which would be wanting in universality. If a wig, it is a compromise between the more modern scratch and the departed glory of the toupee. If his own hair, it is white, in spite of his favourite grandson, who used to get on the chair behind him, and pull the silver hairs out, ten years ago. If he is bald at top, the hairdresser, hovering and breathing about him like a second youth, takes care to give the bald place as much powder as the covered; in order that he may convey to the sensorium within a pleasing indistinctness of idea respecting the exact limits of skin and hair. He is very clean and neat; and in warm weather, is proud of open-

LEIGH HUNT

ing his waistcoat half way down, and letting so much of his frill be seen; in order to show his hardiness as well as taste. His watch and shirt-buttons are of the best; and he does not care if he has two rings on a finger. If his watch ever failed him at the club or coffee-house, he would take a walk every day to the nearest clock of good character, purely to keep it right. He has a cane at home, but seldom uses it, on finding it out of fashion with his elderly juniors. He has a small cocked hat for gala days, which he lifts higher from his head than the round one, when made a bow to. In his pockets are two handkerchiefs (one for the neck at night-time), his spectacles, and his pocket-book. The pocket-book, among other things, contains a receipt for a cough, and some verses cut out of an odd sheet of an old magazine, on the lovely Duchess of A., beginning—

When beauteous Mira walks the plain.

He intends this for a common-place book which he keeps, consisting of passages in verse and prose cut out of newspapers and magazines, and pasted in columns; some of them rather gay. His principal other books are Shakespeare's *Plays* and Milton's *Paradise Lost;* the *Spectator,* the *History of England;* the works of Lady M. W. Montague, Pope, and Churchill; Middleton's *Geography, The Gentleman's Magazine;* Sir John Sinclair on Longevity; several plays with portraits in character; *Account of Elizabeth Canning, Memoirs of George Ann Bellamy, Poetical Amusements at Bath-Easton,* Blair's *Works, Elegant Extracts; Junius* as originally published; a few pamphlets on the American War and Lord George Gordon, &c. and one on the French Revolution. In his sitting rooms are some engravings from Hogarth and Sir Joshua; an engraved portrait of the Marquis of Granby; ditto of M. le Comte

THE OLD GENTLEMAN 267

de Grasse surrendering to Admiral Rodney; a humorous piece after Penny; and a portrait of himself, painted by Sir Joshua. His wife's portrait is in his chamber, looking upon his bed. She is a little girl, stepping forward with a smile and a pointed toe, as if going to dance. He lost her when she was sixty.

The Old Gentleman is an early riser, because he intends to live at least twenty years longer. He continues to take tea for breakfast, in spite of what is said against its nervous effects; having been satisfied on that point some years ago by Dr. Johnson's criticism on Hanway, and a great liking for tea previously. His china cups and saucers have been broken since his wife's death, all but one, which is religiously kept for his use. He passes his morning in walking or riding, looking in at auctions, looking after his India bonds or some such money securities, furthering some subscription set on foot by his excellent friend Sir John, or cheapening a new old print for his portfolio. He also hears of the newspapers; not caring to see them till after dinner at the coffee-house. He may also cheapen a fish or so; the fishmonger soliciting his doubting eye as he passes, with a profound bow of recognition. He eats a pear before dinner.

His dinner at the coffee-house is served up to him at the accustomed hour, in the old accustomed way, and by the accustomed waiter. If William did not bring it, the fish would be sure to be stale, and the flesh new. He eats no tart; or if he ventures on a little, takes cheese with it. You might as soon attempt to persuade him out of his senses, as that cheese is not good for digestion. He takes port; and if he has drank more than usual, and in a more private place, may be induced by some respectful inquiries respecting the old style of

music, to sing a song composed by Mr. Oswald or Mr. Lampe, such as—

> Chloe, by that borrowed kiss,

or

> Come, gentle god of soft repose;

or his wife's favourite ballad beginning—

> At Upton on the Hill
> There lived a happy pair.

Of course, no such exploit can take place in the coffee-room; but he will canvass the theory of that matter there with you, or discuss the weather, or the markets, or the theatres, or the merits of 'my Lord North' or 'my Lord Rockingham'; for he rarely says simply, lord; it is generally 'my lord,' trippingly and genteelly off the tongue. If alone after dinner, his great delight is the newspaper; which he prepares to read by wiping his spectacles, carefully adjusting them on his eyes, and drawing the candle close to him, so as to stand sideways betwixt his ocular aim and the small type. He then holds the paper at arm's length, and dropping his eyelids half down and his mouth half open, takes cognizance of the day's information. If he leaves off, it is only when the door is opened by a new-comer, or when he suspects somebody is over-anxious to get the paper out of his hand. On these occasions, he gives an important hem! or so; and resumes.

In the evening, our Old Gentleman is fond of going to the theatre, or of having a game of cards. If he enjoys the latter at his own house or lodgings, he likes to play with some friends whom he has known for many years; but an elderly stranger may be introduced, if quiet and scientific; and the privilege is extended to younger men of letters; who, if ill players, are good losers. Not that he is a miser; but to win money at cards is like proving

THE OLD GENTLEMAN 269

his victory by getting the baggage; and to win of a younger man is a substitute for his not being able to beat him at rackets. He breaks up early, whether at home or abroad.

At the theatre, he likes a front row in the pit. He comes early, if he can do so without getting into a squeeze, and sits patiently waiting for the drawing up of the curtain, with his hands placidly lying one over the other on the top of his stick. He generously admires some of the best performers, but thinks them far inferior to Garrick, Woodward, and Clive. During splendid scenes, he is anxious that the little boy should see.

He has been induced to look in at Vauxhall again, but likes it still less than he did years back, and cannot bear it in comparison with Ranelagh. He thinks everything looks poor, flaring, and jaded. 'Ah!' says he, with a sort of triumphant sigh, 'Ranelagh was a noble place! Such taste, such elegance, such beauty! There was the Duchess of A., the finest woman in England, Sir; and Mrs. L., a mighty fine creature; and Lady Susan what's her name, that had that unfortunate affair with Sir Charles. Sir, they came swimming by you like the swans.'

The Old Gentleman is very particular in having his slippers ready for him at the fire, when he comes home. He is also extremely choice in his snuff, and delights to get a fresh boxful in Tavistock Street, in his way to the theatre. His box is a curiosity from India. He calls favourite young ladies by their Christian names, however slightly acquainted with them; and has a privilege also of saluting all brides, mothers, and indeed every species of lady on the least holiday occasion. If the husband, for instance, has met with a piece of luck, he instantly moves forward, and gravely kisses the wife on

the cheek. The wife then says, 'My niece, Sir, from the country'; and he kisses the niece. The niece, seeing her cousin biting her lips at the joke, says, 'My cousin Harriet, Sir'; and he kisses the cousin. He never recollects such weather, except during the Great Frost, or when he rode down with Jack Skrimshire to Newmarket. He grows young again in his little grandchildren, especially the one which he thinks most like himself; which is the handsomest. Yet he likes best perhaps the one most resembling his wife; and will sit with him on his lap, holding his hand in silence, for a quarter of an hour together. He plays most tricks with the former, and makes him sneeze. He asks little boys in general who was the father of Zebedee's children. If his grandsons are at school, he often goes to see them; and makes them blush by telling the master or the upper-scholars, that they are fine boys, and of a precocious genius. He is much struck when an old acquaintance dies, but adds that he lived too fast; and that poor Bob was a sad dog in his youth; 'a very sad dog, Sir, mightily set upon a short life and a merry one.'

When he gets very old indeed, he will sit for whole evenings, and say little or nothing; but informs you, that there is Mrs. Jones (the housekeeper),—'*She'll* talk.'

COLOUR

[*London Journal,* August 29, 1835]

In this beloved, beautiful, but sometimes foggy, and too often not very brilliant country of ours, we are not fond enough of *colours*,—not fond enough of a beauty, of which Nature herself is evidently *very fond,* and with which, like all the rest of her beauties, it is the business of civilized man to adorn and improve his own well-being. The summer season is a good time for becoming

COLOUR 271

acquainted with them, for it is then we see them best, and may acquire a relish for them against the insipidity of winter. We remember a dyer in Genoa, who used to hang out his silks upon a high wall opposite his shop, where they shone with such lustre under the blue sky (we particularly remember some yellow ones) that it was a treat to pass that way. You hailed them at a distance, like

> another sun
> Risen at noonday;

or as if Nature herself had been making some araperies out of buttercups, and had just presented the world with the phenomenon. It is the blue sky and clear air of their native land which have made the Italian painters so famous for colouring; and Rubens and Watteau, likewise men, saw the good of transferring the beauty to the less fortunate climate of Flanders. One of the first things that attracted our notice in Italy was a red cap on the head of a boatman. In England, where nobody else wears such a cap, we should have thought of a butcher; in Italy the sky set it off to such advantage, that it reminded us of a scarlet bud.

The Puritans, who did us a great deal of good, helped to do this harm for us. They degraded material beauty and gladness, as if essentially hostile to what was spiritually estimable; whereas the desirable thing is to show the compatibility of both, and vindicate the hues of the creation. Thus the finest colours in men's dresses have at last come almost exclusively to livery footmen and soldiers. A soldier's wife, or a market-woman, is the only female that ventures to wear a scarlet cloak; and we have a favourite epithet of vituperation, *gaudy,* which we bestow upon all colours that do not suit our melancholy. It is sheer want of heart and animal

spirits. We were not always so. Puritanism, and wars, and debts, and the Dutch succession, and false ideas of utility, have all conspired to take gladness out of our eyesight, as well as jollity out of our pockets. We shall recover a better taste, and we trust exhibit it to better advantage than before; but we must begin by having faith in as many good things as possible, and not think ill of any one of Heaven's means of making us cheerful, because in itself it is cheerful. 'If a merry meeting is to be wished,' says the man in Shakespeare, 'may God prohibit it.' So, the more obviously cheerful and desirable anything is, the more we seem to beg the question in its disfavour. Reds, and yellows, and bright blues are 'gaudy'; we must have nothing but browns, and blacks, and drab-colour, or stone. Earth is not of this opinion; nor the heavens either. Gardens do not think so; nor the fields, nor the skies, nor the mountains, nor dawn, nor sunset, nor light itself, which is made of colours, and holds them always ready in its crystal quiver, to shoot forth and divide into loveliness. The beautiful attracts the beautiful. Colours find homes of colour. To red go the red rays, and to purple the purple. The rainbow reads its beauteous lecture in the clouds, showing the sweet division of the hues; and the mechanical 'philosopher,' as he calls himself, smiles with an air of superiority, and thinks he knows all about it, because the division is made.

The little child, like the real philosopher, *knows more*, for his 'heart leaps up,' and he acknowledges a glad mystery. He feels the immensity of what he does *not* know; and though the purely mechanical-minded man admits that such immensity exists with regard to himself, he does not feel it as the child or the wiser man does, and therefore he does not truly perceive—does not thoroughly take it into his consciousness. He talks and

COLOUR

acts as if he had come to the extent of his knowledge—and he has so. But beyond the dry line of knowledge lies beauty, and all of which is beautiful in hope, and exalting in imagination.

We feel as if there were a moral as well as material beauty in colour,—an inherent gladness,—an intention on the part of Nature to share with us a pleasure felt by herself. Colours are the smiles of Nature. When they are extremely smiling, and break forth into other beauty besides, they are her laughs, as in the flowers. The 'laughing flowers,' says the poet; and it is the business of the poet to feel truths beyond the proof of the mechanician. Nature, at all events, humanly speaking, is manifestly very fond of colour, *for she has made nothing without it*. Her skies are blue; her fields green; her waters vary with her skies; her animals, minerals, vegetables, are all coloured. She paints a great many of them in apparently superfluous hues, as if to show the dullest eye how she loves colour. The pride of the peacock, or some stately exhibition of a quality very like pride, is a singular matter of fact, evidently connected with it. Youthful beauty in the human being is partly made up of it. One of the three great arts with which Providence has adorned and humanized the mind—Painting—is founded upon the love and imitation of it. And the magnificence of empire can find nothing more precious, either to possess or to be proud of wearing, than

> Fiery opals, sapphires, amethysts,
> Jacinths, hard topaz, grass-green emeralds,
> Beauteous rubies, sparkling diamonds,
> And seld-seen costly stones of so great price,
> As one of them, indifferently rated,
> May serve in peril of calamity
> To ransom great kings from captivity.

A CAT BY THE FIRE

[*London Journal*, Nov. 26, 1834]

A BLAZING fire, a warm rug, candles lit and curtains drawn, the kettle on for tea (if rich, you may have a silver kettle, and so partake the pleasures of the poor), and finally, the cat before you, attracting your attention,—it is a scene which everybody likes unless he has a morbid aversion to cats; which is not common. There are some nice inquirers, it is true, who are apt to make uneasy comparisons of cats with dogs,—to say they are not so loving, that they prefer the house to the man, &c. But agreeably to the good old maxim, that 'comparisons are odious,' our readers, we hope, will continue to like what is likeable in anything, for its own sake, without trying to render it unlikeable from its inferiority to something else,—a process by which we might ingeniously contrive to put soot into every dish that is set before us, and to reject one thing after another, till we were pleased with nothing. Here is a good fireside, and a cat to it; and it would be our own fault, if, in removing to another house and another fireside, we did not take care that the cat removed with us. Cats cannot look to the moving of goods, as men do. If we would have creatures considerate towards us, we must be so towards them. It is not to be expected of everybody, quadruped or biped, that they should stick to us in spite of our want of merit, like a dog or a benevolent sage. Besides, stories have been told of cats very much to the credit of their benignity; such as their following a master about like a dog, waiting at a gentleman's door to thank him for some obligation over-night, &c. And our readers may remember the history of the famous Arabian Godolphin, upon whose

A CAT BY THE FIRE

275

grave a cat that had lived with him in the stable, went and stretched itself, and died.

The cat purrs, as if it applauded our consideration,— and gently moves its tail. What an odd expression of the power to be irritable and the will to be pleased there is in its face, as it looks up at us. We must own, that we do not prefer a cat in the act of purring, or of looking in that manner. It reminds us of the sort of smile, or *simmer* (*simper* is too weak and fleeting a word) that is apt to be in the faces of irritable people, when they are pleased to be in a state of satisfaction. We prefer, for a general expression, the cat in a quiet unpretending state, and the human countenance with a look indicative of habitual grace and composure, as if it were not necessary to take any violent steps to prove its amiability,—the 'smile without a smile,' as the poet beautifully calls it.*

Furthermore (in order to get rid at once of all that may be objected to poor Pussy, as boys at school get down their bad dumpling as fast as possible, before the meat comes) we own we have an objection to the way in which a cat sports with a mouse before she kills it, tossing and jerking it about like a ball, and letting it go, in order to pounce upon it with the greater relish. And yet what right have we to apply human measures of cruelty to the inferior reflectability of a cat? Perhaps she has no idea of the mouse's being alive, in the sense that we have,—most likely she looks upon it as a pleasant movable toy, made to be eaten,—a sort of lively pudding, that oddly jumps hither and thither. It would be hard to beat into the head of a country squire, of the old class, that there is any cruelty in hunting a hare; and most assuredly it would be still harder to beat mouse-sparing into the head of a cat. You

* Knowles, in *The Beggar of Bethnal Green*.

might read the most pungent essay on the subject into her ear, and she would only sneeze at it.

As to the unnatural cruelties, which we sometimes read of, committed by cats upon their offspring, they are exceptions to the common and beautiful rules of nature, and accordingly we have nothing to do with them. They are traceable to some unnatural circumstances of breeding or position. Enormities as monstrous are to be found among human beings, and argue nothing against the general character of the species. Even dogs are not always immaculate; and sages have made slips. Dr. Franklin cut off his son with a shilling, for differing with him in politics.

But cats resemble tigers? They are tigers in miniature? Well,—and very pretty miniatures they are. And what has the tiger himself done, that he has not a right to his dinner, as well as Jones? A tiger treats a man much as a cat does a mouse;—granted; but we have no reason to suppose that he is aware of the man's sufferings, or means anything but to satisfy his hunger; and what have the butcher and poulterer been about meanwhile? The tiger, it is true, lays about him a little superfluously sometimes, when he gets into a sheepfold, and kills more than he eats; but does not the Squire or the Marquis do pretty much like him in the month of September? Nay, do we not hear of venerable judges, that would not hurt a fly, going about in that refreshing month, seeking whom they may lame? See the effect of habit and education! And you can educate the tiger in no other way than by attending to his stomach. Fill that, and he will want no men to eat, probably not even to lame. On the other hand, deprive Jones of his dinner for a day or two, and see what a state he will be in, especially if he is by nature irascible. Nay, keep him from it for half an hour, and observe the tiger

A CAT BY THE FIRE

propensities of his stomach and fingers,—how worthy of killing he thinks the cook, and what boxes of the ear he feels inclined to give the footboy.

Animals, by the nature of things, in their present state, dispose of one another into their respective stomachs, without any ill-will on any side. They keep down the several populations of their neighbours, till the time may come when superfluous population of any kind need not exist, and predatory appearances may vanish from the earth, as the wolves have done from England. But whether they may or not, is not a question by a hundred times so important to moral inquirers as into the possibilities of human education and the nonsense of ill-will. Show the nonsensity of that, and we may all get our dinners as jovially as we can, sure of these three undoubted facts,—that life is long, death short, and the world beautiful. And so we bring our thoughts back again to the fireside, and look at the cat.

Poor Pussy! she looks up at us again, as if she thanked us for those vindications of dinner; and symbolically gives a twist of a yawn, and a lick to her whiskers. Now she proceeds to clean herself all over, having a just sense of the demands of her elegant person,—beginning judiciously with her paws, and fetching amazing tongues at her hind-hips. Anon, she scratches her neck with a foot of rapid delight, leaning her head towards it, and shutting her eyes, half to accommodate the action of the skin, and half to enjoy the luxury. She then rewards her paws with a few more touches;—look at the action of her head and neck, how pleasing it is, the ears pointed forward, and the neck gently arching to and fro. Finally she gives a sneeze, and another twist of mouth and whiskers, and then, curl-

ing her tail towards her front claws, settles herself on her hind quarters, in an attitude of bland meditation.

What does she think of?—Of her saucer of milk at breakfast? or of the thump she got yesterday in the kitchen, for stealing the meat? or of her own meat, the Tartar's dish, noble horse-flesh? or of her friend the cat next door, the most impassioned of serenaders? or of her little ones, some of whom are now large, and all of them gone? Is *that* among her recollections when she looks pensive? Does she taste of the noble prerogative sorrows of man?

She is a sprightly cat, hardly past her youth; so happening to move the fringe of the rug a little with our foot, she darts out a paw, and begins plucking it and inquiring into the matter, as if it were a challenge to play, or something lively enough to be eaten. What a graceful action of that foot of hers, between delicacy and petulance,—combining something of a thrust out, a beat, and a scratch. There seems even something of a little bit of fear in it, as if just enough to provoke her courage, and give her the excitement of a sense of hazard. We remember being much amused with seeing a kitten manifestly making a series of experiments upon the patience of its mother,—trying how far the latter would put up with positive bites and thumps. The kitten ran at her every moment, gave her a knock or a bite of the tail; and then ran back again, to recommence the assault. The mother sat looking at her, as if betwixt tolerance and admiration, to see how far the spirit of the family was inherited or improved by her sprightly offspring. At length, however, the 'little Pickle' presumed too far, and the mother, lifting up her paw, and meeting her at the very nick of the moment, gave her one of the most unsophisticated boxes of the ear we ever beheld. It sent her rolling half over

A CAT BY THE FIRE

the room, and made her come to a most ludicrous pause, with the oddest little look of premature and wincing meditation.

That lapping of the milk out of the saucer is what one's human thirst cannot sympathize with. It seems as if there could be no satisfaction in such a series of atoms of drink. Yet the saucer is soon emptied; and there is a refreshment to one's ears in that sound of plashing with which the action is accompanied, and which seems indicative of a like comfort to Pussy's mouth. Her tongue is thin, and can make a spoon of itself. This, however, is common to other quadrupeds with the cat, and does not, therefore, more particularly belong to our feline consideration. Not so the electricity of its coat, which gives out sparks under the hand; its passion for the herb valerian (did the reader ever see one roll in it? it is a mad sight) and other singular delicacies of nature, among which perhaps is to be reckoned its taste for fish, a creature with whose element it has so little to do, that it is supposed even to abhor it; though lately we read somewhere of a swimming cat, that used to fish for itself. And this reminds us of an exquisite anecdote of dear, dogmatic, diseased, thoughtful, surly, charitable Johnson, who would go out of doors himself, and buy oysters for his cat, because his black servant was too proud to do it! Not that we condemn the black, in those enslaving, unliberating days. He had a right to the mistake, though we should have thought better of him had he seen farther, and subjected his pride to affection for such a master. But Johnson's true practical delicacy in the matter is beautiful. Be assured that he thought nothing of 'condescension' in it, or of being eccentric. He was singular in some things, because he could not help it. But he hated eccentricity. No: in his best moments he felt

LEIGH HUNT

himself simply to be a man, and a good man too, though a frail,—one that in virtue as well as humility, and in a knowledge of his ignorance as well as his wisdom, was desirous of being a Christian philosopher; and accordingly he went out, and bought food for his hungry cat, because his poor negro was too proud to do it, and there was nobody else in the way whom he had a right to ask. What must anybody that saw him have thought, as he turned up Bolt Court! But doubtless he went as secretly as possible,—that is to say if he considered the thing at all. His friend Garrick could not have done as much! He was too grand, on the great 'stage' of life. Goldsmith could; but he would hardly have thought of it. Beauclerc might; but he would have thought it necessary to excuse it with a jest or a wager, or some such thing. Sir Joshua Reynolds, with his fashionable, fine-lady-painting hand, would certainly have shrunk from it. Burke would have reasoned himself into its propriety, but he would have reasoned himself out again. Gibbon! Imagine its being put into the head of Gibbon!! He and his bag-wig would have started with all the horror of a gentleman-usher; and he would have rung the bell for the cook's-deputy's-under-assistant-errand-boy.

Cats at firesides live luxuriously, and are the picture of comfort; but lest they should not bear their portion of trouble in this world, they have the drawbacks of being liable to be shut out of doors on cold nights, beatings from the 'aggravated' cooks, over-pettings of children (how should we like to be squeezed and pulled about in that manner by some great patronizing giants?), and last, not least, horrible, merciless tramples of unconscious human feet and unfeeling legs of chairs. Elegance, comfort, and security seem the order of the day on all sides, and you are going to sit down to dinner, or to music, or to take tea, when all of a sudden the cat

MY BOOKS

gives a squall as if she was mashed; and you are not sure that the fact is otherwise. Yet she gets in the way again, as before; and dares all the feet and mahogany in the room. Beautiful present sufficingness of a cat's imagination! Confined to the snug circle of her own sides, and the two next inches of rug or carpet.

MY BOOKS

[*Literary Examiner,* July 5 and 12, 1823]

SITTING, last winter, among my books, and walled round with all the comfort and protection which they and my fireside could afford me; to wit, a table of high-piled books at my back, my writing-desk on one side of me, some shelves on the other, and the feeling of the warm fire at my feet; I began to consider how I loved the authors of those books: how I loved them, too, not only for the imaginative pleasures they afforded me, but for their making me love the very books themselves, and delight to be in contact with them. I looked sideways at my Spenser, my Theocritus, and my *Arabian Nights;* then above them at my Italian poets; then behind me at my Dryden and Pope, my romances, and my Boccaccio; then on my left side at my Chaucer, who lay on a writing-desk; and thought how natural it was in C[harles] L[amb] to give a kiss to an old folio, as I once saw him do to Chapman's *Homer.* At the same time I wondered how he could sit in that front room of his with nothing but a few unfeeling tables and chairs, or at best a few engravings in trim frames, instead of putting a couple of arm-chairs into the backroom with the books in it, where there is but one window. Would I were there, with both the chairs properly filled, and one or two more besides! 'We had talk,

Sir,'—the only talk capable of making one forget the books.

Good God! I could cry like one of the Children in the Wood to think how far I and mine are from home; but this would not be 'decent or manly'; so I smile instead, and am philosophical enough to make your heart ache. Besides, I shall love the country I am in more and more, and on the very account for which it angers me at present.

This is confessing great pain in the midst of my books. I own it; and yet I feel all the pleasure in them which I have expressed.

Take me, my book-shelves, to your arms,
And shield me from the ills of life.

No disparagement to the arms of Stella; but in neither case is pain a reason why we should not have a high enjoyment of the pleasure.

I entrench myself in my books equally against sorrow and the weather. If the wind comes through a passage I look about to see how I can fence it off by a better disposition of my movables; if a melancholy thought is importunate, I give another glance at my Spenser. When I speak of being in contact with my books, I mean it literally. I like to lean my head against them. Living in a southern climate, though in a part sufficiently northern to feel the winter, I was obliged, during that season, to take some of the books out of the study, and hang them up near the fireplace in the sitting-room, which is the only room that has such a convenience. I therefore walled myself in, as well as I could, in the manner above-mentioned. I took a walk every day, to the astonishment of the Genoese, who used to huddle against a bit of sunny wall, like flies on a chimney-piece; but I did this only that

MY BOOKS

I might so much the more enjoy my *English* evening. The fire was a wood fire instead of a coal; but I imagined myself in the country. I remembered at the very worst, that one end of my native land was not nearer the other than England is to Italy.

While writing this article I am in my study again. Like the rooms in all houses in this country which are not hovels, it is handsome and ornamented. On one side it looks towards a garden and the mountains; on another, to the mountains and the sea. What signifies all this? I turn my back upon the sea; I shut up even one of the side windows looking upon the mountains, and retain no prospect but that of the trees. On the right and left of me are book-shelves; a bookcase is affectionately open in front of me; and thus kindly enclosed with my books and the green leaves, I write. If all this is too luxurious and effeminate, of all luxuries it is the one that leaves you the most strength. And this is to be said for scholarship in general. It unfits a man for activity, for his bodily part in the world; but it often doubles both the power and the sense of his mental duties; and with much indignation against his body, and more against those who tyrannize over the intellectual claims of mankind, the man of letters, like the magician of old, is prepared 'to play the devil' with the great men of this world, in a style that astonishes both the sword and the toga.

I do not like this fine large study. I like elegance. I like room to breathe in, and even walk about, when I want to breathe and walk about. I like a great library next my study; but for the study itself, give me a small snug place, almost entirely walled with books. There should be only one window in it, looking upon trees. Some prefer a place with few, or no books at all—nothing but a chair or a table, like Epictetus; but

I should say that these were philosophers, not lovers of books, if I did not recollect that Montaigne was both. He had a study in a round tower, walled as aforesaid. It is true, one forgets one's books while writing—at least they say so. For my part, I think I have them in a sort of sidelong mind's eye; like a second thought, which is none—like a waterfall, or a whispering wind.

I dislike a grand library to study in. I mean an immense apartment, with books all in Museum order, especially wire-safed. I say nothing against the Museum itself, or public libraries. They are capital places to go to, but not to sit in; and talking of this, I hate to read in public, and in strange company. The jealous silence; the dissatisfied looks of the messengers; the inability to help yourself; the not knowing whether you really ought to trouble the messengers, much less the Gentleman in black, or brown, who is, perhaps, half a trustee; with a variety of other jarrings between privacy and publicity, prevent one's settling heartily to work. They say 'they manage these things better in France'; and I dare say they do; but I think I should feel still more *distrait* in France, in spite of the benevolence of the servitors, and the generous profusion of pen, ink, and paper. I should feel as if I were doing nothing but interchanging amenities with polite writers.

A grand private library, which the master of the house also makes his study, never looks to me like a real place of books, much less of authorship. I cannot take kindly to it. It is certainly not out of envy; for three parts of the books are generally trash, and I can seldom think of the rest and the proprietor together. It reminds me of a fine gentleman, of a collector, of a patron, of Gil Blas and the Marquis of Marialva; of anything but genius and comfort. I have a particular

MY BOOKS

hatred of a round table (not *the* Round Table, for that was a dining one) covered and irradiated with books, and never met with one in the house of a clever man but once. It is the reverse of Montaigne's Round Tower. Instead of bringing the books around you, they all seem turning another way, and eluding your hands.

Conscious of my propriety and comfort in these matters, I take an interest in the bookcases as well as the books of my friends. I long to meddle, and dispose them after my own notions. When they see this confession, they will acknowledge the virtue I have practised. I believe I did mention his book-room to C. L., and I think he told me that he often sat there when alone. It would be hard not to believe him. His library, though not abounding in Greek or Latin (which are the only things to help some persons to an idea of literature), is anything but superficial. The depths of philosophy and poetry are there, the innermost passages of the human heart. It has some Latin too. It has also a handsome contempt for appearance. It looks like what it is, a selection made at precious intervals from the book-stalls;—now a Chaucer at nine and two-pence; now a Montaigne or a Sir Thomas Browne at two shillings; now a Jeremy Taylor; a Spinoza; an old English Dramatist, Prior, and Sir Philip Sidney; and the books are 'neat as imported.' The very perusal of the backs is a 'discipline of humanity.' There Mr. Southey takes his place again with an old Radical friend: there Jeremy Collier is at peace with Dryden: there the lion, Martin Luther, lies down with the Quaker lamb, Sewell: there Guzman de Alfarache thinks himself fit company for Sir Charles Grandison, and has his claims admitted. Even the 'high fantastical' Duchess of Newcastle, with her laurel on her head, is

286 LEIGH HUNT

received with grave honours, and not the less for declining to trouble herself with the constitutions of her maids. There is an approach to the library of W. C., who also includes Italian among his humanities. W[illiam] H[azlitt], I believe, has no books, except mine; but he has Shakespeare and Rousseau by heart. V[incent] N[ovello], who though not a bookman by profession, is fond of those who are, and who loves his volume enough to read it across the fields, has his library in the common sitting-room, which is hospitable. H. R.'s books are all too modern and finely bound, which however is not his fault, for they were left him by will,—not the most kindly act of the testator. Suppose a man were to bequeath us a great japan chest three feet by four, with an injunction that it was always to stand on the tea-table. I remember borrowing a book of H. R. which, having lost, I replaced with a copy equally well bound. I am not sure I should have been in such haste, even to return the book, had it been a common-looking volume; but the splendour of the loss dazzled me into this ostentatious piece of propriety. I set about restoring it as if I had diminished his fortunes, and waived the privilege a friend has to use a man's things as his own. I may venture upon this ultra-liberal theory, not only because candour compels me to say that I hold it to a greater extent, with Montaigne, but because I have been a meek son in the family of book-losers. I may affirm, upon a moderate calculation, that I have lent and lost in my time (and I am eight-and-thirty), half-a-dozen decent-sized libraries,—I mean books enough to fill so many ordinary bookcases. I have never complained; and self-love, as well as gratitude, makes me love those who do not complain of me.

MY BOOKS

But, like other patient people, I am inclined to burst out now that I grow less strong,—now that writing puts a hectic to my cheek. Publicity is nothing nowadays 'between friends.' There is R., not H. R., who in return for breaking my set of English Poets, makes a point of forgetting me, whenever he has poets in his eye; which is carrying his conscience too far. But W[illiam] H[azlitt] treated me worse; for not content with losing other of said English Poets, together with my Philip Sidney, (all in one volume) and divers pieces of Bacon, he vows I never lent them to him; which is 'the unkindest cut of all.' This comes of being magnanimous. It is a poor thing after all to be 'pushed from a level consideration' of one's superiority in matters of provocation. But W[illiam] H[azlitt] is not angry on this occasion though he is forgetful; and in spite of his offences against me and mine (not to be done away with by his good word at intervals), I pardon the irritable patriot and metaphysician, who would give his last penny to an acquaintance, and his last pulse to the good of mankind. Why did he fire up at an idle word from one of the few men who thought as deeply as himself, and who 'died daily' in the same awful cause? But I forgive him, because *he* forgave him, and yet I know not if I can do it for that very reason.

Come, my best friends, my books, and lead me on:
'Tis time that I were gone.

I own I borrow books with as much facility as I lend. I cannot see a work that interests me on another person's shelf, without a wish to carry it off: but, I repeat, that I have been much more sinned against than sinning in the article of non-return; and am scrupulous in the article of intention. I never had a felonious

intent upon a book but once; and then I shall only say, it was under circumstances so peculiar, that I cannot but look upon the conscience that induced me to restore it, as having sacrificed the spirit of its very self to the letter; and I have a grudge against it accordingly. Some people are unwilling to lend their books. I have a special grudge against them, particularly those who accompany their unwillingness with uneasy professions to the contrary, and smiles like Sir Fretful Plagiary. The friend who helped to spoil my notions of property, or rather to make them too good for the world 'as it goes,' taught me also to undervalue my squeamishness in refusing to avail myself of the books of these gentlemen. He showed me how it was doing good to all parties to put an ordinary face on the matter; though I know his own blushed not a little sometimes in doing it, even when the good to be done was for another. (Dear S[helley], in all thy actions, small as well as great, how sure was the beauty of thy spirit to break forth.) I feel, in truth, that even when anger inclines me to exercise this privilege of philosophy, it is more out of revenge than contempt. I fear that in allowing myself to borrow books, I sometimes make extremes meet in a very sinful manner, and do it out of a refined revenge. It is like eating a miser's beef at him.

I yield to none in my love of bookstall urbanity. I have spent as many happy moments over the stalls (until the woman looked out) as any literary apprentice boy who ought to be moving onwards. But I confess my weakness in liking to see some of my favourite purchases neatly bound. The books I like to have about me most are, Spenser, Chaucer, the minor poems of Milton, the *Arabian Nights,* Theocritus, Ariosto, and such old good-natured speculations as Plutarch's *Morals.* For most of these I like a plain good old

MY BOOKS

binding, never mind how old, provided it wears well; but my *Arabian Nights* may be bound in as fine and flowery a style as possible, and I should love an engraving to every dozen pages. Book-prints of all sorts, bad and good, take with me as much as when I was a child: and I think some books, such as Prior's *Poems,* ought always to have portraits of the authors. Prior's airy face with his cap on, is like having his company. From early association, no edition of Milton pleases me so much, as that in which there are pictures of the Devil with brute ears, dressed like a Roman General: nor of Bunyan, as the one containing the print of the Valley of the Shadow of Death, with the Devil whispering in Christian's ear, or old Pope by the wayside, and

> Vanity Fair,
> With the Pilgrims . suffering there.

I delight in the recollection of the puzzle I used to have with the frontispiece of the *Tale of a Tub,* of my real horror at the sight of that crawling old man representing Avarice, at the beginning of *Enfield's Speaker,* the *Looking Glass,* or some such book; and even of the careless schoolboy hats, and the prim stomachers and cottage bonnets, of such golden-age antiquities as the *Village School.* The oldest and most worn-out woodcut, representing King Pippin, Goody Two Shoes, or the grim Soldan, sitting with three staring blots for his eyes and mouth, his sceptre in one hand, and his other five fingers raised and spread in admiration at the feats of the Gallant London Prentice, cannot excite in me a feeling of ingratitude. Cooke's edition of the *British Poets and Novelists* came out when I was at school: for which reason I never could put up with Suttaby's or Walker's publications, except in the case of such

works as the *Fairy Tales,* which Mr. Cooke did not publish. Besides, they are too cramped, thick, and mercenary; and the pictures are all frontispieces. They do not come in at the proper places. Cooke realized the old woman's *beau ideal* of a prayer-book,—'A little book, with a great deal of matter, and a large type':— for the type was really large for so small a volume. Shall I ever forget his Collins and his Gray, books at once so 'superbly ornamented' and so inconceivably cheap? Sixpence could procure much before; but never could it procure so much as then, or was at once so much respected, and so little cared for. His artist Kirk was the best artist, except Stothard, that ever designed for periodical works; and I will venture to add (if his name rightly announces his country) the best artist Scotland ever produced, except Wilkie, but he unfortunately had not enough of his country in him to keep him from dying young. His designs for Milton and the *Arabian Nights,* his female extricated from the water in the *Tales of the Genii,* and his old hag issuing out of the chest of the Merchant Abadah in the same book, are before me now, as vividly as they were then. He possessed elegance and the sense of beauty in no ordinary degree; though they sometimes played a trick or so of foppery. I shall never forget the gratitude with which I received an odd number of Akenside, value sixpence, one of the set of that poet, which a boarder distributed among three or four of us, 'with his mother's compliments.' The present might have been more lavish, but I hardly thought of that. I remember my number. It was the one in which there is a picture of the poet on a sofa, with Cupid coming to him, and the words underneath, 'Tempt me no more, insidious Love!' The picture and the number appeared to me equally divine. I cannot help thinking

MY BOOKS

to this day, that it is right and natural in a gentleman to sit in a stage dress, on that particular kind of sofa, though on no other, with that exclusive hat and feathers on his head, telling Cupid to begone with a tragedy air. Cowley says that even when he was 'a very young boy at school, instead of his running about on holidays, and playing with his fellows, he was wont to steal from them and walk into the fields, either alone with a book, or with some one companion, if he could find one of the same temper.' When I was at school, I had no fields to run into, or I should certainly have gone there; and I must own to having played a great deal; but then I drew my sports as much as possible out of books, playing at Trojan wars, chivalrous encounters with coal-staves, and even at religious mysteries. When I was not at these games, I was either reading in a corner, or walking round the cloisters with a book under one arm and my friend linked with the other, or with my thoughts. It has since been my fate to realize all the romantic notions I had of a friend at that time, and just as I had embraced him in a distant country, to have him torn from me. This it is that sprinkles the most cheerful of my speculations now with tears, and that must obtain me the reader's pardon for a style unusually chequered and egotistical. No man was a greater lover of books than he. He was rarely to be seen, unless attending to other people's affairs, without a volume of some sort, generally of Plato or one of the Greek tragedians. Nor will those who understand the real spirit of his scepticism, be surprised to hear that one of his companions was the Bible. He valued it for the beauty of some of its contents, for the dignity of others, and the curiosity of all; though the philosophy of Solomon he thought too *Epicurean,* and the inconsistencies of other parts afflicted him. His

LEIGH HUNT

favourite part was the book of Job, which he thought the grandest of tragedies. He projected founding one of his own upon it; and I will undertake to say, that Job would have sat in that tragedy with a patience and profundity of thought worthy of the original. Being asked on one occasion, what book he would save for himself if he could save no other? he answered, 'The oldest book, the Bible.' It was a monument to him of the earliest, most lasting, and most awful aspirations of humanity. But more of this on a fitter occasion.*

I love an author the more for having been himself a lover of books. The idea of an ancient library perplexes our sympathy by its map-like volumes, rolled upon cylinders. Our imagination cannot take kindly to a yard of wit, or to thirty inches of moral observation, rolled out like linen in a draper's shop. But we conceive of Plato as a lover of books; of Aristotle certainly; of Plutarch, Pliny, Horace, Julian, and Marcus Aurelius. Virgil, too, must have been one; and, after a fashion, Martial. May I confess, that the passage which I recollect with the greatest pleasure in Cicero, is where he says that books delight us at home, *and are no impediment abroad; travel with us, ruralize with us.* His period is rounded off to some purpose: '*Delectant domi, non impediunt foris; peregrinantur rusticantur.*'

---

* I will mention, however, in this place, that an advantage of a very cunning and vindictive nature was taken of Mr. Shelley's known regard for the Bible, to represent him as having one with him at the time he was drowned. Nothing was more probable: and it is true that he had a book in his pocket, the remains of which, at the request of the author of this article, were buried with him, but it was the volume of Mr. Keats' poems, containing *Hyperion,* of which he was a great admirer. He borrowed it of me when I went away, and knowing how I valued it also, said that he would not let it quit him till he saw me again.

MY BOOKS

I am so much of this opinion, that I do not care to be anywhere without having a book or books at hand, and like Dr. Orkborne, in the novel of *Camilla,* stuff the coach or post-chaise with them whenever I travel. As books, however, become ancient, the love of them becomes more unequivocal and conspicuous. The ancients had little of what we call learning. They made it. They were also no very eminent buyers of books— they made books for posterity. It is true, that it is not at all necessary to love many books, in order to love them much. The scholar, in Chaucer, who would rather have

> At his beddes head
> A twenty bokes, clothed in black and red,
> Of Aristotle and his philosophy,
> Than robès rich, or fiddle, or psaltry—

doubtless beat all our modern collectors in his passion for reading; but books must at least exist, and have acquired an eminence, before their lovers can make themselves known. There must be a possession, also, to perfect the communion; and the mere contact is much, even when our mistress speaks an unknown language. Dante puts Homer, the great ancient, in his Elysium, upon trust; but a few years afterwards, *Homer,* the book, made its appearance in Italy, and Petrarch, in a transport, put it upon his bookshelves, where he adored it, like 'the unknown God.' Petrarch ought to be the god of the Bibliomaniacs, for he was a collector and a man of genius, which is an union that does not often happen. He copied out, with his own precious hand, the manuscripts he rescued from time, and then produced others for time to reverence. With his head upon a book he died. Boccaccio, his friend, was another; nor can one look upon the longest and

LEIGH HUNT

most tiresome works he wrote (for he did write some tiresome ones, in spite of the gaiety of his *Decameron*), without thinking, that in that resuscitation of the world of letters, it must have been natural to a man of genius to add to the existing stock of volumes, at whatsoever price. I always pitch my completest idea of a lover of books, either in these dark ages, as they are called,

(Cui cieco a torto il cieco volgo appella—)

or in the gay town days of Charles II, or a little afterwards. In both times the portrait comes out by the force of contrast. In the first, I imagine an age of iron warfare and energy, with solitary retreats, in which the monk or the hooded scholar walks forth to meditate, his precious volume under his arm. In the other, I have a triumphant example of the power of books and wit to contest the victory with sensual pleasure:—Rochester, staggering home to pen a satire in the style of Monsieur Boileau; Butler, cramming his jolly duodecimo with all the learning that he laughed at; and a new race of book poets come up, who, in spite of their periwigs and petit-maîtres, talk as romantically of 'the bays,' as if they were priests of Delphos. It was a victorious thing in books to beguile even the old French of their egotism, or at least to share it with them. Nature never pretended to do as much. And here is the difference between the two ages, or between any two ages in which genius and art predominate. In the one, books are loved because they are the records of nature and her energies; in the other, because they are the records of those records, or evidences of the importance of the individuals, and proofs of our descent in the new and imperishable aristocracy. This is the reason why rank (with few exceptions) is so jealous of literature, and loves to appropriate or withhold the honours of it, as if they

MY BOOKS

were so many toys and ribbons, like its own. It has an instinct that the two pretensions are incompatible. When Montaigne (a real lover of books) affected the order of St. Michael, and pleased himself with possessing that fugitive little piece of importance, he did it because he would pretend to be above nothing that he really felt, or that was felt by men in general; but at the same time he vindicated his natural superiority over this weakness by praising and loving all higher and lasting things, and by placing his best glory in doing homage to the geniuses that had gone before him. He did not endeavour to think that an immortal renown was a fashion, like that of the cut of his scarf; or that by undervaluing the one, he should go shining down to posterity in the other, perpetual lord of Montaigne and of the ascendant.

There is a period of modern times, at which the love of books appears to have been of a more decided nature than at either of these—I mean the age just before and after the Reformation, or rather all that period when book-writing was confined to the learned languages. Erasmus is the god of it. Bacon, a mighty book-man, saw, among his other sights, the great advantage of loosening the vernacular tongue, and wrote both Latin and English. I allow this is the greatest closeted age of books; of old scholars sitting in dusty studies; of heaps of 'illustrious obscure,' rendering themselves more illustrious and more obscure by retreating from the 'thorny queaches' of Dutch and German names into the 'vacant interlunar caves' of appellations latinized or translated. I think I see all their volumes now, filling the shelves of a dozen German convents. The authors are bearded men, sitting in old woodcuts, in caps and gowns, and their books are dedicated to princes and statesmen, as illustrious as themselves. My old friend Wierus, who wrote a thick book, *De Praestigiis Dae-*

monum, was one of them, and had a fancy worthy of his sedentary stomach. I will confess, once for all, that I have a liking for them all. It is my link with the bibliomaniacs, whom I admit into our relationship, because my love is large, and my family pride nothing. But still I take my idea of books read with a gusto, of companions for bed and board, from the two ages before-mentioned. The other is of too book-worm a description. There must be both a judgment and a fervour; a discrimination and a boyish eagerness; and (with all due humility) something of a point of contact between authors worth reading and the reader. How can I take Juvenal into the fields, or Valcarenghius *De Aortae Aneurismate* to bed with me? How could I expect to walk before the face of nature with the one; to tire my elbow properly with the other, before I put out my candle, and turn round deliciously on the right side? Or how could I stick up *Coke upon Littleton* against something on the dinner-table, and be divided between a fresh paragraph and a mouthful of salad?

I take our four great English poets to have all been fond of reading. Milton and Chaucer proclaim themselves for hard sitters at books. Spenser's reading is evident by his learning; and if there were nothing else to show for it in Shakespeare, his retiring to his native town, long before old age, would be a proof of it. It is impossible for a man to live in solitude without such assistance, unless he is a metaphysician or mathematician, or the dullest of mankind; and any country town would be solitude to Shakespeare, after the bustle of a metropolis and a theatre. Doubtless he divided his time between his books, and his bowling-green, and his daughter Susanna. It is pretty certain, also, that he planted, and rode on horseback; and there is evidence of all sorts to make it clear that he must have occasion-

MY BOOKS

ally joked with the blacksmith, and stood godfather
for his neighbours' children. Chaucer's account of himself must be quoted, for the delight and sympathy of
all true readers:—

> As for me, though that I can but lite,
> On bookès for to rede I me delite,
> And to hem yeve I faith and full credènce,
> And in mine herte have hem in reverence
> So hertèly, that there is gamè none,
> That fro my bookès maketh me to gone,
> But it is seldome on the holy daie;
> Save certainly whan that the month of May
> Is comen, and that I hear the foulès sing,
> And that the flourès ginnen for to spring.
> Farewell my booke and my devociön.
>
> > *The Legend of Good Women.*

And again, in the second book of his *House of Fame,*
where *the eagle* addresses him:—

> ——Thou wilt make
> At night full oft thine head to ake,
> And in thy study as thou writest,
> And evermore of Love enditest,
> In honour of him and his praisings,
> And in his folkès furtherings,
> And in his matter all devisest,
> And not him ne his folke despisest,
> Although thou mayst go in the daunse
> Of hem, that him list not advance;
> Therefore as I said, ywis,
> Jupiter considreth well this.
> And also, beausire, of other things;
> That is, thou hast no tidings
> Of Lovès folke, if they be glade,

Ne of nothing else that God made,
And not only fro ferre countree,
But no tidings commen to thee,
Not of thy very neighbouris,
That dwellen almost at thy dores;
Thou hearest neither that ne this,
For whan thy labour all done is,
And hast made all thy rekenings,*
Instead of rest and of new things,
Thou goest home to thine house anone,
And all so dombe as anie stone,
Thou sittest at another booke,
Till fully dazed is thy looke.

After I think of the bookishness of Chaucer and Milton, I always make a great leap to Prior and Fenton. Prior was first noticed, when a boy, by Lord Dorset, sitting in his uncle's tavern, and reading Horace. He describes himself, years after, when Secretary of Embassy at the Hague, as taking the same author with him in the Saturday's chaise, in which he and his mistress used to escape from town cares into the country, to the admiration of Dutch beholders. Fenton was a martyr to contented scholarship (including a sirloin and a bottle of wine), and died among his books, of inactivity. 'He rose late,' says Johnson, 'and when he had risen, sat down to his books and papers.' A woman that once waited on him in a lodging, told him, as she said, that he would 'lie a-bed and be fed with a spoon.' He must have had an enviable liver, if he was happy. I must own (if my conscience would let me), that I should like to lead, half the year, just such a life (woman included, though not that woman), the other half being passed in the fields and woods, with a cottage

* Chaucer at this time had an office under the government.

MY BOOKS

just big enough to hold us. Dacier and his wife had a pleasant time of it; both fond of books, both scholars, both amiable, both wrapt up in the ancient world, and helping one another at their tasks. If they were not happy, matrimony would be a rule even without an exception. Pope does not strike me as being a bookman; he was curious rather than enthusiastic; more nice than wise; he dabbled in modern Latin poetry, which is a bad symptom. Swift was decidedly a reader; the *Tale of a Tub,* in its fashion as well as substance, is the work of a scholarly wit; the *Battle of the Books* is the fancy of a lover of libraries. Addison and Steele were too much given up to Button's and the town. Periodical writing, though its demands seem otherwise, is not favourable to reading; it becomes too much a matter of business and will either be attended to at the expense of the writer's books, or books, the very admonishers of his industry, will make him idle. Besides, a periodical work, to be suitable to its character, and warrant its regular recurrence, must involve something of a gossiping nature, and proceed upon experiences familiar to the existing community, or at least likely to be received by them in consequence of some previous tinge of inclination. You do not pay weekly visits to your friends to lecture them, whatever good you may do their minds. There will be something compulsory in reading the *Ramblers,* as there is in going to church. Addison and Steele undertook to regulate the minor morals of society, and effected a world of good, with which scholarship had little to do. Gray was a bookman; he wished to be always lying on sofas, reading 'eternal new novels of Crebillon and Marivaux.' This is a true hand. The elaborate and scientific look of the rest of his reading was owing to the necessity of employing himself: he had not health and spirits for the literary

voluptuousness he desired. Collins, for the same reason, could not employ himself; he was obliged to dream over Arabian tales, to let the light of the supernatural world half in upon his eyes. 'He loved,' as Johnson says (in that strain of music, inspired by tenderness), 'fairies, genii, giants, and monsters; he delighted to rove through the meanders of enchantment, to gaze on the magnificence of golden palaces, to repose by the waterfalls of Elysian gardens.' If Collins had had a better constitution, I do not believe that he would have written his projected work upon the *Restoration of Literature,* fit as he was by scholarship for the task, but he would have been the greatest poet since the days of Milton. If his friend Thomas Warton had had a little more of his delicacy of organization, the love of books would almost have made him a poet. His edition of the minor poems of Milton is a wilderness of sweets. It is the only one in which a true lover of the original can pardon an exuberance of annotation; though I confess I am inclined enough to pardon any notes that resemble it, however numerous. The 'builded rhyme' stands at the top of the page, like a fair edifice with all sorts of flowers and fresh waters at its foot. The young poet lives there, served by the nymphs and fauns.

Hinc atque hinc glomerantur Oreades.

Huc ades, o formose puer: tibi lilia plenis
Ecce ferunt Nymphae calathis: tibi candida Nais,
Pallentes violas et summa papavera carpens,
Narcissum et florem jungit bene olentis anethi.

Among the old writers I must not forget Ben Jonson and Donne. Cowley has been already mentioned. His boyish love of books, like all the other inclinations of his early life, stuck to him to the last; which is the

MY BOOKS

greatest reward of virtue. I would mention Izaak Walton, if I had not a grudge against him. His brother fishermen, the divines, were also great fishers of books. I have a grudge against them and their divinity. They talked much of the devil and divine right, and yet forgot what Shakespeare says of the devil's friend Nero, that he is 'an angler in the lake of darkness.' Selden was called 'the walking library of our nation.' It is not the pleasantest idea of him; but the library included poetry and wit, as well as heraldry and the Jewish doctors. His *Table Talk* is equally pithy and pleasant, and truly worthy of the name, for it implies other speakers. Indeed it was actually what it is called, and treasured up by his friends. Selden wrote complimentary verses to his friends the poets, and a commentary on Drayton's *Polyolbion*. Drayton was himself a reader, addicted to all the luxuries of scholarship. Chapman sat among his books, like an astrologer among his spheres and altitudes.

How pleasant it is to reflect, that all these lovers of books have themselves become books! What better metamorphosis could Pythagoras have desired! How Ovid and Horace exulted in anticipating theirs! And how the world have justified their exultation! They had a right to triumph over brass and marble. It is the only visible change which changes no farther, which generates and yet is not destroyed. Consider: mines themselves are exhausted; cities perish; kingdoms are swept away, and man weeps with indignation to think that his own body is not immortal.

> Muoiono le città, muoiono i regni,
> E l' uom d' esser mortal par che si sdegni.

Yet this little body of thought, that lies before me in the shape of a book, has existed thousands of years, nor

since the invention of the press can anything short of an universal convulsion of nature abolish it. To a shape like this, so small yet so comprehensive, so slight yet so lasting, so insignificant yet so venerable, turns the mighty activity of Homer, and so turning, is enabled to live and warm us for ever. To a shape like this turns the placid sage of Academus: to a shape like this the grandeur of Milton, the exuberance of Spenser, the pungent elegance of Pope, and the volatility of Prior. In one small room, like the compressed spirits of Milton, can be gathered together

> The assembled souls of all that men held wise.

May I hope to become the meanest of these existences? This is a question which every author who is a lover of books, asks himself some time in his life; and which must be pardoned, because it cannot be helped. I know not. I cannot exclaim with the poet,

> Oh that my name were number'd among theirs,
> Then gladly would I end my mortal days.

For my mortal days, few and feeble as the rest of them may be, are of consequence to others. But I should like to remain visible in this shape. The little of myself that pleases myself, I could wish to be accounted worth pleasing others. I should like to survive so, were it only for the sake of those who love me in private, knowing as I do what a treasure is the possession of a friend's mind, when he is no more. At all events, nothing while I live and think, can deprive me of my value for such treasures. I can help the appreciation of them while I last, and love them till I die; and perhaps, if fortune turns her face once more in kindness upon me before I go, I may chance, some quiet day, to lay my overbeating temples on a book, and so have the death I most envy.

WALTER SAVAGE LANDOR

JOEL CHANDLER HARRIS, I have somewhere read, professed himself a great admirer of Landor's prose; surely the least expected among those guests with whom, Landor prophesied, he should belatedly dine. Yet one remembers that Dickens, too, admired him, as man if not as stylist, and has left a portrait of him in characteristic vein as Roger Boythorne. Carlyle's appreciation and the hero-worship of Swinburne are less surprising. It is among writers that Landor is held in highest esteem, as it is among poets that Spenser is most beloved. For Landor scorned the tricks of popularity; there is in him no easy diffuseness; the solid virtues of his style are such as only those who have sought to acquire them can appreciate to the full.

Compression is chief of his stylistic merits. Freedom from extrinsic ornamentation is the inevitable adjunct; his prose has the simplicity and purity of line to be found in Greek architecture of the best period. Figures of speech—and Landor's are often remarkable—are not decorative in purpose but are short cuts to his meaning; they are spontaneous and swift. His diction does not strike the reader by its singularity but derives from the soundest English tradition. And that his idiom might be pure he studied the Elizabethan prose masters, Ben Jonson in chief. Hazlitt and Landor as stylists have much in common, but Hazlitt's style is the more personal, colloquial, and easy.

The *Imaginary Conversations*, Landor's chief prose work, number over one hundred and fifty, and the

WALTER SAVAGE LANDOR

range of reading and historical knowledge which they display is enormous. Landor, who wrote Latin with as much ease as English, was deeply versed in several literatures. The *Conversations* aim to portray character and also to suggest the quality of a particular civilization or epoch. Famous men and women and periods the most notable in history are thus characterized. Appreciation of the dialogues is dependent upon the degree of knowledge which the reader possesses. Thus it is the English conversations or the relatively modern ones of other literatures which I most enjoy, a limitation born of an inadequate acquaintance with remote and alien characters and cultures.

To Landor's mastery of restraint is due the moving quality of his pathos evident in such a dialogue as that of Lady Lisle with Elizabeth Gaunt. His power in this is the same as in his *Iphegenia and Agamemnon* in verse. Restraint, compression, subordination of detail and freedom from extrinsic ornament are virtues which are associated usually with classical literature and art. Yet there is evident also in Landor a romantic strain. He neither worships tradition nor discards it. His knowledge of the best that has been said and done in the world permits the widest range of models. In some respects he resembles Matthew Arnold; but he is untroubled by Arnold's pessimism and doubt, and in prose certainly, if not indisputably in verse, is the superior of the younger man. Unlike Arnold he is not wholly the product of, nor characteristic of, his time. Goethe, of all modern writers, he most resembles in that balance of qualities which marks an author as independent of his age. Landor's work, one feels, would have been much as it is had he lived at any time during the last three or four hundred years.

IMAGINARY CONVERSATIONS

HENRY VIII AND ANNE BOLEYN

Henry. Dost thou know me, Nanny, in this yeoman's dress? 'S blood! does it require so long and vacant a stare to recollect a husband after a week or two? No tragedy-tricks with me! a scream, a sob, or thy kerchief a trifle wetter, were enough. Why, verily the little fool faints in earnest. These whey faces, like their kinsfolk the ghosts, give us no warning. (*Sprinkling water over her.*) Hast had water enough upon thee? Take that, then: art thyself again?

Anne. Father of mercies! do I meet again my husband, as was my last prayer on earth? Do I behold my beloved lord—in peace—and pardoned, my partner in eternal bliss? It was his voice. I cannot see him: why cannot I? Oh why do these pangs interrupt the transports of the blessed?

Henry. Thou openest thy arms: faith! I came for that. Nanny, thou art a sweet slut. Thou groanest, wench: art in labour? Faith! among the mistakes of the night, I am ready to think almost that thou hast been drinking, and that I have not.

Anne. God preserve your Highness: grant me your forgiveness for one slight offence. My eyes were heavy; I fell asleep while I was reading. I did not know of your presence at first; and, when I did, I could not speak. I strove for utterance: I wanted no respect for my liege and husband.

Henry. My pretty warm nestling, thou wilt then lie! Thou wert reading, and aloud too, with thy saintly cup of water by thee, and—what! thou art still girlishly fond of those dried cherries!

Anne. I had no other fruit to offer your Highness the first time I saw you, and you were then pleased

305

WALTER SAVAGE LANDOR

to invent for me some reason why they should be **acceptable**. I did not dry these: may I present them, such as they are? We shall have fresh next month.

Henry. Thou art always driving away from the discourse. One moment it suits thee to know me, another not.

Anne. Remember, it is hardly three months since I miscarried: I am weak, and liable to swoons.

Henry. Thou hast, however, thy bridal cheeks, with lustre upon them when there is none elsewhere, and obstinate lips resisting all impression; but, now thou talkest about miscarrying, who is the father of the boy?

Anne. The Father is yours and mine; he who hath taken him to his own home, before (like me) he could struggle or cry for it.

Henry. Pagan, or worse, to talk so! He did not come into the world alive: there was no baptism.

Anne. I thought only of our loss: my senses are confounded. I did not give him my milk, and yet I loved him tenderly; for I often fancied had he lived, how contented and joyful he would have made you and England.

Henry. No subterfuges and escapes. I warrant, thou canst not say whether at my entrance thou wert waking or wandering.

Anne. Faintness and drowsiness came upon me suddenly.

Henry. Well, since thou really and truly sleepedst, what didst dream of?

Anne. I begin to doubt whether I did indeed sleep.

Henry. Ha! false one—never two sentences of truth together! But come, what didst think about, asleep or awake?

Anne. I thought that God had pardoned me my offences, and had received me unto him.

IMAGINARY CONVERSATIONS

Henry. And nothing more?

Anne. That my prayers had been heard and my wishes were accomplishing: the angels alone can enjoy more beatitude than this.

Henry. Vexatious little devil! she says nothing now about me, merely from perverseness. Hast thou never thought about me, nor about thy falsehood and adultery?

Anne. If I had committed any kind of falsehood, in regard to you or not, I should never have rested until I had thrown myself at your feet and obtained your pardon; but, if ever I had been guilty of that other crime, I know not whether I should have dared to implore it, even of God's mercy.

Henry. Thou hast heretofore cast some soft glances upon Smeaton; hast thou not?

Anne. He taught me to play on the virginals, as you know, when I was little, and thereby to please your Highness.

Henry. And Brereton and Norris, what have they taught thee?

Anne. They are your servants, and trusty ones.

Henry. Has not Weston told thee plainly that he loved thee?

Anne. Yes; and—

Henry. What didst thou?

Anne. I defied him.

Henry. Is that all?

Anne. I could have done no more if he had told me that he hated me. Then, indeed, I should have incurred more justly the reproaches of your Highness: I should have smiled.

Henry. We have proofs abundant: the fellows shall one and all confront thee.—Ay, clap thy hands and kiss thy sleeve, harlot!

WALTER SAVAGE LANDOR

Anne. Oh, that so great a favour is vouchsafed me. My honour is secure; my husband will be happy again; he will see my innocence.

Henry. Give me now an account of the moneys thou hast received from me within these nine months. I want them not back; they are letters of gold in record of thy guilt. Thou hast had no fewer than fifteen thousand pounds in that period, without even thy asking; what hast done with it, wanton?

Anne. I have regularly placed it out to interest.

Henry. Where? I demand of thee.

Anne. Among the needy and ailing. My Lord Archbishop has the account of it, sealed by him weekly. I also had a copy myself: those who took away my papers may easily find it; for there are few others, and they lie open.

Henry. Think on my munificence to thee; recollect who made thee. Dost sigh for what thou hast lost?

Anne. I do, indeed.

Henry. I never thought thee ambitious; but thy vices creep out one by one.

Anne. I do not regret that I have been a queen and am no longer one; nor that my innocence is called in question by those who never knew me: but I lament that the good people who loved me so cordially, hate and curse me; that those who pointed me out to their daughters for imitation, check them when they speak about me; and that he whom next to God I have served with most devotion is my accuser.

Henry. Wast thou conning over something in that dingy book for thy defence? Come, tell me, what wast thou reading?

Anne. This ancient chronicle. I was looking for some one in my own condition, and must have missed the page. Surely in so many hundred years there shall

IMAGINARY CONVERSATIONS

have been other young maidens, first too happy for exaltation, and after too exalted for happiness,—not, perchance, doomed to die upon a scaffold, by those they ever honoured and served faithfully: that, indeed, I did not look for nor think of; but my heart was bounding for any one I could love and pity. She would be unto me as a sister dead and gone; but hearing me, seeing me, consoling me, and being consoled. O my husband! it is so heavenly a thing—

Henry. To whine and whimper, no doubt, is vastly heavenly.

Anne. I said not so; but those, if there be any such, who never weep, have nothing in them of heavenly or of earthly. The plants, the trees, the very rocks and unsunned clouds, show us at least the semblances of weeping; and there is not an aspect of the globe we live on, nor of the waters and skies around it, without a reference and a similitude to our joys or sorrows.

Henry. I do not remember that notion anywhere. Take care no enemy rake out of it something of materialism. Guard well thy empty hot brain: it may hatch more evil. As for those odd words, I myself would fain see no great harm in them, knowing that grief and frenzy strike out many things which would else lie still, and neither spirt nor sparkle. I also know that thou hast never read any thing but Bible and history,—the two worst books in the world for young people, and the most certain to lead astray both prince and subject. For which reason I have interdicted and entirely put down the one, and will (by the blessing of the Virgin and of holy Paul) commit the other to a rigid censor. If it behooves us kings to enact what our people shall eat and drink,—of which the most unruly and rebellious spirit can entertain no doubt,—greatly more doth it behoove us to examine

what they read and think. The body is moved according to the mind and will: we must take care that the movement be a right one, on pain of God's anger in this life and the next.

Anne. O my dear husband! it must be a naughty thing, indeed, that makes him angry beyond remission. Did you ever try how pleasant it is to forgive any one? There is nothing else wherein we can resemble God perfectly and easily.

Henry. Resemble God perfectly and easily! Do vile creatures talk thus of the Creator?

Anne. No, Henry, when his creatures talk thus of him, they are no longer vile creatures! When they know that he is good, they love him; and, when they love him, they are good themselves. O Henry! my husband and King! the judgments of our Heavenly Father are righteous: on this, surely, we must think alike.

Henry. And what, then? Speak out: again I command thee, speak plainly! thy tongue was not so torpid but this moment. Art ready? must I wait?

Anne. If any doubt remains upon your royal mind of your equity in this business; should it haply seem possible to you that passion or prejudice, in yourself or another, may have warped so strong an understanding,—do but supplicate the Almighty to strengthen and enliven it, and he will hear you.

Henry. What! thou wouldst fain change thy quarters, ay?

Anne. My spirit is detached and ready, and I shall change them shortly, whatever your Highness may determine. Ah! my native Bickling is a pleasant place. May I go back to it? Does that kind smile say, *Yes?* Do the hounds ever run that way now? The fruit-trees must be all in full blossom, and the gorse on the

IMAGINARY CONVERSATIONS   311

hill above quite dazzling. How good it was in you
to plant your park at Greenwich after my childish
notion, tree for tree, the very same as at Bickling!
Has the hard winter killed them, or the winds loosened
the stakes about them?

Henry.   Silly child! as if thou shouldst see them
any more.

Anne.   Alas, what strange things happen! But they
and I are nearly of the same age; young alike, and
without hold upon any thing.

Henry.   Yet thou appearest hale and resolute, and
(they tell me) smirkest and smilest to everybody.

Anne.   The withered leaf catches the sun sometimes,
little as it can profit by it; and I have heard stories
of the breeze in other climates that sets in when daylight is about to close, and how constant it is, and how
refreshing. My heart, indeed, is now sustained strangely: it became the more sensibly so from that time forward, when power and grandeur and all things terres-
trial were sunk from sight. Every act of kindness in
those about me gives me satisfaction and pleasure, such
as I did not feel formerly. I was worse before God
chastened me; yet I was never an ingrate. What pains
have I taken to find out the village-girls who placed
their posies in my chamber ere I arose in the morning!
How gladly would I have recompensed the forester
who lit up a brake on my birthnight, which else had
warmed him half the winter! But these are times
past: I was not Queen of England.

Henry.   Nor adulterous, nor heretical.

Anne.   God be praised!

Henry.   Learned saint! thou knowest nothing of the
lighter, but perhaps canst inform me about the graver,
of them.

312 WALTER SAVAGE LANDOR

Anne. Which may it be, my liege?

Henry. Which may it be? Pestilence! I marvel
that the walls of this tower do not crack around thee
at such impiety.

Anne. I would be instructed by the wisest of theologians: such is your Highness.

Henry. Are the sins of the body, foul as they are,
comparable to those of the soul?

Anne. When they are united, they must be worse.

Henry. Go on, go on: thou pushest thy own breast
against the sword. God hath deprived thee of thy
reason for thy punishment. I must hear more: proceed,
I charge thee.

Anne. An aptitude to believe one thing rather than
another, from ignorance or weakness, or from the more
persuasive manner of the teacher, or from his purity
of life, or from the strong impression of a particular
text at a particular time, and various things beside,
may influence and decide our opinion; and the hand of
the Almighty, let us hope, will fall gently on human
fallibility.

Henry. Opinion in matters of faith! rare wisdom!
rare religion! Troth, Anne! thou hast well sobered
me. I came rather warmly and lovingly; but these
light ringlets, by the holy rood, shall not shade this
shoulder much longer. Nay, do not start; I tap it for
the last time, my sweetest. If the Church permitted
it, thou shouldst set forth on thy long journey with
the eucharist between thy teeth, however loath.

Anne. Love your Elizabeth, my honoured lord, and
God bless you! She will soon forget to call me. Do
not chide her: think how young she is.

Could I, could I kiss her, but once again! it would
comfort my heart,—or break it.

IMAGINARY CONVERSATIONS 313

THE LADY LISLE AND ELIZABETH GAUNT

Lady Lisle. Madam, I am confident you will pardon me; for affliction teaches forgiveness.

Elizabeth Gaunt. From the cell of the condemned we are going, unless my hopes mislead me, where alone we can receive it.

Tell me, I beseech you, lady! in what matter or manner do you think you can have offended a poor sinner such as I am. Surely we come into this dismal place for our offences; and it is not here that any can be given or taken.

Lady Lisle. Just now, when I entered the prison, I saw your countenance serene and cheerful; you looked upon me for a time with an unaltered eye: you turned away from me, as I fancied, only to utter some expressions of devotion; and again you looked upon me, and tears rolled down your face. Alas that I should, by any circumstance, any action or recollection, make another unhappy! Alas that I should deepen the gloom in the very shadow of death!

Elizabeth Gaunt. Be comforted: you have not done it. Grief softens and melts and flows away with tears.

I wept because another was greatly more wretched than myself. I wept at that black attire,—at that attire of modesty and of widowhood.

Lady Lisle. It covers a wounded, almost a broken, heart,—an unworthy offering to our blessed Redeemer.

Elizabeth Gaunt. In his name let us now rejoice! Let us offer our prayers and our thanks at once together! We may yield up our souls, perhaps, at the same hour.

Lady Lisle. Is mine so pure? Have I bemoaned, as I should have done, the faults I have committed? Have my sighs arisen for the unmerited mercies of my God;

WALTER SAVAGE LANDOR

and not rather for him, the beloved of my heart, the adviser and sustainer I have lost?

Open, O gates of Death!

Smile on me, approve my last action in this world, O virtuous husband! O saint and martyr! my brave, compassionate, and loving Lisle.

Elizabeth Gaunt. And cannot you too smile, sweet lady? Are not you with him even now? Doth body, doth clay, doth air, separate and estrange free spirits? Bethink you of his gladness, of his glory; and begin to partake them.

Oh! how could an Englishman, how could twelve, condemn to death—condemn to so great an evil as they thought it and may find it—this innocent and helpless widow?

Lady Lisle. Blame not *that* jury!—blame not the jury which brought against me the verdict of guilty. I was so: I received in my house a wanderer who had fought under the rash and giddy Monmouth. He was hungry and thirsty, and I took him in. My Saviour had commanded, my King had forbidden, it.

Yet the twelve would not have delivered me over to death, unless the judge had threatened them with an accusation of treason in default of it. Terror made them unanimous: they redeemed their properties and lives at the stated price.

Elizabeth Gaunt. I hope, at least, the unfortunate man whom you received in the hour of danger may avoid his penalty.

Lady Lisle. Let us hope it.

Elizabeth Gaunt. I, too, am imprisoned for the same offence; and I have little expectation that he who was concealed by me hath any chance of happiness, although he hath escaped. Could I find the means of conveying

IMAGINARY CONVERSATIONS 315

to him a small pittance, I should leave the world the more comfortably.

Lady Lisle. Trust in God; not in one thing or another, but in all. Resign the care of this wanderer to *his* guidance.

Elizabeth Gaunt. He abandoned that guidance.

Lady Lisle. Unfortunate! how can money then avail him?

Elizabeth Gaunt. It might save him from distress and from despair, from the taunts of the hard-hearted and from the inclemency of the godly.

Lady Lisle. In godliness, O my friend! there cannot be inclemency.

Elizabeth Gaunt. You are thinking of perfection, my dear lady; and I marvel not at it, for what else hath ever occupied your thoughts! But godliness, in almost the best of us, often is austere, often uncompliant and rigid,—proner to reprove than to pardon, to drag back or thrust aside than to invite and help onward.

Poor man! I never knew him before; I cannot tell how he shall endure his self-reproach, or whether it will bring him to calmer thoughts hereafter.

Lady Lisle. I am not a busy idler in curiosity; nor, if I were, is there time enough left me for indulging in it; yet gladly would I learn the history of events, at the first appearance so resembling those in mine.

Elizabeth Gaunt. The person's name I never may disclose; which would be the worst thing I could betray of the trust he placed in me. He took refuge in my humble dwelling, imploring me in the name of Christ to harbour him for a season. Food and raiment were afforded him unsparingly; yet his fears made him shiver through them. Whatever I could urge of prayer and exhortation was not wanting; still, although he prayed,

he was disquieted. Soon came to my ears the declaration of the King, that his Majesty would rather pardon a rebel than the concealer of a rebel. The hope was a faint one; but it *was* hope, and I gave it him. His thanksgivings were now more ardent, his prayers more humble, and oftener repeated. They did not strengthen his heart: it was unpurified and unprepared for them. Poor creature! he consented with it to betray me; and I am condemned to be burned alive. Can we believe, can we encourage the hope, that in his weary way through life he will find those only who will conceal from him the knowledge of this execution? Heavily, too heavily, must it weigh on so irresolute and infirm a breast.

Let it not move you to weeping.

Lady Lisle. It does not; oh! it does not.

Elizabeth Gaunt. What, then?

Lady Lisle. Your saintly tenderness, your heavenly tranquillity.

Elizabeth Gaunt. No, no: abstain! abstain! It was I who grieved; it was I who doubted. Let us now be firmer: we have both the same rock to rest upon. See! I shed no tears.

I saved his life, an unprofitable and (I fear) a joyless one; he, by God's grace, has thrown open to me, and at an earlier hour than ever I ventured to expect it, the avenue to eternal bliss.

Lady Lisle. O my good angel! that bestrewest with fresh flowers a path already smooth and pleasant to me, may those timorous men who have betrayed, and those misguided ones who have persecuted, us, be conscious on their death-beds that we have entered it! and they too will at last find rest.

IMAGINARY CONVERSATIONS 317

THE EMPRESS CATHARINE AND PRINCESS DASHKOF

Catharine. Into his heart! into his heart! If he escapes, we perish.

Do you think, Dashkof, they can hear me through the double door? Yes; hark! they heard me: they have done it.

What bubbling and gurgling! he groaned but once.

Listen! his blood is busier now than it ever was before. I should not have thought it could have splashed so loud upon the floor, although our bed, indeed, is rather of the highest.

Put your ear against the lock.

Dashkof. I hear nothing.

Catharine. My ears are quicker than yours, and know these notes better. Let me come.—Hear nothing! You did not wait long enough, nor with coolness and patience. There!—there again! The drops are now like lead: every half-minute they penetrate the eider-down and the mattress.—How now! which of these fools has brought his dog with him? What tramping and lapping! the creature will carry the marks all about the palace with his feet and muzzle.

Dashkof. Oh, heavens!

Catharine. Are you afraid?

Dashkof. There is a horror that surpasses fear, and will have none of it. I knew not this before.

Catharine. You turn pale and tremble. You should have supported me, in case I had required it.

Dashkof. I thought only of the tyrant. Neither in life nor in death could any one of these miscreants make me tremble. But the husband slain by his wife!—I saw not into my heart; I looked not into it, and it chastises me.

Catharine. Dashkof, are you, then, really unwell?

318   WALTER SAVAGE LANDOR

Dashkof.   What will Russia, what will Europe, say?

Catharine.   Russia has no more voice than a whale. She may toss about in her turbulence; but my artillery (for now, indeed, I can safely call it mine) shall stun and quiet her.

Dashkof.   God grant—

Catharine.   I cannot but laugh at thee, my pretty Dashkof! God grant, forsooth! He has granted all we wanted from him at present,—the safe removal of this odious Peter.

Dashkof.   Yet Peter loved *you;* and even the worst husband must leave, surely, the recollection of some sweet moments. The sternest must have trembled, both with apprehension and with hope, at the first alteration in the health of his consort; at the first promise of true union, imperfect without progeny. Then, there are thanks rendered together to heaven, and satisfactions communicated, and infant words interpreted; and when the one has failed to pacify the sharp cries of babyhood, pettish and impatient as sovereignty itself, the success of the other in calming it, and the unenvied triumph of this exquisite ambition, and the calm gazes that it wins upon it.

Catharine.   Are these, my sweet friend, your lessons from the Stoic school? Are not they, rather, the pale-faced reflections of some kind epithalamiast from Livonia or Bessarabia? Come, come away. I am to know nothing at present of the deplorable occurrence. Did not you wish his death?

Dashkof.   It is not his death that shocks me.

Catharine.   I understand you: besides, you said as much before.

Dashkof.   I fear for your renown.

Catharine.   And for your own good name,—ay, Dashkof?

IMAGINARY CONVERSATIONS 319

Dashkof. He was not, nor did I ever wish him to be, my friend.

Catharine. You hated him.

Dashkof. Even hatred may be plucked up too roughly.

Catharine. Europe shall be informed of my reasons, if she should ever find out that I countenanced the conspiracy. She shall be persuaded that her repose made the step necessary; that my own life was in danger; that I fell upon my knees to soften the conspirators; that, only when I had fainted, the horrible deed was done. She knows already that Peter was always ordering new exercises and uniforms; and my ministers can evince at the first audience my womanly love of peace.

Dashkof. Europe may be more easily subjugated than duped.

Catharine. She shall be both, God willing.

Dashkof. The majesty of thrones will seem endangered by this open violence.

Catharine. The majesty of thrones is never in jeopardy by those who sit upon them. A sovereign may cover one with blood more safely than a subject can pluck a feather out of the cushion. It is only when the people does the violence that we hear an ill report of it. Kings poison and stab one another in pure legitimacy. Do your republican ideas revolt from such a doctrine?

Dashkof. I do not question this right of theirs, and never will oppose their exercise of it. But if you prove to the people how easy a matter it is to extinguish an emperor, and how pleasantly and prosperously we may live after it, is it not probable that they also will now and then try the experiment; particularly, if any one in Russia should hereafter hear of glory and honour, and how immortal are these by the consent of mankind, in

all countries and ages, in him who releases the world, or any part of it, from a lawless and ungovernable despot? The chances of escape are many, and the greater if he should have no accomplices. Of his renown there is no doubt at all: that is placed above chance and beyond time, by the sword he hath exercised so righteously.

Catharine. True; but we must reason like democrats no longer. Republicanism is the best thing we can have, when we cannot have power; but no one ever held the two together. I am now autocrat.

Dashkof. Truly, then, may I congratulate you. The dignity is the highest a mortal can attain.

Catharine. I know and feel it.

Dashkof. I wish you always may.

Catharine. I doubt not the stability of power: I can make constant both fortune and love. My Dashkof smiles at this conceit: she has here the same advantage, and does not envy her friend even the autocracy.

Dashkof. Indeed I do, and most heartily.

Catharine. How?

Dashkof. I know very well what those intended who first composed the word; but they blundered egregiously. In spite of them, it signifies power over oneself,—of all power the most enviable, and the least consistent with power over others.

I hope and trust there is no danger to you from any member of the council-board inflaming the guards or other soldiery.

Catharine. The members of the council-board did not sit *at* it, but *upon* it; and their tactics were performed cross-legged. What partisans are to be dreaded of that commander-in-chief whose chief command is over pantaloons and facings, whose utmost glory is perched on loops and feathers, and who fancies that battles are

IMAGINARY CONVERSATIONS   321

to be won rather by pointing the hat than the cannon?

Dashkof.   Peter was not insensible to glory; few men
are: but wiser heads than his have been perplexed in
the road to it, and many have lost it by their ardour
to attain it.   I have always said that, unless we devote
ourselves to the public good, we may perhaps be celebrated; but it is beyond the power of fortune, or even
of genius, to exalt us above the dust.

Catharine.   Dashkof, you are a sensible, sweet
creature; but rather too romantic on *principle,* and
rather too visionary on glory.   I shall always both
esteem and love you; but no other woman in Europe
will be great enough to endure you, and you will really
put the men *hors de combat.*   Thinking is an enemy
to beauty, and no friend to tenderness.   Men can ill
brook it one in another; in women it renders them what
they would fain call "scornful" (vain assumption of
high prerogative!) and what you would find bestial and
outrageous.   As for my reputation, which I know is dear
to you, I can purchase all the best writers in Europe
with a snuffbox each, and all the remainder with its
contents.   Not a gentleman of the Academy but is
enchanted by a toothpick, if I deign to send it him.   A
brilliant makes me Semiramis; a watch-chain, Venus;
a ring, Juno.   Voltaire is my friend.

Dashkof.   He was Frederick's.

Catharine.   I shall be the *Pucelle* of Russia.   No!
I had forgotten: he has treated her scandalously.

Dashkof.   Does your Majesty value the flatteries of
a writer who ridicules the most virtuous and glorious of
his nation; who crouched before that monster of infamy,
Louis XV.; and that worse monster, the king his prede-
cessor?   He reviled, with every indignity and indecency,
the woman who rescued France; and who alone, of all
that ever led the armies of that kingdom, made its con-

querors—the English—tremble. Its monarchs and marshals cried and ran like capons, flapping their fine crests from wall to wall, and cackling at one breath defiance and surrender. The village girl drew them back into battle, and placed the heavens themselves against the enemies of Charles. She seemed supernatural: the English recruits deserted; they would not fight against God.

Catharine. Fools and bigots!

Dashkof. The whole world contained none other, excepting those who fed upon them. The Maid of Orleans was pious and sincere: her life asserted it: her death confirmed it. Glory to her, Catharine, if you love glory. Detestation to him who has profaned the memory of this most holy martyr,—the guide and avenger of her king, the redeemer and saviour of her country.

Catharine. Be it so; but Voltaire buoys me up above some impertinent, troublesome qualms.

Dashkof. If Deism had been prevalent in Europe, he would have been the champion of Christianity; and, if the French had been Protestants, he would have shed tears upon the papal slipper. He buoys up no one; for he gives no one hope. He may amuse: dulness itself must be amused, indeed, by the versatility and brilliancy of his wit.

Catharine. While I was meditating on the great action I have now so happily accomplished, I sometimes thought his wit feeble. This idea, no doubt, originated from the littleness of everything in comparison with my undertaking.

Dashkof. Alas! we lose much when we lose the capacity of being delighted by men of genius, and gain little when we are forced to run to them for incredulity.

Catharine. I shall make some use of my philosopher at Ferney. I detest him as much as you do; but where

IMAGINARY CONVERSATIONS 323

will you find me another who writes so pointedly? You really, then, fancy that people care for truth? Innocent Dashkof! Believe me, there is nothing so delightful in life as to find a liar in a person of repute. Have you never heard good folk rejoicing at it? Or, rather, can you mention to me any one who has not been in raptures when he could communicate such glad tidings? The goutiest man would go on foot without a crutch to tell his friend of it at midnight; and would cross the Neva for the purpose, when he doubted whether the ice would bear him. Men, in general, are so weak in truth, that they are obliged to put their bravery under it to prop it. Why do they pride themselves, think you, on their courage, when the bravest of them is by many degrees less courageous than a mastiff-bitch in the straw? It is only that they may be rogues without hearing it, and make their fortunes without rendering an account of them.

Now we chat again as we used to do. Your spirits and your enthusiasm have returned. Courage, my sweet Dashkof; do not begin to sigh again. We never can want husbands while we are young and lively. Alas! I cannot always be so. Heigho! But serfs and preferment will do: none shall refuse me at ninety,—Paphos or Tobolsk.

Have not you a song for me?

Dashkof. German or Russian?

Catharine. Neither, neither. Some frightful word might drop—might remind me—no, nothing shall remind me. French, rather: French songs are the liveliest in the world.

Is the rouge off my face?

Dashkof. It is rather in streaks and mottles; excepting just under the eyes, where it sits as it should do.

Catharine. I am heated and thirsty: I cannot imagine how. I think we have not yet taken our coffee.

Was it so strong? What am I dreaming of? I could eat only a slice of melon at breakfast; my duty urged me *then,* and dinner is yet to come. Remember, I am to faint at the midst of it when the intelligence comes in, or rather when, in despite of every effort to conceal it from me, the awful truth has flashed upon my mind. Remember, too, you are to catch me, and to cry for help, and to tear those fine flaxen hairs which we laid up together on the toilet; and we are both to be as inconsolable as we can be for the life of us. Not now, child, not now. Come, sing. I know not how to fill up the interval. Two long hours yet!—how stupid and tiresome! I wish all things of the sort could be done and be over in a day. They are mightily disagreeable when by nature one is not cruel. People little know my character. I have the tenderest heart upon earth. I am courageous, but I am full of weaknesses. I possess in perfection the higher part of men, and—to a friend I may say it—the most amiable part of women. Ho, ho! at last you smile: now, your thoughts upon that.

Dashkof. I have heard fifty men swear it.

Catharine. They lied, the knaves! I hardly knew them by sight. We were talking of the sad necessity.— Ivan must follow next: he is heir to the throne. I have a wild, impetuous, pleasant little *protégé,* who shall attempt to rescue him. I will have him persuaded and incited to it, and assured of pardon on the scaffold. He can never know the trick we play him; unless his head, like a bottle of Bordeaux, ripens its contents in the sawdust. Orders are given that Ivan be dispatched at the first disturbance in the precincts of the castle; in short, at the fire of the sentry. But not now,—another time: two such scenes together, and without some interlude, would perplex people.

I thought we spoke of singing: do not make me wait,

IMAGINARY CONVERSATIONS

my dearest creature! Now cannot you sing as usual, without smoothing your dove's-throat with your handkerchief, and taking off your necklace? Give it me, then; give it me. I will hold it for you: I must play with something.

Sing, sing; I am quite impatient.

THE MAID OF ORLEANS AND AGNES SOREL

Agnes. If a boy could ever be found so beautiful and so bashful, I should have taken you for a boy about fifteen years old. Really and without flattery, I think you very lovely.

Jeanne. I hope I shall be greatly more so.

Agnes. Nay, nay: do not expect to improve, except a little in manner. Manner is the fruit, blushes are the blossom: these must fall off before the fruit sets.

Jeanne. By God's help, I may be soon more comely in the eyes of men.

Agnes. Ha, ha! even in piety there is a spice of vanity. The woman can only cease to be the woman when angels have disrobed her in Paradise.

Jeanne. I shall be far from loveliness, even in my own eyes, until I execute the will of God in the deliverance of his people.

Agnes. Never hope it.

Jeanne. The deliverance that is never hoped, seldom comes. We conquer by hope and trust.

Agnes. Be content to have humbled the proud islanders. Oh, how I rejoice that a mere child has done so!

Jeanne. A child of my age, or younger, chastised the Philistines, and smote down the giant their leader.

Agnes. But Talbott is a giant of another mould: his will is immovable; his power is irresistible; his word of command is, *Conquer.*

326 WALTER SAVAGE LANDOR

Jeanne. It shall be heard no longer. The tempest of battle drowns it in English blood.

Agnes. Poor simpleton! The English will recover from the stupor of their fright, believing thee no longer to be a sorceress. Did ever sword or spear intimidate them? Hast thou never heard of Crecy? Hast thou never heard of Agincourt? Hast thou never heard of Poitiers, where the chivalry of France was utterly vanquished by sick and starving men, one against five? The French are the eagle's plume; the English are his talon.

Jeanne. The talon and the plume shall change places.

Agnes. Too confident!

Jeanne. O lady! is any one too confident in God?

Agnes. We may mistake his guidance. Already, not only the whole host of the English, but many of our wisest and most authoritative Churchmen, believe you on their consciences to act under the instigation of Satan.

Jeanne. What country or what creature has the Evil One ever saved? With what has he tempted me?—with reproaches, with scorn, with weary days, with slumberless nights, with doubts, distrusts, and dangers, with absence from all who cherish me, with immodest, soldierly language, and perhaps an untimely and a cruel death.

Agnes. But you are not afraid.

Jeanne. Healthy and strong, yet always too timorous, a few seasons ago I fled away from the lowings of a young steer, if he ran opposite; I awaited not the butting of a full-grown kid; the barking of a house-dog at our neighbour's gate turned me pale as ashes; and (shame upon me!) I scarcely dared kiss the child, when he called on me with burning tongue in the pestilence of a fever.

IMAGINARY CONVERSATIONS 327

Agnes. No wonder! A creature in a fever! what a frightful thing!

Jeanne. It would be, were it not so piteous.

Agnes. And did you kiss it? Did you really kiss the lips?

Jeanne. I fancied mine would refresh them a little.

Agnes. And did they? I should have thought mine could do but trifling good in such cases.

Jeanne. Alas! when I believed I had quite cooled them, it was death had done it.

Agnes. Ah! this is courage.

Jeanne. The courage of the weaker sex, inherent in us all, but as deficient in me as in any until an infant taught me my duty by its cries. Yet never have I quailed in the front of the fight, where I directed our ranks against the bravest. God pardon me, if I err! but I believe his Spirit flamed within my breast, strengthened my arm, and led me on to victory.

Agnes. Say not so, or they will burn thee alive, poor child!

Why fallest thou before me? I have some power, indeed; but in this extremity I could little help thee: the priest never releases the victim.

What! how! thy countenance is radiant with a heavenly joy: thy humility is like an angel's at the feet of God; I am unworthy to behold it.

Rise, Jeanne, rise!

Jeanne. Martyrdom too! The reward were too great for such an easy and glad obedience. France will become just and righteous; France will praise the Lord for her deliverance.

Agnes. Sweet enthusiast! I am confident, I am certain, of thy innocence.

Jeanne. O Lady Agnes!

Agnes. Why fixest thou thy eyes on me so piteously?

WALTER SAVAGE LANDOR

Why sobbest thou,—thou, to whom the representation of an imminent death to be apprehended for thee left untroubled, joyous, exulting? Speak; tell me.

Jeanne. I must. This also is commanded me. You believe me innocent?

Agnes. In truth, I do; why, then, look abashed? Alas! alas! could I mistake the reason? I spoke of innocence!

Leave me, leave me. Return another time. Follow thy vocation.

Jeanne. Agnes Sorel! be thou more than innocent, if innocence is denied thee. In the name of the Almighty, I call on thee to earn his mercy.

Agnes. I implore it incessantly, by day, by night.

Jeanne. Serve him as thou mayest best serve him; and thy tears, I promise thee, shall soon be less bitter than those which are dropping on this jewelled hand, and on the rude one which has dared to press it.

Agnes. What can I,—what can I do?

Jeanne. Lead the King back to his kingdom.

Agnes. The King is in France.

Jeanne. No, no, no!

Agnes. Upon my word of honour.

Jeanne. And at such a time, O Heaven! in idleness and sloth?

Agnes. Indeed, no. He is busy (this is the hour) in feeding and instructing two young hawks. Could you but see the little miscreants, how they dare to bite and claw and tug at him! He never hurts or scolds them for it; he is so good-natured: he even lets them draw blood; he is so very brave!

Running away from France! Who could have raised such a report? Indeed, he is here. He never thought of leaving the country; and his affairs are becoming more and more prosperous ever since the battle. Can

IMAGINARY CONVERSATIONS   329

you not take my asseverations? Must I say it? he is
now in this very house.

Jeanne. Then, not in France. In France, all love
their country. Others of our kings, old men tell us,
have been captives; but less ignominiously. Their
enemies have respected their misfortunes and their
honour.

Agnes. The English have always been merciful and
generous.

Jeanne. And will you be less generous, less merciful?

Agnes. I?

Jeanne. You; the beloved of Charles.

Agnes. This is too confident. No, no, do not draw
back; it is not too confident: it is only too reproachful.
But your actions have given you authority. I have,
nevertheless, a right to demand of you what creature on
earth I have ever treated ignominiously or unkindly.

Jeanne. Your beloved; your King.

Agnes. Never. I owe to him all I have, all I am.

Jeanne. Too true! But let him in return owe to
you, O Lady Agnes, eternal happiness, eternal glory.
Condescend to labour with the humble handmaiden of
the Lord, in fixing his throne and delivering his people.

Agnes. I cannot fight; I abominate war.

Jeanne. Not more than I do; but men love it.

Agnes. Too much.

Jeanne. Often too much, for often unjustly. But
when God's right hand is visible in the vanguard, we
who are called must follow.

Agnes. I dare not; indeed, I dare not.

Jeanne. You dare not?—you who dare withhold the
King from his duty!

Agnes. We must never talk of their duties to our
princes.

Jeanne. Then, we omit to do much of our own. It is now mine; but, above all, it is yours.

Agnes. There are learned and religious men who might more properly.

Jeanne. Are these learned and religious men in the court? Pray tell me: since, if they are, seeing how poorly they have sped, I may peradventure, however unwillingly, however blamably, abate a little of my reverence for learning, and look for pure religion in lower places.

Agnes. They are modest; and they usually ask of me in what manner they may best please their master.

Jeanne. They believe, then, that your affection is proportional to the power you possess over him. I have heard complaints that it is usually quite the contrary. But can such great men be loved? And do you love him? Why do you sigh so?

Agnes. Life is but sighs; and, when they cease, 'tis over.

Jeanne. Now deign to answer me: do you truly love him?

Agnes. From my soul, and above it.

Jeanne. Then, save him!

Lady, I am grieved at your sorrow, although it will hereafter be a source of joy unto you. The purest water runs from the hardest rock. Neither worth nor wisdom come without an effort; and patience and piety and salutary knowledge spring up and ripen from under the harrow of affliction. Before there is wine or there is oil, the grape must be trodden and the olive must be pressed.

I see you are framing in your heart the resolution.

Agnes. My heart can admit nothing but his image.

Jeanne. It must fall thence at last.

Agnes. Alas! alas! Time loosens man's affections.

IMAGINARY CONVERSATIONS 331

I may become unworthy. In the sweetest flower there is much that is not fragrance, and which transpires when the freshness has passed away.

Alas, if he should ever cease to love me!

Jeanne. Alas, if God should!

Agnes. Then, indeed, he might afflict me with so grievous a calamity.

Jeanne. And none worse after?

Agnes. What can there be?

O Heaven! mercy! mercy!

Jeanne. Resolve to earn it: one hour suffices.

Agnes. I am lost. Leave me, leave me.

Jeanne. Do we leave the lost? Are they beyond our care? Remember who died for them, and them only.

Agnes. You subdue me. Spare me: I would only collect my thoughts.

Jeanne. Cast them away. Fresh herbage springs from under the withered. Be strong; and, if you love, be generous. Is it more glorious to make a captive than to redeem one?

Agnes. Is he in danger? Oh!—you see all things— is he? is he? is he?

Jeanne. From none but you.

Agnes. God, it is evident, has given to thee alone the power of rescuing both him and France. He has bestowed on thee the mightiness of virtue.

Jeanne. Believe, and prove thy belief, that he has left no little of it still in thee.

Agnes. When we have lost our chastity, we have lost all, in his sight and in man's. But man is unforgiving; God is merciful.

Jeanne. I am so ignorant, I know only a part of my duties: yet those which my Maker has taught me I am earnest to perform. He teaches me that divine love has less influence over the heart than human; He teaches

me that it ought to have more; finally, He commands me to announce to thee, not His anger, but His will.

Agnes. Declare it; Oh! declare it. I do believe His holy word is deposited in thy bosom.

Jeanne. Encourage the King to lead his vassals to the field.

Agnes. When the season is milder.

Jeanne. And bid him leave you for ever.

Agnes. Leave me! one whole campaign! one entire summer! Oh, anguish! it sounded in my ears as if you said, "for ever."

Jeanne. I say it again.

Agnes. Thy power is superhuman; mine is not.

Jeanne. It ought to be, in setting God at defiance. The mightiest of the angels rued it.

Agnes. We did not make our hearts.

Jeanne. But we can mend them.

Agnes. Oh! mine (God knows it) bleeds.

Jeanne. Say rather it expels from it the last stagnant drop of its rebellious sin. Salutary pangs may be painfuller than mortal ones.

Agnes. Bid him leave me! wish it! permit it! think it near! believe it ever can be! Go, go.—I am lost eternally.

Jeanne. And Charles too.

Agnes. Hush! hush! What has he done that other men have not done also?

Jeanne. He has left undone what others do. Other men fight for their country.

I always thought it was pleasant to the young and beautiful to see those they love victorious and applauded. Twice in my lifetime I have been present at wakes, where prizes were contended for,—what prizes I quite forget; certainly not kingdoms. The winner was made happy; but there was one made happier. Village maids

IMAGINARY CONVERSATIONS   333

love truly: ay, they love glory too; and not their own. The tenderest heart loves best the courageous one: the gentle voice says, "Why wert thou so hazardous?" The deeper-toned replies, "For thee, for thee."

Agnes. But if the saints of heaven are offended, as I fear they may be, it would be presumptuous in the King to expose his person in battle until we have supplicated and appeased them.

Jeanne. One hour of self-denial, one hour of stern exertion against the assaults of passion, outvalues a life of prayer.

Agnes. Prayer, if many others will pray with us, can do all things. I will venture to raise up that arm which has only one place for its repose; I will steal away from that undivided pillow, fragrant with fresh and unextinguishable love.

Jeanne. Sad earthly thoughts!

Agnes. You make them sad; you cannot make them earthly. There is a divinity in a love descending from on high, in theirs who can see into the heart and mold it to their will.

Jeanne. Has man that power?

Agnes. Happy, happy girl! to ask it, and unfeignedly.

Jeanne. Be happy too.

Agnes. How? how?

Jeanne. By passing resolutely through unhappiness. It must be done.

Agnes. I will throw myself on the pavement, and pray until no star is in the heavens. Oh, I will so pray, so weep!

Jeanne. Unless you save the tears of others, in vain you shed your own.

Agnes. Again I ask you, What *can* I do?

Jeanne. When God has told you what you ought to do, he has already told you what you can.

Agnes. I will think about it seriously.

Jeanne. Serious thoughts are folded up, chested, and unlooked-at: lighter, like dust, settle all about the chamber. The promise to think seriously dismisses and closes the door on the thought. Adieu! God pity and pardon you. Through you the wrath of Heaven will fall upon the kingdom.

Agnes. Denouncer of just vengeance, recall the sentence! I tremble before that countenance severely radiant: I sink amid that calm, more appalling than the tempest. Look not into my heart with those gentle eyes! Oh, how they penetrate! They ought to see no sin: sadly must it pain them.

Jeanne. Think not of me; pursue thy destination; save France.

Agnes (*after a long pause*). Glorious privilege! divine appointment! Is it thus, O my Redeemer, my crimes are visited?

Come with me, blessed Jeanne! come instantly with me to the King: come to him whom thy virtue and valour have rescued.

Jeanne. Not now; nor ever with thee. Again I shall behold him,—a conqueror at Orleans, a king at Rheims. Regenerate Agnes! be this thy glory, if there be any that is not God's.

ADMIRAL BLAKE AND HUMPHREY BLAKE

Blake. Humphrey! it hath pleased God, upon this day, to vouchsafe unto the English arms a signal victory. Brother! it grieves my heart that neither of us can rejoice in it as we should do. Evening is closing on the waters: our crews are returning thanks and offering up prayers to the Almighty. Alas! Alas! that we, who ought to be the most grateful for his protection, and

IMAGINARY CONVERSATIONS 335

for the spirit he hath breathed into our people, should be the only men in this vast armament whom he hath sorely chastened!—that we of all others should be ashamed to approach the throne of grace among our countrymen and comrades! There are those who accuse you, and they are brave and honest men—there are those, O Humphrey! Humphrey!—was the sound ever heard in our father's house?—who accuse you, brother! brother!—how can I ever find utterance for the word?—yea, of cowardice.

Stand off! I want no help: let me be.

Humphrey. To-day, for the first time in my life, I was in the midst of many ships of superior force firing upon mine, at once and incessantly.

Blake. The very position where most intrepidity was required. Were none with you?—were none in the same danger? Shame, shame! You owed many an example, and you defrauded them of it. They could not gain promotion, the poor seamen! they could not hope for glory in the wide world: example they might have hoped for. You would not have robbed them of their prize-money—

Humphrey. Brother! was ever act of dishonesty imputed to a Blake?

Blake. Until now. You have robbed them even of the chance they had of winning it; you have robbed them of the pride, the just and chastened pride, awaiting them at home; you have robbed their children of their richest inheritance, a father's good repute.

Humphrey. Despite of calumniators, there are worthy men ready to speak in my favour, at least in extenuation—

Blake. I will hear them, as becomes me, although I myself am cognizant of your default; for during the conflict how anxiously, as often as I could, did I look

WALTER SAVAGE LANDOR

toward your frigate! Especial care could not be fairly taken that aid at the trying moment should be at hand: other vessels were no less exposed than yours; and it was my duty to avoid all partiality in giving my support.

Humphrey. Grievous as my short-coming may be, surely I am not precluded from what benefit the testimony of my friends may afford me.

Blake. Friends!—ah, thou hast many, Humphrey! and many hast thou well deserved. In youth, in boyhood, in childhood, thy honied temper brought ever warm friends about thee. Easiness of disposition conciliates bad and good alike; it draws affections to it, and relaxes enmities: but that same easiness renders us, too often, negligent of our graver duties. God knows, I may without the same excuse (if it is any) be impeached of negligence in many of mine; but never where the honour or safety of my country was concerned. Wherefore the Almighty's hand, in this last battle, as in others no less prosperous, hath conducted and sustained me.

Humphrey! did thy heart wax faint within thee through want of confidence in our sole Deliverer?

Humphrey. Truly I have no such plea.

Blake. It were none; it were an aggravation.

Humphrey. I confess I am quite unable to offer any adequate defence for my backwardness, my misconduct. Oh! could the hour return, the battle rage again! How many things are worse than death!—how few things better! I am twelve years younger than you are, brother, and want your experience.

Blake. Is that your only want? Deplorable is it to know, as now I know, that you will never have it, and that you will have a country which you can never serve.

Humphrey. Deplorable it is, indeed. God help me!

Blake. Worse evil soon may follow,—worse to me,

IMAGINARY CONVERSATIONS 337

remembering thy childhood. Merciful Father! after all the blood that hath been shed this day, must I devote a brother's?

Humphrey. O Robert!—always compassionate, always kind and generous!—do not inflict on yourself so lasting a calamity, so unavailing a regret.

Listen!—not to me—but listen. I hear under your bow the sound of oars. I hear them drawn into boats: verily do I believe that several of the captains are come to intercede for me, as they said they would do.

Blake. Intercession is vain. Honourable men shall judge you. A man to be honourable must be strictly just, at the least. Will brave men spare you? It lies with them. Whatever be their sentence, my duty is (God give me strength!) to execute it.

Gentlemen! who sent for you? [*Officers come aboard*].

Senior Officer. General! we, the captains of your fleet, come before you upon the most painful of duties.

Blake (*to himself*). I said so: his doom is sealed. (*To Senior Officer.*) Speak, sir! speak out, I say. A man who hath fought so bravely as you have fought to-day ought never to hesitate and falter.

Senior Officer. General! we grieve to say that Captain Humphrey Blake, commanding a frigate in the service of the Commonwealth, is accused of remissness in his duty.

Blake. I know it. Where is the accuser? What! no answer from any of you? Then I am he. Captain Humphrey Blake is here impleaded of neglecting to perform his uttermost in the seizure or destruction of the enemy's galleons. Is the crime—write it, write it down!—no need to speak it here—capital? Negligence? no worse? But worse can there be?

Senior Officer. We would humbly represent—

Blake. Representations, if made at all, must be made

elsewhere. He goes forthwith to England. Return each of you to his vessel. Delinquency, grave delinquency, there hath been, of what nature and to what extent you must decide. Take him away. (*Alone.*) Just God! am I the guilty man, that I should drink to the very dregs such a cup of bitterness?

Forgive, forgive, O Lord! the sinful cry of thy servant! Thy will be done! Thou hast shown thy power this day, O Lord! now show, and make me worthy of, thy mercy!

Various and arduous as were Blake's duties, such on all occasions were his circumspection and discretion, that no fault could be detected or invented in him. His victories were won against all calculation but his own. Recollecting, however late, his services; recollecting that in private life, in political, in military, his purity was ever the same,—England will place Robert Blake the foremost and the highest of her defenders. He was the archetype of her Nelsons, Collingwoods, and Pellews. Of all the men that ever bore a sword, none was worthier of that awful trust.

METELLUS AND MARIUS

Metellus. Well met, Caius Marius! My orders are to find instantly a centurion who shall mount the walls; one capable of observation, acute in remark, prompt, calm, active, intrepid. The Numantians are sacrificing to the gods in secrecy; they have sounded the horn once only,—and hoarsely, and low, and mournfully.

Marius. Was that ladder I see yonder among the caper-bushes and purple lilies, under where the fig-tree grows out of the rampart, left for me?

Metellus. Even so, wert thou willing. Wouldst thou mount it?

Marius. Rejoicingly. If none are below or near, may I explore the state of things by entering the city?

Metellus. Use thy discretion in that.

IMAGINARY CONVERSATIONS 339

What seest thou? Wouldst thou leap down? Lift the ladder.

Marius. Are there spikes in it where it sticks in the turf? I should slip else.

Metellus. How! bravest of our centurions, art even thou afraid? Seest thou any one by?

Marius. Ay; some hundreds close beneath me.

Metellus. Retire, then. Hasten back; I will protect thy descent.

Marius. May I speak, O Metellus, without an offence to discipline?

Metellus. Say.

Marius. Listen! Dost thou not hear?

Metellus. Shame on thee! alight, alight! my shield shall cover thee.

Marius. There is a murmur like the hum of bees in the beanfield of Cereate;* for the sun is hot, and the ground is thirsty. When will it have drunk up for me the blood that has run, and is yet oozing on it, from those fresh bodies!

Metellus. How! We have not fought for many days; what bodies, then, are fresh ones?

Marius. Close beneath the wall are those of infants and of girls; in the middle of the road are youths, emaciated; some either unwounded or wounded months ago; some on their spears, others on their swords: no few have received in mutual death the last interchange of friendship; their daggers unite them, hilt to hilt, bosom to bosom.

Metellus. Mark rather the living,—what are they about?

Marius. About the sacrifice, which portends them, I conjecture, but little good,—it burns sullenly and

* The farm of Marius, near Arpinum.

WALTER SAVAGE LANDOR

slowly. The victim will lie upon the pyre till morning, and still be unconsumed, unless they bring more fuel.

I will leap down and walk on cautiously, and return with tidings, if death should spare me.

Never was any race of mortals so unmilitary as these Numantians: no watch, no stations, no palisades across the streets.

Metellus. Did they want, then, all the wood for the altar?

Marius. It appears so,—I will return anon.

Metellus. The gods speed thee, my brave, honest, Marius!

Marius (returned). The ladder should have been better spiked for that slippery ground. I am down again safe, however. Here a man may walk securely, and without picking his steps.

Metellus. Tell me, Caius, what thou sawest.

Marius. The streets of Numantia.

Metellus. Doubtless; but what else?

Marius. The temples and markets and places of exercise and fountains.

Metellus. Art thou crazed, centurion? what more? Speak plainly, at once, and briefly.

Marius. I beheld, then, all Numantia.

Metellus. Has terror maddened thee? hast thou descried nothing of the inhabitants but those carcasses under the ramparts?

Marius. Those, O Metellus, lie scattered, although not indeed far asunder. The greater part of the soldiers and citizens—of the fathers, husbands, widows, wives, espoused—were assembled together.

Metellus. About the altar?

Marius. Upon it.

Metellus. So busy and earnest in devotion! but how all upon it?

IMAGINARY CONVERSATIONS

Marius. It blazed under them, and over them, and round about them.

Metellus. Immortal gods! Art thou sane, Caius Marius? Thy visage is scorched: thy speech may wander after such an enterprise; thy shield burns my hand.

Marius. I thought it had cooled again. Why, truly, it seems hot: I now feel it.

Metellus. Wipe off those embers.

Marius. 'Twere better: there will be none opposite to shake them upon, for some time.

The funereal horn, that sounded with such feebleness, sounded not so from the faint heart of him who blew it. Him I saw; him only of the living. Should I say it? there was another: there was one child whom its parent could not kill, could not part from. She had hidden it in her robe, I suspect; and, when the fire had reached it, either it shrieked or she did. For suddenly a cry pierced through the crackling pinewood, and something of round in figure fell from brand to brand, until it reached the pavement, at the feet of him who had blown the horn. I rushed toward him, for I wanted to hear the whole story, and felt the pressure of time. Condemn not my weakness, O Cæcilius! I wished an enemy to live an hour longer; for my orders were to explore and bring intelligence. When I gazed on him, in height almost gigantic, I wondered not that the blast of his trumpet was so weak: rather did I wonder that Famine, whose hand had indented every limb and feature, had left him any voice articulate. I rushed toward him, however, ere my eyes had measured either his form or strength. He held the child against me, and staggered under it.

"Behold," he exclaimed, "the glorious ornament of a Roman triumph!"

WALTER SAVAGE LANDOR

I stood horror-stricken; when suddenly drops, as of rain, pattered down from the pyre. I looked; and many were the precious stones, many were the amulets and rings and bracelets, and other barbaric ornaments, unknown to me in form or purpose, that tinkled on the hardened and black branches, from mothers and wives and betrothed maids; and some, too, I can imagine, from robuster arms,—things of joyance, won in battle. The crowd of incumbent bodies was so dense and heavy, that neither the fire nor the smoke could penetrate upward from among them; and they sank, whole and at once, into the smouldering cavern eaten out below. He at whose neck hung the trumpet felt this, and started.

"There is yet room," he cried, "and there is strength enough yet, both in the element and in me."

He extended his withered arms, he thrust forward the gaunt links of his throat, and·upon gnarled knees, that smote each other audibly, tottered into the civic fire. It—like some hungry and strangest beast on the innermost wild of Africa, pierced, broken, prostrate, motionless, gazed at by its hunter in the impatience of glory, in the delight of awe—panted once more, and seized him.

I have seen within this hour, O Metellus, what Rome in the cycle of her triumphs will never see, what the Sun in his eternal course can never show her, what the Earth has borne but now, and must never rear again for her, what Victory herself has envied her—a Numantian.

Metellus. We shall feast to-morrow. Hope, Caius Marius, to become a tribune: trust in fortune.

Marius. Auguries are surer: surest of all is perseverance.

Metellus. I hope the wine has not grown vapid in my tent: I have kept it waiting, and must now report

IMAGINARY CONVERSATIONS 343

to Scipio the intelligence of our discovery. Come after me, Caius.

Marius (*alone*). The tribune is the discoverer! the centurion is the scout! Caius Marius must enter more Numantias. Light-hearted Cæcilius, thou mayest perhaps hereafter, and not with humbled but with exulting pride, take orders from this hand. If Scipio's words are fate, and to me they sound so, the portals of the Capitol may shake before my chariot, as my horses plunge back at the applauses of the people, and Jove in his high domicile may welcome the citizen of Arpinum.

SYDNEY SMITH

SYDNEY SMITH'S name is one frequently encountered
in literary reminiscences of the early nineteenth century, and some of his witticisms are still remembered.
But lacking a Boswell to immortalize him, his good
talk and sound sense are now scarcely more than a
tradition. His literary work was unfortunately limited
to public letters upon controversial questions of the
day and to a series of articles in the *Edinburgh Review*.
To this magazine he was chief contributor in the years
1802-1827; therein, with some current book as a text,
he wrote upon a vast number of social, political, and
religious questions. He was not, however, a literary
critic, the books which he reviewed are for the most
part dead, and the public questions which he debated
have now in most instances only an historical interest.
To a student who desires an intimate knowledge of
English society during the first quarter of the nineteenth century the essays republished from the *Edinburgh* are valuable, but they can hardly be so to the
general reader.

There is, nevertheless, much good sense and pungent
comment in them which should be preserved in some
little volume of excerpts. The questions with which
he concerned himself are not wholly dead issues, though
today they have assumed other forms. Sanity, tolerance, and humor are none too common in the world;
we can afford to lose no conspicuous examples of them.
Nor are Sydney Smith's prejudices, with which he

SYDNEY SMITH 345

was well endowed, without their savour. Had he cast his views of life in a volume of familiar essays he might take rank, with Cobbett and Hunt, only a little below the best prose writers of his time. The fragment here reprinted, *A Little Moral Advice,* is evidence of his abilities in a field he did not attempt.

Noodle's Oration is an excerpt from a review of Jeremy Bentham's *The Book of Fallacies.* Smith remarks of this book, "Neither Gods, men, nor booksellers can doubt the necessity of a middleman between Mr. Bentham and the public. Mr. Bentham is long; Mr. Bentham is occasionally involved and obscure; Mr. Bentham invents new and alarming expressions; Mr. Bentham loves division and subdivision—and he loves method itself, more than its consequences. Those only, therefore, who know his originality, his knowledge, his vigour, and his boldness, will recur to the works themselves." In a review of considerable length Sydney Smith thereupon interprets Bentham to his public, concluding with *Noodle's Oration,* a burlesque parliamentary address in which he contrives to exhibit most of the political fallacies which Bentham had sought to puncture, fallacies advanced by those who, under the pretense of caution and good sense, combat every effort of progress and reform. These fallacies are always with us. So, too, are societies for the suppression of this, that, and the other diversion of our fellowmen. Sydney Smith was doubtful both of the aims and methods of suppression. Progress, he conceived, did not lie that way. American readers should peruse his review of the *Proceedings of the Society for the Suppression of Vice* with peculiar edification.

A LITTLE MORAL ADVICE

**A FRAGMENT ON THE CULTIVATION AND IMPROVEMENT
OF THE ANIMAL SPIRITS.**

It is surprising to see for what foolish causes men hang themselves. The most silly repulse, the most trifling ruffle of temper, or derangement of stomach, anything seems to justify an appeal to the razor or the cord. I have a contempt for persons who destroy themselves. Live on, and look evil in the face; walk up to it, and you will find it less than you imagined, and often you will not find it at all; for it will recede as you advance. Any fool may be a suicide. When you are in a melancholy fit, first suspect the body, appeal to rhubarb and calomel, and send for the apothecary; a little bit of gristle sticking in the wrong place, an untimely consumption of custard, excessive gooseberries, often cover the mind with clouds and bring on the most distressing views of human life.

I start up at two o'clock in the morning, after my first sleep, in an agony of terror, and feel all the weight of life upon my soul. It is impossible that I can bring up such a family of children, my sons and daughters will be beggars; I shall live to see those whom I loved exposed to the scorn and contumely of the world!—But stop, thou child of sorrow, and humble imitator of Job, and tell me on what you dined. Was not there soup and salmon, and then a plate of beef, and then duck, blanc-mange, cream cheese, diluted with beer, claret, champagne, hock, tea, coffee, and noyeau? And after all this, you talk of the *mind* and the evils of life! These kind of cases do not need meditation, but magnesia. Take short views of life. What am I to do in these times with such a family of children? So I argued, and lived dejected and with

346

A LITTLE MORAL ADVICE

little hope; but the difficulty vanished as life went on.
An uncle died, and left me some money; an aunt died,
and left me more; my daughter married well; I had
two or three appointments, and before life was half
over became a prosperous man. And so will you. Every
one has uncles and aunts who are mortal; friends start
up out of the earth; time brings a thousand chances
in your favour; legacies fall from the clouds. Nothing
so absurd as to sit down and wring your hands because
all the good which may happen to you in twenty years
has not taken place at this precise moment.

The greatest happiness which can happen to any
one is to cultivate a love of reading. Study is often
dull because it is improperly managed. I make no
apology for speaking of myself, for as I write anon-
ymously nobody knows who I am, and if I did not,
very few would be the wiser—but every man speaks
more firmly when he speaks from his own experience.
I read four books at a time; some classical book perhaps on Monday, Wednesday, and Friday mornings.
The "History of France," we will say, on the evenings
of the same days. On Tuesday, Thursday, and Saturday, Mosheim or Lardner, and in the evening of
those days, Reynolds' Lectures, or Burns' Travels.
Then I have always a standing book of poetry, and a
novel to read when I am in the humour to read nothing
else. Then I translate some French into English one
day, and re-translate it the next; so that I have seven
or eight pursuits going on at the same time, and this
produces the cheerfulness of diversity, and avoids that
gloom which proceeds from hanging a long while over
a single book. I do not recommend this as a receipt
for becoming a learned man, but for becoming a cheerful one.

Nothing contributes more certainly to the animal

SYDNEY SMITH

spirits than benevolence. Servants and common people are always about you; make moderate attempts to please everybody, and the effort will insensibly lead you to a more happy state of mind. Pleasure is very reflective, and if you give it you will feel it. The pleasure you give by kindness of manner returns to you, and often with compound interest. The receipt for cheerfulness is not to have one motive only in the day for living, but a number of little motives; a man who from the time he rises till bedtime conducts himself like a gentleman, who throws some little condescension into his manner to superiors, and who is always contriving to soften the distance between himself and the poor and ignorant, is always improving his animal spirits, and adding to his happiness.

I recommend lights as a great improver of animal spirits. How is it possible to be happy with two mould candles ill snuffed? You may be virtuous, and wise, and good, but two candles will not do for animal spirits. Every night the room in which I sit is lighted up like a town after a great naval victory, and in this cereous galaxy and with a blazing fire, it is scarcely possible to be low-spirited, a thousand pleasing images spring up in the mind, and I can see the little blue demons scampering off like parish boys pursued by the beadle.

NOODLE'S ORATION

"What would our ancestors say to this, Sir? How does this measure tally with their institutions? How does it agree with their experience? Are we to put the wisdom of yesterday in competition with the wisdom of centuries? (*Hear, hear!*) Is beardless youth to show no respect for the decisions of mature age? (*Loud cries of hear! hear!*) If this measure be right,

NOODLE'S ORATION

would it have escaped the wisdom of those Saxon progenitors to whom we are indebted for so many of our best political institutions? Would the Dane have passed it over? Would the Norman have rejected it? Would such a notable discovery have been reserved for these modern and degenerate times? Besides, Sir, if the measure itself is good, I ask the honourable gentleman if this is the time for carrying it into execution—whether, in fact, a more unfortunate period could have been selected than that which he has chosen? If this were an ordinary measure, I should not oppose it with so much vehemence; but, Sir, it calls in question the wisdom of an irrevocable law—of a law passed at the memorable period of the Revolution. What right have we, Sir, to break down this firm column, on which the great men of that day stamped a character of eternity? Are not all authorities against this measure—Pitt, Fox, Cicero, and the Attorney and Solicitor General? The proposition is new, Sir; it is the first time it was ever heard in this House. I am not prepared, Sir—this house is not prepared, to receive it. The measure implies a distrust of his Majesty's government; their disapproval is sufficient to warrant opposition. Precaution only is requisite where danger is apprehended. Here the high character of the individuals in question is a sufficient guarantee against any ground of alarm. Give not, then, your sanction to this measure; for, whatever be its character, if you do give your sanction to it, the same man by whom this is proposed, will propose to you others to which it will be impossible to give your consent. I care very little, Sir, for the ostensible measure, but what is there behind? What are the honourable gentleman's future schemes? If we pass this bill, what fresh concessions may he not require? What further deg-

350 SYDNEY SMITH

radation is he planning for his country? Talk of evil and inconvenience, Sir! Look to other countries—study other aggregations and societies of men, and then see whether the laws of this country demand a remedy or deserve a panegyric. Was the honourable gentleman (let me ask him) always of this way of thinking? Do I not remember when he was the advocate in this House of very opposite opinions? I not only quarrel with his present sentiments, Sir, but I declare very frankly, I do not like the party with which he acts. If his own motives were as pure as possible, they cannot but suffer contamination from those with whom he is politically associated. This measure may be a boon to the constitution; but I will accept no favour to the constitution from such hands. (*Loud cries of hear! hear!*) I profess myself, Sir, an honest and upright member of the British Parliament, and I am not afraid to profess myself an enemy to all change and all innovation. I am satisfied with things as they are; and it will be my pride and pleasure to hand down this country to my children as I received it from those who preceded me. The honourable gentleman pretends to justify the severity with which he has attacked the noble Lord who presides in the Court of Chancery; but I say such attacks are pregnant with mischief to Government itself. Oppose Ministers, you oppose Government: disgrace Ministers, you disgrace Government: bring Ministers into contempt, you bring Government into contempt; and anarchy and civil war are the consequences. Besides, Sir, the measure is unnecessary. Nobody complains of disorder in that shape in which it is the aim of your measure to propose a remedy to it. The business is one of the greatest importance; there is need of the greatest caution and circumspection.

NOODLE'S ORATION

Do not let us be precipitate, Sir. It is impossible to foresee all consequences. Every thing should be gradual: the example of a neighbouring nation should fill us with alarm! The honourable gentleman has taxed me with illiberality, Sir. I deny the charge. I hate innovation; but I love improvement. I am an enemy to the corruption of Government; but I defend its influence. I dread reform; but I dread it only when it is intemperate. I consider the liberty of the Press as the great Palladium of the Constitution; but, at the same time, I hold the licentiousness of the Press in the greatest abhorrence. Nobody is more conscious than I am of the splendid abilities of the honourable mover; but I tell him at once, his scheme is too good to be practicable. It savours of Utopia. It looks well in theory; but it won't do in practice. It will not do, I repeat, Sir, in practice; and so the advocates of the measure will find, if unfortunately, it should find its way through Parliament. (*Cheers*) The source of that corruption to which the honourable member alludes, is in the minds of the people: so rank and extensive is that corruption, that no political reform can have any effect in removing it. Instead of reforming others—instead of reforming the State, the Constitution, and every thing that is most excellent, let each man reform himself! let him look at home; he will find there enough to do, without looking abroad, and aiming at what is out of his power. (*Loud cheers*) And now, Sir, as it is frequently the custom in this House to end with a quotation, and as the gentleman who preceded me in the debate has anticipated me in my favourite quotation of, 'The strong pull and the long pull,'—I shall end with the memorable words of the assembled Barons—'*Nolumus leges Angliae mutari*'."

PROCEEDINGS OF THE SOCIETY FOR THE SUPPRESSION OF VICE. (E. Review, 1809)

Statement of the Proceedings of the Society for the Suppression of Vice, from July 9. to November 12., read at their General Meeting, held November 12, 1804. With an Appendix, containing the Plan of the Society, etc., etc. London, 1804.

An Address to the Public from the Society for the Suppression of Vice, instituted in London 1802. Part the Second. Containing an Account of the Proceedings of the Society from its original Institution. London, 1804.

A SOCIETY, that holds out as its object the suppression of vice, must at first sight conciliate the favour of every respectable person; and he who objects to an institution calculated apparently to do so much good, is bound to give very clear and satisfactory reasons for his dissent from so popular an opinion. We certainly have, for a long time, had doubts of its utility; and now think ourselves called upon to state the grounds of our distrust.

Though it were clear that individual informers are useful auxiliaries to the administration of the laws, it would by no means follow that these informers should be allowed to combine,—to form themselves into a body,—to make a public purse,—and to prosecute under a common name. An informer, whether he is paid by the week, like the agents of this society—or by the crime, as in common cases,—is, in general, a man of a very indifferent character. So much fraud and deception are necessary for carrying on his trade—it is so odious to his fellow-subjects,—that no man of respectability will ever undertake it. It is evidently impossible to make such a character otherwise than odious. A man who receives weekly pay for prying into the transgressions of mankind, and bringing them to consequent punishment, will always be hated by

352

SOCIETY FOR SUPPRESSION OF VICE 353

mankind; and the office must fall to the lot of some man of desperate fortunes and ambiguous character. The multiplication, therefore, of such officers, and the extensive patronage of such characters, may, by the management of large and opulent societies, become an evil nearly as great as the evils they would suppress. The alarm which a private and disguised accuser occasions in a neighbourhood, is known to be prodigious, not only to the guilty, but to those who may be at once innocent, and ignorant, and timid. The destruction of social confidence is another evil, the consequence of information. An informer gets access to my house or family,—worms my secret out of me,—and then betrays me to the magistrate. Now, all these evils may be tolerated in a small degree, while, in a greater degree, they would be perfectly intolerable. Thirty or forty informers roaming about the metropolis, may frighten the mass of offenders a little, and do some good: ten thousand informers would either create an insurrection, or totally destroy the confidence and cheerfulness of private life. Whatever may be said, therefore, of the single and insulated informer, it is quite a new question when we come to a corporation of informers supported by large contributions. The one may be good, the other a very serious evil; the one legal, the other wholly out of the contemplation of law,—which often, and very wisely, allows individuals to do, what it forbids to many individuals assembled.

If once combination is allowed for the suppression of vice, where are its limits to be? Its capital may as well consist of 100,000 *l. per annum,* as of a thousand: its members may increase from a thousand subscribers, which this society, it seems, had reached in its second year, to twenty thousand: and in that case, what accused person of an inferior condition of life would

SYDNEY SMITH

have the temerity to stand against such a society?
Their mandates would very soon be law; and there is
no compliance into which they might not frighten the
common people, and the lower orders of tradesmen.
The idea of a society of gentlemen, calling themselves
an Association for the Suppression of Vice, would
alarm any small offender, to a degree that would make
him prefer any submission to any resistance. He would
consider the very fact of being accused by them as
almost sufficient to ruin him.

An individual accuser accuses at his own expense;
and the risk he runs is a good security that the subject
will not be harassed by needless accusations,—a security which, of course, he cannot have against such a
society as this, to whom pecuniary loss is an object
of such little consequence. It must never be forgotten,
that this is not a society for *punishing* people who have
been found to transgress the law, but for *accusing* persons of transgressing the law; and that, before trial,
the accused person is to be considered as innocent, and
is to have every fair chance of establishing his innocence. He must be no common defendant, however,
who does not contend against such a society with very
fearful odds;—the best counsel engaged for his oppo-
nents,—great practice in the particular court and particular species of cause,—witnesses thoroughly hack-
neyed in a court of justice,—and an unlimited command
of money. It by no means follows, that the legislature,
in allowing individuals to be informers, meant to subject the accused person to the superior weight and
power of such societies. The very influence of names
must have a considerable weight with the jury. Lord
Dartmouth, Lord Radstock, and the Bishop of Durham, versus a Whitechapel butcher or a publican! Is
this a fair contest before a jury? It is not so even in

SOCIETY FOR SUPPRESSION OF VICE   355

London; and what must it be in the country, where a society for the suppression of vice may consist of all the principal persons in the neighbourhood? These societies are now established in York, in Reading, and in many other large towns. Wherever this is the case, it is far from improbable that the same persons, at the Quarter or Town Sessions, may be both judges and accusers; and still more fatally so, if the offence is tried by a special jury. This is already most notoriously the case in societies for the preservation of game. They prosecute a poacher;—the jury is special; and the poor wretch is found guilty by the very same persons who have accused him.

If it be lawful for respectable men to combine for the purpose of turning informers, it is lawful for the lowest and most despicable race of informers to do the same thing; and then it is quite clear that every species of wickedness and extortion would be the consequence. We are rather surprised that no society of perjured attorneys and fraudulent bankrupts has risen up in this metropolis for the suppression of vice. A chairman, deputy-chairman, subscriptions, and an annual sermon, would give great dignity to their proceedings; and they would soon begin to take some rank in the world.

It is true that it is the duty of grand juries to inform against vice; but the law knows the probable number of grand jurymen, the times of their meeting, and the description of persons of whom they consist. Of voluntary societies it can know nothing,—their numbers, their wealth, or the character of their members. It may therefore trust to a grand jury what it would by no means trust to an unknown combination. A vast distinction is to be made, too, between official duties and voluntary duties. The first are commonly carried

SYDNEY SMITH

on with calmness and moderation; the latter often characterised, in their execution, by rash and intemperate zeal.

The present Society receives no members but those who are of the Church of England. As we are now arguing the question generally, we have a right to make any supposition. It is equally free, therefore, upon general principles, for a society of sectarians to combine and exclude members of the Church of England; and the suppression of vice may thus come in aid of Methodism, Jacobinism, or of any set of principles, however perilous, either to Church or State. The present Society may perhaps consist of persons whose sentiments on these points are rational and respectable. Combinations, however, of this sort may give birth to something far different; and such a supposition is the fair way of trying the question.

We doubt if there be not some mischief in averting the fears and hopes of the people from the known and constituted authorities of the country to those self-created powers;—a society that punishes in the Strand, another which rewards at Lloyd's Coffeehouse! If these things get to any great height, they throw an air of insignificance over those branches of the government to whom these cares properly devolve, and whose authority is by these means assisted, till it is superseded. It is supposed that a project must necessarily be good, because it is intended for the aid of law and government. At this rate, there should be a society in aid of the government, for procuring intelligence from foreign parts, with accredited agents all over Europe. There should be a voluntary transport board, and a gratuitous victualling office. There should be a duplicate, in short, of every department of the State, —the one appointed by the King, and the other by itself.

SOCIETY FOR SUPPRESSION OF VICE 357

There should be a real Lord Glenbervie in the woods and forests,—and with him a monster, a voluntary Lord Glenbervie, serving without pay, and guiding *gratis,* with secret counsel, the axe of his prototype. If it be asked, who are the constituted authorities who are legally appointed to watch over morals, and whose functions the Society usurp? our answer is, that there are in England about 12,000 clergy, not unhandsomely paid for persuading the people, and about 400 justices, 30 grand juries, and 40,000 constables, whose duty and whose inclination it is to compel them to do right. Under such circumstances, a voluntary moral society does indeed seem to be the purest result of volition; for there certainly is not the smallest particle of necessity mingled with its existence.

It is hardly possible that a society for the suppression of vice can ever be kept within the bounds of good sense and moderation. If there are many members who have really become so from a feeling of duty, there will necessarily be some who enter the Society to hide a bad character, and others whose object it is to recommend themselves to their betters by a sedulous and bustling inquisition into the immoralities of the public. The loudest and noisiest suppressors will always carry it against the more prudent part of the community; the most violent will be considered as the most moral; and those who see the absurdity will, from the fear of being thought to encourage vice, be reluctant to oppose it.

It is of great importance to keep public opinion on the side of virtue. To their authorised and legal correctors, mankind are, on common occasions, ready enough to submit; but there is something in the self-erection of a voluntary magistracy which creates so much disgust that it almost renders vice popular, and

SYDNEY SMITH

puts the offence at a premium. We have no doubt but that the immediate effect of a voluntary combination for the suppression of vice, is an involuntary combination in favour of the vices to be suppressed; and this is a very serious drawback from any good of which such societies may be the occasion; for the state of morals, at any one period, depends much more upon opinion than law; and to bring odious and disgusting auxiliaries to the aid of virtue, is to do the utmost possible good to the cause of vice. We regret that mankind are as they are; and we sincerely wish that the species at large were as completely devoid of every vice and infirmity as the President, Vice-President, and Committee of the Suppressing Society; but, till they are thus regenerated, it is of the greatest consequence to teach them virtue and religion in a manner which will not make them hate both the one and the other. The greatest delicacy is required in the application of violence to moral and religious sentiment. We forget, that the object is, not to produce the outward compliance, but to raise up the inward feeling, which secures the outward compliance. You may drag men into church by main force, and prosecute for buying a pot of beer,—and cut them off from the enjoyment of a leg of mutton;—and you may do all this, till you make the common people hate Sunday, and the clergy, and religion, and every thing which relates to such subjects. There are many crimes, indeed, where persuasion cannot be waited for, and where the untaught feelings of all men go along with the violence of the law. A robber and a murderer must be knocked on the head like mad dogs; but we have no great opinion of the possibility of indicting men into piety, or of calling in the Quarter Sessions to the aid of religion. You may produce outward conformity by these means; but you are so far from producing (the only thing worth

SOCIETY FOR SUPPRESSION OF VICE 359

producing) the inward feeling, that you incur a great risk of giving birth to a totally opposite sentiment.

The violent modes of making men good, just alluded to, have been resorted to at periods when the science of legislation was not so well understood as it now is; or when the manners of the age have been peculiarly gloomy or fanatical. The improved knowledge, and the improved temper of later times, push such laws into the background, and silently repeal them. A Suppressing Society, hunting every where for penalty and information, has a direct tendency to revive ancient ignorance and fanaticism,—and to re-enact laws which, if ever they ought to have existed at all, were certainly calculated for a very different style of manners, and a very different degree of information. To compel men to go to church under a penalty appears to us to be absolutely absurd. The bitterest enemy of religion will necessarily be that person who is driven to a compliance with its outward ceremonies, by informers and justices of the peace. In the same manner, any constable who hears another swear an oath has a right to seize him, and carry him before a magistrate, where he is to be fined so much for each execration. It is impossible to carry such laws into execution; and it is lucky that it is impossible,—for their execution would create an infinitely greater evil than it attempted to remedy. The common sense, and common feeling of mankind, if left to themselves, would silently repeal such laws; and it is one of the evils of these societies, that they render absurdity eternal, and ignorance indestructible. Do not let us be misunderstood: upon the object to be accomplished, there can be but one opinion;—it is only upon the means employed, that there can be the slightest difference of sentiment. To go to church is a duty of the greatest possible importance; and on the blasphemy and vul-

garity of swearing, there can be but one opinion. But such duties are not the objects of legislation; they must be left to the general state of public sentiment; which sentiment must be influenced by example, by the exertions of the pulpit and the press, and, above all, by education. The fear of God can never be taught by constables, nor the pleasures of religion be learnt from a common informer.

Beginning with the best intentions in the world, such societies must in all probability degenerate into a receptacle for every species of tittle-tattle, impertinence, and malice. Men, whose trade is rat-catching, love to catch rats; the bug-destroyer seizes on his bug with delight; and the suppressor is gratified by finding his vice. The last soon becomes a mere tradesman like the others; none of them moralise, or lament that their respective evils should exist in the world. The public feeling is swallowed up in the pursuit of a daily occupation, and in the display of a technical skill. Here, then, is a society of men, who invite accusation,—who receive it (almost unknown to themselves) with pleasure,—and who, if they hate dulness and inoccupation, can have very little pleasure in the innocence of their fellow creatures. The natural consequence of all this is, that (besides that portion of rumour which every member contributes at the weekly meeting) their table must be covered with anonymous lies against the characters of individuals. Every servant discharged from his master's service,—every cowardly assassin of character,—now knows where his accusations will be received, and where they cannot fail to produce some portion of the mischievous effects which he wishes. The very first step of such a Society should be, to declare, in the plainest manner, that they would never receive any anonymous accusation. This would be the only security

SOCIETY FOR SUPPRESSION OF VICE   361

to the public, that they were not degrading themselves into a receptacle for malice and falsehood. Such a declaration would inspire some species of confidence; and make us believe that their object was neither the love of power, nor the gratification of uncharitable feelings. The Society for the Suppression, however, have done no such thing. They request, indeed, the signature of the informers whom they invite; but they do not (as they ought) make that signature an indispensable condition.

Nothing has disgusted us so much in the proceedings of this Society, as the control which they exercise over the amusements of the poor. One of the specious titles under which this legal meanness is gratified is, *Prevention of Cruelty to Animals.*

Of cruelty to animals, let the reader take the following specimens:—

Running an iron hook in the intestines of an animal; presenting this first animal to another as his food; and then pulling this second creature up and suspending him by the barb in his stomach.

Riding a horse till he drops, in order to see an innocent animal torn to pieces by dogs.

Keeping a poor animal upright for many weeks, to communicate a peculiar hardness to his flesh.

Making deep incisions into the flesh of another animal while living, in order to make the muscles more firm.

Immersing another animal, while living, in hot water.

Now we do fairly admit, that such abominable cruelties as these are worthy the interference of the law; and that the Society should have punished them, cannot be matter of surprise to any feeling mind.—But stop, gentle reader! these cruelties are the cruelties of the Suppressing Committee, not of the poor. You must not

SYDNEY SMITH

think of punishing these.—The first of these cruelties passes under the pretty name of *angling;*—and therefore there can be no harm in it—the more particularly as the President himself has one of the best preserved trout streams in England.—The next is *hunting;*—and as many of the Vice-Presidents and of the Committee hunt, it is not possible there can be any cruelty in hunting. The next is, a process for making *brawn*—a dish never tasted by the poor, and therefore not to be disturbed by indictment. The fourth is the mode of *crimping* cod; and the fifth, of boiling lobsters; all high-life cruelties, with which a justice of the peace has no business to meddle. The real thing which calls forth the sympathies, and harrows up the soul, is to see a number of boisterous artisans baiting a bull, or a bear; not a savage hare, or a carnivorous stag,—but a poor, innocent, timid bear;—not pursued by magistrates, and deputy lieutenants, and men of education,—but by those who must necessarily seek their relaxation in noise and tumultuous merriment,—by men whose feelings are blunted, and whose understanding is wholly devoid of refinement. The Society detail, with symptoms of great complacency, their detection of a bear-baiting in Black-boy Alley, Chick Lane, and the prosecution of the offenders before a magistrate. It appears to us, that nothing can be more partial and unjust than this kind of proceedings. A man of ten thousand a year may worry a fox as much as he pleases,—may encourage the breed of a mischievous animal on purpose to worry it; and a poor labourer is carried before a magistrate for paying sixpence to see an exhibition of courage between a dog and a bear! Any cruelty may be practised to gorge the stomachs of the rich,—none to enliven the holidays of the poor. We venerate those feelings which really protect creatures susceptible of pain, and incapa-

SOCIETY FOR SUPPRESSION OF VICE 363

ble of complaint. But heaven-born pity, now-a-days, calls for the income-tax, and the court guide; and ascertains the rank and fortune of the tormentor before she weeps for the pain of the sufferer. It is astonishing how the natural feelings of mankind are distorted by false theories. Nothing can be more mischievous than to say, that the pain inflicted by the dog of a man of quality is not (when the strength of the two animals is the same) equal to that produced by the cur of a butcher. Haller, in his Pathology, expressly says, *that the animal bitten knows no difference in the quality of the biting animal's master;* and it is now the universal opinion among all enlightened men, that the misery of the brawner would be very little diminished, if he could be made sensible that he was to be eaten up only by persons of the first fashion. The contrary supposition seems to us to be absolute nonsense; it is the desertion of the true *Baconian* philosophy and the substitution of mere unsupported conjecture in its place. The trespass, however, which calls forth all the energies of a suppresser, is the sound of a fiddle. That the common people are really enjoying themselves, is now beyond all doubt: and away rush Secretary, President, and Committee, to clap the cotillon into the Compter, and to bring back the life of the poor to its regular standard of decorous gloom. The gambling houses of St. James's remain untouched. The peer ruins himself and his family with impunity; while the Irish labourer is privately whipped for not making a better use of the excellent moral and religious education which he has received in the days of his youth!

It is not true, as urged by the Society, that the vices of the poor are carried on in houses of public resort, and those of the rich in their own houses. The Society cannot be ignorant of the innumerable gambling houses

SYDNEY SMITH

resorted to by men of fashion. Is there one they have suppressed, or attempted to suppress? Can any thing be more despicable than such distinctions as these? Those who make them seem to have for other persons' vices all the rigour of the ancient Puritans—without a particle of their honesty or their courage. To suppose that any society will ever attack the vices of people of fashion, is wholly out of the question. If the Society consisted of tradesmen, they would infallibly be turned off by the vicious customers whose pleasures they interrupted: and what gentleman so fond of suppressing, as to interfere with the vices of good company, and inform against persons who were really genteel? He knows very well that the consequence of such interference would be a complete exclusion from elegant society; that the upper classes could not, and would not, endure it; and that he must immediately lose his rank in the world, if his zeal subjected fashionable offenders to the slightest inconvenience from the law. Nothing, therefore, remains, but to rage against the Sunday dinners of the poor, and to prevent a bricklayer's labourer from losing, on the seventh day, that beard which has been augmenting the other six. We see at the head of this Society the names of several noblemen, and of other persons moving in the fashionable world. Is it possible they can be ignorant of the innumerable offences against the law and morality which are committed by their own acquaintances and connections? Is there one single instance where they have directed the attention of the Society to this higher species of suppression, and sacrificed men of consideration to that zeal for virtue which watches so acutely over the vices of the poor? It would give us very little pleasure to see a duchess sent to the Poultry Compter; but if we saw the Society flying at such high game, we should at least say they were honest

SOCIETY FOR SUPPRESSION OF VICE 365

and courageous, whatever judgment we might form of their good sense. At present they should denominate themselves a Society for suppressing the vices of persons whose income does not exceed £500 *per annum;* and then, to put all classes upon an equal footing, there must be another society of barbers, butchers, and bakers, to return to the higher classes that moral character, by which they are so highly benefited.

To show how impossible it is to keep such societies within any kind of bounds, we shall quote a passage respecting circulating libraries, from their Proceedings.

> "Your Committee have good reasons for believing, that the circulation of their notices among the printsellers, warning them against the sale or exhibition of indecent representations, has produced, and continues to produce, the best effects.
>
> "But they have to lament that the extended establishment of circulating libraries, however useful they may be, in a variety of respects, to the easy and general diffusion of knowledge, are extremely injurious to morals and religion, by the indiscriminate admission which they give to the works of a prurient and immoral nature. It is a toilsome task to any virtuous and enlightened mind, to wade through the catalogues of these collections, and much more to select such books from them as have only an apparent bad tendency. But your Committee being convinced that their attention ought to be directed to those institutions which possess such powerful and numerous means of poisoning the minds of young persons, and especially of the female youth, have therefore begun to make some endeavours towards their better regulation."
> —*Statement of the Proceedings for* 1804, pp. 11, 12.

In the same spirit we see them writing to a country magistrate in Devonshire, respecting a wake advertised in the public papers. Nothing can be more presumptuous than such conduct, or produce, in the minds of impartial men, a more decisive impression against the Society.

The natural answer from the members of the Society (the only answer they have ever made to the enemies

SYDNEY SMITH

of their institution) will be, that we are lovers of vice,—desirous of promoting indecency, of destroying the Sabbath, and of leaving mankind to the unrestrained gratification of their passions. We have only very calmly to reply, that we are neither so stupid nor so wicked as not to concur in every scheme which has for its object the preservation of rational religion and sound morality; —but the scheme must be well concerted,—and those who are to carry it into execution must deserve our confidence, from their talents and their character. Upon religion and morals depends the happiness of mankind; —but the fortune of knaves and the power of fools is sometimes made to rest on the same apparent basis; and we will never (if we can help it) allow a rogue to get rich, or a blockhead to get powerful, under the sanction of these awful words. We do not by any means intend to apply these contemptuous epithets to the Society for the Suppression. That there are among their numbers some very odious hypocrites, is not impossible; that many men who believe they come there from the love of virtue, do really join the Society from the love of power, we do not doubt; but we see no reason to doubt that the great mass of subscribers consists of persons who have very sincere intentions of doing good. That they have, in some instances, done a great deal of good, we admit with the greatest pleasure. We believe, that in the hands of truly honest, intrepid, and, above all, discreet men, such a society might become a valuable institution, improve in some degree the public morals, and increase the public happiness. So many qualities, however, are required to carry it on well,—the temptations to absurdity and impertinence are so very great,— that we ever despair of seeing our wishes upon this subject realised. In the present instance, our object has been to suppress the arrogance of suppressors,—to

SOCIETY FOR SUPPRESSION OF VICE 367

keep them within due bounds,—to show them that to do good requires a little more talent and reflection than they are aware of,—and, above all, to impress upon them that true zeal for virtue knows no distinction between the rich and the poor; and that the cowardly and the mean can never be the true friends of morality, and the promoters of human happiness. If they attend to these rough doctrines they will ever find in the writers of this Journal their warmest admirers, and their most sincere advocates and friends.

ROBERT SOUTHEY

EVERY family has its mainstay, some hard-working conscientious member on whom all the incompetents and visionaries impose. Southey unwittingly cast himself for this role when he and Coleridge, dreaming of pantisocracy, married the Misses Edith and Sarah Fricker, "two milliners of Bath." Literature stands a little self-conscious in the presence of Robert Southey, aware of her own indifferent morals and yet desirous of being seen in such respectable company. Surely never was there a more industrious man nor one with more distinguished domestic virtues.

I find it hard to say more of him. Professor Zeitlin has salvaged a sizable volume of extracts from his innumerable histories, biographies, essays, and criticisms. *The Doctor,* Southey's labor of love, written to please himself in a manner reminiscent of *Tristram Shandy,* is heavily drawn upon. It is customary, when mentioning Southey, to remark that the *Life of Nelson* is a classic, and *The Doctor* the happiest expression in prose of his varied talents. The *Life of Nelson* is to me a dry book, and *The Doctor,* in which I have wandered, irritates and depresses me. So much labored humor, so vast an array of variegated learning, leaves me cold. Why must the man be so diffuse? Why must he display so ostentatiously his Spanish and Portuguese, his Latin, Italian, and Greek? The reader suffers from an inferiority complex, always a distressing experience.

Southey is a sound writer in the main. No intelligent man could write so much as did he and not become facile in the use of his tools. But great literature asks more than this—work that is individual, different, and char-

DERWENTWATER 369

acterized by a peculiar and ingratiating temperament. Southey's epics, I believe, have a better chance to live than his prose. *The Curse of Kehama* excites very much the interest of a concerto written for the kettle-drums. To read it once is a diverting experience. I do not find his prose exciting, though in occasional instances it is pleasing. The extracts which follow are not, I feel, wholly characteristic but rather exceptional. I have chosen them because I prefer them to his usual manner. That charming story, *Goldilocks and the Three Bears,* which it seemed not practicable to include, I like best of all. Perhaps this story, beloved of every genera-tion of little children, will do more to preserve his name from the dust than all the weighty and solemn volumes in whose composition he spent his life.

DERWENTWATER

THE best general view of Derwentwater is from the terrace, between Applethwaite and Milbeck, a little beyond the former hamlet. The old roofs and chimnies of that hamlet come finely in the foreground, and the trees upon the Ormathwaite estate give there a richness to the middle ground, which is wanting in other parts of the vale. From that spot, I once saw three artists sketching at the same time; William Westall (who has engraved it among his admirable views of Keswick), Glover, and Edward Nash, my dear, kind-hearted friend and fellow-traveller, whose death has darkened some of the blithest recollections of my latter life. I know not from which of the surrounding heights it is seen to most advantage; any one will amply repay the labor of the ascent; and often as I have ascended them all, it has never been without a fresh delight. The best near view is from the field adjoining Friar's Crag. There it is,

that if I had Aladdin's lamp or Fortunatus's purse,—
(with leave of Greenwich Hospital be it spoken,) I
would build myself a house.

Thither I had strolled on one of those first genial
days of spring which seem to affect the animal, not less
than the vegetable creation. At such times, even I,
sedentary as I am, feel a craving for the open air and
sunshine, and creep out as instinctively as snails after
a shower. Such seasons, which have an exhilarating
effect upon youth, produce a soothing one when we are
advanced in life. The root of an ash tree, on the bank
which bends round the little bay, had been half bared
by the waters during one of the winter floods, and
afforded a commodious resting place, whereon I took
my seat, at once basking in the sun, and bathing as it
were in the vernal breeze. But delightful as all about
me was to eye, and ear, and feeling, it brought with it a
natural reflection,—that the scene which I now beheld
was the same which it had been and would continue to
be, while so many of those, with whom I had formerly
enjoyed it, were passed away. Our day dreams become
retrospective as we advance in years, and the heart
feeds as naturally upon remembrance in age, as upon
hope in youth.

"Where are they gone, the old familiar faces?"

(Lamb)

I thought of her whom I had so often seen plying her
little skiff upon the glassy water,—the Lady of the
Lake. It was like a poet's dream, or a vision of romance,
to behold her,—and like a vision or a dream she had
departed!

O gentle Emma, o'er a lovelier form
Than thine, earth never closed; nor e'er did Heaven
Receive a purer spirit from the world!

DERWENTWATER

I thought of D.* the most familiar of my friends during those years when we lived near enough to each other for familiar intercourse;—my friend, and the friend of all who were dearest to me;—a man of whom all who knew him will concur with me in saying, that they never knew nor could conceive of one more strictly dutiful, more actively benevolent, more truly kind, more thoroughly good;—the pleasantest companion, the sincerest counsellor, the most considerate friend, the kindest host, the welcomest guest. After our separation, he had visited me here three summers: with him it was that I had first explored this Land of Lakes in all directions; and again and again should we have retraced our steps in the wildest recesses of these vales and mountains, and lived over the past again, if he had not, too early for all who loved him—

Began the travel of eternity.

I called to mind my hopeful H——,† too, so often the sweet companion of my morning walks to this very spot;—in whom I had fondly thought my better part should have survived me, and

"With whom, it seemed, my very life
Went half away.
But we shall meet,—but we shall meet
Where parting tears shall never flow;
And when I think thereon, almost
I long to go!"††

"Thy dead shall live," O Lord! "together with my

---

* Charles Danvers.

† His son Herbert.

†† These lines are quoted from a little volume, entitled *Solitary Hours,* which, with the "Widow's Tale," etc., of the same authoress, I recommend to all admirers of that poetry that proceeds from the heart.

dead body shall they arise. Awake and sing, ye that dwell in dust! for Thy dew is as the dew of herbs, and the earth shall cast out the dead!"

Surely to the sincere believer death would be an object of desire instead of dread, were it not for those ties,—those heart-strings—by which we are attached to life. Nor indeed do I believe it is natural to fear death, however generally it may be thought so. From my own feelings I have little right to judge; for, although habitually mindful that the hour cometh, and even now may be, it has never appeared actually near enough to make me duly apprehend its effect upon myself. But from what I have observed, and what I have heard those persons say whose professions lead them to the dying, I am induced to infer that the fear of death is not common, and that where it exists, it proceeds rather from a diseased or enfeebled mind, than from any principle in our nature. Certain it is that, among the poor, the approach of dissolution is usually regarded with a quiet and natural composure which it is consolatory to contemplate, and which is as far removed from the dead palsy of unbelief, as it is from the delirious raptures of fanaticism. Theirs is a true unhesitating faith; and they are willing to lay down the burthen of a weary life in the sure and certain hope of a blessed immortality. Who indeed is there that would not gladly make the exchange, if he lived only for himself, and were to leave none who stood in need of him, no eyes to weep at his departure, no hearts to ache for his loss? The day of death, says the Preacher, is better than the day of one's birth,—a sentence to which whoever has lived long, and may humbly hope that he has not lived ill, must heartily assent. The excellent Henry Scougal used to say that "abstracted from the will of God, mere curiosity would make him long for another world." How

MEMOIR OF THE CATS AT GRETA HALL 373

many of the ancients committed suicide from the mere weariness of life, a conviction of the vanity of human enjoyments, or to avoid the infirmities of old age! This, too, in utter uncertainty concerning a future state; not with the hope of change, for in their prospect there was no hope; but for the desire of death.

"SIR THOMAS MORE," Colloquy IX.

MEMOIR OF THE CATS OF GRETA HALL

For as much, most excellent Edith May, as you must always feel a natural and becoming concern in whatever relates to the house wherein you were born, and in which the first part of your life has thus far so happily been spent, I have, for your instruction and delight, composed these Memoirs of the Cats of Greta Hall: to the end that the memory of such worthy animals may not perish, but be held in deserved honour by my children, and those who shall come after them. And let me not be supposed unmindful of Beelzebub of Bath, and Senhor Thomaz de Lisboa, that I have not gone back to an earlier period, and included them in my design. Far be it from me to intend any injury or disrespect to their shades! Opportunity of doing justice to their virtues will not be wanting at some future time, but for the present I must confine myself within the limits of these precincts.

In the autumn of the year 1803, when I entered upon this place of abode, I found the hearth in possession of two cats, whom my nephew Hartley Coleridge, (then in the 7th year of his age,) had named Lord Nelson and Bona Marietta. The former, as the name implies, was of the worthier gender: it is as decidedly so in Cats, as in grammar and in law. He was an ugly specimen of the streaked-carrotty, or Judas-coloured

kind; which is one of the ugliest varieties. But *nimium ne crede colori*. In spite of his complection, there was nothing treacherous about him. He was altogether a good Cat, affectionate, vigilant, and brave; and for services performed against the Rats was deservedly raised in succession to the rank of Baron, Viscount, and Earl. He lived to a good old age; and then being quite helpless and miserable, was in mercy thrown into the river. I had more than once interfered to save him from this fate; but it became at length plainly an act of compassion to consent to it. And here let me observe that in a world wherein death is necessary, the law of nature by which one creature preys upon another is a law of mercy, not only because death is thus made instrumental to life, and more life exists in consequence, but also because it is better for the creatures themselves to be cut off suddenly, than to perish by disease or hunger,—for these are the only alternatives.

There are still some of Lord Nelson's descendants in the town of Keswick. Two of the family were handsomer than I should have supposed any Cats of this complection could have been; but their fur was fine, the colour a rich carrot, and the striping like that of the finest tyger or tabby kind. I named one of them William Rufus; the other Danayn le Roux, after a personage in the Romance of Gyron le Courtoys.

Bona Marietta was the mother of Bona Fidelia, so named by my nephew aforesaid. Bona Fidelia was a tortoise-shell cat. She was filiated upon Lord Nelson, others of the same litter having borne the unequivocal stamp of his likeness. It was in her good qualities that she resembled him, for in truth her name rightly bespoke her nature. She approached as nearly as possible in disposition to the ideal of a perfect cat:—he who supposes that animals have not their difference of

MEMOIR OF THE CATS AT GRETA HALL 375

disposition as well as men, knows very little of animal nature. Having survived her daughter Madame Catalani, she died of extreme old age, universally esteemed and regretted by all who had the pleasure of her acquaintance.

Bona Fidelia left a daughter and a granddaughter; the former I called Madame Bianchi—the latter Pulcheria. It was impossible ever to familiarize Madame Bianchi, though she had been bred up in all respects like her gentle mother, in the same place, and with the same persons. The nonsense of that arch-philosophist Helvetius would be sufficiently confuted by this single example, if such rank folly, contradicted as it is by the experience of every family, needed confutation. She was a beautiful and singular creature, white, with a fine tabby tail, and two or three spots of tabby, always delicately clean; and her wild eyes were bright and green as the Duchess de Cadaval's emerald necklace. Pulcheria did not correspond, as she grew up, to the promise of her kittenhood and her name; but she was as fond as her mother was shy and intractable. Their fate was extraordinary as well as mournful. When good old Mrs. Wilson died, who used to feed and indulge them, they immediately forsook the house, nor could they be allured to enter it again, though they continued to wander and moan around it, and came for food. After some weeks Madame Bianchi disappeared, and Pulcheria soon afterwards died of a disease endemic at that time among cats.

For a considerable time afterwards, an evil fortune attended all our attempts at reestablishing a Cattery. Ovid disappeared and Virgil died of some miserable distemper. You and your cousin are answerable for these names: the reasons which I could find for them were, in the former case, the satisfactory one that the

ROBERT SOUTHEY

said Ovid might be presumed to be a master in the Art of Love; and in the latter, the probable one that something like Ma-ro might be detected in the said Virgil's notes of courtship. There was poor Othello: most properly named, for black he was, and jealous undoubtedly he would have been, but he in his kittenship followed Miss Wilbraham into the street, and there in all likelihood came to an untimely end. There was the Zombi—(I leave the Commentators to explain that title, and refer them to my History of Brazil to do it,)—his marvellous story was recorded in a letter to Bedford,—and after that adventure he vanished. There was Prester John, who turned out not to be of John's gender, and therefore had the name altered to Pope Joan. The Pope I am afraid came to a death of which other Popes have died. I suspect that some poison which the rats had turned out of their holes proved fatal to their enemy. For some time I feared we were at the end of our Cat-a-logue: but at last Fortune, as if to make amends for her late severity, sent us two at once,—the-never-to-be-enough-praised Rumpelstilzchen, and the equally-to-be-admired Hurlyburlybuss.

And "first for the first of these" as my huge favourite, and almost namesake, Robert South, says in his Sermons.

When the Midgeleys went away from the next house, they left this creature to our hospitality, cats being the least moveable of all animals because of their strong local predilections;—they are indeed in a domesticated state the serfs of the animal creation, and properly attached to the soil. The change was gradually and therefore easily brought about, for he was already acquainted with the children and with me; and having the same precincts to prowl in was hardly sensible of any other difference in his condition than that of obtain-

MEMOIR OF THE CATS AT GRETA HALL   377

ing a name; for when he was consigned to us he was
an anonymous cat; and I having just related at breakfast, with universal applause, the story of Rumpelstilzchen from a German tale in Grimm's Collection, gave
him that strange and magnisonant appellation; to which,
upon its being ascertained that he came when a kitten
from a bailiff's house, I added the patronymic of Mac-
bum. Such is his history; his character may with most
propriety be introduced after the manner of Plutarch's
parallels, when I shall have given some previous account
of his great compeer and rival Hurlyburlybuss—that
name also is of Germanic and Grimmish extraction.

Whence Hurlyburlybuss came was a mystery when
you departed from the Land of Lakes, and a mystery
it long remained. He appeared here, as Mango Capac
did in Peru and Quetzalcohuatl among the Aztecas, no
one knew from whence. He made himself acquainted
with all the philofelists of the family—attaching himself
more particularly to Mrs. Lovell, but he never attempted
to enter the house, frequently disappeared for days, and
once, since my return, for so long a time that he was
actually believed to be dead, and veritably lamented as
such. The wonder was whither did he return at such
times—and to whom did he belong; for neither I in my
daily walks, nor the children, nor any of the servants,
ever by any chance saw him anywhere except in our
own domain. There was something so mysterious in
this, that in old times it might have excited strong suspicion, and he would have been in danger of passing for
a Witch in disguise, or a familiar. The mystery, however, was solved about four weeks ago, when, as we
were returning from a walk up the Greta, Isabel saw
him on his transit across the road and the wall from
Shulicrow, in a direction toward the Hill. But to this
day we are ignorant who has the honour to be his owner

ROBERT SOUTHEY

in the eye of the law; and the owner is equally ignorant of the high favour in which Hurlyburlybuss is held, of the heroic name which he has obtained, and that his fame has extended far and wide—even unto Norwich in the East, and Escott and Crediton and Kellerton in the West, yea—that with Rumpelstilzchen he has been celebrated in song, by some hitherto undiscovered poet, and that his glory will go down to future generations.

The strong enmity which unhappily subsists between these otherwise gentle and most amiable cats is not unknown to you. Let it be imputed, as in justice it ought, not to their individual characters, (for Cats have characters,—and for the benefit of philosophy, as well as *felisophy,* this truth ought generally to be known,) but to the constitution of Cat nature,—an original sin, or an original necessity, which may be only another mode of expressing the same thing:

> Two stars keep not their motion in one sphere,
> Nor can one purlieu brook a double reign
> Of Hurlyburlybuss and Rumpelstilzchen.

When you left us, the result of many a fierce conflict was, that Hurly remained master of the green and garden, and the whole of the out of door premises; Rumpel always upon the appearance of his victorious enemy retiring into the house as a citadel or sanctuary. The conquerer was perhaps in part indebted for this superiority to his hardier habits of life, living always in the open air, and providing for himself; while Rumpel, (who though born under a bumbailiff's roof was nevertheless kittened with a silver spoon in his mouth,) passed his hours in luxurious repose beside the fire, and looked for his meals as punctually as any two-legged member of the family. Yet I believe that the advantage on Hurly's side is in a great degree con-

MEMOIR OF THE CATS AT GRETA HALL 379

stitutional also, and that his superior courage arises from a confidence in his superior strength, which, as you well know, is visible in his make. What Bento and Maria Rosa used to say of my poor Thomaz, that he was *muito fidalgo,* is true of Rumpelstilzchen, his countenance, deportment, and behaviour being such that he is truly a gentleman-like Tom-cat. Far be it from me to praise him beyond his deserts,—he is not beautiful, the mixture, tabby and white, is not good, (except under very favourable combinations,) and the tabby is not good of its kind. Nevertheless he is a fine cat, handsome enough for his sex, large, well-made, with good features, and an intelligent countenance, and carrying a splendid tail, which in Cats and Dogs is undoubtedly the seat of honour. His eyes, which are soft and expressive, are of a hue between chrysolite and emerald. Hurlyburlybuss's are between chrysolite and topaz. Which may be the more esteemed shade for the *olho de gato* I am not lapidary enough to decide. You should ask my Uncle. But both are of the finest water. In all his other features Hurly must yield the palm, and in form also; he has no pretensions to elegance, his size is ordinary and his figure bad: but the character of his face and neck is so masculine, that the Chinese, who use the word bull as synonymous with male, and call a boy a bull-child, might with great propriety denominate him a bull-cat. His make evinces such decided marks of strength and courage, that if cat-fighting were as fashionable as cock-fighting, no Cat would stand a fairer chance for winning a Welsh main. He would become as famous as the Dog Billy himself, whom I look upon as the most distinguished character that has appeared since Buonaparte.

Some weeks ago Hurlyburlybuss was manifestly emaciated and enfeebled by ill health, and Rumpel-

stilzchen with great magnanimity made overtures of peace. The whole progress of the treaty was seen from the parlour window. The caution with which Rumpel made his advances, the sullen dignity with which they were received, their mutual uneasiness when Rumpel, after a slow and wary approach, seated himself whisker-to-whisker with his rival, the mutual fear which restrained not only teeth and claws, but even all tones of defiance, the mutual agitation of their tails which, though they did not expand with anger, could not be kept still for suspense, and lastly the manner in which Hurly retreated, like Ajax still keeping his face toward his old antagonist, were worthy to have been represented by that painter who was called the Rafaelle of Cats. The overture I fear was not accepted as generously as it was made; for no sooner had Hurlyburlybuss recovered strength than hostilities were recommenced with greater violence than ever; Rumpel, who had not abused his superiority while he possessed it, had acquired mean time a confidence which made him keep the field. Dreadful were the combats which ensued, as their ears, faces and legs bore witness. Rumpel had a wound which went through one of his feet. The result has been so far in his favour that he no longer seeks to avoid his enemy, and we are often compelled to interfere and separate them. Oh it is aweful to hear the "dreadful note of preparation" with which they prelude their encounters!—the long low growl slowly rises and swells till it becomes a high sharp yowl,—and then it is snapped short by a sound which seems as if they were spitting fire and venom at each other. I could half persuade myself that the word felonious is derived from the feline temper as displayed at such times. All means of reconciling them and making them understand how goodly a thing it is for cats to dwell together in

THE MANUFACTURING SYSTEM 381

peace, and what fools they are to quarrel and tear each
other, are in vain. The proceedings of the Society for
the Abolition of War are not more utterly ineffectual
and hopeless.

All we can do is to act more impartially than the
Gods did between Achilles and Hector, and continue to
treat both with equal regard.

And thus having brought down these Memoirs of the
Cats of Greta Hall to the present day, I commit the
precious memorial to your keeping, and remain

Most dissipated and light-heeled daughter,

Your most diligent and light-hearted father,

ROBERT SOUTHEY.

Keswick, 18 *June,* 1824.

THE MANUFACTURING SYSTEM

J. HAD provided us with letters to a gentleman in
Manchester; we delivered them after breakfast, and
were received with that courtesy which a foreigner
when he takes with him the expected recommendations
is sure to experience in England. He took us to one
of the great cotton manufactories, showed us the number
of children who were at work there, and dwelt with
delight on the infinite good which resulted from employing them at so early an age. I listened without contra-
dicting him, for who would lift up his voice against
Diana in Ephesus!—proposed my questions in such a
way as not to imply, or at least not to advance, any
difference of opinion, and returned with a feeling at
heart which makes me thank God I am not an Englishman.

There is a shrub in some of the East Indian islands
which the French call *veloutier;* it exhales an odour
that is agreeable at a distance, becomes less so as you

draw nearer, and, when you are quite close to it, is insupportably loathsome. Alciatus himself could not have imagined an emblem more appropriate to the commercial prosperity of England.

Mr. —— remarked that nothing could be so beneficial to a country as manufactures. "You see these children, sir," said he. "In most parts of England poor children are a burthen to their parents and to the parish; here the parish, which would else have to support them, is rid of all expense; they get their bread almost as soon as they can run about, and by the time they are seven or eight years old bring in money. There is no idleness among us:—they come at five in the morning; we allow them half an hour for breakfast, and an hour for dinner; they leave work at six, and another set relieves them for the night; the wheels never stand still." I was looking while he spoke, at the unnatural dexterity with which the fingers of these little creatures were playing in the machinery, half giddy myself with the noise and the endless motion; and when he told me there was no rest in these walls, day nor night, I thought that if Dante had peopled one of his hells with children, here was a scene worthy to have supplied him with new images of torment.

"These children, then," said I, "have no time to receive instruction." "That, sir," he replied, "is the evil which we have found. Girls are employed here from the age you see them till they marry, and then they know nothing about domestic work, not even how to mend a stocking or boil a potatoe. But we are remedying this now, and send the children to school for an hour after they have done work." I asked if so much confinement did not injure their health. "No," he replied, "they are as healthy as any children in the world could be. To be sure, many of them as they

THE MANUFACTURING SYSTEM

grew up went off in consumptions, but consumption was the disease of the English." I ventured to inquire afterwards concerning the morals of the people who were trained up in this monstrous manner, and found, what was to be expected, that in consequence of herding together such numbers of both sexes, who are uninstructed in the commonest principles of religion and morality, they were as debauched and profligate as human beings under the influence of such circumstances must inevitably be; the men drunken, the women dissolute; that however high the wages they earned, they were too improvident ever to lay-by for a time of need; and that, though the parish was not at the expense of maintaining them when children, it had to provide for them in diseases induced by their mode of life, and in premature debility and old age; the poor-rates were oppressively high, and the hospitals and workhouses always full and overflowing. I inquired how many persons were employed in the manufactory, and was told, children and all about two hundred. What was the firm of the house?—There were two partners. So! thought I,—a hundred to one!

"We are well off for hands in Manchester," said Mr. ——; "manufactures are favourable to population, the poor are not afraid of having a family here, the parishes therefore have always plenty to apprentice, and we take them as fast as they can supply us. In new manufacturing towns they find it difficult to get a supply. Their only method is to send people round the country to get children from their parents. Women usually undertake this business; they promise the parents to provide for the children; one party is glad to be eased of a burthen, and it answers well to the other to find the young ones in food, lodging and clothes, and receive their wages." "But if these children should

be ill-used?" said I. "Sir," he replied, "it never can be the interest of the women to use them ill, nor of the manufacturers to permit it."

It would have been in vain to argue had I been disposed to it. Mr. —— was a man of humane and kindly nature, who would not himself use anything cruelly, and judged of others by his own feelings. I thought of the cities in Arabian romance, where all the inhabitants were enchanted: here Commerce is the queen witch, and I had no talisman strong enough to disenchant those who were daily drinking of the golden cup of her charms.

We purchase English cloth, English muslins, English buttons, &c., and admire the excellent skill with which they are fabricated, and wonder that from such a distance they can be afforded to us at so low a price, and think what a happy country is England! A happy country indeed it is for the higher orders; no where have the rich so many enjoyments, no where have the ambitious so fair a field, no where have the ingenious such encouragement, no where have the intellectual such advantages; but to talk of English happiness is like talking of Spartan freedom, the Helots are overlooked. In no other country can such riches be acquired by commerce, but it is the one who grows rich by the labour of the hundred. The hundred, human beings like himself, as wonderfully fashioned by Nature, gifted with the like capacities, and equally made for immortality, are sacrificed body and soul. Horrible as it must needs appear, the assertion is true to the very letter. They are deprived in childhood of all instruction and all enjoyment; of the sports in which childhood instinctively indulges, of fresh air by day and of natural sleep by night. Their health, physical and moral, is alike destroyed; they die of diseases induced by unremitting

THE MANUFACTURING SYSTEM

task work, by confinement in the impure atmosphere of crowded rooms, by the particles of metallic or vegetable dust which they are continually inhaling; or they live to grow up without decency, without comfort, and without hope, without morals, without religion, and without shame, and bring forth slaves like themselves to tread in the same path of misery.

The dwellings of the labouring manufacturers are in narrow streets and lanes, blocked up from light and air, not as in our country to exclude an insupportable sun, but crowded together because every inch of land is of such value, that room for light and air cannot be afforded them. Here in Manchester a great proportion of the poor lodge in cellars, damp and dark, where every kind of filth is suffered to accumulate, because no exertions of domestic care can ever make such homes decent. These places are so many hotbeds of infection; and the poor in large towns are rarely or never without an infectious fever among them, a plague of their own, which leaves the habitations of the rich, like a Goshen of cleanliness and comfort, unvisited.

Wealth flows into the country, but how does it circulate there? Not equally and healthfully through the whole system; it sprouts into wens and tumours, and collects in aneurisms which starve and palsy the extremities. The government indeed raises millions now as easily as it raised thousands in the days of Elizabeth: the metropolis is six times the size which it was a century ago; it has nearly doubled during the present reign; a thousand carriages drive about the streets of London, where, three generations ago, there were not an hundred; a thousand hackney coaches are licensed in the same city, where at the same distance of time there was not one; they whose grandfathers dined at noon from wooden trenchers, and upon the produce of

ROBERT SOUTHEY

their own farms, sit down by the light of waxen tapers to be served upon silver, and to partake of delicacies from the four quarters of the globe. But the number of the poor, and the sufferings of the poor, have continued to increase; the price of every thing which they consume has always been advancing, and the price of labour, the only commodity which they have to dispose of, remains the same. Work-houses are erected in one place, and infirmaries in another; the poor-rates increase in proportion to the taxes; and in times of dearth the rich even purchase food, and retail it to them at a reduced price, or supply them with it gratuitously: still every year adds to their number. Necessity is the mother of crimes; new prisons are built, new punishments enacted; but the poor become year after year more numerous, more miserable, and more depraved; and this is the inevitable tendency of the manufacturing system.

This system is the boast of England,—long may she continue to boast it before Spain shall rival her! Yet this is the system which we envy, and which we are so desirous to imitate. Happily our religion presents one obstacle; that incessant labour which is required in these task-houses can never be enacted in a Catholic country, where the Church has wisely provided so many days of leisure for the purposes of religion and enjoyment. Against the frequency of these holy days much has been said; but Heaven forbid that the clamour of philosophizing commercialists should prevail, and that the Spaniard should ever be brutalized by unremitting task-work, like the negroes in America and the labouring manufacturers in England! Let us leave to England the boast of supplying all Europe with her wares; let us leave to these lords of the sea the distinction of which they are so tenacious, that of being the white slaves of

THE MANUFACTURING SYSTEM

the rest of the world, and doing for it all its dirty work. The poor must be kept miserably poor, or such a state of things could not continue; there must be laws to regulate their wages, not by the value of their work, but by the pleasures of their masters; laws to prevent their removal from one place to another within the kingdom, and to prohibit their emigration out of it. They would not be crowded in hot task-houses by day, and herded together in damp cellars at night; they would not toil in unwholesome employments from sun-rise till sun-set, whole days, and whole days and quarters, for with twelve hours labour the avidity of trade is not satisfied; they would not sweat night and day, keeping up this *laus perennis* of the Devil, before furnaces which are never suffered to cool, and breathing-in vapours which inevitably produce disease and death; the poor would never do these things unless they were miserably poor, unless they were in that state of abject poverty which precludes instruction, and, by destroying all hope for the future, reduces man, like the brutes, to seek for nothing beyond the gratification of present wants.

How England can remedy this evil, for there are not wanting in England those who perceive and confess it to be an evil, it is not easy to discover, nor is it my business to inquire. To us it is of more consequence to know how other countries may avoid it, and, as it is the prevailing system to encourage manufacturers everywhere, to inquire how we may reap as much good and as little evil as possible. The best methods appear to be by extending to the utmost the use of machinery, and leaving the price of labour to find its own level: the higher it is the better. The introduction of machinery in an old manufacturing country always produces distress by throwing workmen out of employ, and it is

ROBERT SOUTHEY

seldom effected without riots and executions. Where new fabrics are to be erected it is obvious that this difficulty does not exist, and equally obvious that, when hard labour can be performed by iron and wood, it is desirable to spare flesh and blood. High wages are a general benefit, because money thus distributed is employed to the greatest general advantage. The labourer, lifted up one step in society, acquires the pride and the wants, the habits and the feelings, of the class now next above him. Forethought, which the miserably poor necessarily and instinctively shun, is to him who earns a comfortable competence, new pleasure; he educates his children, in the hope that they may rise higher than himself, and that he is fitting them for better fortunes. Prosperity is said to be more dangerous than adversity to human virtue; both are wholesome when sparingly distributed, both in the excess perilous always, and often deadly: but if prosperity be thus dangerous, it is a danger which falls to the lot of few; and it is sufficiently proved by the vices of those unhappy wretches who exist in slavery, under whatever form or in whatever disguise, that hope is as essential to prudence, and to virtue, as to happiness.

Letters of Espriella, XXXVIII.

SIEGE OF ZARAGOZA (1808)

IMPORTANT as the battle of Baylen was in its direct and immediate consequences to the Spaniards, their cause derived greater celebrity and more permanent strength from the defence of Zaragoza.

Order had been restored in that city from the hour when Palafox assumed the command. Implicit confidence in the commander produced implicit and alert

SIEGE OF ZARAGOZA

obedience, and preparations were made with zeal and
activity proportioned to the danger. When the new
Captain-General declared war against the French, the
troops which he mustered amounted only to 220 men,
and the public treasury could furnish him with no more
than one hundred dollars; sixteen ill-mounted guns were
all the artillery in the place, and the arsenal contained
but few muskets. Fowling-pieces were put in requisi-
tion, pikes were forged, powder was supplied from the
mills at Villafeliche, which were some of the most considerable in Spain,—for everything else Palafox trusted
to his country and his cause. And his trust was not in
vain; the Zaragozans were ready to endure any suffering
and make any sacrifice in the discharge of their duty;
the same spirit possessed the whole country, and from
all those parts of Spain which were under the yoke of
the enemy, officers and soldiers repaired to Zaragoza
as soon as it was seen that an army was collecting there;
many came from Madrid and from Pamplona, and some
officers of engineers from the military academy at
Alcala. And the spirits of the people were encouraged
by the discovery of a depot of fire arms walled up in
the Aljafaria; they had probably been secreted there
in the succession war, when one party resigned that city
to its enemies, and their discovery in this time of need
was regarded by the Zaragozans as a manifestation of
divine Providence in their favour. The defeats which
their undisciplined levies sustained at Tudela, Mallen,
and Alagon abated not their resolution; and in the last
of these actions a handful of regular troops protected
their retreat with great steadiness. The French general,
Lefebvre Desnouettes, pursuing his hitherto uninterrupted success, advanced, and took up a position very
near the city, and covered by a rising ground planted
with olive trees.

ROBERT SOUTHEY

Zaragoza was not a fortified town; the brick wall which surrounded it was from ten to twelve feet high, and three feet thick, and in many places it was interrupted by houses, which formed part of the inclosure. The city had no advantages of situation for its defence, and would not have been considered capable of resistance by any men but those whose courage was sustained by a virtuous and holy principle of duty. It stands in an open plain, which was then covered with olive grounds, and is bounded on either hand by high and distant mountains; but it is commanded by some high ground called the Torrero, about a mile to the southwest, upon which there was a convent, with some smaller buildings. The canal of Aragon divides this elevation from another rising ground, where the Spaniards had erected a battery. The Ebro bathes the walls of the city, and separates it from the suburbs; it has two bridges, within musket-shot of each other; one of wood, said to be more beautiful than any other of the like materials in Europe; the other of freestone, consisting of seven arches, the largest of which is 122 feet in diameter; the river is fordable above the city. Two smaller rivers, the Galego and the Guerva, flow at a little distance from the city, the one on the east, the other on the west; the latter being separated from the walls only by the breadth of the common road; both are received into the Ebro. Unlike most other places of the peninsula, Zaragoza has neither aqueduct nor fountains, but derives its water wholly from the river. The people of Tortosa, (and probably of the other towns upon its course,) drink also of the Ebro, preferring it to the finest spring; the water is of a dirty red colour, but having stood a few hours, it becomes perfectly clear, and has a softness and pleasantness of taste, which soon induces strangers to agree with the

SIEGE OF ZARAGOZA 391

natives in their preference of it. The population was stated in the census of 1787 at 42,600; that of 1797, excellent as it is in all other respects, has the fault of not specifying the places in each district; later accounts computed its inhabitants at 60,000, and it was certainly one of the largest cities in the peninsula. It had twelve gates, four of them in the old wall of Augustus, by whom the older town of Salduba upon the same site was enlarged, beautified, and called Cæsarea-Augusta, or Cæsaraugusta; a word easily corrupted into its present name.*

The whole city is built of brick; even the convents and churches were of this coarse material, which was bad of its kind, so that there were cracks in most of these edifices from top to bottom. The houses are not so high as they usually are in old Spanish towns, their general height being only three stories; the streets are, as usual, very narrow and crooked; there are, however, open market-places; and one very wide, long, and regularly built street, formerly called the Calle Santa, having been the scene of many martyrdoms, but now more commonly known by the name of Cozo. The people, like the rest of the Aragonese, and their neighbours, the Catalans, have been always honourably distinguished in Spanish history for their love of liberty; and the many unavailing struggles which they have made during the last four centuries, had not abated their attachment to the good principles of their forefathers. Within the peninsula, (and once indeed throughout the whole of Catholic Europe,) Zaragoza was famous as the city of our Lady of the Pillar, whose legend is still so firmly believed by the people, and most of the clergy in Spain, that it was frequently appealed to in the proclamations

---

* The Spaniards, by a more curious corruption, call Syracuse, Zaragoza de Sicilia.

of the different generals and Juntas, as one of the most popular articles of the national faith. The legend is this: when the apostles, after the resurrection, separated and went to preach the gospel in different parts of the world, St. James the elder, (or Santiago as he may more properly be called in his mythological history,) departed for Spain, which province Christ himself had previously commended to his care. When he went to kiss the hand of the Virgin, and request her leave to set off, and her blessing, she commanded him, in the name of her Son, to build a church to her honour in that city of Spain wherein he should make the greatest number of converts, adding, that she would give him farther instructions concerning the edifice upon the spot. Santiago set sail, landed in Galicia, and, having preached with little success through the northern provinces, reached Cæsarea-Augusta, where he made eight disciples. One night, after he had been conversing and praying with them as usual on the banks of the river, they fell asleep, and just at midnight the apostle heard heavenly voices sing, *Ave Maria gratia plena!* He fell on his knees, and instantly beheld the Virgin upon a marble pillar in the midst of a choir of angels, who went through the whole of the matin service. When this was ended, she bade him build her church around that pillar, which his Lord, her blessed Son, had sent him by the hands of his angels; there, she told him, that pillar was to remain till the end of the world, and great mercies would be vouchsafed there to those who supplicated for them in her name. Having said this, the angels transported her back to her house at Jerusalem, (for this was before the Assumption,) and Santiago, in obedience, erected upon that spot the first church which was ever dedicated to the Virgin. Cathedral service was performed both in this church and in the see, and

SIEGE OF ZARAGOZA 393

the meetings of the chapter were held alternately in each. The interior of each was of the most imposing kind. When the elder of these joint cathedrals was erected, Pope Gelasius granted indulgences to all persons who would contribute toward the work, and thus introduced a practice which contributed as much to the grandeur and magnificence of ecclesiastical architecture, as to laxity of morals and the prevalence of superstition.

Many mournful scenes of bigotry and superstition have been exhibited in Zaragoza; but, in these fiery trials which Buonaparte's tyranny was preparing for the inhabitants, the dross and tinsel of their faith disappeared, and its pure gold remained. The French, accustomed as they were to undervalue the Spanish character, had spoken with peculiar contempt of the Zaragozans. "Few persons," they said, "are to be seen among them who distinguish themselves by their dress; there is little of that elegant attire so observable in large cities. All is serious and regular,—dull and monotonous. The place seems without any kind of resource, because the inhabitants use no effort to obtain any;—accustomed to a state of apathy and languor, they have not an idea of the possibility of shaking it off." With this feeling, equally despising the strength of the place, and the character of the people, the French proceeded to besiege the capital of Aragon. A party of their cavalry entered the town on the 14th, perhaps in pursuit of the retreating patriots; they thought to scour the streets, but they were soon made to feel, that the superiority of disciplined soldiers to citizens exists only in the field.

On the following morning, the French, with part of their force, attacked the outposts upon the canal, and, with their main body, attempted to storm the city by the gate called Portillo. A desperate conflict ensued.

The Aragonese fought with a spirit worthy of their cause. They had neither time, nor room, nor necessity for order. Their cannon, which they had hastily planted before the gates, and in the best situations without the town, were served by any persons who happened to be near them; any one gave orders who felt himself competent to take the command. A party of the enemy entered the city, and were all slain. Lefebvre perceived that it was hopeless to persist in the attack with his present force, and drew off his troops, having suffered great loss. The patriots lost about 2000 men killed, and as many wounded. In such a conflict the circumstances are so materially in favour of the defendants, that the carnage made among the French must have been much greater. Some part of their baggage and plunder was abandoned in their retreat. The conquerors would have exposed themselves by a rash pursuit, but Palafox exhorted them not to be impatient, telling them, that the enemy would give them frequent opportunities to display their courage. While he thus restrained their impetuosity, he continued to excite their zeal. This victory, he said, was but the commencement of the triumphs which they were to expect under the powerful assistance of their divine patrons. The precious blood of their brethren had been shed in the field of glory,—on their own soil. Those blessed martyrs required new victims; let us, he added, be prepared for the sacrifice!

The Zaragozans had obtained only a respite; defeated as he was, Lefebvre had only removed beyond the reach of their guns; his troops were far superior to any which they could bring against him; and it was not to be doubted that he would soon return in greater force, to take vengeance for the repulse and the disgrace which he had suffered. A regular siege was to be expected;

SIEGE OF ZARAGOZA

how were the citizens to sustain it with their brick walls, without heavy artillery, and without troops who could sally to interrupt the besiegers in their works? In spite of all these discouraging circumstances, confiding in God and their own courage, they determined to defend the streets to the last extremity. Palafox, immediately after the repulse of the enemy, set out to muster reinforcements, to provide such resources for the siege as he could, and to place the rest of Aragon in a state of defence, if the capital should fall. He was accompanied by Colonel Burton, his friend and aide-de-camp; Lieut.-Colonel Beillan, of the engineers; Padre Basilio, and Tio Jorge. With these companions and a small escort he left the city by the suburbs, crossed the Ebro at Pina, and collecting on the way about 1400 soldiers who had escaped from Madrid, formed a junction at Belchite with Baron Versage and some newly raised troops from Calatayud. Their united numbers amounted to some 7000 men, with 100 horse and four pieces of artillery. Small as this force was, and still more inefficient for want of discipline than of numerical strength, Palafox resolved upon making an attempt with it to succour the city. The prudence of this determination was justly questioned by some; others proposed the strange measure of marching to Valencia: this probably originated with some of the stray soldiers who were at liberty to seek their fortune where they pleased, and the proposal was so well received that a considerable party prepared to set off in that direction, without orders. But Palafox called them together, exhorted them to do their duty, and offered passports to as many as chose to leave him in the moment of danger. The consequence of this offer was that not a man departed. From Almunia, where he had rested a day, he then marched towards Épila, thinking to advance to the vil-

ROBERT SOUTHEY

lage of La Muela, and thus place the invaders between his little army and the city, in the hope of cutting them off from their reinforcements. Lefebvre prevented this, by suddenly attacking him at Epila, on the night of the 23d: after a most obstinate resistance, the superior arms and discipline of the French were successful. The wreck of this gallant band retreated to Calatayud, and afterwards, with great difficulty, threw themselves into Zaragoza.

The besiegers' army was soon reinforced by General Verdier, with 2500 men, besides some battalions of Portugueze, who, according to the devilish system of Buonaparte's tyranny, had been forced out of their own country, to be pushed on in the foremost ranks, wherever the first fire of a battery was to be received, a line of bayonets clogged, or a ditch filled, with bodies. They occupied the best positions in the surrounding plain, and, on the 27th, attacked the city and the Torrero; but they were repulsed with the loss of 800 men, six pieces of artillery, and five carts of ammunition. By this time, they had invested nearly half the town. The next morning they renewed the attack at both places; from the city they were again repulsed, losing almost all the cavalry who were engaged. But the Torrero was lost through the alleged misconduct of an artillery officer, who was charged with having made his men abandon the batteries at the most critical moment. For this he was condemned to run the gauntlet six times, the soldiers beating him with their ramrods, and after this cruelty he was shot.

The French, having now received a train of mortars, howitzers, and twelve-pounders, which were of sufficient calibre against mud walls, kept up a constant fire, and showered down shells and grenades from the Torrero. About twelve hundred were thrown into the town, and

SIEGE OF ZARAGOZA

there was not one building that was bomb proof within the walls. After a time, the inhabitants placed beams of timber together, endways, against the houses, in a sloping direction, behind which those who were near when a shell fell, might shelter themselves. The enemy continued also to invest the city more closely, while the Aragonese made every effort to strengthen their means of defence. They tore down the awnings from their windows, and formed them into sacks, which they filled with sand, and piled up before the gates, in the form of a battery, digging round it a deep trench. They broke holes for musketry in the walls and intermediate buildings, and stationed cannon where the position was favourable for it. The houses in the environs were destroyed. "Gardens and olive grounds," says an eye-witness, "that in better times had been the recreation and support of their owners, were cheerfully rooted up by the proprietors themselves, wherever they impeded the defence of the city, or covered the approach of the enemy." Women of all ranks assisted; they formed themselves into companies, some to relieve the wounded, some to carry water, wine, and provisions, to those who defended the gates. The Countess Burita instituted a corps for this service; she was young, delicate, and beautiful. In the midst of the most tremendous fire of shot and shells, she was seen coolly attending to those occupations which were now become her duty; nor throughout the whole of a two months' siege did the imminent danger, to which she incessantly exposed herself, produce the slightest apparent effect upon her, or in the slightest degree bend her from her heroic purpose. Some of the monks bore arms; others exercised their spiritual offices to the dying: others, with the nuns, were busied in making cartridges which the children distributed.

ROBERT SOUTHEY

Among threescore thousand persons there will always be found some wicked enough for any employment, and the art of corrupting has constituted great part of the French system of war. During the night of the 28th the powder magazine, in the area where the bull-fights were performed, which was in the very heart of the city, was blown up, by which fourteen houses were destroyed, and about 200 persons killed. This was the signal for the enemy to appear before three gates which had been sold to them. And while the inhabitants were digging out their fellow-citizens from the ruins, a fire was opened upon them with mortars, howitzers, and cannons, which had now been received for battering the town. Their attack seemed chiefly to be directed against the gate called Portillo, and a large square building near it, without the walls, and surrounded by a deep ditch; though called a castle, it served only for a prison. The sand-bag battery before this gate was frequently destroyed, and as often reconstructed under the fire of the enemy. The carnage here throughout the day was dreadful. Augustina Zaragoza, a handsome woman of the lower class, about twenty-two years of age, arrived at this battery with refreshments, at the time when not a man who defended it was left alive, so tremendous was the fire which the French kept up against it. For a moment the citizens hesitated to re-man the guns. Augustina sprung forward over the dead and dying, snatched a match from the hand of a dead artilleryman, and fired off a six-and-twenty pounder; then, jumping upon the gun, made a solemn vow never to quit it alive during the siege. Such a sight could not but animate with fresh courage all who beheld it. The Zaragozans rushed into the battery, and renewed their fire with greater vigour than ever, and the French were repulsed here, and at all other points, with great slaughter. **On**

SIEGE OF ZARAGOZA 399

the morning of this day a fellow was detected going out of the city with letters to Murat. It was not till after these repeated proofs of treasonable practices, that the French residents in Zaragoza, with other suspected persons, were taken into custody.

Lefebvre now supposing that his destructive bombardment must have dismayed the people, and convinced them how impossible it was for so defenceless a city to persist in withstanding him, again attempted to force his way into the town, thinking that, as soon as his troops could find a lodgement within the gates, the Zaragozans would submit. On the 2d of July, a column of his army marched out of their battery, which was almost within musket-shot of the Portillo, and advanced towards it with fixed bayonets, and without firing a shot. But when they reached the castle, such a discharge of grape and musketry was opened upon their flank, that, notwithstanding the most spirited exertions of their officers, the column immediately dispersed. The remainder of their force had been drawn up to support their attack, and follow them into the city; but it was impossible to bring them a second time to the charge. The general, however, ordered another column instantly to advance against the gate of the Carmen, on the left of the Portillo. This entrance was defended by a sand-bag battery and by musketeers, who lined the walls on each side, and commanded two out of three approaches to it; and here also the French suffered great loss, and were repulsed.

The military men in Zaragoza considered these attacks as extremely injudicious. Lefebvre probably was so indignant at meeting with any opposition from a people whom he despised, and a place which, according to the rules and pedantry of war, was not tenable, that he lost his temper, and thought to subdue them

the shortest way, by mere violence and superior force. Having found his mistake, he proceeded to invest the city still more closely. In the beginning of the siege, the besieged received some scanty succours; yet, however scanty, they were of importance. Four hundred soldiers from the regiment of Estremadura, small parties from other corps, and a few artillerymen got in. Two hundred of the militia of Logrono were added to these artillerymen, and soon learnt their new service, being in the presence of an enemy whom they had such righteous reason to abhor. Two four-and-twenty-pounders and a few shells, which were much wanted, were procured from Lerida. The enemy, meantime, were amply supplied with stores from the magazine in the citadel of Pamplona, which they had so perfidiously seized on their first entrance, as allies, into Spain. Hitherto they had remained on the right bank of the Ebro. On the 11th of July they forced the passage of the ford, and posted troops enough on the opposite side to protect their workmen while forming a floating bridge. In spite of all the efforts of the Aragonese, this bridge was completed on the 14th; a way was thus made for their cavalry, to their superiority in which the French were mostly indebted for all their victories in Spain. This gave them the command of the surrounding country; they destroyed the mills, levied contributions on the villages, and cut off every communication by which the besieged had hitherto received supplies. These new difficulties called out new resources in this admirable people and their general,—a man worthy of commanding such a people in such times. Corn mills, worked by horses, were erected in various parts of the city; the monks were employed in manufacturing gun-powder, materials for which were obtained by immediately collecting all the sulphur in the place, by washing the soil

SIEGE OF ZARAGOZA 401

of the streets to extract its nitre, and making charcoal from the stalks of hemp, which in that part of Spain grows to a magnitude that would elsewhere be thought very unusual.

By the end of July the city was completely invested, the supply of food was scanty, and the inhabitants had no reason to expect succour. Their exertions had now been unremitted for forty-six days, and nothing but the sense of duty could have supported their bodily strength and their spirit under such trials. They were in hourly expectation of another general attack, or another bombardment. They had not a single place of security for the sick and the children, and the number of wounded was daily increased by repeated skirmishes, in which they engaged for the purpose of opening a communication with the country. At this juncture they made one desperate effort to recover the Torrero. It was in vain; and convinced by repeated losses, and especially by this repulse, that it was hopeless to make any effectual sally, they resolved to abide the issue of the contest within the walls, and conquer or perish there.

On the night of the second of August, and on the following day, the French bombarded the city from their batteries opposite the gate of the Carmen. A foundling hospital, which was now filled with the sick and wounded, took fire, and was rapidly consumed. During this scene of horror, the most intrepid exertions were made to rescue these helpless sufferers from the flames. No person thought of his own property or individual concerns,—every one hastened thither. The women were eminently conspicuous in their exertions, regardless of the shot and shells which fell about them, and braving the flames of the building. It has often been remarked, that the wickedness of women exceeds that of the other sex;—for the same reason, when cir-

cumstances, forcing them out of the sphere of their ordinary nature, compel them to exercise manly virtues, they display them in the highest degree, and, when they are once awakened to a sense of patriotism, they carry the principle to its most heroic pitch. The loss of women and boys, during this siege, was very great, fully proportionate to that of men; they were always the more forward, and the difficulty was to teach them a prudent and proper sense of their danger.

On the following day, the French completed their batteries upon the right flank of the Guerva, within pistol-shot of the gate of St. Engracia, so called from a splendid church and convent of Jeronimites, situated on one side of it. This convent was, on many accounts, a remarkable place. Men of letters beheld it with reverence, because the excellent historian Zurita spent the last years of his life there, observing the rules of the community, though he had not entered into the order; and because he was buried there, and his countryman and fellow-labourer, Geronymo de Blancas, after him. Devotees revered it, even in the neighbourhood of our Lady of the Pillar, for its relics and the saint to whom it was dedicated. . . .

On the 4th of August, the French opened batteries within pistol-shot of this church and convent. The mud walls were levelled at the first discharge; and the besiegers, rushing through the opening, took the batteries before the adjacent gates in reverse. Here General Mori, who had distinguished himself on many former occasions, was made prisoner. The street of St. Engracia, which they had thus entered, leads into the Cozo, and the corner buildings where it thus terminated, were on the one hand the convent of St. Francisco, and on the other the General Hospital. Both were stormed and set on fire; the sick and the wounded

SIEGE OF ZARAGOZA 403

threw themselves from the windows to escape the flames, and the horror of the scene was aggravated by the maniacs, whose voices raving or singing in paroxysms of wilder madness, or crying in vain to be set free, were heard amid the confusion of dreadful sounds. Many fell victims to the fire, and some to the indiscriminating fury of the assailants. Those who escaped were conducted as prisoners to the Torrero; but when their condition had been discovered, they were sent back on the morrow, to take their chance in the siege. After a severe contest and dreadful carnage, the French forced their way into the Cozo, in the very centre of the city, and, before the day closed, were in possession of one half of Zaragoza. Lefebvre now believed that he had effected his purpose, and required Palafox to surrender, in a note containing only these words: "Headquarters, St. Engracia. Capitulation!" The heroic Spaniard immediately returned this reply: "Headquarters, Zaragoza. War to the knife's point!"

The contest which was now carried on is unexampled in history. One side of the Cozo, a street about as wide as Pall-mall, was possessed by the French; and, in the centre of it, their general, Verdier, gave his orders from the Franciscan convent. The opposite side was maintained by the Aragonese, who threw up batteries at the openings of the cross streets, within a few paces of those which the French erected against them. The intervening space was presently heaped with dead, either slain upon the spot, or thrown out from the windows. Next day the ammunition of the citizens began to fail; the French were expected every moment to renew their efforts for completing the conquest, and even this circumstance occasioned no dismay, nor did any one think of capitulation. One cry was heard from the people, wherever Palafox rode among them, that,

if powder failed they were ready to attack the enemy with their knives,—formidable weapons in the hands of desperate men. Just before the day closed, Don Francisco Palafox, the general's brother, entered the city with a convoy of arms, and ammunition, and a reinforcement of three thousand men, composed of Spanish guards, Swiss, and volunteers of Aragon,—a succour as little expected by the Zaragozans, as it had been provided against by the enemy.

The war was now continued from street to street, from house to house, and from room to room; pride and indignation having wrought up the French to a pitch of obstinate fury, little inferior to the devoted courage of the patriots. During the whole siege, no man distinguished himself more remarkably than the curate of one of the parishes, within the walls, by name P. Santiago Sass. He was always to be seen in the streets, sometimes fighting with the most determined bravery against the enemies, not of his country alone, but of freedom, and of all virtuous principles, wherever they were to be found; at other times, administering the sacrament to the dying, and confirming with the authority of faith, that hope, which gives to death, under such circumstances, the joy, the exultation, the triumph, and the spirit of martyrdom. Palafox reposed the utmost confidence in this brave priest, and selected him whenever anything peculiarly difficult or hazardous was to be done. At the head of forty chosen men, he succeeded in introducing a supply of powder into the town, so essentially necessary for its defence.

This most obstinate and murderous contest was continued for eleven successive days and nights, more indeed by night than by day; for it was almost certain death to appear by daylight within reach of those houses which were occupied by the other party. But

SIEGE OF ZARAGOZA 405

under cover of darkness, the combatants frequently dashed across the street to attack each other's batteries; and the battles which began there, were often carried on into the houses beyond, where they fought from room to room, and floor to floor. The hostile batteries were so near each other, that a Spaniard in one place made way under cover of the dead bodies, which completely filled the space between them, and fastened a rope to one of the French cannons; in the struggle which ensued, the rope broke, and the Zaragozans lost their prize at the very moment when they thought themselves sure of it.*

A new horror was added to the dreadful circumstances of war in this ever memorable siege. In general engagements the dead are left upon the field of battle, and the survivors remove to clear ground and an untainted atmosphere; but here—in Spain, and in the month of August, there where the dead lay the struggle was still carried on, and pestilence was dreaded from the enormous accumulation of putrifying bodies. Nothing in the whole course of the siege so embarrassed Palafox

---

* It is asserted by the French, in their official account, that, after many days' fighting, they won possession of many cloisters which had been fortified, three-fourths of the city, the arsenal, and all the magazines; and that the peaceable inhabitants, encouraged by these advantages, hoisted a white flag, and came forward to offer terms of capitulation; but that they were murdered by the insurgents; for this is the name which the French, and the tyrant whom they served, applied to a people fighting in defence of their country, and of whatever could be dear to them. Unquestionably, if any traitors had thus ventured to show themselves in the heat of the contest, they would have been put to death as certainly as they would have deserved it; and, if the thing had occurred, it would be one fact more to be recorded in honour of the Zaragozans; but there is no other authority for it than the French official account, in which account the result of the siege is totally suppressed. The circumstance, had it really taken place, would not have been omitted in Mr. Vaughan's Narrative, and in the accounts published by the Spaniards.

as this evil. The only remedy was to tie ropes to the French prisoners, and push them forward amid the dead and dying, to remove the bodies, and bring them away for interment. Even for this necessary office there was no truce, and it would have been certain death to the Aragonese who should have attempted to perform it; but the prisoners were in general secured by the pity of their own soldiers, and in this manner the evil was, in some degree, diminished.

A council of war was held by the Spaniards on the 8th, not for the purpose which is too usual in such councils, but that their heroic resolution might be communicated with authority to the people. It was, that in those quarters of the city where the Aragonese still maintained their ground, they should continue to defend themselves with the same firmness: should the enemy at last prevail, they were then to retire over the Ebro into the suburbs, break down the bridge, and defend the suburbs till they perished. When this resolution was made public, it was received with the loudest acclamations. But in every conflict the citizens now gained ground upon the soldiers, winning it inch by inch, till the space occupied by the enemy, which on the day of their entrance was nearly half the city, was gradually reduced to about an eighth part. Meantime, intelligence of the events in other parts of Spain was received by the French,—all tending to dishearten them; the surrender of Dupont, the failure of Moncey before Valencia, and the news that the Junta of that province had dispatched six thousand men to join the levies in Aragon, which were destined to relieve Zaragoza. During the night of the 13th, their fire was particularly fierce and destructive; after their batteries had ceased, flames burst out in many parts of the buildings which they had won; their last act was to blow up the church of St. Engracia;

SIEGE OF ZARAGOZA 407

the powder was placed in the subterranean church,—and this remarkable place,—this monument of fraud and credulity,—the splendid theatre wherein so many feelings of deep devotion had been excited,—which so many thousands had visited in faith, and from which unquestionably many had departed with their imaginations elevated, their principles ennobled, and their hearts strengthened, was laid in ruins. In the morning the French columns, to the great surprise of the Spaniards, were seen at a distance, retreating over the plain, on the road to Pamplona.

The history of a battle, however skilfully narrated, is necessarily uninteresting to all except military men; but in the detail of a siege, when time has destroyed those considerations, which prejudice or pervert our natural sense of right and wrong, every reader sympathizes with the besieged, and nothing, even in fictitious narratives, excites so deep and animating an interest. There is not, either in the annals of ancient or of modern times, a single event recorded more worthy to be held in admiration, now and for evermore, than the siege of Zaragoza. Will it be said that this devoted people obtained for themselves, by all this heroism and all these sacrifices, nothing more than a short respite from their fate? Woe be to the slavish heart that conceives the thought, and shame to the base tongue that gives it utterance! They purchased for themselves an everlasting remembrance upon earth,—a place in the memory and love of all good men in all ages that are yet to come. They performed their duty; they redeemed their souls from the yoke; they left an example to their country, never to be forgotten, never to be out of mind, and sure to contribute to and hasten its deliverance.

History of the Peninsular War, ch. IX.

THOMAS PAINE

FEW patriots have deserved so well of posterity as Tom Paine; yet he is remembered almost in dishonor in the country which he helped to free. One popular president, a man of some pretensions as an historian, even has characterized him as a "dirty little atheist" and suffered no rebuke. Paine's services to the Colonial cause in the American Revolution would be precisely what they were, invaluable, had he been Christian or atheist, Mohammedan or fire-worshipper. It so happens, however, that he was not an atheist but a deist, a believer in God and in immortality. Today he would be thought of as a liberal Christian. The epithet "atheist" fastened upon him was expressive of the opprobrium in which he was held by his political enemies. Paine was a radical, Paine was a revolutionist; anticipating the ways of modern thought he studied his Bible as a work of historical, ethical, and literary significance. Blackest of his sins, he was in his last days, which he passed in the United States, an abolitionist. In 1800 an abolitionist was more execrated than a Bolshevist today. Paine's services to his adopted country were forgotten and he died repudiated by his contemporaries. Times changed: it was no longer infamous to be an abolitionist; a liberal Christianity such as his became the faith of millions. But the old defamations clung and still cling to his name.

Paine was hated because he was feared. If not a great writer in the narrow sense, he was at least a great propagandist, one who did more than any other one man to popularize French revolutionary ideas among English

THOMAS PAINE 409

readers. His *Rights of Man,* proscribed by the English government, had a vast surreptitious circulation among the working classes and fostered the radicalism which found later expression in the Chartist movement. To-day one reads it with surprise, finding in it nothing wild or hare-brained. It is a calm clear statement of democratic political doctrine; it is temperate and free from bombast and sentimentality. One sentence at least is widely and deservedly known. Burke, indifferent to the fate of peasants, had lamented the sufferings and death of Marie Antoinette. Paine wrote, "he pities the plumage but forgets the dying bird."

Paine was no irresponsible revolutionist but a constructive critic of political and social institutions. The practical program of his reforms as outlined in the second part of the *Rights of Man* makes interesting reading in the light of one hundred years of halting progress. He advocates among other innovations these: the limitation of armaments by agreement with rival nations; the establishment of a steeply graduated income tax to prevent the concentration of vast fortunes in a few hands; the adoption of a system of universal popular education; the provision by the state of work for the unemployed on roads and other public enterprises; the provision from the taxes of old age pensions. In terms that should have given his proposals weight with any far-seeing prime-minister or chancellor he demonstrated a feasible redistribution of the national income to these ends. But few prime ministers and chancellors have ever been so genuinely concerned for the welfare of the common man as was Tom Paine. Though some of his proposals have since been realized and others are now the theme of political debate, it is the common man himself whose political enfranchisement has made them possible.

From THE RIGHTS OF MAN

I AM not contending for nor against any form of Government, nor for nor against any party, here or elsewhere. That which a whole Nation chooses to do, it has a right to do. Mr. Burke says, No. Where, then, does the right exist? I am contending for the rights of the *living,* and against their being willed away, and controuled and contracted for, by the manuscript assumed authority of the dead; and Mr. Burke is contending for the authority of the dead over the rights and freedom of the living. There was a time when Kings disposed of their Crowns by will upon their death-beds, and consigned the people, like beasts of the field, to whatever successor they appointed. This is now so exploded as scarcely to be remembered, and so monstrous as hardly to be believed; but the Parliamentary clauses upon which Mr. Burke builds his political church are of the same nature.

The laws of every country must be analogous to some common principle. In England no parent or master, nor all the authority of Parliament, omnipotent as it has called itself, can bind or controul the personal freedom even of an individual beyond the age of twenty-one years. On what ground of right, then, could the Parliament of 1688, or any other Parliament, bind all posterity for ever?

Those who have quitted the world, and those who are not yet arrived at it, are as remote from each other as the utmost stretch of mortal imagination can conceive. What possible obligation, then, can exist between them; what rule or principle can be laid down that of two non-entities, the one out of existence and the other not in, and who never can meet in this world, the one should controul the other to the end of time?

410

THE RIGHTS OF MAN   411

In England it is said that money cannot be taken out of the pockets of the people without their consent. But who authorised, or who could authorise, the Parliament of 1688 to controul and take away the freedom of posterity (who were not in existence to give or to withhold their consent), and limit and confine their right of acting in certain cases for ever?

A greater absurdity cannot present itself to the understanding of man than what Mr. Burke offers to his readers. He tells them, and he tells the world to come, that a certain body of men who existed a hundred years ago, made a law, and that there does not now exist in the Nation, nor ever will, nor ever can, a power to alter it. Under how many subtilties or absurdities has the divine right to govern been imposed on the credulity of mankind! Mr. Burke has discovered a new one, and he has shortened his journey to Rome by appealing to the power of this infallible Parliament of former days; and he produces what it has done as of divine authority, for that power must certainly be more than human which no human power to the end of time can alter.

*   *   . *   *   *   *   *

Through the whole of Mr. Burke's book I do not observe that the Bastille is mentioned more than once, and that with a kind of implication as if he were sorry it was pulled down, and wished it were built up again. "We have rebuilt Newgate," says he, "and tenanted the mansion; and we have prisons almost as strong as the Bastille for those who dare to libel the Queens of France."*   As to what a madman like the person called

---

* Since writing the above, two other places occur in Mr. Burke's pamphlet in which the name of the Bastille is mentioned, but in the same manner. In the one he introduces it in a sort of obscure question, and asks: "Will any ministers who now serve such a king, with but a decent appearance of respect, cordially obey the orders of those whom but the

THOMAS PAINE

Lord G—— G—— might say, to whom Newgate is rather a bedlam than a prison, it is unworthy a rational consideration. It was a madman that libelled, and that is sufficient apology; and it afforded an opportunity for confining him, which was the thing that was wished for. But certain it is that Mr. Burke, who does not call himself a madman (whatever other people may do), has libelled in the most unprovoked manner, and in the grossest stile of the most vulgar abuse, the whole representative authority of France, and yet Mr. Burke takes his seat in the British House of Commons! From his violence and his grief, his silence on some points and his excess on others, it is difficult not to believe that Mr. Burke is sorry, extremely sorry, that arbitrary power, the power of the Pope and the Bastille, are pulled down.

Not one glance of compassion, not one commiserating reflection that I can find throughout his book, has he bestowed on those who lingered out the most wretched of lives, a life without hope in the most miserable of prisons. It is painful to behold a man employing his talents to corrupt himself. Nature has been kinder to Mr. Burke than he is to her. He is not affected by the reality of distress touching his heart, but by the showy resemblance of it striking his imagination. He pities the plumage, but forgets the dying bird. Accustomed to kiss the aristocratical hand that hath purloined him from himself, he degenerates into a composition of art, and the genuine soul of nature forsakes him. His hero or his heroine must be a tragedy-victim expiring in

---

other day, *in his name,* they had committed to the Bastille?" In the other the taking it is mentioned as implying criminality in the French guards, who assisted in demolishing it. "They have not," says he, "forgot the taking the king's castles at Paris." This is Mr. Burke, who pretends to write on constitutional freedom.

THE RIGHTS OF MAN 413

show, and not the real prisoner of misery, sliding into death in the silence of a dungeon.

* * * * * * *

Every history of the creation, and every traditionary account, whether from the lettered or unlettered world, however they may vary in their opinion or belief of certain particulars, all agree in establishing one point, *the unity of man;* by which I mean that men are all of *one degree,* and consequently that all men are born equal, and with equal natural rights, in the same manner as if posterity had been continued by *creation* instead of *generation,* the latter being only the mode by which the former is carried forward; and consequently every child born into the world must be considered as deriving its existence from God. The world is as new to him as it was to the first man that existed, and his natural right in it is of the same kind.

The Mosaic account of the creation, whether taken as divine authority or merely historical, is fully up to this point, *the unity or equality of man.* The expressions admit of no controversy. "And God said, Let us make man in our own image. In the image of God created he him; male and female created he them." The distinction of sexes is pointed out, but no other distinction is even implied. If this be not divine authority, it is at least historical authority, and shows that the equality of man, so far from being a modern doctrine, is the oldest upon record.

It is also to be observed that all the religions known in the world are founded, so far as they relate to man, on the *unity of man,* as being all of one degree. Whether in heaven or in hell, or in whatever state man may be supposed to exist hereafter, the good and the bad are the only distinctions. Nay, even the laws of Govern-

ments are obliged to slide into this principle, by making degrees to consist in crimes and not in persons.

It is one of the greatest of all truths, and of the highest advantage to cultivate. By considering man in this light, and by instructing him to consider himself in this light, it places him in a close connection with all his duties, whether to his Creator or to the creation, of which he is a part; and it is only when he forgets his origin, or, to use a more fashionable phrase, his *birth and family,* that he becomes dissolute. It is not among the least of the evils of the present existing Governments in all parts of Europe that man, considered as man, is thrown back to a vast distance from his Maker, and the artificial chasm filled up by a succession of barriers, or sort of turnpike gates, through which he has to pass. I will quote Mr. Burke's catalogue of barriers that he has set up between Man and his Maker. Putting himself in the character of a herald, he says: *We fear God—we look with* AWE *to kings—with affection to Parliaments— with duty to magistrates—with reverence to priests, and with respect to nobility.* Mr. Burke has forgotten to put in *"chivalry."* He has also forgotten to put in Peter.

The duty of man is not a wilderness of turnpike gates, through which he is to pass by tickets from one to the other. It is plain and simple, and consists but of two points. His duty to God, which every man must feel; and with respect to his neighbour, to do as he would be done by. If those to whom power is delegated do well, they will be respected; if not, they will be despised; and with regard to those to whom no power is delegated, but who assume it, the rational world can know nothing of them.

* * * * * * *

Titles are but nicknames, and every nickname is a title. The thing is perfectly harmless in itself, but it

THE RIGHTS OF MAN 415

marks a sort of foppery in the human character, which degrades it. It reduces man into the diminutive of man in things which are great, and the counterfeit of woman in things which are little. It talks about its fine *blue ribbon* like a girl, and shows its new *garter* like a child. A certain writer, of some antiquity, says: *"When I was a child, I thought as a child; but when I became a man, I put away childish things."*

It is, properly, from the elevated mind of France that the folly of titles has fallen. It has outgrown the baby cloaths of *Count* and *Duke*, and breeched itself in manhood. France has not levelled, it has exalted. It has put down the dwarf, to set up the man. The punyism of a senseless word like *Duke* or *Count* or *Earl* has ceased to please. Even those who possessed them have disowned the gibberish, and as they outgrew the rickets, have despised the rattle. The genuine mind of man, thirsting for its native home, society, contemns the gewgaws that separate him from it. Titles are like circles drawn by the magician's wand, to contract the sphere of man's felicity. He lives immured within the Bastille of a word, and surveys at a distance the envied life of man.

Is it, then, any wonder that titles should fall in France? Is it not a greater wonder they should be kept up anywhere? What are they? What is their worth, and "what is their amount"?

When we think or speak of a *Judge* or a *General*, we associate with it the ideas of office and character; we think of gravity in the one and bravery in the other; but when we use a word *merely as a title*, no ideas associate with it. Through all the vocabulary of Adam there is not such an animal as a Duke or a Count; neither can we connect any certain idea with the words. Whether they mean strength or weakness, wisdom or folly, a child

or a man, or the rider or the horse, is all equivocal. What respect then can be paid to that which describes nothing, and which means nothing? Imagination has given figure and character to centaurs, satyrs, and down to all the fairy tribe; but titles baffle even the powers of fancy, and are a chimerical nondescript.

But this is not all. If a whole country is disposed to hold them in contempt, all their value is gone, and none will own them. It is common opinion only that makes them anything or nothing, or worse than nothing. There is no occasion to take titles away, for they take themselves away when society concurs to ridicule them. This species of imaginary consequence has visibly declined in every part of Europe, and it hastens to its exit as the world of reason continues to rise. There was a time when the lowest class of what are called *nobility* was more thought of than the highest is now, and when a man in armour riding through Christendom in quest of adventures was more stared at than a modern Duke. The world has seen this folly fall, and it has fallen by being laughed at, and the farce of titles will follow its fate. The patriots of France have discovered in good time that rank and dignity in society must take a new ground. The old one has fallen through. It must now take the substantial ground of character, instead of chimerical ground of titles; and they have brought their titles to the altar, and made of them a burnt-offering to Reason.

*   *   *   *   *   *   *

The French Constitution hath abolished or renounced *Toleration* and *Intoleration* also, and hath established UNIVERSAL RIGHT OF CONSCIENCE.

Toleration is not the *opposite* of Intolerance, but is the *counterfeit* of it. Both are despotisms. The one assumes to itself the right of withholding Liberty of

THE RIGHTS OF MAN 417

Conscience, and the other of granting it. The one is the Pope armed with fire and faggot, and the other is the Pope selling or granting indulgences. The former is Church and State, and the latter is Church and traffic.

But Toleration may be viewed in a much stronger light. Man worships not himself, but his Maker; and the liberty of conscience which he claims is not for the service of himself, but of his God. In this case, therefore, we must necessarily have the associated idea of two beings; the *mortal* who renders the worship, and the IMMORTAL BEING who is worshipped. Toleration, therefore, places itself, not between man and man, nor between Church and Church, nor between one denomination of religion and another, but between God and man; between the being who worships, and the BEING who is worshipped; and by the same act of assumed authority by which it tolerates man to pay his worship, it presumptuously and blasphemously sets itself up to tolerate the Almighty to receive it.

Were a Bill brought into any Parliament, entitled, *"An Act to tolerate or grant liberty to the Almighty to receive the worship of a Jew or a Turk,"* or "to prohibit the Almighty from receiving it," all men would startle and call it blasphemy. There would be an uproar. The presumption of toleration in religious matters would then present itself unmasked; but the presumption is not the less because the name of "Man" only appears to those laws, for the associated idea of the *worshipped* and the *worshipper* cannot be separated. Who then art thou, vain dust and ashes! by whatever name thou art called, whether a King, a Bishop, a Church, or a State, a Parliament, or anything else, that obtrudest thine insignificance between the soul of a man and its maker? Mind thine own concerns. If he believes not as thou believest, it is a proof that thou believest not as he

THOMAS PAINE

believeth, and there is no earthly power can determine between you.

With respect to what are called denominations of religion, if every one is left to judge of his own religion, there is no such thing as a religion that is wrong; but if they are to judge of each other's religion, there is no such thing as a religion that is right; and therefore all the world is right, or all the world is wrong. But with respect to religion itself, without regard to names, and as directing itself from the universal family of mankind to the Divine object of all adoration, *it is man bringing to his Maker the fruits of his heart;* and though those fruits may differ from each other like the fruits of the earth, the grateful tribute of every one is accepted.

A Bishop of Durham, or a Bishop of Winchester, or the Archbishop who heads the Dukes, will not refuse a tythe-sheaf of wheat because it is not a cock of hay, nor a cock of hay because it is not a sheaf of wheat; nor a pig, because it is neither one nor the other; but these same persons, under the figure of an established church, will not permit their Maker to receive the varied tythes of man's devotion.

One of the continual choruses of Mr. Burke's book is "Church and State." He does not mean some one particular Church, or some one particular State, but any Church and State; and he uses the term as a general figure to hold forth the political doctrine of always uniting the Church with the State in every country, and he censures the National Assembly for not having done this in France. Let us bestow a few thoughts on this subject.

All religions are in their nature kind and benign, and united with principles of morality. They could not have made proselytes at first by professing anything that was vicious, cruel, persecuting, or immoral. Like every-

THE RIGHTS OF MAN 419

thing else, they had their beginning; and they proceeded by persuasion, exhortation, and example. How then is it that they lose their native mildness, and become morose and intolerant?

It proceeds from the connection which Mr. Burke recommends. By engendering the Church with the State, a sort of mule-animal, capable only of destroying, and not of breeding up, is produced, called *The Church established by Law*. It is a stranger, even from its birth, to any parent mother, on whom it is begotten, and whom in time it kicks out and destroys.

The Inquisition in Spain does not proceed from the religion originally professed but from this mule-animal engendered between the Church and the State. The burnings in Smithfield proceeded from the same heterogeneous production; and it was the regeneration of this strange animal in England afterwards that renewed rancour and irreligion among the inhabitants, and that drove the people called Quakers and Dissenters to America. Persecution is not an original feature in *any* religion; but it is always the strongly-marked feature of all law-religions, or religions established by law. Take away the law-establishment and every religion reassumes its original benignity. In America a Catholic priest is a good citizen, a good character, and a good neighbour; an Episcopalian minister is of the same description; and this proceeds, independently of the men, from there being no law establishment in America.

If also we view this matter in a temporal sense we shall see the ill effects it has had on the prosperity of nations. The union of Church and State has impoverished Spain. The revoking the Edict of Nantes drove the silk manufacture from France into England; and Church and State are driving the cotton manufacture from England to America and France. Let then Mr.

420   THOMAS PAINE

Burke continue to preach his antipolitical doctrine of Church and State. It will do some good. The National Assembly will not follow his advice, but will benefit by his folly. It was by observing the ill effects of it in England, that America has been warned against it; and it is by experiencing them in France, that the National Assembly have abolished it, and, like America, have established UNIVERSAL RIGHT OF CONSCIENCE AND UNIVERSAL RIGHT OF CITIZENSHIP.

*   *   *   *   *   *   *

As Mr. Burke has not written on Constitutions so neither has he written on the French Revolution. He gives no account of its commencement or its progress. He only expresses his wonder. "It looks," says he, "to me, as if I were in a great crisis, not of the affairs of France alone, but of all Europe, perhaps of more than Europe. All circumstances taken together, the French Revolution is the most astonishing that has hitherto happened in the world."

As wise men are astonished at foolish things, and other people at wise ones, I know not on which ground to account for Mr. Burke's astonishment; but certain it is, that he does not understand the French Revolution. It has apparently burst forth like a creation from a chaos, but it is no more than the consequence of a mental Revolution priorily existing in France. The mind of the Nation had changed beforehand, and the new order of things has naturally followed the new order of thoughts. I will here, as concisely as I can, trace out the growth of the French Revolution, and mark the circumstances that have contributed to produce it.

The despotism of Louis XIV., united with the gaiety of his Court, and the gaudy ostentation of his character had so humbled, and at the same time so fascinated the mind of France, that the people appear to have lost all

THE RIGHTS OF MAN

sense of their own dignity, in contemplating that of their Grand Monarch; and the whole reign of Louis XV., remarkable only for weakness and effeminacy, made no other alteration than that of spreading a sort of lethargy over the nation, from which it showed no disposition to rise.

The only signs which appeared of the spirit of Liberty during those periods, are to be found in the writings of the French philosophers. Montesquieu, President of the Parliament of Bordeaux, went as far as a writer under a despotic Government could well proceed; and being obliged to divide himself between principle and prudence, his mind often appears under a veil, and we ought to give him credit for more than he has expressed.

Voltaire, who was both the flatterer and the satirist of despotism, took another line. His forte lay in exposing and ridiculing the superstitions which priestcraft, united with witchcraft, had interwoven with Governments. It was not from the purity of his principles, or his love of mankind (for satire and philanthropy are not naturally concordant), but from his strong capacity of seeing folly in its true shape, and his irresistible propensity to expose it, that he made those attacks. They were, however, as formidable as if the motives had been virtuous; and he merits the thanks rather than the esteem of mankind.

On the contrary, we find in the writings of Rousseau, and the Abbé Raynal, a loveliness of sentiment in favour of liberty, that excites respect, and elevates the human faculties; but having raised this animation, they do not direct its operations, and leave the mind in love with an object, without describing the means of possessing it.

The writings of Quesnay, Turgot, and the friends of those authors, are of the serious kind; but they laboured under the same disadvantage with Montesquieu; their

writings abound with moral maxims of Government, but are rather directed to œconomise and reform the administration of the Government, than the Government itself.

But all those writings and many others had their weight; and by the different manner in which they treated the subject of Government, Montesquieu by his judgment and knowledge of laws, Voltaire by his wit, Rousseau and Raynal by their animation, and Quesnay and Turgot by their moral maxims and systems of œconomy, readers of every class met with something to their taste, and a spirit of political inquiry began to diffuse itself through the Nation at the time the dispute between England and the then colonies of America broke out.

In the war which France afterwards engaged in, it is very well known that the nation appeared to be beforehand with the French ministry. Each of them had its view: but those views were directed to different objects; the one sought liberty, and the other retaliation on England. The French officers and soldiers, who after this went to America, were eventually placed in the school of Freedom, and learned the practice as well as the principles of it by heart.

As it was impossible to separate the military events which took place in America from the principles of the American Revolution, the publication of those events in France necessarily connected themselves with the principles which produced them. Many of the facts were in themselves principles; such as the Declaration of American Independence, and the treaty of alliance between France and America, which recognised the natural right of man, and justified resistance to oppression. The then Minister of France, Count Vergennes, was not the friend of America; and it is both justice and

THE RIGHTS OF MAN   423

gratitude to say, that it was the Queen of France who gave the cause of America a fashion at the French Court. Count Vergennes was the personal and social friend of Dr. Franklin; and the Doctor had obtained, by his sensible gracefulness, a sort of influence over him; but with respect to principles Count Vergennes was a despot.

The situation of Dr. Franklin, as Minister from America to France, should be taken into the chain of circumstances. The diplomatic character is of itself the narrowest sphere of society that man can act in. It forbids intercourse by the reciprocity of suspicion; and a diplomatic is a sort of unconnected atom, continually repelling and repelled. But this was not the case with Dr. Franklin. He was not the diplomatic of a Court, but of MAN. His character as a philosopher had been long established, and his circle of society in France was universal. Count Vergennes resisted for a considerable time the publication in France of the American Constitutions translated into the French language: but even in this he was obliged to give way to public opinion, and a sort of propriety in admitting to appear what he had undertaken to defend. The American Constitutions were to Liberty what a grammar is to language: they define its parts of speech, and practically construct them into syntax. The peculiar situation of the then Marquis de la Fayette is another link in the great chain. He served in America as an American officer under a commission of Congress, and by the universality of his acquaintance was in close friendship with the civil government of America, as well as with the military line. He spoke the language of the country, entered into the discussions on the principles of Government, and was always a welcome friend at any election.

When the war closed, a vast reinforcement to the

THOMAS PAINE

cause of Liberty spread itself over France, by the return of the French officers and soldiers. A knowledge of the practice was then joined to the theory; and all that was wanting to give it real existence was opportunity. Man cannot, properly speaking, make circumstances for his purpose, but he always has it in his power to improve them when they occur, and this was the case in France.

* * * * * * *

When we survey the wretched condition of Man, under the monarchical and hereditary system of Government, dragged from his home by one power, or driven by another, and impoverished by taxes more than by enemies, it becomes evident that those systems are bad, and that a general Revolution in the principle and construction of Governments is necessary.

What is Government more than the management of the affairs of a Nation? It is not, and from its nature cannot be, the property of any particular man or family, but of the whole community, at whose expence it is supported; and though by force and contrivance it has been usurped into an inheritance, the usurpation cannot alter the right of things. Sovereignty, as a matter of right, appertains to the Nation only, and not to any individual; and a Nation has at all times an inherent, indefeasible right to abolish any form of Government it finds inconvenient, and to establish such as accords with its interest, disposition, and happiness. The romantic and barbarous distinction of men into Kings and subjects, though it may suit the conditions of courtiers, cannot that of citizens; and is exploded by the principle upon which Governments are now founded. Every citizen is a member of the sovereignty, and, as such, can acknowledge no personal subjection: and his obedience can be only to the laws.

When men think of what Government is, they must

THE RIGHTS OF MAN   425

necessarily suppose it to possess a knowledge of all the objects and matters upon which its authority is to be exercised. In this view of Government, the Republican system, as established by America and France, operates to embrace the whole of a Nation; and the knowledge necessary to the interest of all the parts, is to be found in the centre, which the parts by representation form; but the old Governments are on a construction that excludes knowledge as well as happiness; Government by monks, who know nothing of the world beyond the walls of a convent, is as inconsistent as Government by Kings.

What we formerly called Revolutions, were little more than a change of persons, or an alteration of local circumstances. They rose and fell like things of course, and had nothing in their existence or their fate that could influence beyond the spot that produced them. But what we now see in the world, from the Revolutions of America and France, are a renovation of the natural order of things, a system of principles as universal as truth and the existence of man, and combining moral with political happiness and national prosperity.

I. *Men are born, and always continue, free and equal in respect of their rights. Civil distinctions, therefore, can be founded only on public utility.*

II. *The end of all political associations is the preservation of the natural and imprescriptible rights of man; and these rights are liberty, property, security, and resistance of oppression.*

III. *The Nation is essentially the source of all sovereignty; nor can* ANY INDIVIDUAL, *or* ANY BODY OF MEN, *be entitled to any authority which is not expressly derived from it."*

In these principles there is nothing to throw a Nation

into confusion by inflaming ambition. They are calculated to call forth wisdom and abilities, and to exercise them for the public good, and not for the emolument or aggrandisement of particular descriptions of men or families. Monarchical sovereignty, the enemy of mankind, and the source of misery, is abolished; and sovereignty itself is restored to its natural and original place, the Nation. Were this the case throughout Europe, the cause of wars would be taken away.

* * * * * * *

All hereditary Government is in its nature tyranny. An heritable crown, or an heritable throne, or by what other fanciful name such things may be called, have no other significant explanation than that mankind are heritable property. To inherit a Government, is to inherit the people, as if they were flocks and herds.

With respect to the second head, that of being inadequate to the purposes for which Government is necessary, we have only to consider what Government essentially is, and compare it with the circumstances to which hereditary succession is subject.

Government ought to be a thing always in full maturity. It ought to be so constructed as to be superior to all the accidents to which individual man is subject; and, therefore, hereditary succession, by being *subject to them all,* is the most irregular and imperfect of all the systems of Government.

We have heard the *Rights of Man* called a *levelling* system; but the only system to which the word *levelling* is truly applicable, is the hereditary monarchical system. It is the system of *mental levelling.* It indiscriminately admits every species of character to the same authority. Vice and virtue, ignorance and wisdom, in short, every quality, good or bad, is put on the same level. Kings succeed each other, not as rationals, but as animals.

THE RIGHTS OF MAN 427

It signifies not what their mental or moral characters are. Can we then be surprised at the abject state of the human mind in monarchical countries, when the Government itself is formed on such an abject levelling system? It has no fixed character. Today it is one thing; tomorrow it is something else. It changes with the temper of every succeeding individual, and is subject to all the varieties of each. It is Government through the medium of the passions and accidents. It appears under all the various characters of childhood, decrepitude, dotage; a thing at nurse, in leading-strings, or in crutches. It reverses the wholesome order of nature. It occasionally puts children over men, and the conceits of nonage over wisdom and experience. In short, we cannot conceive a more ridiculous figure of Government, than hereditary succession, in all its cases, presents.

Could it be made a decree in nature, or an edict registered in heaven, and man could know it, that virtue and wisdom should invariably appertain to hereditary succession, the objections to it would be removed; but when we see that nature acts as she disowned and sported with the hereditary system; that the mental characters of successors, in all countries, are below the average of human understanding; that one is a tyrant, another an idiot, a third insane, and some all three together, it is impossible to attach confidence to it, when reason in man has power to act.

* * * * * * *

The representative system takes society and civilisation for its basis; nature, reason, and experience for its guide.

Experience, in all ages and in all countries, has demonstrated that it is impossible to control nature

THOMAS PAINE

in her distribution of mental powers. She gives them as she pleases. Whatever is the rule by which she, apparently to us, scatters them among mankind, that rule remains a secret to man. It would be as ridiculous to attempt to fix the hereditaryship of human beauty as of wisdom. Whatever wisdom constituently is, it is like a seedless plant; it may be reared when it appears, but it cannot be voluntarily produced. There is always a sufficiency somewhere in the general mass of society for all purposes; but with respect to the parts of society, it is continually changing its place. It rises in one to-day, in another to-morrow, and has most probably visited in rotation every family of the earth, and again withdrawn.

As this is in the order of nature, the order of Government must necessarily follow it, or Government will, as we see it does, degenerate into ignorance. The hereditary system, therefore, is as repugnant to human wisdom as to human rights; and is as absurd as it is unjust.

As the republic of letters brings forward the best literary productions, by giving to genius a fair and universal chance; so the representative system of Government is calculated to produce the wisest laws, by collecting wisdom from where it can be found. I smile to myself when I contemplate the ridiculous insignificance into which literature and all the sciences would sink, were they made hereditary; and I carry the same idea into Governments. An hereditary governor is as inconsistent as an hereditary author. I know not whether Homer or Euclid had sons; but I will venture an opinion that if they had, and had left their works unfinished, those sons could not have completed them.

Do we need a stronger evidence of the absurdity of hereditary Government than is seen in the descendants

THE RIGHTS OF MAN 429

of those men, in any line of life, who once were famous? Is there scarcely an instance in which there is not a total reverse of the character? It appears as if the tide of mental faculties flowed as far as it could in certain channels, and then forsook its course and arose in others. How irrational then is the hereditary system, which establishes channels of power, in company with which wisdom refuses to flow! By continuing this absurdity, man is perpetually in contradiction with himself; he accepts, for a King, or a chief magistrate, or a legislator, a person whom he would not elect for a constable.

It appears to general observation that Revolutions create genius and talents; but those events do no more than bring them forward. There is existing in man a mass of sense lying in a dormant state, and which, unless something excites to action, will descend with him, in that condition, to the grave. As it is to the advantage of society that the whole of the faculties should be employed, the construction of Government ought to be such as to bring forward by a quiet and regular operation, all that extent of capacity which never fails to appear in Revolutions.

This cannot take place in the insipid state of hereditary Government, not only because it prevents, but because it operates to benumb. When the mind of a Nation is bowed down by any political superstition in its Government, such as hereditary succession is, it loses a considerable portion of its powers on all other subjects and objects. Hereditary succession requires the same obedience to ignorance as to wisdom; and when once the mind can bring itself to pay this indiscriminate reverence, it descends below the stature of mental manhood. It is fit to be great only in little things. It acts

a treachery upon itself, and suffocates the sensations that urge to detection.

* * * * * * *

The Constitutions of America, and also that of France, have either affixed a period for their revision, or laid down the mode by which improvement shall be made. It is perhaps impossible to establish anything that combines principles with opinions and practice, which the progress of circumstances, through a length of years, will not in some measure derange, or render inconsistent; and, therefore, to prevent inconveniences accumulating, till they discourage reformations or provoke Revolutions, it is best to provide the means of regulating them as they occur. The Rights of Man are the rights of all generations of men, and cannot be monopolized by any. That which is worth following will be followed for the sake of its worth, and it is in this that its security lies, and not in any conditions with which it may be encumbered. When a man leaves property to his heirs, he does not connect it with an obligation that they shall accept it. Why, then, should we do otherwise with respect to Constitutions?

The best Constitution that could now be devised, consistent with the condition of the present moment, may be far short of that excellence which a few years may afford. There is a morning of reason rising upon man on the subject of Government that has not appeared before. As the barbarism of the present old Governments expires, the moral condition of Nations with respect to each other will be changed. Man will not be brought up with the savage idea of considering his species as an enemy, because the accident of birth gave the individuals existence in countries distinguished by different names; and as Constitutions have always

THE RIGHTS OF MAN 431

some relation to external as well as to domestic circumstances, the means of benefiting by every change, foreign or domestic, should be a part of every Constitution.

We already see an alteration in the national disposition of England and France towards each other, which, when we look back to only a few years, is itself a Revolution. Who could have foreseen, or who would have believed, that a French National Assembly would ever have been a popular toast in England, or that a friendly alliance of the two Nations should become the wish of either? It shews that man, were he not corrupted by Governments, is naturally the friend of man, and that human nature is not of itself vicious. That spirit of jealousy and ferocity, which the Governments of the two countries inspired, and which they rendered subservient to the purpose of taxation, is now yielding to the dictates of reason, interest, and humanity. The trade of courts is beginning to be understood, and the affectation of mystery, with all the artificial sorcery by which they imposed upon mankind, is on the decline. It has received its death wound; and though it may linger, it will expire.

Government ought to be as much open to improvement as anything which appertains to man, instead of which it has been monopolized from age to age, by the most ignorant and vicious of the human race. Need we any other proof of their wretched management, than the excess of debts and taxes with which every nation groans, and the quarrels into which they have precipitated the world?

Just emerging from such a barbarous condition, it is too soon to determine to what extent of improvement Government may yet be carried. For what we can

foresee, all Europe may form but one great Republic, and man be free of the whole.

* * * * * * *

Civil Government does not consist in executions; but in making that provision for the instruction of youth and the support of age, as to exclude, as much as possible, profligacy from the one and despair from the other. Instead of this, the resources of a country are lavished upon kings, upon Courts, upon hirelings, imposters and prostitutes; and even the poor themselves, with all their wants upon them, are compelled to support the fraud that oppresses them.

Why is it that scarcely any are executed but the poor? The fact is a proof, among other things, of a wretchedness in their condition. Bred up without morals, and cast upon the world without a prospect, they are the exposed sacrifice of vice and legal barbarity. The millions that are superfluously wasted upon Governments are more than sufficient to reform those evils, and to benefit the condition of every man in a Nation, not included within the purlieus of a Court. This I hope to make appear in the progress of this work.

It is the nature of compassion to associate with misfortune. In taking up this subject I seek no recompence —I fear no consequence. Fortified with that proud integrity that disdains to triumph or to yield, I will advocate the Rights of Man.

It is to my advantage that I have served an apprenticeship to life. I know the value of moral instruction, and I have seen the danger of the contrary.

At an early period, little more than sixteen years of age, raw and adventurous, and heated with the false

THE RIGHTS OF MAN   433

heroism of a master* who had served in a man of war, I began the carver of my own fortune, and entered on board the Terrible Privateer, Captain Death. From this adventure I was happily prevented by the affectionate and moral remonstrance of a good father, who, from his own habits of life, being of the Quaker profession, must begin to look upon me as lost. But the impression, much as it affected at the time, began to wear away, and I entered afterwards in the King of Prussia Privateer, Captain Mendez, and went with her to sea. Yet from such a beginning, and with all the inconvenience of early life against me, I am proud to say that with a perseverance undismayed by difficulties, a disinterestedness that compelled respect, I have not only contributed to raise a new empire in the world, founded on a new system of Government, but I have arrived at an eminence in political literature, the most difficult of all lines to succeed and excel in, which Aristocracy with all its aids has not been able to reach or to rival.

*   *   *   *   *   *   *

Many a youth comes up to London full of expectations, and with little or no money, and unless he get immediate employment he is already half-undone; and boys bred up in London without any means of a livelihood, and as it often happens of dissolute parents, are in a still worse condition; and servants long out of place are not much better off. In short, a world of little cases is continually arising, which busy or affluent life knows not of, to open the first door to distress. Hunger is not among the postponeable wants, and a day, even a few hours, in such a condition is often the crisis of a life of ruin.

* Rev. William Knowles, master of the grammar school of Thetford, in Norfolk.

THOMAS PAINE

These circumstances which are the general cause of the little thefts and pilferings that lead to greater, may be prevented. There yet remain twenty thousand pounds out of the four millions of surplus taxes, which with another fund hereafter to be mentioned, amounting to about twenty thousand pounds more, cannot be better applied than to this purpose. The plan then will be:

First,—To erect two or more buildings, or take some already erected, capable of containing at least six thousand persons, and to have in each of these places as many kinds of employment as can be contrived, so that every person who shall come may find something which he or she can do.

Secondly,—To receive all who shall come, without inquiring who or what they are. The only condition to be, that for so much, or so many hours' work each person shall receive so many meals of wholesome food and a warm lodging, at least as good as a barrack. That a certain portion of what each person's work shall be worth shall be reserved, and given to him or her, on their going away; and that each person shall stay as long or as short a time, or come as often as he chuse, on these conditions.

If each person stayed three months, it would assist by rotation twenty-four thousand persons annually, though the real number, at all times, would be but six thousand. By establishing an asylum of this kind, persons to whom temporary distresses occur would have an opportunity to recruit themselves, and be enabled to look out for better employment.

Allowing that their labour paid but one half the expence of supporting them, after reserving a portion of their earnings for themselves, the sum of forty thousand pounds additional would defray all other charges for even a greater number than six thousand.

THE RIGHTS OF MAN

The fund very properly convertible to this purpose, in addition to the twenty thousand pounds remaining of the former fund, will be the produce of the tax upon coals, so iniquitously and wantonly applied to the support of the Duke of Richmond. It is horrid that any man, more especially at the price coals now are, should live on the distresses of a community; and any Government permitting such an abuse deserves to be dismissed. This fund is said to be about twenty thousand pounds per annum.

I shall now conclude this plan with enumerating the several particulars, and then proceed to other matters. The enumeration is as follows:—

First—Abolition of two million poor-rates.

Secondly—Provision for two hundred and fifty-two thousand poor families.

Thirdly—Education for one million and thirty thousand children.

Fourthly—Comfortable provision for one hundred and forty thousand aged persons.

Fifthly—Donation of twenty shillings each for fifty thousand births.

Sixthly—Donation of twenty shillings each for twenty thousand marriages.

Seventhly—Allowance of twenty thousand pounds for the funeral expences of persons travelling for work, and dying at a distance from their friends.

Eighthly—Employment, at all times, for the casual poor in the cities of London and Westminster.

By the operation of this plan, the poor laws, those instruments of civil torture, will be superseded, and the wasteful expence of litigation prevented. The hearts of the humane will not be shocked by ragged and hungry children, and persons of seventy or eighty years of age, begging for bread. The dying poor will not be dragged from place to place to breathe their last, as a reprisal

of parish upon parish. Widows will have a maintenance for their children, and not be carted away, on the death of their husbands, like culprits and criminals; and children will no longer be considered as increasing the distresses of their parents. The haunts of the wretched will be known, because it will be to their advantage, and the number of petty crimes, the offspring of distress and poverty, will be lessened. The poor, as well as the rich, will then be interested in the support of Government, and the cause and apprehension of riots and tumults will cease. Ye who sit in ease, and solace yourselves in plenty—and such there are in Turkey and Russia, as well as in England—and who say to yourselves, "Are we not well off?" have ye thought of these things? When ye do, ye will cease to speak and feel for yourselves alone.

The plan is easy in practice. It does not embarrass trade by a sudden interruption in the order of taxes, but effects the relief by changing the application of them; and the money necessary for the purpose can be drawn from the excise collections, which are made eight times a year in every market town in England.

WILLIAM GODWIN

UPON the publication of *Political Justice* it is said that Pitt's cabinet considered indicting Godwin for fostering sedition, but refrained because of the book's considerable cost. The wide circulation of Paine's *The Rights of Man* was then causing perturbation in official breasts. It was a period of anti-Red hysteria. Paine and Godwin were regarded much as anarchists and communists have been regarded in later periods. Godwin, however, was the scholarly radical, the theorist, much less to be feared than one of proved practical skill in revolutions; and this consideration no doubt was weighed together with the cost of his book. Nevertheless it is to Godwin's personal credit that he took his chance and awaited with composure the action of the ministry. He was in later life not incapable of pettiness and meanness as his correspondence with Shelley reveals, but his passion for justice and his willingness to suffer in its behalf go far to redeem him in the eyes of posterity.

Political Justice is the best expression of the French Revolutionary philosophy as reformulated by an English mind. The influence of all the chief revolutionary thinkers is manifest. Godwin, however, is no slavish follower. For Rousseau's social contract theory he has little use. He believes in the perfectibility of man but is under no illusion that Utopia is to be won at a blow. It is to the slow processes of education that he looks for the improvement of human society. Violence he deprecates and pins his faith to the persuasive force of human reason.

437

WILLIAM GODWIN

His theories are, roughly, those of philosophical anarchism. The ideal of society is one freed of all institutional government and regulated solely by public opinion. The world will ultimately, he conceives, be composed of a vast number of little communities in the management of which very man, as in a town meeting, will have a voice. Some sort of a national parliament to meet one day a year and pass upon questions arising from the relation of one community to another he grudgingly concedes as perhaps necessary. But the difficult questions of economic relationships among groups he totally ignores. He was, obviously, no economist. Within the group his solution of the problem of wealth and its distribution is delightfully simple. He who has what another needs will naturally share his excess with that other. Men will work half an hour a day, or possibly as much as two hours, in the creation of wealth. So much labor should suffice for the simple wants of a race of philosophers which mankind will ultimately be. Life will be passed in a round of intellectual pursuits. Its pleasures will largely consist of stimulating conversation. We shall learn perhaps to do without sleep and by the exercise of will protract our lives far beyond the present span. In his rather dry and academic manner Godwin anticipates some of the ideas which Bernard Shaw expresses in *Back to Methuselah,*

Godwin pushes theory to absurd lengths at times. So passionate an individualist was he that he deprecates orchestras and theatrical companies because members of these organizations must submit to the will of a director. Arguing a hypothetical case he contends that if we can rescue but one occupant from a burning house we should select the one of greatest value to society regardless of our personal preference whether for wife or child. Abstract speculation has seldom reached

WILLIAM GODWIN 439

such sublime and unemotional heights. It must be remarked that in his family relations, especially when his daughter Mary eloped with Shelley, he fell short of his stoical ideals. He was a human, crotchety, academic man, often rather ridiculous but with a touch of genius. *Political Justice* is eminently clear and well written and in his novels he displays more talent for narrative than one would expect.

The very center of his argument in *Political Justice,* the point to which he repeatedly returns, is this: freedom of thought, freedom of speech, freedom of the press are the basis of a proper society. Given these, and the realization in every man that it is his duty to tell the full and unqualified truth on all occasions, and mankind will cast aside all false ideals, all worship of rank, wealth, and ostentation. These are the offspring of a debased and servile society. All social progress springs from the conscientious individual bravely speaking his mind unintimidated by the powers of tyranny.

It is impossible to estimate the influence of Godwin's thought upon posterity. That he was one of those who fostered the democratic ideal and thus was instrumental in political reform is clear. Yet his practical influence was probably much less than Tom Paine's. It is his influence upon the youthful Shelley which is his chief claim to the consideration of posterity. Shelley's early work is deeply coloured by the Godwinian influence. This indebtedness Shelley never forgot nor ceased to repay.

In the following paragraphs selected from the two volumes of *Political Justice* I have endeavored to illustrate Godwin's basic ideas, those to which he repeatedly returns and upon which he rears the structure of his speculations. Despite their episodic character

they cohere more closely than might be anticipated, for Godwin's ideas are essentially simple and congruous even when extreme.

From POLITICAL JUSTICE

The real enemies of liberty in any country are not the people, but those higher orders who profit by a contrary system. Infuse just views of society into a certain number of the liberally educated and reflecting members; give to the people guides and instructors; and the business is done. This however is not to be accomplished but in a gradual manner, as will more fully appear in the sequel. The error lies, not in tolerating the worst forms of government for a time, but in supposing a change impracticable, and not incessantly looking forward to its accomplishment.

* * * * * * *

Is there a country in which a prudent director of education would propose some other object for his labours than to make his pupil temperate and just and wise? Is there a climate that requires its inhabitants to be hard drinkers or horse-jockies or gamesters or bullies, rather than men? Can there be a corner of the world, where the lover of justice and truth would find himself out of his element and useless? If no; then liberty must be every where better than slavery, and the government of rectitude and impartiality better than the government of caprice.

* * * * * * *

Man is in a state of perpetual progress. He must grow either better or worse, either correct his habits or confirm them. The government proposed must either increase our passions and prejudices by fanning the flame, or by gradually discouraging tend to extir-

POLITICAL JUSTICE 441

pate them. In reality, it is sufficiently difficult to imagine a government that shall have the latter tendency. By its very nature political institution has a tendency to suspend the elasticity, and put an end to the advancement of mind. Every scheme for embodying imperfection must be injurious. That which is today a considerable melioration, will at some future period, if preserved unaltered, appear a defect and disease in the body politic. It were earnestly to be desired that each man was wise enough to govern himself without the intervention of any compulsory restraint; and, since government even in its best state is an evil, the object principally to be aimed at is, that we should have as little of it as the general peace of human society will permit.

*   *   *   *   *   *   *

It follows that the promoting of the best interests of mankind eminently depends upon the freedom of social communication. Let us imagine to ourselves a number of individuals, who, having first stored their minds with reading and reflection, proceed afterwards in candid and unreserved conversation to compare their ideas, to suggest their doubts, to remove their difficulties, and to cultivate a collected and striking manner of delivering their sentiments. Let us suppose these men, prepared by mutual intercourse, to go forth to the world, to explain with succinctness and simplicity, and in a manner well calculated to arrest attention, the true principles of society. Let us suppose their hearers instigated in their turn to repeat these truths to their companions. We shall then have an idea of knowledge as perpetually gaining ground, unaccompanied with peril in the means of its diffusion. Reason will spread itself, and not a brute and unintelligent

WILLIAM GODWIN

sympathy. Discussion perhaps never exists with so much vigour and utility as in the conversation of two persons. It may be carried on with advantage in small and friendly societies. Does the fewness of their numbers imply the rarity of their existence? Far otherwise: the time perhaps will come when such institutions will be universal. Shew to mankind by a few examples the advantages of political discussion undebauched by political enmity and vehemence, and the beauty of the spectacle will soon render the example contagious. Every man will commune with his neighbour. Every man will be eager to tell and to hear what the interest of all requires them to know. The bolts and fortifications of the temple of truth will be removed. The craggy steep of science, which it was before difficult to ascend, will be levelled with the plain. Knowledge will be accessible to all. Wisdom will be the inheritance of man, from which none will be excluded but by their own heedlessness and prodigality. If these ideas cannot completely be realised, till the inequality of conditions and the tyranny of government are rendered somewhat less oppressive, this affords no reason against the setting afloat so generous a system. The improvement of individuals and the melioration of political institutions are destined mutually to produce and reproduce each other. Truth, and above all political truth, is not hard of acquisition, but from the superciliousness of its possessors. It has been slow and tedious of improvement, because the study of it has been relegated to doctors and civilians. It has produced little effect upon the practice of mankind, because it has not been allowed a plain and direct appeal to their understandings. Remove these obstacles, render it the common property, bring it into daily use, and you may reason-

POLITICAL JUSTICE 443

ably promise yourself consequences of the most inestimable value.

* * * * * * *

What is it that at this day enables a thousand errors to keep their station in the world, priestcraft, tests, bribery, war, cabal, and whatever else is the contempt and abhorrence of the enlightened and honest mind? Cowardice. Because, while vice walks erect with an unabashed countenance, men less vicious dare not paint her with that truth of colouring, which should at once confirm the innocent and reform the guilty. Because the majority of those who are not involved in the busy scene, and who, possessing some discernment, see that things are not altogether right, yet see in so frigid a way, and with so imperfect a view. Many, who detect the imposture, are yet absurd enough to imagine that imposture is necessary to keep the world in awe, and that truth being too weak to curb the turbulent passions of mankind, it is exceedingly proper to call in knavery and artifice as the abettors of her power. If every man today would tell all the truth he knows, three years hence there would be scarcely a falsehood of any magnitude remaining in the civilized world.

* * * * * * *

Considering then the doctrine of moral necessity as sufficiently established, let us proceed to the consequences that are to be deduced from it. This view of things presents us with an idea of the universe as connected and cemented in all its parts, nothing in the boundless progress of things being capable of happening otherwise than it has actually happened. In the life of every human being there is a chain of causes, generated in that eternity which preceded his birth, and going on in regular procession through the whole period of his existence, in consequence of which it was

WILLIAM GODWIN

impossible for him to act in any instance otherwise than he has acted.

* * * * * * *

The system of disinterested benevolence proves to us, that it is possible to be virtuous, and not merely to talk of virtue; that all which has been said by philosophers and moralists respecting impartial justice is not an unmeaning rant; and that, when we call upon mankind to divest themselves of selfish and personal considerations, we call upon them for something which they are able to practise. An idea like this reconciles us to our species; teaches us to regard with enlightened admiration the men who have appeared to lose the feeling of their personal existence in the pursuit of general advantage; and gives us reason to expect, that, as men collectively advance in science and useful institution, they will proceed more and more to consolidate their private judgment and their individual will with abstract justice and the unmixed approbation of general happiness.

* * * * * *

Virtue was never yet held in much honour and esteem in a monarchical country. It is the inclination and the interest of courtiers and kings to bring it into disrepute; and they are but too successful in the attempt. Virtue is in their conception arrogant, intrusive, unmanageable and stubborn. It is an assumed outside, by which those who pretend to it intend to gratify their rude tempers or their secret views. Within the circle of monarchy virtue is always regarded with dishonourable incredulity. The philosophical system which affirms self love to be the first mover of all our actions and the falsity of human virtues, is the growth of these countries. Why is it that the language of integrity and public spirit is constantly regarded among us a hypocrisy? It was not

POLITICAL JUSTICE 445

always thus. It was not till the usurpation of Caesar, that books were written by the tyrant and his partisans to prove that Cato was no better than a snarling pretender.

*   *   *   *   *   *

Of all the principles of justice there is none so material to the moral rectitude of mankind as this, that no man can be distinguished but by his personal merit. Why not endeavour to reduce to practice so simple and sublime a lesson? When a man has proved himself a benefactor to the public, when he has already by laudable perseverance cultivated in himself talents, which need only encouragement and public favour to bring them to maturity, let that man be honoured. In a state of society where fictitious distinctions are unknown, it is impossible he should not be honoured. But that a man should be looked up to with servility and awe, because the king has bestowed on him a spurious name, or decorated him with a ribband; that another should wallow in luxury, because his ancestor three centuries ago bled in the quarrel of Lancaster and York; do we imagine that these iniquities can be practised without injury?

*   *   *   *   *   *

Let us for a moment give the reins to reflexion, and endeavour accurately to conceive the state of mankind where justice should form the public and general principle. In that case our moral feelings would assume a firm and wholesome tone, for they would not be perpetually counteracted by examples that weakened their energy and confounded their clearness. Men would be fearless, because they would know that there were no legal snares lying in wait for their lives. They would be courageous, because no man would be pressed to the earth that another might enjoy immoderate luxury,

WILLIAM GODWIN

because every one would be secure of the just reward of his industry and prize of his exertions. Jealousy and hatred would cease, for they are the offspring of injustice. Every man would speak truth with his neighbour, for there would be no temptation to falsehood and deceit. Mind would find its level, for there would be every thing to encourage and to animate. Science would be unspeakably improved, for understanding would convert into a real power, no longer an *ignis fatuus,* shining and expiring by turns, and leading us into sloughs of sophistry, false science and specious mistake. All men would be disposed to avow their dispositions and actions: none would endeavour to suppress the just eulogium of his neighbour, for, so long as there were tongues to record, the suppression would be impossible; none fear to detect the misconduct of his neighbour, for there would be no laws converting the sincere expression of our convictions into a libel.

*　　*　　*　　*　　*　　*

Is all this nothing? Is all this necessary for the maintenance of civil order? Let it be recollected that for this distinction there is not the smallest foundation in the nature of things, that, as we have already said, there is no particular mould for the construction of lords, and that they are born neither better nor worse than the poorest of their dependents. It is this structure of aristocracy in all its sanctuaries and fragments against which reason and philosophy have declared war. It is alike unjust, whether we consider it in the casts of India, the villainage of the feudal system, or the despotism of the patricians of ancient Rome dragging their debtors into personal servitude to expiate loans they could not repay. Mankind will never be in an eminent degree virtuous and happy, till each man shall possess that portion of distinction and no more, to which he is

POLITICAL JUSTICE 447

entitled by his personal merits. The dissolution of aristocracy is equally the interest of the oppressor and the oppressed. The one will be delivered from the listlessness of tyranny, and the other from the brutalising operation of servitude. How long shall we be told in vain, "that mediocrity of fortune is the true rampart of personal happiness"?

*　　*　　*　　*　　*　　*

The road to the improvement of mankind is in the utmost degree simple, to speak and act the truth. If the Athenians had had more of this, it is impossible they should have been so flagrantly erroneous. To tell the truth in all cases without reserve, to administer justice without partiality, are principles which, when once rigorously adopted, are of all others the most prolific. They enlighten the understanding, give energy to the judgment, and strip misrepresentation of its speciousness and plausibility. In Athens men suffered themselves to be dazzled by splendour and show. If the error in their constitution which led to this defect can be discovered, if a form of political society can be devised in which men shall be accustomed to judge strictly and soberly, and habitually exercised to the plainness and simplicity of truth, democracy would in that society cease from the turbulence, instability, fickleness and violence that have too often characterised it. Nothing can be more certain than the omnipotence of truth, or, in other words, than the connexion between the judgment and the outward behaviour. If science be capable of perpetual improvement, men will also be capable of perpetually advancing in practical wisdom and justice. Once establish the perfectibility of man, and it will inevitably follow that we are advancing to a state, in which truth will be too well known to be easily mistaken, and justice too habitually practised to

be voluntarily counteracted. Nor shall we see reason to think upon severe reflection, that this state is so distant as we might at first be inclined to imagine. Error is principally indebted for its permanence to social institution. Did we leave individuals to the progress of their own minds, without endeavouring to regulate them by any species of public foundation, mankind would in no very long period convert to the obedience of truth. The contest between truth and falsehood is of itself too unequal, for the former to stand in need of support from any political ally. The more it be discovered, especially that part of it which relates to man in society, the more simple and self evident will it appear; and it will be found impossible any otherwise to account for its having been so long concealed, than from the pernicious influence of positive institution.

*   *   *   *   *   *

The nature of anarchy has never been sufficiently understood. It is undoubtedly a horrible calamity, but it is less horrible than despotism. Where anarchy has slain its hundreds, despotism has sacrificed millions upon millions, with this only effect, to perpetuate the ignorance, the vices and the misery of mankind. Anarchy is a short lived mischief, while despotism is all but immortal. It is unquestionably a dreadful remedy, for the people to yield to all their furious passions, till the spectacle of their effects gives strength to recovering reason: but, though it be a dreadful remedy, it is a sure one. No idea can be supposed, more pregnant with absurdity, than that of a whole people taking arms against each other till they are all exterminated. It is to despotism that anarchy is indebted for its sting. If despotism were not ever watchful for its prey, and mercilessly prepared to take advantage of the errors

POLITICAL JUSTICE 449

of mankind, this ferment, like so many others, being left to itself, would subside into an even, clear and delightful calm. Reason is at all times progressive. Nothing can give permanence to error, that does not convert it into an establishment, and arm it with powers to resist an invasion.

*　　*　　*　　*　　*　　*

The desire to gain a more extensive territory, to conquer or to hold in awe our neighbouring states, to surpass them in arts or arms, is a desire founded in prejudice and error. Power is not happiness. Security and peace are more to be desired than a name at which nations tremble. Mankind are brethren. We associate in a particular district or under a particular climate, because association is necessary to our internal tranquillity, or to defend us against the wanton attacks of a common enemy. But the rivalship of nations is a creature of the imagination. If riches be our object, riches can only be created by commerce; and the greater is our neighbour's capacity to buy, the greater will be our opportunity to sell. The prosperity of all is the interest of all.

The more accurately we understand our own advantage, the less shall we be disposed to disturb the peace of our neighbour. The same principle is applicable to him in return. It becomes us therefore to desire that he may be wise. But wisdom is the growth of equality and independence, not of injury and oppression. If oppression had been the school of wisdom, the improvement of mankind would have been inestimable, for they have been in that school for many thousand years. We ought therefore to desire that our neighbour should be independent. We ought to desire that he should be free; for wars do not originate in the unbiassed propensities

of nations, but in the cabals of government and the propensities that governments inspire into the people at large. If our neighbour invade our territory, all we should desire is to repel him from it; and for that purpose it is not necessary we should surpass him in prowess, since upon our own ground his match is unequal. Not to say that to conceive a nation attacked by another, so long as its own conduct is sober, equitable and moderate, is an exceedingly improbable supposition.

* * * * * *

Government can have no more than two legitimate purposes, the suppression of injustice against individuals within the community, and the common defense against external invasion. The first of these purposes, which alone can have an uninterrupted claim upon us, is sufficiently answered by an association of such an extent as to afford room for the institution of a jury, to decide upon the offences of individuals within the community, and upon the questions and controversies respecting property which may chance to arise. It might be easy indeed for an offender to escape from the limits of so petty a jurisdiction; and it might seem necessary at first that the neighbouring parishes or jurisdictions should be governed in a similar manner, or at least should be willing, whatever was their form of government, to co-operate with us in the removal or reformation of an offender, whose present habits were alike injurious to us and to them. But there will be no need of any express compact, and still less of any common centre of authority, for this purpose. General justice and mutual interest are found more capable of binding men than signatures and seals. In the mean time all necessity for causing the punishment of the crime to pursue the criminal, would socn at least cease,

POLITICAL JUSTICE 451

if it ever existed. The motives to offence would become rare: its aggravations few; and rigour superfluous. The principal object of punishment is restraint upon a dangerous member of the community; and the end of this restraint would be answered, by the general inspection that is exercised by the members of a limited circle over the conduct of each other, and by the gravity and good sense that would characterise the censures of men, from whom all mystery and empiricism were banished. No individual would be hardy enough in the cause of vice, to defy the general consent of sober judgment that would surround him. It would carry despair to his mind, or, which is better, it would carry conviction. He would be obliged, by a force not less irresistible than whips and chains, to reform his conduct.

* * * * * *

All that is to be asked on the part of government in behalf of morality and virtue is a clear stage upon which for them to exert their own energies, and perhaps some restraint for the present upon the violent disturbers of the peace of society, that the efforts of these principles may be allowed to go on uninterrupted to their natural conclusion. Who ever saw an instance in which error unaided by power was victorious over truth? Who is there so absurd as to believe, that with equal arms truth can be ultimately defeated? Hitherto every instrument of menace or influence has been employed to counteract her. Has she made no progress?—Has the mind of man the capacity to chuse falsehood and reject truth, when her evidence is fairly presented? When it has been once thus presented and has gained a few converts, does she ever fail to go on perpetually increasing the number of her votaries? Exclusively of the fatal interference of government, and the violent irruptions of barbarism

WILLIAM GODWIN

threatening to sweep her from the face of the earth, has not this been in all instances the history of science?

* * * * * *

The just conclusion from the above reasonings is nothing more than a confirmation, with some difference in the mode of application, of the fundamental principle, that government is little capable of affording benefit of the first importance to mankind. It is calculated to induce us to lament, not the apathy and indifference, but the inauspicious activity of government. It incites us to look for the moral improvement of the species, not in the multiplying of regulations, but in their repeal. It teaches us that truth and virtue, like commerce, will then flourish most, when least subjected to the mistaken guardianship of authority and laws. This maxim will rise upon us in its importance, in proportion as we connect it with the numerous departments of political justice to which it will be found to have relation. As fast as it shall be adopted into the practical system of mankind, it will go on to deliver us from a weight intolerable to mind, and in the highest degree inimical to the progress of truth.

* * * * * *

There is no criterion of duty to any man but in the exercise of his private judgment. Has coercion any tendency to enlighten the judgment? Certainly not. Judgment is the perceived agreement or disagreement of two ideas, the perceived truth or falsehood of any proposition. Nothing can aid this perception, that does not set the ideas in a clearer light, that does not afford new evidence of the substantialness or unsubstantialness of the proposition. The direct tendency of coercion is to set our understanding and our fears, our duty and our weakness at variance with each other. And how poor spirited a refuge does coercion afford? If what you

POLITICAL JUSTICE 453

require of me is duty, are there no reasons that will prove it to be such? If you understand more of eternal justice than I, and are thereby fitted to instruct me, cannot you convey the superior knowledge you possess from your understanding into mine? Will you set your wit against one who is intellectually a child, and because you are better informed than I, assume, not to be my preceptor, but my tyrant? Am I not a rational being? Could I resist your arguments, if they were demonstrative? The odious system of coercion, first annihilates the understanding of the subject, and then of him that adopts it. Dressed in the supine prerogatives of a master, he is excused from cultivating the faculties of a man. What would not man have been, long before this, if the proudest of us had no hopes but in argument, if he knew of no resort beyond, and if he were obliged to sharpen his faculties, and collect his powers, as the only means of effecting his purposes?

* * * * * *

Having seen the justice of an equal distribution of property, let us next consider the benefits with which it would be attended. And here with grief it must be confessed, that, however great and extensive are the evils that are produced by monarchies and courts, by the imposture of priests and the iniquity of criminal laws, all these are imbecile and impotent compared with the evils that arise out of the established system of property.

Its first effect is that which we have already mentioned, a sense of dependence. It is true that courts are mean spirited, intriguing and servile, and that this disposition is transferred by contagion from them to all ranks of society. But property brings home a servile and truckling spirit by no circuitous method to every house in the nation. Observe the pauper fawning with

abject vileness upon his rich benefactor, and speechless with sensations of gratitude for having received that, which he ought to have claimed with an erect mien, and with a consciousness that his claim was irresistible. Observe the servants that follow in a rich man's train, watchful of his looks, anticipating his commands, not daring to reply to his insolence, all their time and their efforts under the direction of his caprice. Observe the tradesman, how he studies the passions of his customers, not to correct, but to pamper them, the vileness of his flattery and the systematical constancy with which he exaggerates the merit of his commodities. Observe the practices of a popular election, where the great mass are purchased by obsequiousness, by intemperance and bribery, or driven by unmanly threats of poverty and persecution. Indeed "the age of chivalry is" not "gone"! The feudal spirit still survives, that reduced the great mass of mankind to the rank of slaves and cattle for the service of a few.

*   *   *   *   *   *

A second evil that arises out of the established system of property is the perpetual spectacle of injustice it exhibits. This consists partly in luxury and partly in caprice. There is nothing more pernicious to the human mind than luxury. Mind, being in its own nature essentially active, necessarily fixes on some object public or personal, and in the latter case on the attainment of some excellence, or something which shall command the esteem and deference of others. No propensity, absolutely considered, can be more valuable than this. But the established system of property directs it into the channel of the acquisition of wealth. The ostentation of the rich perpetually goads the spectator to the desire of opulence. Wealth, by the sentiments of servility and dependence it produces, makes the rich man stand for-

POLITICAL JUSTICE

ward as the only object of general esteem and deference. In vain are sobriety, integrity and industry, in vain the sublimest powers of mind and the most ardent benevolence, if their possessor be narrowed in his circumstances. To acquire wealth and to display it, is therefore the universal passion. The whole structure of human society is made a system of the narrowest selfishness. If self love and benevolence were apparently reconciled as to their object, a man might set out with the desire of eminence, and yet every day become more generous and philanthropical in his views. But the passion we are here describing is accustomed to be gratified at every step, by inhumanly trampling upon the interest of others. Wealth is acquired by over-reaching our neighbours, and is spent in insulting them.

*   *   *   *   *   *

This leads us to observe, thirdly, that the established system of property, is the true leveling system with respect to the human species, by as much as the cultivation of intellect and truth, is more valuable and more characteristic of man, than the gratifications of vanity or appetite. Accumulated property treads the powers of thought in the dust, extinguishes the sparks of genius, and reduces the great mass of mankind to be immersed in sordid cares; beside depriving the rich, as we have already said, of the most salubrious and effectual motives to activity. If superfluity were banished, the necessity for the greater part of the manual industry of mankind would be superseded; and the rest, being amicably shared among all the active and vigorous members of the community, would be burthensome to none. Every man would have a frugal, yet wholesome diet; every man would go forth to that moderate exercise of his corporal functions that would give hilarity to the spirits; none would be made torpid with fatigue,

WILLIAM GODWIN

but all would have leisure to cultivate the kindly and philanthropical affections of the soul, and to let loose his faculties in the search of intellectual improvement. What a contrast does this scene present us with the present state of human society, where the peasant and the labourer work, till their understandings are benumbed with toil, their sinews contracted and made callous by being for ever on the stretch, and their bodies invaded with infirmities and surrendered to an untimely grave? What is the fruit of this disproportioned and unceasing toil? At evening they return to a family, famished with hunger, exposed half naked to the inclemencies of the sky, hardly sheltered, and denied the slenderest instruction, unless in a few instances, where it is dispensed by the hands of ostentatious charity, and the first lesson communicated is unprincipled servility. All this while their rich neighbour— but we visited him before.

*　　*　　*　　*　　*　　*

The spirit of oppression, the spirit of servility, and the spirit of fraud, these are the immediate growth of the established system of property. These are alike hostile to intellectual and moral improvement. The other vices of envy, malice and revenge are their inseparable companions. In a state of society where men lived in the midst of plenty, and where all shared alike the bounties of nature, these sentiments would inevitably expire. The narrow principle of selfishness would vanish. No man being obliged to guard his little store, or provide with anxiety and pain for his restless wants, each would lose his own individual existence in the thought of the general good. No man would be an enemy to his neighbour, for they would have nothing for which to contend; and of consequence philanthropy would resume the empire which reason assigns her. Mind

POLITICAL JUSTICE 457

would be delivered from her perpetual anxiety about
corporal support, and free to expatiate in the field of
thought which is congenial to her. Each man would
assist the enquiries of all.

Let us fix our attention for a moment upon the revolution of principles and habits that immediately grow
out of an unequal distribution of property. Till it was
thus distributed men felt what their wants required,
and sought the supply of those wants. All that was
more than this, was regarded as indifferent. But no
sooner is accumulation introduced, than they begin to
study a variety of methods, for disposing of their
superfluity with least emolument to their neighbour, or
in other words by which it shall appear to be most their
own. They do not long continue to buy commodities,
before they begin to buy men. He that possesses or is
the spectator of superfluity soon discovers the hold
which it affords us on the minds of others. Hence the
passions of vanity and ostentation. Hence the despotic
manners of them who recollect with complacence the
rank they occupy, and the restless ambition of those
whose attention is engrossed by the possible future.

*   *   *   *   *   *

This argument will be strengthened, if we reflect on
the amount of labour that a state of equal property will
require. What is this quantity of exertion from which
we are supposing many members of the community to
shrink? It is so light a burthen as rather to assume the
appearance of agreeable relaxation and gentle exercise,
than of labour. In this community scarcely any can be
expected in consequence of their situation or avocations
to consider themselves as exempted from manual industry. There will be no rich men to recline in indolence
and fatten upon the labour of their fellows. The
mathematician, the poet and the philosopher will derive

WILLIAM GODWIN

a new stock of cheerfulness and energy from the recurring labour that makes them feel they are men. There will be no persons employed in the manufacture of trinkets and luxuries; and none in directing the wheels of the complicated machine of government, tax-gatherers, beadles, excisemen, tide-waiters, clerks and secretaries. There will be neither fleets nor armies, neither courtiers nor footmen. It is the unnecessary employments that at present occupy the great mass of the inhabitants of every civilised nation, while the peasant labours incessantly to maintain them in a state more pernicious than idleness.

* * * * * *

Force in such a state of society would be unknown; I should part with nothing without a full consent. Caprice would be unknown; no man would covet that which I used, unless he distinctly apprehended, that it would be more beneficial in his possession than it was in mine. My apartment would be as sacred to a certain extent, as it is at present. No man would obtrude himself upon me to interrupt the course of my studies and meditations. No man would feel the whim of occupying my apartment, while he could provide himself another as good as his own. That which was my apartment yesterday would probably be my apartment today. We have few pursuits that do not require a certain degree of apparatus; and it would be for the general good that I should find in ordinary cases the apparatus ready for my use today that I left yesterday. But, though the idea of property thus modified would remain, the jealousy and selfishness of property would be gone. Bolts and locks would be unknown. Every man would be welcome to make every use of my accommodations, that did not interfere with my own use of them. Novices as we are, we may figure to ourselves a thousand dis-

POLITICAL JUSTICE 459

putes, where property was held by so slight a tenure. But disputes would in reality be impossible. They are the offspring of a misshapen and disproportioned love of ourselves. Do you want my table? Make one for yourself; or if I be more skilful in that respect than you, I will make one for you. Do you want it immediately? Let us compare the urgency of your wants and mine, and let justice decide.

MARY WOLLSTONECRAFT

An "hyena in petticoats" Horace Walpole called her. Yet she must, I believe, have possessed charm besides her beauty and her high intelligence. Her letters to Imlay portray her as a creature only too feminine for her own happiness. If her mind was masculine (as males in compliment to their sex assert) there was nothing else about her to justify the caricatures of her enemies. The first great woman's suffragist, she stood almost alone, with few of her sex to lend her moral support and with little hope that her dreams of woman's economic and political liberty would so soon be realized. A century after her death found thousands of her countrywomen supporting themselves in the professions and in business; and political enfranchisement very soon thereafter was realized. Of "these dissentions" she was "the parent and original."

Horace Walpole was quite right to fear and detest her. She was the natural enemy of him and his kind. Had she and her revolutionary associates their way, he and his friends, whether in England or France, who held sinecures and led the fashions in dress or architecture or letters, would have no longer opportunity to live at the expense of society. Mary Wollstonecraft was a true daughter of the Revolution and though her concern is with the rights of woman, she perceived that these were but one aspect of the rights of man. She sought to correct a mistaken emphasis.

She was a realist for all her ardent advocacy of radical doctrine. The obstacles which beset a woman who sought a career she knew from her own hard experience.

MARY WOLLSTONECRAFT 461

The misery of an unhappy marriage in a society which offered women no redress, in which the laws were man-made and were tyrannically harsh to women, she knew from the lives both of her mother, of her sister, and of her most intimate friend. It is not surprising that when she married Godwin for the sake of her unborn child she felt that she was sacrificing her principles. For herself she was willing to endure social obloquy in a cause she thought sacred.

Extremists and martyrs are usually thought of as narrow and one-sided, as perceiving in the mirror of the ideal a distorted reality. It was Mary Wollstone-craft's distinction to see social facts more clearly than did her contemporaries. Her views upon education, upon the rightful equality of the sexes, and upon the need of economic opportunity for women reveal the truth of her insight. But her observations are not confined to this, her peculiar province. I recall no contemporary observation upon the French Revolution so shrewd as hers to the effect that the destruction of a titled nobility was of little significance when wealth remained as before in the hands of a restricted class. She perceived that the French Revolution transferred power from the nobility to the bourgeoisie; had she lived long enough she would have witnessed in the English movement for reform culminating in the Reform Bill of 1832 a similar readjustment.

Her writing in the *Vindication of the Rights of Woman* is not notably good. It is a little impetuous and careless. But it is always readable. She has much to say, she is profoundly in earnest, and her ideas, though in part derived from the general revolutionary fund, are constantly verified and illustrated by facts drawn from her own experience. Her book comes much closer to life than Godwin's smooth but theoretical

treatise. The force of her personality and the warmth of her feelings are both greater than his. She would, I conceive, had she lived many years with him, have found him unsatisfactory.

A VINDICATION OF THE RIGHTS OF WOMAN

CHAPTER IX
OF THE PERNICIOUS EFFECTS WHICH ARISE FROM THE UNNATURAL DISTINCTIONS ESTABLISHED IN SOCIETY

From the respect paid to property flow, as from a poisoned fountain, most of the evils and vices which render this world such a dreary scene to the contemplative mind. For it is in the most polished society that noisome reptiles and venomous serpents lurk under the rank herbage; and there is voluptuousness pampered by the still sultry air, which relaxes every good disposition before it ripens into virtue.

One class presses on another; for all are aiming to procure respect on account of their property: and property, once gained, will procure the respect due only to talents and virtue. Men neglect the duties incumbent on man, yet are treated like demi-gods; religion is also separated from morality by a ceremonial veil, yet men wonder that the world is almost, literally speaking, a den of sharpers or oppressors.

There is a homely proverb, which speaks a shrewd truth, that whoever the devil finds idle he will employ. And what but habitual idleness can hereditary wealth and titles produce? For man is so constituted that he can only attain a proper use of his faculties by exercising them, and will not exercise them unless necessity, of some kind, first set the wheels in motion. Virtue likewise can only be acquired by the discharge of rela-

THE RIGHTS OF WOMAN

tive duties; but the importance of these sacred duties will scarcely be felt by the being who is cajoled out of his humanity by the flattery of sycophants. There must be more equality established in society, or morality will never gain ground, and this virtuous equality will not rest firmly even when founded on a rock, if one half of mankind are chained to its bottom by fate, for they will be continually undermining it through ignorance or pride.

It is vain to expect virtue from women till they are, in some degree, independent of men; nay, it is vain to expect that strength of natural affection, which would make them good wives and mothers. Whilst they are absolutely dependent on their husbands they will be cunning, mean, and selfish, and the men who can be gratified by the fawning fondness of spaniel-like affection, have not much delicacy, for love is not to be bought, in any sense of the words, its silken wings are instantly shrivelled up when any thing beside a return in kind is sought. Yet whilst wealth enervates men; and women live, as it were, by their personal charms, how can we expect them to discharge those ennobling duties which equally require exertion and self-denial. Hereditary property sophisticates the mind, and the unfortunate victims to it, if I may so express myself, swathed from their birth, seldom exert the locomotive faculty of body or mind; and, thus viewing everything through one medium, and that a false one, they are unable to discern in what true merit and happiness consist. False, indeed, must be the light when the drapery of situation hides the man, and makes him stalk in masquerade, dragging from one scene of dissipation to another the nerveless limbs that hang with stupid listlessness, and rolling round the vacant eye which plainly tells us that there is no mind at home.

I mean, therefore, to infer that the society is not properly organized which does not compel men and women to discharge their respective duties, by making it the only way to acquire that countenance from their fellow-creatures, which every human being wishes some way to attain. The respect, consequently, which is paid to wealth and mere personal charms, is a true north-east blast, that blights the tender blossoms of affection and virtue. Nature has wisely attached affections to duties, to sweeten toil, and to give that vigour to the exertions of reason which only the heart can give. But, the affection which is put on merely because it is the appropriated insignia of a certain character, when its duties are not fulfilled, is one of the empty compliments which vice and folly are obliged to pay to virtue and the real nature of things.

To illustrate my opinion, I need only observe, that when a woman is admired for her beauty, and suffers herself to be so far intoxicated by the admiration she receives, as to neglect to discharge the indispensable duty of a mother, she sins against herself by neglecting to cultivate an affection that would equally tend to make her useful and happy. True happiness, I mean all the contentment, and virtuous satisfaction, that can be snatched in this imperfect state, must arise from well regulated affections; and an affection includes a duty. Men are not aware of the misery they cause, and the vicious weakness they cherish, by only inciting women to render themselves pleasing; they do not consider that they thus make natural and artificial duties clash, by sacrificing the comfort and respectability of a woman's life to voluptuous notions of beauty, when in nature they all harmonize.

Cold would be the heart of a husband, were he not rendered unnatural by early debauchery, who did not

THE RIGHTS OF WOMAN 465

feel more delight at seeing his child suckled by its mother, than the most artful wanton tricks could ever raise; yet this natural way of cementing the matrimonial tie, and twisting esteem with fonder recollections, wealth leads women to spurn. To preserve their beauty, and wear the flowery crown of the day, that gives them a kind of right to reign for a short time over the sex, they neglect to stamp impressions on their husbands' hearts, that would be remembered with more tenderness when the snow on the head began to chill the bosom, than even their virgin charms. The maternal solicitude of a reasonable affectionate woman is very interesting, and the chastened dignity with which a mother returns the caresses that she and her child receive from a father who has been fulfilling the serious duties of his station, is not only a respectable, but a beautiful sight. So singular, indeed, are my feelings, and I have endeavoured not to catch factitious ones, that after having been fatigued with the sight of insipid grandeur and the slavish ceremonies that with cumberous pomp supplied the place of domestic affections, I have turned to some other scene to relieve my eye by resting it on the refreshing green everywhere scattered by nature. I have then viewed with pleasure a woman nursing her children, and discharging the duties of her station with, perhaps, merely a servant maid to take off her hands the servile part of the household business. I have seen her prepare herself and children, with only the luxury of cleanliness, to receive her husband, who returning weary home in the evening found smiling babes and a clean hearth. My heart has loitered in the midst of the group, and has even throbbed with sympathetic emotion, when the scraping of the well known foot has raised a pleasing tumult.

Whilst my benevolence has been gratified by contem-

plating this artless picture, I have thought that a couple of this description, equally necessary and independent of each other, because each fulfilled the respective duties of their station, possessed all that life could give.— Raised sufficiently above abject poverty not to be obliged to weigh the consequence of every farthing they spend, and having sufficient to prevent their attending to a frigid system of economy, which narrows both heart and mind. I declare, so vulgar are my conceptions, that I know not what is wanted to render this the happiest as well as the most respectable situation in the world, but a taste for literature, to throw a little variety and interest into social converse, and some superfluous money to give to the needy and to buy books. For it is not pleasant when the heart is opened by compassion and the head active in arranging plans of usefulness, to have a prim urchin continually twitching back the elbow to prevent the hand from drawing out an almost empty purse, whispering at the same time some prudential maxim about the priority of justice.

Destructive, however, as riches and inherited honours are to the human character, women are more debased and cramped, if possible, by them, than men, because men may still, in some degree, unfold their faculties by becoming soldiers and statesmen.

As soldiers, I grant, they can now only gather, for the most part, vain glorious laurels, whilst they adjust to a hair the European balance, taking especial care that no bleak northern nook or sound incline the beam. But the days of true heroism are over, when a citizen fought for his country like a Fabricius or a Washington, and then returned to his farm to let his virtuous fervour run in a more placid, but not a less salutary, stream. No, our British heroes are oftener sent from the gaming table than from the plow; and their passions have been

THE RIGHTS OF WOMAN

rather inflamed by hanging with dumb suspense on the turn of a die, than sublimated by panting after the adventurous march of virtue in the historic page.

The statesman, it is true, might with more propriety quit the Faro Bank, or card-table, to guide the helm, for he has still but to shuffle and trick. The whole system of British politics, if system it may courteously be called, consisting in multiplying dependents and contriving taxes which grind the poor to pamper the rich; thus a war, or any wild goose chace is, as the vulgar use the phrase, a lucky turn-up of patronage for the minister, whose chief merit is the art of keeping himself in place.

It is not necessary then that he should have bowels for the poor, so he can secure for his family the odd trick. Or should some shew of respect, for what is termed with ignorant ostentation an Englishman's birthright, be expedient to bubble the gruff mastiff that he has to lead by the nose, he can make an empty shew, very safely, by giving his single voice, and suffering his light squadron to file off to the other side. And when a question of humanity is agitated he may dip a sop in the milk of human kindness, to silence Cerberus, and talk of the interest which his heart takes in an attempt to make the earth no longer cry for vengeance as it sucks in its children's blood, though his cold hand may at the very moment rivet their chains, by sanctioning the abominable traffick. A minister is no longer a minister than while he can carry a point, which he is determined to carry.—Yet it is not necessary that a minister should feel like a man, when a bold push might shake his seat.

But, to have done with these episodical observations, let me return to the more specious slavery which chains

the very soul of woman, keeping her for ever under the bondage of ignorance.

The preposterous distinctions of rank, which render civilization a curse, by dividing the world between voluptuous tyrants, and cunning envious dependents, corrupt, almost equally, every class of people, because respectability is not attached to the discharge of the relative duties of life, but to the station, and when the duties are not fulfilled the affections cannot gain sufficient strength to fortify the virtue of which they are the natural reward. Still there are some loop-holes out of which a man may creep, and dare to think and act for himself; but for a woman it is an herculean task, because she has difficulties peculiar to her sex to overcome, which require almost superhuman powers.

A truly benevolent legislator always endeavours to make it the interest of each individual to be virtuous; and thus private virtue becoming the cement of public happiness, an orderly whole is consolidated by the tendency of all the parts towards a common centre. But, the private or public virtue of woman is very problematical; for Rousseau, and a numerous list of male writers, insist that she should all her life be subjected to a severe restraint, that of propriety. Why subject her to propriety—blind propriety if she be capable of acting from a nobler spring, if she be an heir of immortality? Is sugar always to be produced by vital blood? Is one half of the human species, like the poor African slaves, to be subject to prejudices that brutalize them, when principles would be a surer guard, only to sweeten the cup of man? Is not this indirectly to deny woman reason? for a gift is a mockery, if it be unfit for use.

Women are, in common with men, rendered weak and luxurious by the relaxing pleasures which wealth pro-

THE RIGHTS OF WOMAN 469

cures; but added to this they are made slaves to their persons, and must render them alluring that man may lend them his reason to guide their tottering steps aright. Or should they be ambitious, they must govern their tyrants by sinister tricks, for without rights there cannot be any incumbent duties. The laws respecting woman, which I mean to discuss in a future part, make an absurd unit of a man and his wife; and then, by the easy transition of only considering him as responsible, she is reduced to a mere cypher.

The being who discharges the duties of its station is independent; and, speaking of women at large, their first duty is to themselves as rational creatures, and the next, in point of importance, as citizens, is that, which includes so many, of a mother. The rank in life which dispenses with their fulfilling this duty, necessarily degrades them by making them mere dolls. Or, should they turn to something more important than merely fitting drapery upon a smooth block, their minds are only occupied by some soft platonic attachment; or, the actual management of an intrigue may keep their thoughts in motion; for when they neglect domestic duties, they have it not in their power to take the field and march and counter-march like soldiers, or wrangle in the senate to keep their faculties from rusting.

I know that as a proof of the inferiority of the sex, Rousseau has exultingly exclaimed, How can they leave the nursery for the camp!—And the camp has by some moralists been termed the school of the most heroic virtues; though, I think, it would puzzle a keen casuist to prove the reasonableness of the greater number of wars that have dubbed heroes. I do not mean to consider this question critically; because, having frequently viewed these freaks of ambition as the first natural mode of civilization, when the ground must be torn

MARY WOLLSTONECRAFT

up, and the woods cleared by fire and sword, I do not choose to call them pests; but surely the present system of war has little connection with virtue of any denomination, being rather the school of *finesse* and effeminacy, than of fortitude.

Yet, if defensive war, the only justifiable war, in the present advanced state of society, where virtue can shew its face and ripen amidst the rigours which purify the air on the mountain's top, were alone to be adopted as just and glorious, the true heroism of antiquity might again animate female bosoms.——But fair and softly, gentle reader, male or female, do not alarm thyself, for though I have contrasted the character of a modern soldier with that of a civilized woman, I am not going to advise them to turn their distaff into a musket, though I sincerely wish to see the bayonet converted into a pruning-hook. I only recreated an imagination, fatigued by contemplating the vices and follies which all proceed from a feculent stream of wealth that has muddied the pure rills of natural affection, by supposing that society will some time or other be so constituted, that man must necessarily fulfil the duties of a citizen, or be despised, and that while he was employed in any of the departments of civil life, his wife, also an active citizen, should be equally intent to manage her family, educate her children, and assist her neighbours.

But, to render her really virtuous and useful, she must not, if she discharge her civil duties, want, individually, the protection of civil laws; she must not be dependent on her husband's bounty for her subsistence during his life, or support after his death——for how can a being be generous who has nothing of its own? or, virtuous, who is not free? The wife, in the present state of things, who is faithful to her husband, and neither suckles nor educates her children, scarcely deserves

THE RIGHTS OF WOMAN 471

the name of a wife, and has no right to that of a citizen. But take away natural rights, and there is of course an end of duties.

Women thus infallibly become only the wanton solace of men, when they are so weak in mind and body, that they cannot exert themselves, unless to pursue some frothy pleasure, or to invent some frivolous fashion. What can be a more melancholy sight to a thinking mind, than to look into the numerous carriages that drive helter-skelter about this metropolis in a morning full of pale-faced creatures who are flying from themselves. I have often wished, with Dr. Johnson, to place some of them in a little shop with half a dozen children looking up to their languid countenances for support. I am much mistaken, if some latent vigour would not soon give health and spirit to their eyes, and some lines drawn by the exercise of reason on the blank cheeks, which before were only undulated by dimples, might restore lost dignity to the character, or rather enable it to attain the true dignity of its nature. Virtue is not to be acquired even by speculation, much less by the negative supineness that wealth naturally generates.

Besides, when poverty is more disgraceful than even vice, is not morality cut to the quick? Still to avoid misconstruction, though I consider that women in the common walks of life are called to fulfil the duties of wives and mothers, by religion and reason, I cannot help lamenting that women of a superiour cast have not a road open by which they can pursue more extensive plans of usefulness and independence. I may excite laughter, by dropping an hint, which I mean to pursue, some future time, for I really think that women ought to have representatives, instead of being arbitrarily

governed without having any direct share allowed them in the deliberations of government.

But, as the whole system of representation is now, in this country, only a convenient handle for despotism, they need not complain, for they are as well represented as a numerous class of hard working mechanics, who pay for the support of royalty when they can scarcely stop their children's mouths with bread. How are they represented whose very sweat supports the splendid stud of an heir apparent, or varnishes the chariot of some female favourite who looks down on shame? Taxes on the very necessaries of life, enable an endless tribe of idle princes and princesses to pass with stupid pomp before a gaping crowd, who almost worship the very parade which costs them so dear. This is mere gothic grandeur, something like the barbarous useless parade of having sentinels on horseback at Whitehall, which I could never view without a mixture of contempt and indignation.

How strangely must the mind be sophisticated when this sort of state impresses it! But, till these monuments of folly are levelled by virtue, similar follies will leaven the whole mass. For the same character, in some degree, will prevail in the aggregate of society: and the refinements of luxury, or the vicious repinings of envious poverty, will equally banish virtue from society, considered as the characteristic of that society, or only allow it to appear as one of the stripes of the harlequin coat, worn by the civilized man.

In the superiour ranks of life, every duty is done by deputies, as if duties could ever be waived, and the vain pleasures which consequent idleness forces the rich to pursue, appear so enticing to the next rank, that the numerous scramblers for wealth sacrifice everything to tread on their heels. The most sacred trusts

THE RIGHTS OF WOMAN 473

are then considered as sinecures, because they were procured by interest, and only sought to enable a man to keep *good company*. Women, in particular, all want to be ladies. Which is simply to have nothing to do, but listlessly to go they scarcely care where, for they cannot tell what.

But what have women to do in society? I may be asked, but to loiter with easy grace; surely you would not condemn them all to suckle fools and chronicle small beer! No. Women might certainly study the art of healing, and be physicians as well as nurses. And midwifery, decency seems to allot to them, though I am afraid the word midwife, in our dictionaries, will soon give place to *accoucheur,* and one proof of the former delicacy of the sex be effaced from the language. They might, also, study politics, and settle their benevolence on the broadest basis; for the reading of history will scarcely be more useful than the perusal of romances, if read as mere biography; if the character of the times, the political improvements, arts, etc., be not observed. In short, if it be not considered as the history of man; and not of particular men, who filled a niche in the temple of fame, and dropped into the black rolling stream of time, that silently sweeps all before it, into the shapeless void called—eternity. —For shape, can it be called, 'that shape hath none?'

Business of various kinds, they might likewise pursue, if they were educated in a more orderly manner, which might save many from common and legal prostitution. Women would not then marry for a support, as men accept of places under government, and neglect the implied duties; nor would an attempt to earn their own subsistence, a most laudable one! sink them almost to the level of those poor abandoned creatures who live by prostitution. For are not milliners and mantua-

makers reckoned the next class? The few employments open to women, so far from being liberal, are menial; and when a superior education enables them to take charge of the education of children as governesses, they are not treated like the tutors of sons, though even clerical tutors are not always treated in a manner calculated to render them respectable in the eyes of their pupils, to say nothing of the private comfort of the individual. But as women educated like gentlewomen, are never designed for the humiliating situation which necessity sometimes forces them to fill; these situations are considered in the light of a degradation; and they know little of the human heart, who need to be told, that nothing so painfully sharpens the sensibility as such a fall in life.

Some of these women might be restrained from marrying by a proper spirit or delicacy, and others may not have had it in their power to escape in this pitiful way from servitude; is not that government then very defective, and very unmindful of the happiness of one-half of its members, that does not provide for honest, independent women, by encouraging them to fill respectable stations? But in order to render their private virtue a public benefit, they must have a civil existence in the state, married or single; else we shall continually see some worthy women, whose sensibility has been rendered painfully acute by undeserved contempt, droop like 'the lily broken down by a plowshare.'

It is a melancholy truth; yet such is the blessed effect of civilization! the most respectable women are the most oppressed; and, unless they have understandings far superior to the common run of understandings, taking in both sexes, they must, from being treated like contemptible beings, become contemptible. How

THE RIGHTS OF WOMAN

many women thus waste life away the prey of discontent, who might have practiced as physicians, regulated a farm, managed a shop, and stood erect, supported by their own industry, instead of hanging their heads surcharged with the dew of sensibility that consumes the beauty to which it at first gave lustre; nay, I doubt whether pity and love are so near akin as poets feign, for I have seldom seen much compassion excited by the helplessness of females, unless they were fair; then, perhaps, pity was the soft handmaid of love, or the harbinger of lust.

How much more respectable is the woman who earns her own bread by fulfilling any duty, than the most accomplished beauty!—beauty did I say?—so sensible am I of the beauty of moral loveliness, or the harmonious propriety that attunes the passions of a well-regulated mind, that I blush at making the comparison; yet I sigh to think how few women aim at attaining this respectability by withdrawing from the giddy whirl of pleasure, or the indolent calm that stupifies the good sort of women it sucks in.

Proud of their weakness, however, they must always be protected, guarded from care, and all the rough toils that dignify the mind.—If this be the fiat of fate, if they will make themselves insignificant and contemptible, sweetly to waste 'life away,' let them not expect to be valued when their beauty fades, for it is the fate of the fairest flowers to be admired and pulled to pieces by the careless hand that plucked them. In how many ways do I wish, from the purest benevolence, to impress this truth on my sex; yet I fear that they will not listen to a truth that dear-bought experience has brought home to many an agitated bosom, nor willingly resign the privileges of rank and sex for the

MARY WOLLSTONECRAFT

privileges of humanity, to which those have no claim who do not discharge its duties.

Those writers are particularly useful, in my opinion, who make man feel for man, independent of the station he fills, or the drapery of factitious sentiments. I then would fain convince reasonable men of the importance of some of my remarks, and prevail on them to weigh dispassionately the whole tenor of my observations.— I appeal to their understandings; and, as a fellow-creature claim, in the name of my sex, some interest in their hearts. I entreat them to assist to emancipate their companion, to make her a helpmeet for them!

Would men but generously snap our chains, and be content with rational fellowship instead of slavish obedience, they would find us more observant daughters, more affectionate sisters, more faithful wives, more reasonable mothers—in a word, better citizens. We should then love them with true affection, because we should learn to respect ourselves; and the peace of mind of a worthy man would not be interrupted by the idle vanity of his wife, nor his babes sent to nestle in a strange bosom, having never found a home in their mother's.

THE MODERN
STUDENT'S LIBRARY

Each volume edited with an introduction by a leading
American authority

This series is composed of such works as are conspicuous in the
province of literature for their enduring influence. Every volume
is recognized as essential to a liberal education and will tend to infuse a love for true literature and an appreciation of the qualities
which cause it to endure.

A WEEK ON THE CONCORD AND MERRIMAC RIVERS
By HENRY DAVID THOREAU
With an Introduction by
ODELL SHEPARD
Professor of English at Trinity College

". . . Here was a man who stood with his head in the clouds,
perhaps, but with his feet firmly planted on rubble and grit. He
was true to the kindred points of Heaven and Home. Thoreau's
eminently practical thought was really concerned in the last analysis with definite human problems. The major question how to live
was at the end of all his vistas."

EMERSON'S ESSAYS
Selected and edited, with an Introduction, by
ARTHUR HOBSON QUINN
Professor of English and Dean of the College University of
Pennsylvania

"Among the shifting values in our literary history, Emerson stands
secure. As a people we are rather prone to underestimate our native
writers in relation to English and continental authors, but even
among those who have been content to treat our literature as a by-
product of British letters, Emerson's significance has become only
more apparent with time."

THE MODERN STUDENT'S LIBRARY

EVAN HARRINGTON
By George Meredith

With an Introduction by
GEORGE G. REYNOLDS
Professor of English Literature, University of Colorado

Evan Harrington, one of the greatest demonstrations of George Meredith's genius, is an ironic comment on English society and manners in the latter part of the last century, done with amazing penetration and the best of his humor. In the large, it reflects the struggle between spiritual and moral ideals which was constantly going on in Meredith's mind and which ends in the triumph of the spirit of sacrifice.

THE MASTER OF BALLANTRAE
By Robert Louis Stevenson

With an Introduction by
H. S. CANBY
Formerly Professor of English Literature at Yale University, and present editor of the New York *Evening Post* Literary Review

Here is one of the most absorbing of Stevenson's romances, full of the spice of adventure and exciting incident, the thrill of danger and the chill of fear; it is, beside, a powerful and subtle study of Scotch character of different types, and brings into being one of the most amazing of all the dramatis personæ of romantic fiction.

POEMS AND PLAYS
By Robert Browning

Selected with an Introduction and Notes by
HEWETTE ELWELL JOYCE
Assistant Professor of English in Dartmouth College

A volume intended for the student or less-advanced reader of Browning who does not require a complete edition. The introduction suggests an approach to Browning, points out such difficulties as often perplex one who reads Browning for the first time, and states simply a few of the poet's fundamental ideas.

THE MODERN STUDENT'S LIBRARY

ENGLISH POETS OF THE EIGHTEENTH CENTURY

Selected and Edited by

ERNEST BERNBAUM
Professor of English at the University of Illinois

The great age of the eighteenth century is, more than any other, perhaps, mirrored in its poetry, and this anthology reveals its manners and ideals.

While the text of the various poems is authentic, it is not burdened with scholastic editing and marginal comment. The collection and its form is one which satisfies in an unusual way the interest of the general reader as well as that of the specialist.

PILGRIM'S PROGRESS

BY JOHN BUNYAN

With an Introduction and Notes by

DR. S. M. CROTHERS

This book is one of the most vivid and entertaining in the English language, one that has been read more than any other in our language, except the Bible.

PRIDE AND PREJUDICE

BY JANE AUSTEN

With an Introduction by

WILLIAM DEAN HOWELLS

To have this masterpiece of realistic literature introduced by so eminent a critic as William Dean Howells is, in itself, an event in the literary world. We cannot better comment upon the edition than by quoting from Mr. Howells's introduction:

He says: "When I came to read the book the tenth or fifteenth time for the purposes of this introduction, I found it as fresh as when I read it first in 1889, after long shying off from it."

THE MODERN STUDENT'S LIBRARY

NINETEENTH CENTURY LETTERS

Selected and edited by

BYRON JOHNSON REES

Professor of English at Williams College

Contains letters from Blake, Wordsworth, Smith, Southey, Lamb, Irving, Keats, Emerson, Lincoln, Thackeray, Huxley, Meredith, "Lewis Carroll," Phillips Brooks, Sidney Lanier, and Stevenson.

PAST AND PRESENT

By THOMAS CARLYLE

With an Introduction by

EDWIN W. MIMS

Professor of English at Vanderbilt University

"Past and Present," written in 1843, when the industrial revolutions had just taken place in England and when democracy and freedom were the watchwords of liberals and progressives, reads like a contemporary volume on industrial and social problems.

BOSWELL'S LIFE OF JOHNSON

Abridged and edited, with an Introduction and Notes, by

CHARLES G. OSGOOD

Professor of English at Princeton University

Seldom has an abridgment been made with as great skill in omitting nothing vital and keeping proper proportions as this edition by Professor Osgood.

AMERICAN BALLADS AND SONGS

Collected and edited by

LOUISE POUND

Professor of English, University of Nebraska

An anthology intended to present to lovers of traditional songs such selections as illustrate the main classics and types having currency in English-speaking North America. It includes a number of imported ballads and songs, Western songs, dialogue and nursery songs, etc.

THE MODERN STUDENT'S LIBRARY

SELECTIONS FROM "THE FEDERALIST"

Edited with an Introduction by
JOHN SPENCER BASSETT
Professor of History in Smith College

A careful and discriminating selection of the "Essays written in favor of the new constitution, as agreed upon by the federal convention, September 17, 1787."

HISTORICAL ESSAYS

BY LORD MACAULAY

Selected with an Introduction by
CHARLES DOWNER HAZEN
Professor of History at Columbia University

A group of the better-known historical essays which includes "John Hampden," "William Pitt," "The Earl of Chatham," "Lord Clive," "Warren Hastings," "Machiavelli," and "Frederick the Great."

SARTOR RESARTUS

BY THOMAS CARLYLE

Edited with an Introduction by
ASHLEY THORNDIKE
Professor of English at Columbia University

This "Nonsense on Clothes," as Carlyle referred to it in one entry of his journal, reaches into all the human realm and is perhaps the greatest philosophical expression of Carlyle's genius. Surely there is a power of pure thought which he has put into the mind of Professor Teufelsdröckh and a charm of words which he has given him to speak which he has nowhere surpassed.

A glossary in this edition will be of invaluable service to the student.

THE MODERN STUDENT'S LIBRARY

THE ESSAYS OF
ADDISON AND STEELE

Selected and edited by

WILL D. HOWE
Professor of English at Indiana University

With the writings of these two remarkable essayists modern prose began. It is not merely that their style even to-day, after two centuries, commands attention, it is equally noteworthy that these men were among the first to show the possibilities of our language in developing a reading public.

BENJAMIN FRANKLIN AND
JONATHAN EDWARDS

With an Introduction by

CARL VAN DOREN

Franklin and Edwards often sharply contrasted in thought are, however, in the main, complementary to each other. In religion, Franklin was the utilitarian, Edwards the mystic. Franklin was more interested in practical morality than in revelation; Edwards sought a spiritual exaltation in religious ecstasy. In science Franklin was the practical experimenter, Edwards the detached observer, the theoretical investigator of causes.

THE
HEART OF MIDLOTHIAN

By Sir Walter Scott

With an Introduction by

WILLIAM P. TRENT
Professor of English at Columbia University

Universally admitted one of the world's greatest story-tellers, Scott himself considered "The Heart of Midlothian" his masterpiece, and it has been accepted as such by most of his admirers.

THE MODERN STUDENT'S LIBRARY

THE ORDEAL OF RICHARD FEVEREL
By George Meredith

With an Introduction by
FRANK W. CHANDLER
Professor of English at the University of Cincinnati

"The Ordeal of Richard Feverel," published in 1859, was Meredith's first modern novel and probably his best. Certainly it was, and has remained, the most generally popular of all this author's books and among the works of its type it stands pre-eminent. The story embodies in the most beautiful form the idea that in life the whole truth and nothing but the truth is best.

MEREDITH'S ESSAY ON COMEDY

With an Introduction, Notes, and Biographical Sketch by
LANE COOPER
Professor of English at Cornell University

"Good comedies," Meredith tells us, "are such rare productions that, notwithstanding the wealth of our literature in the comic element, it would not occupy us long to run over the English list." The "Essay on Comedy" is in a peculiarly intimate way the exposition of Meredith's attitude toward life and art. It helps us to understand more adequately the subtle delicacies of his novels.

CRITICAL ESSAYS OF THE NINETEENTH CENTURY
Selected and edited, with an Introduction, by
RAYMOND M. ALDEN
Professor of English at Leland Stanford University

The essays in this volume include those of Wordsworth, Copleston, Jeffrey, Scott, Coleridge, Lockhart, Lamb, Hazlitt, Byron, Shelley, Newman, DeQuincey, Macaulay, Wilson, and Hunt.

THE MODERN STUDENT'S LIBRARY

BACON'S ESSAYS

Selected, with an Introduction and Notes, by

MARY AUGUSTA SCOTT
Late Professor of English Literature at Smith College

These essays, the distilled wisdom of a great observer upon the affairs of common life, are of endless interest and profit. The more one reads them the more remarkable seem their compactness and their vitality.

ADAM BEDE
By George Eliot

With an Introduction by

LAURA J. WYLIE
Professor of English at Vassar College

With the publication of "Adam Bede" in 1859, it was evident both to England and America that a great novelist had appeared. "Adam Bede" is the most natural of George Eliot's books, simple in problem, direct in action, with the freshness and strength of the Derbyshire landscape and character and speech in its pages.

THE RING AND THE BOOK
By Robert Browning

With an Introduction by

FREDERICK MORGAN PADELFORD
Professor of English at Washington University

" 'The Ring and the Book,' " says Dr. Padelford in his introduction, "is Browning's supreme literary achievement. It was written after the poet had attained complete mastery of his very individual style; it absorbed his creative activity for a prolonged period; and it issued with the stamp of his characteristic genius on every page."

THE MODERN STUDENT'S LIBRARY

BARCHESTER TOWERS
By Anthony Trollope

With an Introduction by
CLARENCE DIMICK STEVENS
Professor of English at the University of Cincinnati

Trollope covered a wide range of subjects in the more than thirty novels that he wrote, but he was at his best in portraying provincial life among the clergy and the gentry in a cathedral city. "Barchester Towers" (1857), the most widely read of his books, is a classic for its unfailing humor, its distinctly drawn characters, and its unerring accuracy in picturing situations that are true to life.

POEMS BY WILLIAM WORDSWORTH

Selected and edited, with an Introduction, by
GEORGE McLEAN HARPER
Professor of English at Princeton University

Even so sincere a friend of Wordsworth as Matthew Arnold believed that it was essential for the fame of the poet that a selection be made of the poems, and he made one. There is no person better suited to prepare a selection, after his long study and valuable discoveries, than Professor Harper.

CHARLES SCRIBNER'S SONS
PUBLISHERS   NEW YORK

THE MODERN STUDENT'S LIBRARY

ROBERT LOUIS STEVENSON'S ESSAYS

With an Introduction by
WILLIAM LYON PHELPS
Professor of English at Yale University

This volume includes not only essays in formal literary criticism, but also of personal monologue and gossip, as well as philosophical essays on the greatest themes that can occupy the mind of man. All reveal the complex, whimsical, humorous, romantic, imaginative, puritanical personality now known everywhere by the formula R. L. S.

PENDENNIS
By Thackeray

With an Introduction by
ROBERT MORSS LOVETT
Professor of English at the University of Chicago

"Pendennis" stands as a great representative of biographical fiction and reflects more of the details of Thackeray's life than all his other writings. Of its kind there is probably no more interesting book in our literature.

THE RETURN OF THE NATIVE
By Thomas Hardy

With an Introduction and Notes by
JOHN W. CUNLIFFE
Professor of English at Columbia University

"The Return of the Native" is probably Thomas Hardy's great tragic masterpiece. It carries to the highest perfection the rare genius of the finished writer. It presents in the most remarkable way Hardy's interpretation of nature in which there is a perfect unison between the physical world and the human character.

THE MODERN STUDENT'S LIBRARY

EACH VOLUME EDITED BY A LEADING
AMERICAN AUTHORITY

This series is composed of such works as are conspicuous in the province of literature for their enduring influence. Every volume is recognized as essential to a liberal education and will tend to infuse a love for true literature and an appreciation of the qualities which cause it to endure.

A descriptive list of the volumes published in this series appears in the last pages of this volume

CHARLES SCRIBNER'S SONS

THE MODERN STUDENT'S LIBRARY

ROMANTIC PROSE OF THE EARLY NINETEENTH CENTURY